AQA Government and Politics

AS

Exclusively e[...]

D0537400

Duncan Watts

Series consultants
Morton Davies
Lynton Robins

Nelson Thornes

Text © Duncan Watts 2008
Original illustrations © Nelson Thornes Ltd 2008

Published in 2008 by:
Nelson Thornes Ltd
Delta Place
27 Bath Road
CHELTENHAM
GL53 7TH
United Kingdom

08 09 10 11 12 / 10 9 8 7 6 5 4

BLACKBURN COLLEGE
LIBRARY

Acc No. BB42840

Class No. 320.941 WAT

Date JAN '11

A catalogue record for this book is available from the British Library

ISBN 978 0 7487 9821 6

Cover photograph by Photolibrary

Illustrations include artwork drawn by SD Illustrations

Page make-up by Florence Production, Devon

Printed and bound in China by 1010 Printing International Ltd

The author and publishers wish to thank the following for permission to use copyright material:

piv: Getty Images; p2: Getty Images; p14: The Print Collector / Alamy; p18: Getty Images; p23: Getty Images; p34: AFP/Getty Images; p37: Getty Images; p40: Getty Images; p41: Getty Images; p47: AFP/Getty Images; p49: David White / Alamy; p55: Jeff Morgan politics and government / Alamy; p57: vario images GmbH & Co.KG / Alamy; p62: David Robertson / Alamy; p62 Getty Images; p69: Getty Images; p77: Time & Life Pictures/Getty Images; p80: Time & Life Pictures/Getty Images; p80: Time & Life Pictures/Getty Images; p81: Tom Stoddart Archive; p82: AFP/Getty Images; p84: Getty Images; p85: AFP/Getty Images; p86: Getty Images; p88: Getty Images; p89: Gettty Images; p93: AFP/Getty Images; p95: Getty Images; p98: Getty Images; p99: Getty Images; p103: [apply pictures] / Alamy; p116: Getty Images; p117: Getty Images; p121: RSPB; p125: Getty Images; p133: (1) Time & Life Pictures/Getty Images, (2) Time & Life Pictures/Getty Images, (3) Getty Images; Martin Jenkinson / Alamy; p138: Getty Images; p139: Getty Images; p144: Getty Images; p146: Getty Images; p150: Visual Arts Library (London) / Alamy; p153: Roger Viollet/Getty Images; p159: Nikreates / Alamy; p165: Getty Images; p174; Getty Images; p179: STOCKFOLIO / Alamy; p185: Tim Graham/Getty Images; p187: Getty Images; p193: Getty Images; p210: Getty Images; p215: Getty Images; p224: Getty Images; p229: Getty Images; p233: BRIAN HARRIS / Alamy; p248: Getty Images; p251, 254: Adrian Teal / Cartoonstock; p267: David Hoffman Photo Library / Alamy; p268: Getty Images; p283: reproduced with the kind permission of Colin Dobson at m4design and Gerry Pontet at Astec Projects; p289: reproduced with the kind permission of The Campaign for an English Parliament; p291: Roger Viollet/Getty Images; p296: AFP/Getty Images; p297: Getty Images

A rescue plan for politics: The first step in our blueprint is a written constitution - written, that is, by the public Copyright Guardian News & Media Ltd 2007; One good reason to ask the people Copyright Guardian News & Media Ltd 2004; Women MPs bullied and abused in Commons Copyright Jackie Ashley; Militant pressure groups . . . rush to judgment exaggerating their case and in expressing themselves in simplistic terms designed for easy headlines, they can undermine both balanced decision-making and parliamentary democracy. M Dobbs / NI Syndication Limited

Other material appears courtesy Crown Copyright

Contents

AQA introduction

Nelson Thornes has worked in partnership with AQA to ensure this book and the accompanying online resources offer you the best support for your A level course.

All resources have been approved by senior AQA examiners so you can feel assured that they closely match the specification for this subject and provide you with everything you need to prepare successfully for your exams.

These print and online resources together **unlock blended learning**; this means that the links between the activities in the book and the activities online blend together to maximise your understanding of a topic and help you achieve your potential.

These online resources are available on *kerboodle!* which can be accessed via the internet at **http://www.kerboodle.com/live**, anytime, anywhere. If your school or college subscribes to this service you will be provided with your own personal login details. Once logged in, access your course and locate the required activity.

For more information and help visit **http://www.kerboodle.com**

Icons in this book indicate where there is material online related to that topic. The following icons are used:

✓ Progress tracking

These resources include a variety of tests that you can use to check your knowledge on particular topics (Test yourself) and a range of resources that enable you to analyse and understand examination questions (On your marks . . .).

Research support

These resources include WebQuests, in which you are assigned a task and provided with a range of web links to use as source material for research.

How to use this book

This book covers the specification for your course and is arranged in a sequence approved by AQA.

The book content is divided into sections matched to the topics of the AQA Government and Politics AS specification - Participation and Voting Behaviour; Electoral Systems; Political Parties; Pressure Groups and Protest Movements; The British Constitution; Parliament; The Core Executive; Multi-level Governance. Sections are divided into chapters, and then further divided into topics, making them clear and easy to use.

The features in this book include:

Learning objectives:

At the beginning of each section you will find a list of learning objectives that contain targets linked to the requirements of the specification.

Key terms

Terms that you will need to be able to define and understand.

Hint

Hints to aid your understanding of the topics.

Links

This highlights any key areas where topics relate to one another.

In depth

A closer look at a concept, organisation or issue.

Activity

Suggestions for practical investigations you can carry out.

Further information

Statistics, quotations and information to extend your understanding of the subject.

Summary questions

Short questions that test your understanding and encourage you to think more widely about the subject.

Examination-style questions

Questions in the style that you can expect in your exam.

AQA examination questions are reproduced by permission of the Assessment and Qualifications Alliance.

Web links in the book

As Nelson Thornes is not responsible for third party content online, there may be some changes to this material that are beyond our control. In order for us to ensure that the links referred to in the book are as up-to-date and stable as possible, the websites are usually homepages with supporting instructions on how to reach the relevant pages if necessary.

Please let us know at **kerboodle@nelsonthornes.com** if you find a link that doesn't work and we will do our best to redirect the link, or to find an alternative site.

AQA Government and Politics AS

Introduction

This book has been written to assist your preparation as a student for the AQA AS examination in Government and Politics. You will be introduced systematically to the subject matter included in the AQA specification. The primary focus will be on the structures and institutions of British government and participation in politics, but the volume also includes explanations of the theories and concepts needed to make sense of those political structures, institutions and behaviours. In addition to the main text the author provides boxed sections which give explanations and definitions of key terms, examples to accompany the commentary, topics for discussions in class and questions similar to those likely to appear on the examination papers. Charts, tables and other related evidence are provided which will enhance your knowledge and understanding.

The study of politics

Politics is a challenging and exciting subject and this book will help you to get started in developing your knowledge and honing your analytical skills. It will assist greatly in your preparation for the examination. The excitement of this subject, however, is that politics is an all pervasive activity which is constantly changing and developing. It demands constant reappraisal, revision and/or confirmation of the myriad assumptions that are made in explaining political behaviour, institutions, values, objectives and programmes. British politics has changed a great deal in the last quarter of a century. For example, the dominance of Thatcherism in the 1980s led subsequently to profound changes in the nature and focus of the major British parties; the increasing importance of Britain's membership of the EU has had an effect, especially on the Conservative party; the reform of the civil service has affected the ways in which public services are delivered. Similarly the constitutional reforms of the Blair government have had an effect on attitudes to and assessments of devolution, the second chamber and government by coalition.

The message is clear – in a subject like politics there are no unchangeable truths that remain valid for all time and in all circumstances. You must therefore be constantly vigilant in the development of your knowledge and understanding and that you do not rely on perceptions and explanations which may have sufficed in an earlier period but which no longer accommodate the facts or factors in an emerging situation. As politics itself has developed so has the study of politics. Different scholars adopt different approaches. In recent decades many books have been produced reflecting those different approaches, e.g. institutional, behavioural, philosophical, quantitative, pluralist, elitist, Marxist. Similarly different works adopt different normative perspectives on their subject matter – some critical, others supportive. New topics or emphases, such as the study of the media or political culture, have come to the fore in recent years in many publications.

Politics and you

All of these developments in the study of politics are relevant in trying to make sense of the world of politics which surrounds us in almost every aspect of our lives. The public services we receive – education, health, welfare, security, etc. – are all the result of political and governmental action. Clubs and associations to which we belong frequently involve themselves in politics by seeking influence with decision makers, be they local councillors, government ministers, civil servants, EU officials or MPs/MEPs.

Therefore, you should be aware that your appreciation of government and politics can be enhanced in the course of your daily lives. Politics permeates the media – newspapers, radio programmes such as the *Today* programme, and television's *Newsnight* report and comment on politics as it unfolds. Regular monitoring of these will help your understanding of how political stories unfold and develop; how unexpected factors change the significance of, or perspective on, a piece of news. The media stories can augment the examples given within this text and significantly enhance the breadth and depth of your knowledge and understanding of the subject. They will also provide material which exemplifies or modifies some of the theories and concepts introduced in the text.

Unlike many recent introductory textbooks this one does not purport to be a comprehensive introduction to the study of Government and Politics. It has been written specifically to address the topics contained in the AQA Government and Politics AS specification. You may find it helpful to consider some of the generic questions associated with the study of Government and Politics whilst using this volume, such as the following examples.

What is politics?

Politics exists because people are social creatures who choose to exist in groups. This inevitably requires mechanisms and procedures to make decisions because some resources are unavoidably in short supply and conflicts arise about their allocation and use: to whom and in what proportions? The study of politics is a mixture of how those decisions are made and how they ought to be made. It is also a study of *how* society can best exploit, develop and manage its resources (better management; technological advancement; conquest; conflict; and/or competition). Various definitions of the study of politics have appeared in the annals of political science. They do not necessarily contradict each other but they emphasise different aspects of the subject. The following are examples of this.

Politics as the study of power

Power is the capacity to make others do what they would not otherwise do. Various means can be employed in this endeavour ranging from rational persuasion, to subliminal manipulation, to overt threats or violence. This led some to limit their definition to 'Politics as the study of authority', i.e. authority is the exercise of legitimate power, thus distinguishing between, for example, the power of the gangster or hoodlum from that of an elected office holder.

Politics as the study of the State

The state is a legal construct designed specifically for the purpose of government. Within the framework of the state citizens receive legally established rights (e.g. to vote, to receive specified services, no punishment without trial, etc.) and are charged with certain obligations (e.g. to pay taxes, to sit on juries, to obey the law). The study of politics as the study of the State concentrates on the formal and institutional arrangements for conducting the business of government. It distinguishes the State from society in general, but recognises that the activities of the State occur within the social framework and reflect the values, aspirations, culture and behavioural characteristics of that society.

Politics and social life

However politics is defined, there are other fundamental questions which need to be borne in mind. For example, what is the relationship of politics to the non-political dimensions of social life? Some might even question whether there are any significant dimensions of social life that are devoid of a political element. If politics is to be seen as a means of reconciling the different interests in society this raises the question of how best this can be achieved. In which areas of social endeavour should competition be encouraged and where should cooperation be promoted; which decisions must be made by elected politicians and which should be left to experts or officials; when the normal processes of political dialogue and negotiation break down what means are available to participants to promote their cause or their interests; what are the limits of politics? Can violence or physical confrontation ever be justified? Are there any values or standards that cannot or must not be challenged without placing the fundamental features of a society at risk?

These and many other questions are at the heart of the study of politics. There are no absolutely right or wrong answers and all responses will be based on an intricate series of assumptions about human nature, human behaviour and aspiration. The answers can only be defended in a better or worse fashion, in a more or less persuasive manner. The AS study of Government and Politics can lead to more advanced studies in the subject that was once described by Aristotle as 'the master science'. This volume will be an invaluable aid in taking the first step on what will be an enjoyable and challenging journey in that direction.

Whilst this book has been written specifically as an aid to the study of the topics in the AQA Government and Politics AS specification, it has been necessary, in places, to provide important background information which is beyond the strict limits of the specification. This information contextualises the topics and will help candidates to gain a well-rounded appreciation of politics as a subject rather than just a collection of examination topics. However, if used appropriately, this material will enable candidates not only to demonstrate the breadth and depth of their learning in classroom discussions but also to enhance the quality of their examination answers.

Morton R Davies

Lynton Robins

1 Participating in politics

1 Politics, democracy and participation

Learning objectives:

- What do we understand by politics, democracy and participation?
- What is the difference between power and authority?
- What is the difference between a direct and an indirect democracy?
- What is a liberal democracy?
- Why is participation important in any democracy?

Key terms

Politics is concerned with developing a knowledge and understanding of government and society. In particular, it is about the struggle for power and influence between competing individuals and groups.

Democracy is people power, as in Abraham Lincoln's phrase 'government of the people, by the people and for the people'.

Equality is the belief that people should be treated equally and given equal opportunities, as long as there are no grounds for treating them differently.

Authoritarian regimes are non-democratic countries in which there is very strong central direction and control. There may be elections, but the range of candidates is usually limited or the campaigning is made very difficult for those who take an alternative view to those in power.

What is politics?

Politics is about how we are governed. It concerns the ways in which decisions are made about government, state and public affairs: where power lies; how governments and states work; and different theories and practices such as **democracy**, **equality**, tyranny and violence. In the AQA course, we will look at the activities of political parties and politicians as well as the other groups and individuals who take part in political activity and help to shape the society in which we live.

In society, people have different values and ideas about what goals should be pursued and about the best means of achieving those goals. Whenever people are engaged in making decisions, conflict is inevitable. It may be mild verbal disagreement or it may be more dramatic physical confrontation. The process of resolving conflicts about the way in which we organise our society and the priorities we establish is a political process. Those charged with making decisions exercise power and authority over us. They have the ability to determine how our community is run and how we live our lives.

There is a difference between power and authority:

- **Power** is the ability to get things done, if necessary by making others do what they would not do by free choice. Other means of persuasion may be used, but underlying their use is the ability to reward or punish. Power is a key ingredient of politics, enabling collective decisions to be made and enforced. It is the tool that enables rulers to serve or manipulate the people over whom they rule. Hay has described politics as being 'concerned with the distribution, exercise and consequences of power'.

- **Authority** is the ability of governments and individuals to direct others and achieve their goals because the majority of people accept that it is the government's right to tell them what to do, rather than because of the power or force they have at their disposal. If power is the ability to influence or determine the behaviour of others, authority is power cloaked in rightfulness. Usually, the exercise of authority implies that others will obey and force will not have to be used. It is legitimate power, based on respect and recognition that the person exercising it is justified in so doing. A police officer has both power and authority, whereas a blackmailer has power but no authority.

Power can depend on naked force or coercion. It is used in many **authoritarian regimes** to maintain leaders in office, the rule of dictators often ultimately relying on intimidation and physical threat. By contrast, in a democracy, those who govern have the authority to do so. They derive their **legitimate** authority from the consent of those over whom they govern, as determined in periodic, free and meaningful elections in which there is a genuine choice of candidates with a range of differing viewpoints. In a democracy, there is free competition between parties and **participation** by the mass of voters in elections.

What is democracy?

The word 'democracy' derives from two Greek terms: *demos* meaning people and *kratia* signifying 'rule of' or 'by'. Many people therefore see democracy as meaning 'people power', with government resting on the consent of the governed. According to Abraham Lincoln, democracy is 'government of the people, by the people and for the people'. In ancient Athens (between 461 BC and 322 BC), every qualified citizen (this did not include women, slaves and non-Athenians) had the opportunity to participate in political decision making. Citizens gathered together and voted directly on issues of current interest and concern. This was **direct democracy** in action. In today's large and more industrialised societies, people cannot all come together to discuss and vote on issues. They elect representatives to act on their behalf. This is **indirect or representative democracy**.

Key elements of a modern representative democracy include:

- popular control of policy makers
- the existence of open and organised opposition
- political equality ('one person, one vote')
- political freedoms
- majority rule
- free and fair elections
- lawmaking by elected representatives.

A democratic political system is one in which public policies are made, on a majority basis, by representatives subject to effective popular control at periodic elections which are conducted on the principle of political equality and under conditions of political freedom.

Almost all countries claim that they are democratic because the language of democracy presents a good image – so they use the terms or labels

Key terms

A **legitimate** system of government is one in which the authority of the government is widely accepted by those who are subject to it. We speak of the authority of an official, but of the legitimacy of a regime.

Participation is the engagement of the population in forms of political action.

Direct democracy is a form of democracy in which the citizens themselves assemble to debate and decide issues of public importance.

Indirect or representative democracy is where the people elect representatives who make decisions on their behalf.

Elitism is the recognition that society should be governed by an elite or small group.

Activity

Write a paragraph describing the difference between power and authority.

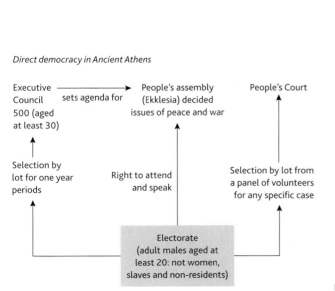

Direct democracy in Ancient Athens

In Athens, the people assembled, listened to/took part in debates and voted.

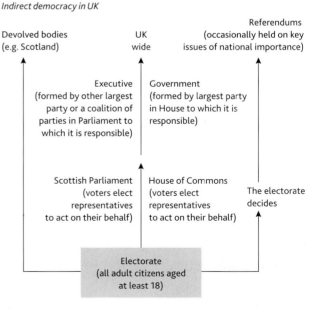

Indirect democracy in UK

In UK (as in Scotland) the voters elect politicians to reach decisions on their behalf. The governing party/parties are answerable to Parliament between elections and to the voters at election time.

Fig. 1 *Direct versus indirect democracy*

Key terms

Pluralism, literally 'rule by the many', relates to a society in which there are diverse and competing centres of power, which seek to exert influence over government.

Pressure groups comprise organisations that do not stand for election themselves, but rather seek to influence those who do gain political office and are therefore in a position to shape public policy.

Electorate relates to all qualified voters.

Franchise (or suffrage) is the right to vote for representatives in a legislative body.

Activities

1 Use the following statement as a basis for class discussion: 'Britain is considered to be a liberal, representative democracy.' Apply the various characteristics of the two forms of democracy to British political life. Make a list of all those features that qualify Britain as a democracy.

2 Do any aspects of our political system lead you to question how good a democracy Britain really is?

Summary questions

1 What do you think the dramatist George Bernard Shaw (1856–1950) meant by saying that democracy substitutes government by the incompetent majority for government by the privileged few?

2 Is democracy too elitist? Is Britain a democracy?

of democracy to some extent. However, we might not recognise their regimes as democratic. Particularly over the last three decades, since the 1970s, democracy has been widely accepted around the world as the most desirable form of government. At one time it was seen mainly as a Western creed, strong in western Europe and former colonies such as Australia, New Zealand and North America, but that is no longer true. Democracies are to be found in southern Europe (Greece and Portugal), most of eastern Europe (Hungary and Slovenia) and parts of Latin America (Argentina), Africa (South Africa) and Asia (Taiwan). The democratic ideal appears to have triumphed.

In a democracy, a few govern and the mass of people follow. The electors cast their vote every few years at election time, but in between they have little say. This is obviously a form of 'people power', but a limited one. In effect, the voters are giving away the right of decision making to a small number of elected representatives who make decisions on their behalf. This is political **elitism**, the few acting on behalf of the many.

Britain and other Western democracies are often described as liberal democracies. In addition to the features of democracy that we have already mentioned (free elections, the right to oppose, etc.), liberal democracies are noted for their commitment to the ideas of:

- **Pluralism** – the existence of diverse centres of economic and political power, involving a choice of political parties and the existence of many **pressure groups**.
- **Limited government** – checks and limitations on the power of government in order to secure essential liberties.
- **Civil liberties and civil rights** – the existence of essential public freedoms that are often written into law (e.g. freedom of assembly and speech, the right to vote and to a fair trial).
- **Open government** – non-secretive government that can be seen to be fair and accountable.
- **Independent judiciary** – a just, impartial and independent legal system based on equal access to the law.
- **Free and open media** – newspapers and broadcasting being allowed to operate freely without government pressure.

Participation, the essence of democracy

All citizens can participate by standing as political candidates. **In politics, participation is an umbrella term that covers the various means by which the public can directly participate in decisions about public policy**.

A country is democratic if the people have the means and opportunity to effectively participate in the way that it is run. Citizen participation is basic to the democratic system. People may not be able to make decisions directly, but those who do make them are accountable to the **electorate** at election time. All adults have gained the **franchise** or right to vote (see p6), sometimes as a result of prolonged struggle. For many of them, this is the extent of their involvement in the political process. But there are plenty of other ways in which they can participate, whether that is by contacting their MP or attending political meetings, signing petitions or going on a demonstration to register their protest. All are forms of 'people power'.

2 Forms of political participation

Learning objectives:

- What do we mean by participation?
- What are the main ways in which people today participate in politics?
- What has happened to turnout at UK elections in recent years?

Key terms

Abstainers are those who do not vote. This may be for involuntary reasons (sickness, not being on the register or the lack of a candidate to represent their particular viewpoint). More often, abstention is a deliberate choice not to vote, perhaps due to the reasons in the 'In depth' section adjacent.

Devolved assemblies are the national parliament in Scotland, the National Assembly in Wales and the Assembly in Northern Ireland.

Further information

The right to vote in Britain

- Some 44 million entitled to vote.
- Exceptions: those under 18; leading members of the Royal Family; peers; non-British citizens; some prisoners serving sentences; mentally ill; those disqualified because of past corrupt practices.
- Only a few hundred thousand could vote in early 1800s.
- In 1832, 1867, 1884 and 1918, vote gradually extended to all men.
- 1918: women over 30 granted vote.
- 1928: vote extended to women over 21.
- 1969: vote extended to 18-year-olds.

Political participation relates to the range of activities by which individuals attempt to influence who should govern and the decisions made by those who do. In established democracies, such action is normally **voluntary participation**, i.e. people choosing whether to vote or otherwise get involved and the means by which they do so. (The main exception is the insistence on compulsory voting in Australia, Belgium, Greece and a few other countries.) In non-democratic regimes, people may be expected to vote and persuaded to do so by the presence of soldiers, or they may feel forced to join a political party in the knowledge that only by party membership will they have any chance of getting a better job (or other privileges). These are examples of **forced** or **manipulated participation**.

Participation via elections

Elections are the main way in which most people participate; indeed for many it is the only political activity in which they engage. In Britain, this probably means voting in a general election, although millions of potential voters are **abstainers**, choosing not to have a say in which party governs. It can also mean voting to choose local councillors; Scottish, Welsh or Northern Irish members of the **devolved assemblies**; and members of the European parliament (MEPs).

In depth

Levels of turnout in British elections

Voting is the most usual form of political participation. Voter turnout refers to the percentage of the qualified voting-age population that actually turns out on polling day. A good turnout of voters is often considered to be a healthy sign in any democracy as it appears to indicate vitality and interest. Many advanced countries have turnouts consistently above 75%, some over 90%, but those with exceptionally high figures (e.g. Australia, Belgium and Italy) have compulsory voting laws.

Britain has usually had lower turnout figures than those recorded in other established European democracies over the last few decades. Turnout in general elections has varied considerably from one general election to the next. The variation from constituency to constituency is also very large (ranging from over 90% to just over 40%). In 2001, 59.4% voted; in 2005, 61.3% voted. Turnouts in elections for local councils, devolved assemblies and the European parliament, have usually been very low, in the region of 30–45%.

The turnout in the 2005 general election was slightly better than in 2001, perhaps the reason being that there was the prospect of a closer contest. Although the Conservatives lacked popular appeal, there was the opportunity to pass a verdict on the then Prime Minister Tony Blair and give him a 'bloody nose'. There was greater reason for interest than in the previous election in which the result seemed to be a foregone conclusion. Significantly, in

Key terms

Apathy is a lack of interest or enthusiasm, in this case for playing a part in the political system. Others might see it as representing broad satisfaction with things as they are, so that there is no need to exert oneself to register one's own viewpoint or take an active role.

Alienation in general means a feeling of separateness, of being alone and apart from others. In this sense, it refers to the feeling of being estranged from the rest of the community, society or the world.

Capitalism generally relates to 'free enterprise' economic systems in which the means of production are mostly privately owned and operated for profit, as in much of the Western world.

Communism is an ideology that seeks to establish a classless society based on common ownership (everything held 'in common') of the means of production. It represents a strand of the broader socialist movement, sometimes being regarded as a revolutionary form of socialism.

The **Cold War** was the state of constant rivalry, suspicion and sometimes extreme tension in the post-1945 era between communist eastern Europe and the Western nations (led by the US).

The **post-materialist age** is an era in which people are less concerned about their material needs (such as the basic requirements of food, clothing and shelter) which are all available to the majority and are more concerned with qualify-of-life issues.

Ecology is the study of the relationships between living organisms and their environment.

those constituencies where there was a genuine prospect of political change, turnout was higher, as the figures in the table indicate.

A general decline in turnout in Europe and the US

Most democracies have found that the figures for turnout have declined in the last few elections and this has led to alarm about the degree of **apathy** towards, or even **alienation** from, the political system that many voters now experience. Many voters across Europe and America seem increasingly disillusioned with the performance of parties in office and with the politicians who represent them. Media analysis has sometimes encouraged the view that promise has not always been matched by outcome, so that in the eyes of many voters the parties and politicians all seem as bad as each other. Moreover, party differences have narrowed as some of the big issues of **capitalism** versus **communism**, and peace and warfare, of the **Cold War** era have ceased to be so relevant. Nowadays, the distinctions between party programmes are often not fundamental ones.

Table 1 *Figures for turnout in UK general and European elections, 1979–2005 (%)*

General elections	European elections
1979 – 76.0	1979 – 31.6
1983 – 72.7	1984 – 32.6
1987 – 75.3	1989 – 36.2
1992 – 77.7	1994 – 36.5
1997 – 71.4	1999 – 23.6
2001 – 59.4	2004 – 38.8
2005 – 61.3	

Source: Adapted from figures provided in the Nuffield election studies (general elections) and N Nugent, The Government and Politics of the European Union, *Palgrave, 2006 (European elections)*

It may be the case that the descendants of the committed voters of yesteryear are today's pressure-group campaigners who see involvement in environmental and community issues as more worthwhile. Perhaps in a **post-materialist age** in which the majority of people live a much better life than their predecessors of yesteryear, what matters more are quality-of-life issues such as **ecology** and minority rights. Pressure groups arguably represent these causes more effectively than do the parties that contest elections.

Finally, some writers would suggest that rather than lower turnouts being a sign of apathy and resentment, they may reflect broad contentment. Abstention or non-voting may amount to general satisfaction with the conduct of affairs, so that voters do not feel stirred to express their feelings at the ballot box. Of course, the motives of voters may vary among different groups, some feeling that they do not need to go out and vote because everything seems to be going along satisfactorily, whilst others – often the young, the poor and members of ethnic minorities – may feel that the parties or candidates have nothing to offer them.

Activity

Should the voting age in the UK be lowered to 16? Write down as many reasons as you can for and against lowering the age. Bear in mind that:

Worldwide voting ages are not consistent, fluctuating between 15 and 21 In Europe, 18 is a common age (e.g. in Belgium, Denmark, France, Germany, Greece, Italy and Luxembourg).

People under the voting age make up 20–50% of the population in some countries, but they have no political representation.

The Greens, Liberal Democrats and the Scottish and Welsh Nationalists think the voting age in the UK should be reduced to 16 (At time of going to press this has also been suggested by Gordon Brown.)

Voting ages in some non-European democracies are:

a Brazil 16

b Croatia 16 (if employed)

c Isle of Man 16.

Voting ages in some non-democracies are:

a Cuba 16

b Indonesia 17

c Iran 18

d North Korea 17

e Sudan 17.

Voting to choose an elected representative is the primary way in which most people participate in an indirect democracy. Where direct democracy exists, they can be more actively involved. We saw that in ancient Greece, people came together at some well-known venue to debate and vote upon the issues of the day. Direct democracy rarely works like that today, but there are other ways to achieve the same effect (see the details about New England's town meetings, p61). Some countries use **initiatives**, **referendums** and **recall votes** to allow for more participation both in policy making and the behaviour of those who represent them. In several US states, all three methods are employed. Switzerland has used referendums for more than a century, in effect offering the Swiss people a modern equivalent of Athenian democracy, as people can vote directly on issues ranging from whether women should have the franchise to whether the country should attempt to join the European Union or United Nations.

In Britain, we have made occasional use of referendums at the national and local levels (see Chapter 4). The turnout varies, but in our national referendums it has averaged an impressive 62.1%. However, for the last decade the turnout in general elections has been markedly lower than in the past. Therefore, referendums are at best an irregular and infrequent means of popular involvement in political life.

Participation via other forms of involvement

There are many other possibilities for involvement. For example, the pensioner who contacts the local authority in order to claim a reduction in the level of council tax; the green activist who lies on the planned

Key terms

An **initiative** is a procedure through which an individual or group may propose legislation by securing the signatures of a required number of qualified voters.

A **referendum** is a vote of the people on a single issue of public policy, e.g. on some proposed law or policy, perhaps to amend the constitution.

A **recall vote** is an infrequently used device that enables a certain number of voters to demand a vote on whether an elected official should be removed from office. A famous recall vote was held in California in 2003. It resulted in the removal of the State Governor and the election in his place of Arnold Schwarzenegger.

Activity

Using the internet to help you, find out about the use of referendums and initiatives in Switzerland. On what sort of issues have the Swiss recently been allowed popular votes?

■ Key terms

The term **London bombings** refers to the terrorist attacks on the capital on 7 July 2005 (52 killed) and 21 July 2005 (none killed).

Suicide bombers are those individuals or groups who are prepared to kill others to register their protest and establish their particular vision and know that they are likely to die in the process.

An **opinion poll** is a survey designed to find out the voting intentions or attitudes of members of the public.

Focus groups are small groups of people whose views are probed on a range of questions.

Direct action is political action outside the constitutional and legal framework.

route of a road in order to prevent construction workers from building a new highway; and even the terrorists who planned the **London bombings** of July 2005. All are forms of individual participation, although the action of the **suicide bombers** in the latter example is very different to the earlier ones and is generally accepted as being a method which is beyond the boundaries of the democratic political system.

Other than by voting in elections or referendums, it is possible to participate by:

- Becoming a member of a political party. This is not common (see Chapter 6). More active membership might involve serving on a committee.
- Wearing a party badge at election time or putting up a campaign poster.
- Seeking election to the Westminster parliament, Scottish/Welsh/Northern Irish devolved bodies or to a local council.
- Membership of one or more pressure groups – this is more common (see Chapter 7). More active membership might involve accepting a key post, for example by becoming a trade union representative rather than just being a passive member.
- Attending a meeting, distributing leaflets, canvassing on the doorstep, writing to elected representatives (or ministers, councillors or a newspaper), taking part in a television or radio phone-in programme, participating in an **opinion poll** or **focus group** survey, or (more actively) setting up a website.

Fig. 2 *The bombers caught on camera*

- Taking **direct action**, ranging from staging or joining in a sit-down protest, taking part in an anti-war march, scribbling political graffiti or painting protest graffiti on a wall, or joining a demonstration in favour of animal rights to going on strike, chaining yourself to the railings of a public building, damaging property or rioting against the government.
- Political violence, ranging from kidnapping a person to hijacking a plane.

  Of course political activity can take place within the home or among friends, whether it involves passively watching a current affairs programme, engaging in family discussion about the Iraq War or about the merits or otherwise of the party leaders, or arguing with or seeking to persuade friends at school or in the pub.

More orthodox forms of participation have declined in recent years. Figures for electoral turnout, party membership and doorstep canvassing for a party are all down. These are signs of public disengagement from the traditional democratic process.

Summary questions

1. Does it matter if turnout figures in general elections have been low recently?

2. What are the most effective ways for young people to participate in politics?

3 Who participates and to what extent?

Learning objectives:

- What do we know about the people who participate in our political life and those who do not?

- Why does the underclass in British society play little part in politics?

- To what extent have some people lost faith in our political system?

- What are Putnam's views on public disengagement?

Link

For more on 'Reasons for non-participation' see p38 and pp257–259, 'Local government, does anyone care?'.

Key term

Anti-globalisation relates to the political outlook of those social movements that protest against global trade agreements and the impact they have on the world's poorest people, on the environment and on the prospects for international peace. One such movement is known as the Global Justice Movement.

In most established democracies such as Britain and the US, the level of popular participation falls well below the ideal. Beyond voting, other major forms of participation are sporadic, confined to a small minority even among the more educated and well-off sections of the community.

Many voters are ill-informed about political issues or indeed any other issues affecting public affairs. In Britain, surveys have shown a lack of knowledge and understanding in many voters. Large numbers are unable to name their MPs, MEPs and local councillors, and are not very interested in what goes on at Westminster or in the European parliament. Crewe's survey of young people in Britain and the US (1996) found that 80% of British pupils engaged in very little or no discussion of public affairs at home, even when including local issues of importance to their own communities.

Two studies, in the US and in Britain, have expanded our knowledge about levels of political participation:

1 In the US, Milbrath and Goel (1977) used the language of Roman gladiatorial contests to label the population according to their levels of involvement:

   a Gladiators are the relatively small percentage of activists who are keen participants.

   b Spectators, in the large majority, are those who observe the contest but who limit their participation to voting.

   c Apathetics are the non-participants who do not even watch the contest and are indifferent to its outcome.

2 In Britain, Parry *et al.* (1992) surveyed more than 1,500 respondents and provided them with a list of 23 different political actions, ranging from attending meetings to contacting an MP. They concluded that not everyone participates, and of those that do they do not participate at the same rate or in the same way. Only a quarter of the population was involved in any significant activity. Three out of four interviewed were active to some degree: many were voters only (of course, considerably fewer voted in 2001 and 2005) and the rest were inactive (see below). However, the fieldwork in Parry's survey was conducted more than 20 years ago. He dealt more with old-style, traditional forms of participation rather than some of the newer forms such as purchase of a product for ethical reasons (e.g. Fair Trade coffee), mass blockades, trespasses, **anti-globalisation** and anti-war demonstrations, and various forms of political violence.

Further information

Parry's findings on levels of participation (based on research in the 1980s)

- **23.2% were involved in a variety of political activities beyond voting.**
- **51% limited their involvement to voting in elections.**
- **25.85% were almost inactive.**

The political participation of the vast majority of the population is either minimal or non-existent.

Table 2 *Political activism in the UK (%)*

Form of participation	Women	Men
Voting		
Voted in 2001 election	68	66
Campaign-oriented		
Contacted a politician	17	20
Donated money to a party	6	9
Worked for a party	2	4
Had been a party member	2	4
Had worn a campaign badge	10	11
Cause-oriented		
Signed a petition	42	36
Bought a product for political reason	36	29
Boycotted a product	27	25
Demonstrated illegally	5	4
Protested illegally	1	1
Civic-oriented		
Member of a church group	18	10
Member of an environmental group	6	6
Member of a humanitarian group	3	4
Member of an educational group	6	7
Member of a trade union	15	16
Member of a hobby group	14	19
Member of a social club	13	19
Member of a consumer group	28	35
Member of a professional group	9	17
Member of a sports club	20	33

Source: Adapted from R Campbell, P Norris and J Lovenduski, 'Gender and political participation', a report published by the Electoral Commission, April 2004

Key term

40:30:30 society A society in which 40% of the population have secure employment and are comfortably or well off, 30% are in insecure employment ('the newly insecure' who have reduced employment protection, including many self-employed and part-time workers) and the remaining 30% are economically and socially marginalised, jobless or working for poverty wages and barely able to subsist.

Activities

1. Study the figures in Table 2. and suggest reasons why, on balance, women participate less than men in political activity.

2. In what sort of political activities do young people most commonly engage? Why do you think that young people are generally reluctant to get involved?

In Britain and the US there is a significant element of the population that forms an under-class, uninformed about, uninterested in and alienated from the political system. There is widespread scepticism about politicians and what they promise and deliver. Those who are alienated feel that politics has nothing to offer them. It seems irrelevant to their lives. This group is concentrated among the least well-off who feel marginalised from the rest of society. Large numbers live below the poverty line, and the minority populations are heavily concentrated in this category. They are at the wrong end of what Will Hutton has called a **40:30:30 society**. Among members of this least-educated and lower-income group, it is easy to feel discouraged and disillusioned. At election time, they may feel that they have no effective political outlet as the two main parties have little to say that is relevant to their predicament.

Disenchantment: a loss of trust in the political system and those who operate within it

Trust in government has declined, and fewer people think that politicians are truthful, reliable and willing to act in the public interest. Parry's study in 1992 found that in comparison with other advanced industrial countries, Britain had a middle-ranking position on the 'trust in government and politicians' scale, the British were 'less trusting and more cynical than West Germany, Austria and Switzerland, but more trusting and less cynical than the USA and Italy'.

Putnam (writing in 2000) has echoed some of Parry's concerns. He detects a really profound change of feeling that is more serious than a sense of apathy and alienation. In his view, there is a decline in civil participation and public trust that together constitute 'a worrying decline in America's **social capital**'. A degree of scepticism about those who govern may be healthy and desirable, but democracy is based on the consent of the governed. If they lack confidence in their political leaders, this may be a sign that the system is not serving the people well.

Table 3 *Some factors affecting levels of participation in elections and via other means*

Factor	Impact on participation
Age	Young people (the under 35s) are less likely to vote and less interested in traditional political outlets, e.g. joining youth wings of main parties. They are more interested in direct action to promote animal rights etc. Middle-aged and older people are more likely to vote and more interested in supporting parties and established pressure groups such as unions.
Ethnic origin	On polling day there is a high turnout of Jewish population, moderate to high turnout of Asians but low turnout of Afro-Caribbeans.
Gender	Men are traditionally more likely to vote and join organisations, but in recent years women have become more active in voting and joining/supporting causes. Some argue that in the past male political scientists did not see what was to them 'invisible' female participation via groups such as the Women's Institute.
Location of residence	Participation more likely in urban areas than in rural areas (difficulties of transport may play a part). In inner cities, turnout is often very low.
Socialisation and personality	Those brought up in families that were politically active and in which children were involved in discussion and making decisions are more likely to participate, as are more outgoing personalities. Family background is an important determinant.
Social class	Professional and business people, with a better education and higher income, are much more likely to participate in various ways, especially on polling day. Education is a strong determinant, as much activity involves organising, talking and writing – skills often associated with higher levels of attainment.

Source: Adapted from findings of Parry (1992) and Evans (1997)

In depth

Putnam and public disengagement from politics: the social capital

- Writing about the US, the 19th-century French writer de Tocqueville (see Chapter 7) observed that 'Americans of all ages, all stations in life, and all types of disposition are forever forming associations'.

- Robert Putnam, author of *Bowling Alone* (2000), doubts whether this still applies and argues that there is now a 'degree of social disengagement and civic connectedness' that has damaging consequences for political life.

- He believes that social participation is declining in the US and elsewhere, observing that today more people spend time watching *Friends* than making them! More seriously, he points to less people engaged in volunteer work, attending church or public meetings, voting in elections and trusting government.

- He uses the term 'social capital' in reference to social networks, the connections among individuals and the feelings of mutuality and trustworthiness that arise from them. In other words, interaction enables people to build communities, to commit themselves to each other and to knit the social fabric. A sense of belonging (and the relationships of trust and tolerance that can be involved) can, it is argued, bring great benefits to people.

- In his words, it is the ability of a community to 'develop the "I" into the "we"'.

Key terms

Social capital relates to the connections between individuals, and the social networks and trustworthiness that arise from them. A strong fund of social capital (i.e. good social ties between individuals who trust each other) is said to enable a community to develop political institutions and processes that have the capacity to solve society's problems.

Socialisation is the instilling of political attitudes and values via agencies such as family upbringing, education, the media, etc.

Social class relates to the hierarchical distinctions between individuals or groups in society. It is the division of people with similar characteristics into strata or distinct levels, e.g. the term 'working class' has traditionally related to the section of society dependent on physical labour, especially those paid by hourly wage.

Putnam has been the focus of seminars hosted by Bill Clinton at Camp David and Tony Blair at 10 Downing Street. His ideas have also been incorporated into speeches by George W Bush and William Hague.

Summary questions

1. Do low levels of participation reflect a general distrust of political life and politicians in Britain?

2. Are there any steps that can or should be taken to encourage greater participation in British political life?

4 Does participation really matter?

Learning objectives:

- Why have some people urged that participation is both a right and duty?

- What is the case for saying that participation in political life matters?

- What is the case against saying that participation matters?

- Should people vote?

Almost every theory relating to democracy involves the idea of political participation. For most people, popular involvement is the essence of democracy. Think back to the idea of Athenian democracy, in which the participation of all citizens in an open meeting was considered highly desirable. It was a badge of citizenship for the privileged minority, and the people who did not turn out were those who were excluded because they were not counted as citizens. Unfortunately, this happened to be the majority, who were either women, male slaves or non-Athenians.

Among those who have argued for greater participation are:

- **Edmund Burke**, a late 18th-century MP who has subsequently been regarded as a father of modern Conservative thinking. He famously said that 'it is necessary only for the good man to do nothing for evil to triumph'.

- **John Stuart Mill (1806–73)**, a British philosopher and liberal thinker, who in his book *On Liberty* argued that 'the general or prevailing opinion in any subject is rarely or never the whole truth; it is only by the collision of adverse opinions that the remainder of the truth has any chance of being supplied'. In other words, the more people debate issues, the more likely it is that the truth will emerge. Political discussion makes people more informed and better able to hold to account for their actions those who govern. Decision making will be improved if those who make decisions know that their actions are being scrutinised by an informed populace.

The *Report of the Advisory Group on Citizenship* (1998) made an interesting contribution to discussion on participation. Known as the Crick Report, the document was influential in paving the way for the introduction of compulsory lessons, in schools, on Citizenship. It observed:

In the political tradition stemming from the Greek city states and the Roman Republic, citizenship has meant involvement in public affairs by those who uphold the rights of citizens to take part in public debate and, directly or indirectly, shape the laws and decisions of a state.

For Crick and his team, such participation was both a right and a duty, the foundation of a democratic society and a safeguard for its preservation and protection.

Participation does matter!

- **In a democracy, it is ultimately the people who hold ministers to account, as democracy involves control of the government by those who are governed**. According to this view, voting is important, but it is not sufficient by itself. An informed, politically aware and active electorate will be better able to see through governmental deception and/or mismanagement.

- **Without effective opportunities for participation, there is a danger of increasing alienation and political exclusion of some social groups**. Several years ago, Sherry Arnstein defined citizen participation as 'the redistribution of power that enables the have-not citizens, presently excluded from the political and economic processes, to be deliberately included in the future'.

- **Participation by the moderate majority is a counter to the rise of political extremism**. Being highly committed and often fanatical in their beliefs, extremists will participate. If other people sit back and do nothing, they in effect surrender the field to those who zealously pursue their goals (see the Burke quotation above).

- **Participation is the way to counter apathy, alienation and ignorance**. By becoming informed and getting involved, people will see that it is possible to effect political and social change through the democratic process. People must get involved to make the system work for them.

- **So-called 'new forms of participation' are sporadic, often focused on single issues, and they quickly fade out of existence**. They may have a high profile for a while, but they are no substitute for the sustained campaigning of established parties and pressure groups, and the active vigilance of voters.

No, it doesn't matter!

- **It is easy to over-emphasise the arguments concerning participation**. Traditional forms may be in long-term decline, but perhaps in a post-materialist age (when bread-and-butter issues have largely passed out of existence) people have different priorities. They may also register their views by different sorts of action, such as joining environmental campaigns and taking part in the mass popular protests of recent years (fuel protests, pro- and anti-hunting demonstrations, the Make Poverty History campaign, etc.), which are made easier by new developments in technology – e-mail and mobile phones. In some cases, groups that seem very non-political can actually occasionally perform a highly political act. Local ramblers' associations cater for the leisure needs of many mainly older people, but when they deliberately walk on a footpath that farmers have been keen to disguise, or roam the countryside to establish traditional rights of access, they are behaving in a political way. Such 'new forms' of participation have the benefit that they allow people to express their views directly, rather than through some hierarchical political party in which ordinary members play only a small part.

Fig. 3 *Famous suffragette Emmeline Pankhurst arrested outside Buckingham Palace in 1914*

Key term

The **suffragettes** were supporters of the Women's Social and Political Union which campaigned for the right of women to vote in the early 20th century. They often used aggressive tactics.

Further reading

Few accessible general introductions to the study of Politics exist.

B Jones (ed.), *Politics UK*, Prentice Hall, 2004. Chapters 2–4 provide useful coverage of the historical, social and economic contexts of British politics. Chapter 5 covers political participation.

For democracy, see M Cole, *Democracy in Britain*, Edinburgh University Press, 2006.

Several of the other themes explored here are discussed further in future chapters, for which recommended reading is given.

For many people, politics is not an important priority in their lives. Particularly now that most people have a job and sufficient to eat, they want to take advantage of the different opportunities that modern society provides. They want to use their leisure to pursue their dreams (travel, sport, partying, attending pop concerts, etc.). Today, young people have more money than their counterparts in earlier generations. They also have the means of transport, so 'have car, will travel'. There is so much more that people can do now, and most of it seems more exciting than forms of political activity.

People only participate in high numbers at times of crisis, as in the two or three years before Hitler and the Nazis took control in Germany. Turnout went up partly because people were alarmed and wanted to protest about the threat of extremism from the Left and Right, and their present situation and future prospects. When they stay at home, it is a sign that they are relaxed and contented about the way that society is operating and how the country is being run. In other words, non-participation is not a sign of apathy, but rather of contentment.

There is little you can do to make people participate. New means of encouraging voting (by making it easier, e.g. by experimenting with setting up polling booths in supermarket car parks) have not had a profound effect. Many people are simply not interested.

Should people at least turn out to vote? Here are some reasons why it is often said they should:

Through voting, everyone gets a chance to express their views – 'no vote, no say'. Those who exercise power can make decisions much affecting everyone's lives, whether it is over the amount of taxation we pay, the financing of the NHS or how we can better protect the environment. It is important that we have a voice in the decisions that shape our lives.

All over the world, people have fought and died for the right to vote in free elections. In countries in which voting rights had either never been granted or had long been denied – Afghanistan, Iraq and South Africa for example – voting is highly valued and as soon as they were able to vote, people have queued up to get to the polls. In early 19th-century Britain, working people struggled to gain the right to vote and later members of organisations such as the **suffragettes** chained themselves to railings to achieve it.

The vote is perhaps the major symbol of citizenship in a democracy and 'one person, one vote' is one of its core principles. As good citizens, it is our duty as well as our right to vote. We expect society to allow us certain rights and freedoms. In return, we should play our part by doing our democratic duty.

✓ Summary questions

1 Are you in favour of greater participation?

2 Many under-30s do not vote. Should they?

3 How do you think that you developed your political attitudes and ideas?

2 Participation through the ballot box

1 Determinants of voting behaviour: recent trends

Learning objectives:

- What theories have been advanced to explain voting behaviour?

- What do we understand by the processes of partisan and class dealignment?

- What are the main long- and short-term factors that influence voting behaviour?

- What have been the trends in voting behaviour over recent decades?

- Why has voting behaviour become more unstable and less predictable over recent decades?

Key terms

Voting behaviour relates to the way that people vote and why they vote the way that they do.

Psephologists are specialists in the study of elections and voting behaviour.

Partisan alignment is the long-term allegiance of voters to a political party.

Partisan dealignment is the breakdown of long-term allegiance of voters to a particular party since the 1970s.

Social class relates to the hierarchical distinctions between individuals or groups in society. It is the division of people with similar characteristics into strata or layers. It is usually assessed on such characteristics as background, education and occupation.

Voting behaviour is concerned with how people vote and why they vote as they do. The study of the subject developed in the mid-20th century and was based on the new developments in survey research. Much has been written about the relationships between voting behaviour and social class, education, religion and social attitudes. **Psephologists** have developed various models to explain changes that have taken place in voting over recent decades, none of which explains voting patterns entirely.

Theories about voting behaviour

Four main theories have been advanced to explain voting behaviour in the post-war era:

1 **The party identification theory**. Supporters of this theory placed much emphasis on political socialisation which explained how people learned their political attitudes and behaviour via the process of growing up, in settings like their family and schools. Children discovered which party their parents favoured and were influenced by their parents' leanings, many of them staying with the party of their parents. In this way, political loyalties were developed. These tended to be confirmed by membership of particular groups and other social experiences. People had a psychological attachment to their parties, a sense of identity often referred to as **partisan alignment**. The way they voted reflected this identification, so that voting was a long-term manifestation of strongly held beliefs and loyalties.

In recent decades, the process of **partisan dealignment** has been much-noted. In Britain and elsewhere, the level of party identification today is markedly less than in the past. Clarke *et al.* have pointed out that the 'very strong' identification levels with Labour or the Conservatives sampled in 1964 (45%) had fallen to 21% by 1979 and 13% by 2001.

2 **The sociological theory**. Sociological theorists pointed to the way in which people's social characteristics influenced their participation in politics. In particular, **social class** was seen as important in shaping political attitudes, especially in Britain. So widely held was this view that in 1967 Pulzer wrote that: 'Class is the basis of British politics; all else is embellishment and detail'. To a large extent the party system was regarded as mirroring the class system. Thus middle-class people were expected to vote Conservative and the working classes were seen as strongly pro Labour. There were always many people who deviated (i.e. departed) from this pattern of voting, and much study was devoted to working-class Conservatives in particular. Other characteristics such as ethnicity, gender, region and religion were also long-term factors often linked to voting behaviour. However, the link between social class and voting (**class alignment**) was by far the most important connection.

Key terms

Class alignment relates to the strong association of membership of a social class with support for a political party.

Class dealignment relates to the breakdown since the 1970s of the long-term association of a social class with support for a particular political party.

Instrumental voting is a one-off assessment of the parties' policies and reputation, based on their past performance as well as a judgement about their ability to deliver what they promise.

Ideology is a system of assumptions, beliefs and values about public issues which are part of a comprehensive vision of society. The concept is central to politics as almost every political tendency has some degree of ideological backing. Ideologies help us to explain the political world and point towards what form of political action should be taken in particular circumstances.

In the same way that partisan dealignment has been a feature of recent decades, so too has its cousin, **class dealignment**. This has occurred in many Western countries, so that the class analysis of politics is less convincing today. Class mobility has increased. The old concepts of class solidarity – that everyone in a particular social class behaved in the same way – have been undermined.

3 **The rational choice theory**. In the 1980s, the emphasis shifted from the psychological and sociological approaches and was instead placed on the role of the individual in making a rational judgement and consequently acting in a calculated and deliberate way. According to Himmelweit *et al.* (1981), this may be a judgement based on the past performance of a particular administration, or it may be more related to the prospects for the individual and his/her family under any alternative. Either way, their assessments of parties were based on self-interest, i.e. the voters' perception of the likely effect on their life and well-being in the present and near future.

In effect, voters were behaving as consumers do in the marketplace, selecting a package that best suits their preferences. They compared products and made their decisions according to cost, quality and usefulness. One version of this consumerist approach was the idea advanced by Sanders (1996) that the state of the economy and the voters' view of how it was impacting on their lives was very important in helping people decide on how to exercise their vote.

Psephologists recognised that voting was becoming a more **instrumental** act, with people using it as a means by which to achieve their goals. If that was so, it was necessary for parties to adjust what they offered the electorate in line with what they believed voters wanted. In order to win support they also needed to place heavy emphasis on selling their potential and achievements to the electorate. Party managers were well aware of the need for careful management and manipulation of the media. In particular, they understood the importance of giving the leader a high profile in the campaign and exploiting his or her assets.

Some studies advanced in the 1980s and 1990s have cast doubt on the rationality of the choice which voters make. If they are exposed to biased presentation of news and current affairs via the media, then their judgement may be affected by any misleading impression that they receive.

4 **Dominant ideology theory**. Dunleavy and Husbands (1985) have argued that individual choices are influenced by media misrepresentation. In their view, the newspapers and television distort the process of political communication, in that they help to determine the agenda for debate and consciously or unconsciously provide a partial coverage of the news. This is even more important in an age of dealignment, because in the absence of traditional factors such as class and party loyalties, voters are more likely to be swayed by what they hear, see and read.

In this theory, the media are seen as reflecting a dominant prevailing **ideology**. If that view is harsh about welfare claimants or the rights of various minorities in society, voters will be influenced to vote for parties that advance policies which conform to the current thinking of the opinion formers.

The credibility of the dominant ideology theory is open to question. Whether or not you think that voters will succumb to a barrage of media manipulation is a matter of opinion. But the other theories are also open to question as they are incomplete or inadequate explanations of voting behaviour. None of them provides a totally convincing explanation of how and why people vote as they do. They all need to be born in mind when considering the subject and they each have their merits. They are not necessarily mutually exclusive.

Determinants of voting behaviour

Long-term influences include:

- **Party identification and loyalty**. Electors identify with a particular party and loyalties are forged, so that there is a strong long-term alignment (partisanship). Family influences are often reinforced by the membership of particular groups and later social experiences.
- **Social class**. In the US, the deep-seated association with a party is often stressed, but in Britain and on the continent more emphasis has been placed upon the person's membership of and identity with a particular social group such as the working or middle class.
- **Other factors relating to the social structure**, such as age, gender, region, occupation, membership of an **ethnic group** and religion.

Short-term influences include:

- **The economy** (see p22). This covers levels of inflation, unemployment and disposable income, and in particular how voters view their future prospects (whether or not they 'feel good'). Governments like to 'go to the country' at a time when people are happy with their present material circumstances and about their future prospects.
- **The personal qualities and appeal of the party leaders** (see p23). These are more important today given the media's infatuation with personalities.
- **The impact of the mass media** (see p29). The media currently play an important part. They may or may not have a direct influence on how voters vote, but they help to determine what the election is about and the issues that are important. They provide information and – in the case of the press – dramatic headlines which can damage the standing of leaders (e.g. the *Sun*'s damaging portrayal of **Neil Kinnock** in 1987 and 1992).
- **The style and effectiveness of party campaigning** (see p25). This is something which has changed considerably over recent decades.
- **The events leading up to the election**. The '**Winter of Discontent**' wrecked Labour's chances in 1979, in the same way that the humiliating circumstances of British withdrawal from the **ERM** (1992) and the connection in the public mind of the **Major** government with **sleaze** seriously undermined faith in the Conservatives in 1997. More recently, the handling of the war with Iraq seriously damaged the reputation of the Labour administration, and made many voters question the truthfulness of Tony Blair. In contrast, the successful outcome of the Falklands War boosted the prospects of **Margaret Thatcher** in 1983 (see p85).

Activity

Using the internet to assist you, find out the percentage of people living in the UK who belong to ethnic minorities and the composition of the ethnic minority population.

Key term

Ethnic group relates to people who share a common sense of identity as a result of kinship, culture, religion or often skin colour. The term 'ethnic minority group' is normally used to refer to non-white ethnic groups that are mainly the product of past immigration.

Further information

Social class in Britain

Table 1 *Categorisation commonly used by opinion-polling companies*

Category (% of pop.)	Groups included
A/B (28)	Higher/lower managerial, professional and administrative
C1 (29)	White collar, skilled, supervisory or lower non-manual
C2 (19)	Skilled manual
D/E (23)	Semi-skilled and unskilled manual/ residual, casual workers, long-term unemployed and very poor

■ Key terms

Mass media is the collective name for the organisations involved in publishing, broadcasting or other forms of political communication that channel information to the electorate.

Neil Kinnock (born 1942) was Labour MP (1970–95) and leader of the Opposition (1983–92).

The **Winter of Discontent** (1978–1979) was the period of widespread industrial unrest that seriously disrupted everyday life and damaged the prospects of the then Labour government.

ERM: the Exchange Rate Mechanism of the then European Community, a mechanism for regulating relationships between the basket of currencies of the member states.

Major government: John Major (born 1943) was a Conservative MP (1979–2001) and Prime Minister (1990–97).

Sleaze is the collective name for the various financial and sexual scandals that have occurred under recent governments.

Margaret Thatcher (born 1925) was a Conservative MP (1959–92) and Prime Minister (1979–90).

Middle England is the political middle ground often seen as being occupied by the aspirational middle, lower middle and working classes of England, those who wanted to better themselves and whose views are often equated with readership of the *Daily Mail*.

Stability of voting patterns describes a period when voting habits seemed to be consistent and predictable.

Fig. 1 *Rubbish piles up during the 'Winter of Discontent'*

■ **Issues and party images** (see p24). Much depends on the ability of the parties to inspire trust in their own policies and their ability to fulfil them, and to cast doubt on their opponents. Voters 'shop around' for the set of policies on offer that best suits their own priorities. They tend to have generalised images of the parties, traditionally seeing Labour as the party of the working class and in favour of higher social spending, and the Conservatives as the party of the middle and upper classes, more committed to lower taxation than to public expenditure on health and welfare. The image is based upon what the parties have done in the past, and a vague impression of policy positions and the qualities projected by the party leadership.

Broadly, long-term influences have become less important in British politics and the short-term influences have become more significant. The breakdown of these traditional associations is very important for the parties as they can no longer count on the support they once took for granted.

■ Post-war trends

As we have seen, the academic literature of the early post-war era pointed to a positive relationship between membership of a social class and the way people cast their vote. However, from the 1970s onwards, the process of class dealignment was reflected in a reduction in Conservative support from the professional and managerial classes and a reduction in Labour support from the working classes. In 1997, Labour increased its support across all social classes and for some years it continued to broaden its appeal in **Middle England**.

The features most noted in the post-war years up to the 1970s were:

■ **The stability of voting patterns, as people stayed loyal to the party they had always supported**. As Punnett put it in 1971: 'For most people, voting behaviour is habitual and ingrained'.

■ **That elections were determined by a body of floating voters in key marginal constituencies**, whose votes needed to be targeted by the parties if they were to have a chance of success.

- **The uniform nature of the percentage swing of votes between the parties across the UK**, which showed that voters in one area tended to behave in much the same way as those elsewhere.

- **The domination of the two main parties which between them could count on the support of the majority of the electorate**. This reached a high point in 1951 when the Conservatives and Labour between them gained 96.8% of the vote; in 1966, they still obtained 89.8%.

In the 30 years since the 1970s, many of those assumptions have proved to be no longer valid. The parties can no longer expect the degree of support they once enjoyed. The rise of **third parties** has made inroads into the share of the vote that the two main parties can command, as the figures in the table indicate.

Voting behaviour in recent years

Crewe's publication *Decade of De-alignment* (1983) was a psephological milestone. Using data from Essex University's British Election Study, Sarlvik and Crewe analysed elections in the 1970s, culminating in the Conservative victory in 1979. They showed the extent to which the two parties had steadily lost their once-reliable supporters, people who voted for the same party at each election. In particular, the writers discovered that **demographic changes** were taking their toll on Labour because the old working-class communities were being destroyed by redevelopment schemes, and inner cities were emptying. Workers moving to new towns and expanding small towns around London were less likely to vote Labour. Areas of population decline (like the North of England and South Wales) were traditionally Labour, while growth areas (mainly in the South East) were strongly Conservative, a point emphasised by changes to the constituency boundaries. Labour's electoral base was being eroded, a point which led Kellner to write in 1983 that the 'sense of class solidarity which propelled Labour to power in 1945 has all but evaporated'.

The Crewe study was particularly famous for its distinction between the old and the new working class. He wrote of 'the traditional working class of the council estates, the public sector, industrial Scotland and the North, and the old industrial unions . . . the affluent and expanding working class of the new estates and new service economy of the South' (the new working class). By the 1980s, it seemed that **embourgeoisement** was a significant factor favouring the Conservatives because in 1979 members of the skilled 'new' working class were won over by Thatcherite support for tax cuts and shared certain Conservative attitudes on race, unions, nationalisation and crime.

Labour's claim to be the party of the working class took a strong blow in the 1980s. It may be true that the Labour vote remained largely working class, but the working class was no longer largely Labour. To be successful again, Labour had to attract more skilled workers. Under the Blair leadership, the position improved dramatically. In 1997 and 2001, New Labour did well in all social categories (as shown in the table), and only among the AB voters did the Conservatives retain a lead.

Summary questions

1. How has the behaviour of voters changed over recent decades?

2. What do you think are the main influences on why people vote as they do?

Key terms

Third parties are ones that are capable of gathering a sizeable percentage of popular support and regularly gain seats in the legislature, but which have no meaningful chance of being the majority party and forming a government after an election, e.g. the British Liberal Democrat party in its early existence.

Demographic changes are changes that relate to the size and distribution of the population.

Embourgeoisement is the tendency of better-off working people with aspirations to become more like the middle classes in their social outlook and voting behaviour.

Table 2 *Average share of the vote for each party in post-war elections (%)*

	Con.	Lab.	Lib/ Lib. Dem.
1945–70	45.3	46.0	7.1
1974–2005	37.9	36.3	19.4

Activity

Table 3 *Labour support by social class in the 1997 and 2001 elections (%)*

Social class	1997	2001
A/B	31	30
C1	39	38
C2	50	49
D/E	59	55

Source: Based on D Butler and D Kavanagh (2005)

Write a couple of paragraphs about the changing basis of Labour electoral support from the 1970s to the present day. Is Labour still the party of the working classes? In its voter appeal, is Labour mainly a working-class party?

2 Social class and voting: is there still a link?

Learning objectives:

- What is social class?
- How important has class voting been traditionally in determining the outcome of British elections?
- Which parties have traditionally gained support from the upper, middle and working classes respectively?
- Why has class voting broken down in recent decades?
- What was the relationship between social class and voting in the 2005 election?

Key term

Volatility relates to the significant changes in voting habits which have resulted in voting becoming less consistent and more unpredictable. It involves a shift of voter support between parties or between voting and abstention, a process sometimes known as 'churning'.

Activities

1. Write a paragraph to suggest reasons why upper- and middle-class voters have traditionally favoured the Conservative party.

2. Write a paragraph to explain why people in social groups D/E tend to vote Labour.

Social class was once a key determinant of voting, with the working classes tending to vote for the more progressive party, and the better-off favouring to the party that would preserve the status quo. It was still important in the 1980s and 1990s. Even in its bleak years of the early–mid 1980s, Labour continued to find core support from the least well-off in the inner cities and in regions such as Scotland and Wales.

Class voting varies considerably between countries. It is relatively significant in some countries, as the table below indicates. However, generally speaking the influence of class is not as strong as it was. There have always been many voters in Britain and the rest of western Europe who deviated from class voting, but that number increased substantially in the 1980s as right-wing administrations managed to increase their appeal among the more skilled working people who wanted to upgrade their lifestyle and prospects. Old class structures have broken down as many sections of the population have become better off and the manual working class has got smaller.

Table 4 *The relative importance of class voting: some examples*

Importance	Examples
Low	US, 'new' democracies, e.g. Hungary, Poland
Relatively low, little evidence of decline	Ireland, Netherlands, Spain
More significant, but in decline	Austria, Belgium, Germany
Relatively high, but in decline	Denmark, Sweden, UK

Source: Based on data provided in T Bale, European Politics: A Comparative Introduction, Falgrave, 2005

Social changes have occurred in all developed countries and voters have become less committed to their long-term allegiances. Stability rather than change was once the established pattern in voting behaviour, with many voters being reluctant or unwilling to deviate from their regular habits. In recent years, as a result of partisan dealignment, there has been a weakening of the old loyalties. A new **volatility** exists within the electorate. However, parties retain their 'core voters', those who will remain loyal under almost any circumstances.

What is social class and which people belong to each class?

Social class relates to the hierarchical distinctions between individuals or groups in society. It is the division of people with similar characteristics into strata (layers). Anthropologists (those who study human beings and the social relations between them), historians and sociologists identify class as universal, although what determines class varies widely from one society to another.

In the UK, class is determined largely by:

- occupation
- background, education and qualifications

20

▩ income (personal and household)

▩ wealth or net worth including the ownership of land and other forms of property.

In spite of the greater volatility in voting behaviour in recent years, class remains an important – if declining – factor in influencing voting choices. It relates to region, with people in the peripheries of Great Britain (the North of England; Scotland and Wales) being more likely to vote Labour than those in the South Midlands, South and South East. These strong regional differences in party support are in part related to the class structure, as the more socially deprived and solidly working-class areas are those furthest from London.

▩ Class and the 2005 election

In 2005, the social class divide was arguably weaker than ever. The Conservative lead in the share of the A/B vote was down to 9% (it was 32% in 1992), though the A/Bs and C1s remain the most significant element in Conservative support. Even in a year when it did badly in comparison with the two previous elections, New Labour was still able to capture 28% of the A/B vote. Although it lagged behind the Conservatives among the C1s, it was well ahead among the C2s and the D/Es.

Table 5 *Party support in the 2005 election by social class (%)*

Class	Labour	Conservative	Lib Dem	Other
A/B	28	37	29	6
C1	32	36	23	9
C2	40	33	19	8
D/E	48	25	18	9

Source: Based on figures provided by the Observer, *8.5.2005*

Regional variations are related to class variations. The outcome in 2005 varied across the country, only the South East becoming evidently more Conservative. Labour had a clear lead over their rivals in Greater London, the North East, North West, Yorkshire/Humberside, Scotland and Wales, and a narrower lead in the West Midlands and East Midlands. It was behind in the East, the South East and the South West.

There remains a broad north-south division in terms of party support, Labour's strongest areas being the three northernmost regions of England, Scotland and Wales, its weakest ones being the three southernmost areas of England. The Conservatives' weakest areas are in the North of England, Scotland and Wales (23 seats in all) and their strongest are in the South. Support for the Liberal Democrats is more evenly spread across the regions, but they are relatively weak in the Midlands and Wales and strongest in the South West. Of course, within these broad regions, there are variations in party support across individual constituencies, reflecting the importance of local factors in some contests. Indeed, several of those who have analysed the 2005 election have pointed to the lack of uniformity within regions on this occasion, which is why Anthony King (2005) was led to observe that making sense of the election 'is like trying to discern patterns in a shattered mosaic'.

▩ Activities

1 Write a paragraph to explain whether the result of the 2005 election confirms or undermines the view that the middle classes lean to the Conservatives and the poorest section of the working classes lean to Labour.

2 Think about the groups who make up the C2s. How important are they in determining the outcome of elections? How have they been voting in recent years?

■ **Summary questions**

1 'Labour is the party of the industrial urban and inner city areas of the North of England, Scotland and Wales. The Conservatives are the party of rural areas and the suburbs in the South'. Is this statement still true?

2 In your view, is voting in Britain today class based?

3 Influences upon British voters today

Learning objectives:

■ Why have factors other than class become more important in shaping voting behaviour today?

■ Does a strong economy make re-election of the government likely?

■ What has been the impact of television on the significance of party leaders in determining the outcome of elections?

■ Why have issues become more important in recent elections than they were a generation or so ago?

We have noted the broad trend in all democracies away from group or party voting. There has not been a complete dealignment, but rather a weakening of existing patterns and attachments. The consequence of this process is that there is now a more volatile and sceptical electorate whose votes are up for grabs; they are liable to be influenced by a range of factors. These include the short-term factors to which we have already referred:

■ the state of the economy
■ the qualities of party leaders
■ political issues and images
■ the effectiveness of party campaigning
■ the impact of the mass media.

In more pragmatic times, voters come to a general assessment of the parties based on what they have done and what they propose to do. They look for indications of competence. The skill of consultants and other marketing people is to create an impression of confidence and trust in the abilities of ministers and would-be ministers and the policies they represent.

Voting is now much influenced by the opinions and judgements of the voters, what Denver (2003) calls 'judgemental voting'. As he concludes:

> People will disagree over what exactly the judgements are about – issues, ideologies, images, personal economic prospects, party leaders – and this may vary from election to election: but it is the transition from an aligned and socialised electorate to a dealigned and judgemental electorate that has underpinned electoral developments in Britain over the past half-century.

■ The state of the economy

In the 1992 US presidential election campaign, the Democrat candidate, Bill Clinton, had a notice on his desk that read: 'It's the economy, stupid!'. The observation seems to encapsulate much conventional thinking about what determines electoral behaviour and awards success to one party or another in most modern democracies. According to this

22

view, all a government needs to do to get itself returned to power is to ensure that the economy is functioning well.

The economy is a classic valence issue, i.e. one where there is broad agreement within the electorate about the goals that government should pursue. Everyone wants prosperity, and few would be opposed to more specific goals such as full employment, stable prices and increasing real incomes. Various academics have developed theories to illustrate how a government's popularity over the lifetime of a parliament varies according to the state of the economy, most notably David Sanders. He put forward a sophisticated theory that did not rely on objective economic indicators, but suggested that:

1 voters see the success of the economy in terms of the level of mortgage interest and inflation, and

2 people are more likely to re-elect a government which makes them 'feel good' about the state of the economy.

According to this view, people's perceptions of how the economy has affected them in the recent past and their personal expectations for the future influence their level of optimism or pessimism. In explaining individual election results, theories can come unstuck. Sanders' model did not apply to the 1997 result, when there was no obvious alarm about the state of the economy yet the governing Conservatives were still heavily defeated. However, in the run-up to the election in 2001 the feel-good factor did have an impact upon party support. In that election, the rising trend in expectations was matched by a strong victory for the ruling party.

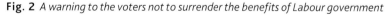
Britain is working. Don't let the Tories take us back to almost 10% inflation. **Labour** www.labour.org.uk

Fig. 2 *A warning to the voters not to surrender the benefits of Labour government*

The impact of party leaders

In the current media age, many people have become more interested in the personalities of those who aspire to lead them. Fifty years ago, it did not matter whether a leader looked good on TV or not, but today it is important. Parties are conscious of the image of any candidate for the leadership. Significantly, it is unusual in any democracy for parties to choose fat, bald or ugly people as leaders. They like to find personable individuals who are likely to charm the voters and who appear relaxed and genial on television. This is not to say that leaders who lack natural and easy charm can never succeed. But if they do not possess it, it is very helpful to have other qualities that the voters can admire. Many may not have warmed to Margaret Thatcher as a person, but nonetheless detected

Activity

Denver, quoted above, feels that party image may be a factor of increasing importance in determining how people vote. A poll by Populus in 2005 mentioned five factors on which Labour was ahead of the Conservatives:

- It has left the past behind and moved on.
- It has leadership prepared to make tough, unpopular decisions.
- Its heart is in the right place, even if the voters do not always share its views.
- It is led by people of real ability.
- Represents the kind of society the voters would like Britain to be.

The Conservatives were still associated with many negatives, being seen as stuck in the past, divisive, extreme, less generous-spirited, old and tired. Potential Conservative voters were turned off by what they perceived as the negativism and aggressiveness of the party's campaign.

The Conservatives appeared to have an 'image problem' in 2005. What do you think are the images presented by Labour and the Conservatives today?

in her remarkable qualities of leadership – toughness, resilience, the willingness to make hard decisions, a sense of direction, etc.

The absence of leadership quality worked against Labour's Michael Foot in the early 1980s. Faced by the formidable Mrs Thatcher, he seemed rather intellectual, aloof and slightly eccentric. Neil Kinnock performed some useful work in remodelling Labour's image, but he was unable to persuade the voters to warm to him personally. He could not successfully compete with Margaret Thatcher in 1987 or with John Major five years later. Major seemed affable, having the image of being a trustworthy, reliable bank manager or accountant.

Labour's decision to choose Tony Blair as leader in 1994 was a very successful one in terms of leader appeal. Young, dynamic and charismatic, he was effective on television and remains one of the most skilful political communicators of our time. As Prime Minister, his levels of popularity remained high for an unusually long time, until the Iraq War and later the '**loans for peerages**' scandal seriously dented his reputation for honesty and trustworthiness. Even at the time of his handover to Gordon Brown, his personal popularity was greater than that of his successor in most of the polls. His three Conservative opponents were no match for him in the contests of 1997, 2001 and 2005. He has been a major factor in Labour's electoral success in recent years, as is evidenced by him being the first Labour leader to be elected in three consecutive elections, each time with a sound or overwhelming majority.

■ The impact of party issues and images

Occasionally there are particular issues in a general election that cause much controversy and interest. It may be that a poor set of unemployment statistics provokes anxiety, or some other event occurs during the campaign. More usually, there is some issue that becomes a broad theme on which the public focus. Sleaze was such an issue in 1997 and it could be again in the next election unless Labour is able to overcome popular impressions of the behaviour of some party figures.

Back in the 1950s and 1960s, when voting behaviour was more predictable and a matter of habit for many people, issues probably counted for less. Most people lacked a real interest in the detail of policy and the level of public knowledge was low. Voters are not very well informed today, but it is likely that the mass coverage of politics on television has contributed to greater public awareness and understanding of particular policies.

Today, in an era when voting behaviour is less stable, issues may play a larger role than in the past, especially given the greater amount of information available. But there is still a great deal of doubt about the importance of issues as a factor in determining voting behaviour.

Ivor Crewe has done a lot of research into issue voting. The salience of an issue is significant, in other words how much it has figured in the public mind. But what is also very important is how voters feel about the ability of the politicians to tackle that issue. Crewe (1988) notes how in Thatcherite Britain in the early 1980s, unemployment was widely seen as a serious problem. This was a valid issue, but many voters seemed to be unconvinced that Labour – the party usually associated with concern for job protection – had any credible, attainable answer. In 1987, voters favoured Labour on three key issues (education, health and unemployment), but this did not prevent the re-election of the Conservative government. Probably many voters were more preoccupied

■ Key term

Loans (cash) **for peerages** (honours) relates to the names given by commentators and politicians to a political scandal in the UK in 2006 and 2007 concerning the alleged connection between loans to political parties and the offer of a seat in the House of Lords.

■ Links

For more on 'loans for peerages', see pp94–95.

■ Activities

1. Write a list of the qualities that make a political leader 'good on television'.

2. Rank these factors in order of their importance as qualities for a party leader:

   a all-round capability

   b calm in crisis

   c down-to-earth

   d effective communicator

   e good grasp of political issues

   f honest and trustworthy

   g intellectual ability

   h personality

   i sound judgement

   j telegenic.

3. Can you identify a politician that you have seen on television and admire very much? What qualities do you admire about him or her?

Activities

Here is a list of the 'top ten' issues that the opinion-polling company Mori listed in the 2005 election:

- asylum/immigration
- crime
- defence
- economy
- education
- Europe
- health
- pensions
- taxation
- transport

1 Are there any other issues that you would have expected to find in the list?

2 Write down the top five issues that you think might help to determine the outcome of the next election.

with their personal prosperity, which they felt was likely to be better protected and promoted by Tory ministers.

David Denver (2003) has suggested that issues are becoming more important at election time. He is not saying that voters carefully weigh up every party policy before making their decision. Rather, now that the electorate has become more dealigned and open to media influence, voters are more likely to base their votes upon a judgement, a one-off assessment of parties' policies and reputations, as well as a guess about what they might deliver in future. Their verdict will be based upon their thinking about current issues, images, ideologies, leaders and government performance than ever before ('judgemental voting'). In many cases, they will have a generalised impression that a particular party is strong on the economy, the NHS or some other policy, or broadly more likely to curb the entry of asylum seekers and 'act tough' on law and order.

In an era of judgemental voting, party image has become more significant than ever before. For the advisers and consultants who determine election strategy in the main parties, the task is to create trust in their own side and doubts about the capacity or integrity of their opponents.

Summary questions

1 In the case of the three main parties, is the current party leader likely to be an asset or liability in the next general election campaign? In each case, give reasons.

2 What current political issues could have a substantial bearing on the outcome of the next election?

4 Election campaigns and their impact

Learning objectives:

- How important have recent election campaigns been in determining the results of the contests?

- What is the purpose of campaigning?

- In what ways has television changed election campaigning?

- How accurate and useful are opinion polls?

Political parties are in one sense always engaged in an **election campaign**, in that they gauge their actions according to the likely impact they will have upon the voters. But during the actual campaign leading up to polling day, their activity becomes more intense and much effort, political skill and professionalism is used to convey the party message. Although the actual campaign must last at least three weeks it usually goes on for four or more – in 1997 it was 44 days.

We have seen that a few decades ago, voting was much more predictable than it is now. Voters tended to have a traditional allegiance and many of them were rarely persuaded to abandon it. They were unlikely to be strongly influenced by the election campaign, unless they were '**floating voters**'. These voters – especially those living in marginal constituencies – determined the outcome, and the parties were keen to identify and target them with their message.

Links

For more on 'Campaigns' see p71, Chapter 5, 'Political parties and the need for them'

Recent elections

Today, voting behaviour is more volatile, so that in theory more votes are up for grabs. David Denver's (2003) analysis of the 1992 election campaign showed that at the beginning of the campaign, only 63% of voters had definitely made up their mind; 21% made up their mind in the last week and 6% on the last day. These findings are consistent with the idea that there was a 'late swing' in the last few days. However, if the campaign in 1992 appeared to have an impact, this was less obvious in 1997. Many voters seem to have decided their vote before the 1997 campaign began. It was time for a change after 18 years of Conservative rule. Labour retained its massive poll lead and won the election.

The 2001 campaign aroused conspicuously less interest than most general elections before. There was little enthusiasm among the voters or in the media once the parties swung into action and the campaign began. This was reflected not only in the poor level of turnout on the day, but also in the lowest viewing figures for election night coverage on television. An ITV poll found that 70% of viewers expressed little or no interest in coverage of the results.

In 2001, the campaign appeared to have only a modest impact, hence the description of it as 'a campaign that changed nothing'. The study of opinion polls shows that support for the parties remained stable during the weeks of the campaign. Labour and Conservative support 'flat-lined', in the sense that there were no major gains or losses for either party, with the campaign appearing to make little difference to voters. The exception was support for the Liberal Democrats, which showed a small increase.

Recent general elections have had bad press. In 2005, the **tabloids** wrote of the alleged dreariness of the campaign. The **broadsheets** complained that it was trivial, nasty or both. Writing of his experiences, Labour MP Tony Wright observed:

> The truth, I think, is that it was the election that nobody really wanted – not the politicians, not the media and certainly not the electorate. It had been going on in a phoney form for so long that most people just wanted it to be over when it finally came.

The purposes of campaigns

Campaigns may have an impact when the outcome is far from clear. The national campaign is now carried out largely on television. It is designed to:

- reinforce the views of those who are already committed to the party
- recruit the genuinely undecided
- convert the waverers in other parties.

In depth

The campaign in 2005

In 2005, there were four weeks for the election campaign proper. For the first time, the Conservatives and Labour had said that there would be none of the traditional early morning press conferences. Instead, the party leaders would meet media interviewers and campaign followers as they journeyed from one venue to another. However, the Liberal Democrats stuck to the usual routine and soon the two main parties held start-of-day gatherings at the national headquarters after all.

As ever, the press conferences were geared to the needs of television, many of the questions coming from the political editors of the main TV channels. Otherwise, there were few large public meetings, rather a series of events in which the leaders met with selected groups of constituents or participated in **photo opportunities** against some background which portrayed their concern about some aspect of life – for example, hospitals and schools. In general, there was little advance publicity for such events because of the opportunities this created for terrorist attacks and organised, aggressive heckling. For the same reason, there were few walkabouts.

Target voters

In a highly professionalised manner, **the leaders targeted those constituencies which they hoped to win or were desperately keen not to lose.** They were concerned with the voters whose reactions might make a difference. They might be persuaded to switch sides or be converted from being abstainers to voters. Experience of US electioneering techniques has shown how such people can be identified, with the social characteristics of each postcode area being carefully recorded and utilised in party propaganda. But of course in total 646 constituency struggles were being conducted around the country – some in marginal constituencies, but many in safe ones.

The complaint was sometimes made that whereas there were some 45 million eligible voters, **the parties concentrated their fire on a few hundred thousand voters in a relatively few seats.** Butler and Kavanagh (2005) quote one Conservative activist who pointed out that 'there are 7.4 million voters in the target seats, but it will be 838,000 who decide the election'.

In 2005, as in 2001, the ratings of the two main parties did not significantly shift in the weeks before polling day. As often happens, the third party benefited from the increased publicity that an election generates.

The local campaign is still important in marginal constituencies where a small number of votes can change party control. Here, the purpose is to get out the maximum vote, by speech making, canvassing and organising postal voting.

Opinion polls and their value

Opinion polling in Britain began in 1938 and since the 1950s it has been carried out on a regular basis. Polls have become a familiar feature of election campaigns. Two main methods of sampling have been tried: random sampling (based on the Electoral Register) and quota sampling (based on face-to-face interviews). In recent elections, random sampling has become more common as there is less chance of an error and it is

Key term

Photo opportunities are carefully stage-managed events where the leading figure is set against a particular background, perhaps to demonstrate concern for the location and those who work within it (e.g. an NHS hospital). This has a humanising effect, showing the person to be in touch with the needs and concerns of ordinary people.

Fig. 3 *The Conservatives use the character issue to damage Labour*

Activity

A Conservative poster in the 2005 campaign used the issue of Iraq to damage the standing of Tony Blair (Fig. 3):

What do you think of negative advertising aimed at undermining the reputation of someone on the other side?

Activities

1. Why are voters in marginal constituencies important to party campaign managers? Write down the ways in which they might try to capture their support.

2. Suggest two reasons why the last two campaigns have failed to ignite voter enthusiasm.

now possible to get higher response rates because of the greater use of telephone contact.

The recent record of the pollsters

In the 1950s and 1960s, pollsters were remarkably successful in pinpointing the actual outcome of elections, often within a small percentage of the result achieved by each party. Since the 1970s, in an age of greater voter volatility, it has proved less easy to gauge the true intentions of the electorate and to be sure that those who favoured one party would actually turn out and vote for it. The performance in 1992 was particularly poor. Most polls predicted a 'hung parliament', in which Labour would be the largest party. The error in the predictions of the likely gap between the two parties was greater than it had ever been.

There are still serious doubts about the performance of the opinion polls. In 1997, they were accurate in predicting the winning party, although bearing in mind the scale of the Labour victory this success was unsurprising. Also in 2001, it was no great achievement to pinpoint the leading party. However, yet again, there was a vast variation in the Labour lead, which ranged from 11% (Rasmussen) to 17% (MORI) in the final polls taken.

Throughout the 2005 campaign, the polls generally agreed that Labour seemed destined to win, but with a reduced majority. They differed on how much the majority might fall. Of the final polls, the one taken by National Opinion Poll (NOP) was the most accurate although none of the major polling companies was far out. Collectively, the surveys were the most accurate predictions ever made of the outcome of any British general election. As can be seen from the table, every individual estimate was within 2% of the result for each party.

Table 6 *Results of polls during the 2005 campaign (%)*

	ICM	MORI	NOP	Populous	YouGov	Result
Labour	38	38	36	38	37	36
Conservatives	32	33	33	32	32	33
Liberal Democrats	22	23	23	21	24	23
Other parties	8	6	9	9	7	8

Source: Information based on data provided on the Mori website and covering surveys conducted wholly or partly after Monday, 2 May 2005

Activity

Using the net to assist you, choose any one polling company and find out about the results of its most recent poll on the state of the parties. See if you can also find out what method of sampling it employs and the number of people it samples.

Do polls matter?

In the early days of polling, the successes of many pollsters led some commentators to accept their findings without question. Problems in some elections since 1970 have led to greater caution in the use of poll findings. However, whatever the reservations, poll results are still viewed with much interest by politicians, the media and many members of the public – especially when an election is looming.

Polls are useful to the parties, enabling them to find out which issues are causing the greatest popular concern, which voters they should target, and the strategies they should devise to maximise their appeal.

Prime Ministers may find polls helpful in determining when to call an election. Some have been skilful at 'playing the polls', in other words

Key terms

The bandwagon effect suggests that the polls encourage voters to climb on the bandwagon of the party that is ahead, so they end up backing the victorious side.

The boomerang effect suggests that electors are encouraged to change sides and support the underdog, the party behind in the polls.

timing the election date to coincide with a period when the polls are showing that their party is 'riding high' in public esteem.

A few countries ban publication of polls in the build-up to polling day in case they influence the way people vote. Some commentators have suggested that there is a **bandwagon effect** in favour of the party in the lead, whilst others have mentioned a contradictory **boomerang effect** in favour of the party in second place. There is no consistent evidence one way or the other. If we do not know for sure what effect polls might have, the case for banning them seems unproven. In any case, to do so might not seem liberal in a free country, as companies have a right to publicise what people think just as the voters have a right to know their findings. Furthermore, if findings are not published, the results may still leak out. It would be hard to stop poll findings from being published abroad.

Summary questions

1. In what ways has television altered the nature of election campaigning?
2. Do election campaigns change anything?
3. Should the publication of opinion polls be banned during an election campaign?

5 The mass media and its impact on popular attitudes and voting

Learning objectives:

- How mass are the mass media?

- Why are campaign managers so concerned to ensure that their parties get a fair deal in TV coverage?

- How important are the media in influencing the outcome of elections?

The term 'mass media' is a catch-all phrase that covers all popular means of communication such as newspapers, periodicals, magazines, posters, the cinema, radio, television and video, as well as more recent innovations such as e-mail and the internet. All of these are concerned with the transmission of ideas and information in one way or another, but today we think mainly of the press and broadcasting when we consider the role of the media in politics.

The mass media certainly are massive:

- A newspaper is delivered or people have access to one in many households: on an average day, nearly 60% of people over the age of 15 read a morning paper. Depending on the newspaper, there is usually considerable discussion of political events and issues – there is less in the popular tabloids and more (though a declining amount) in the quality broadsheets.

- More than 97% of homes have a television, some have two or three. Even though many programmes are for entertainment only, current affairs, documentaries and news bulletins all provide political coverage.

- Internet access in UK homes has grown at an astonishing rate. Some 50% of UK homes now have access to the internet (this is strongly linked to income and education).

Table 7 *UK national daily newspapers: ownership, leanings and circulations*

	Owned by	Support in 1997	Support in 2001	Support in 2005	Average daily circulation March 2007
Popular					
Daily Mirror	Trinity Mirror	Labour	Labour	Labour	1,624,490
Daily Star	Northern and Shell	Labour	Labour	No preference declared	795,451
Sun	News International	Labour	Labour	Labour	3,164,150
Middle market					
Daily Mail	Daily Mail and General Trust	Conservative	Conservative	Anything but a straight Labour victory	2,362,162
Daily Express	Northern and Shell	Conservative	Labour	Conservative	816,046
Qualities					
Financial Times	Pearson	Labour	Labour	Labour	431,242
Daily Telegraph	Telegraph Group	Conservative	Conservative	Conservative	899,923
Guardian	Guardian Media Group	Labour	Labour	Labour	378,378
Independent	Independent Newspapers	Labour	Not Conservative	Inclined to Liberal Democrats	253,878
The Times	News International	Euro-sceptic candidates, especially those of either main party	Labour	Labour	665,764

NB: Circulation figures are as shown. Readership figures for any given newspaper are generally around three times higher than the circulation figures.

For most voters the media – and especially television – is the main source of information. If there is bias in the media, then this could be damaging to the parties and personalities which are the victims of it. **Pluralists** are wary of tales of bias. They do not deny that it exists, but argue that there are many diverse sources of opinion (some representing minority viewpoints); anyway, we cannot assume that biased programmes necessarily change or modify the views of the electorate.

The charters of the BBC and ITV require them to be impartial in their political coverage and to display balance in their coverage of party standpoints. Yet at various times Labour and Conservative politicians have claimed that particular television programmes or interviewers were biased against them. Governments that have been in office for a long time often feel that their spokespersons are badly treated by the interviewers. Inevitably, if problems are exposed they want to know why ministers have not tackled them. Liberal Democrats sometimes complain that they suffer not from biased content but from neglect, their voice failing to get publicity in between general elections.

With television, there is unlikely to be obvious bias in the news as read out by the newsreader. But when he or she goes over to a special correspondent – perhaps on industrial relations or social policy – critics allege that the language used can be 'loaded' (i.e. carry an implication that may influence people one way or another). Choice of language and pictures, intonation, the setting in which words are delivered, can all affect the objectivity of the outcome. Some years ago, the Glasgow University Media Group (GUMG) noted how in industrial disputes strikers were often described as 'militants' or 'wreckers' and pictured haranguing those who wished to work. By contrast, management representatives were interviewed seated calmly behind their desks. In other words, there was a hidden bias in some news presentation.

Newspapers have traditionally been biased towards the Conservative party. In the 1980s and early 1990s, the *Daily Mail*, *Daily Express*, the *Daily Telegraph* and particularly the *Sun* kept up a relentless campaign against the Labour party and especially the leadership of Neil Kinnock. The success of Tony Blair in reversing this anti-Labour bias made it easier for him and his party from 1997 onwards. In the elections of 1997, 2001 and even 2005, the majority of newspaper readership was on Labour's side.

Do the media influence the outcome of elections?

In the 1930s, when European dictators were manipulating the media, propaganda was much used and analysts feared its effects on passive recipients. It was as though they were being injected by a syringe, hence the term 'the hypodermic model of media influence'. The suggestion was that they soaked up the information they were given, like a sponge absorbs water.

After the war, researchers such as Lazarsfeld in the US developed the idea that rather than change popular opinions one way or another, television and newspapers reinforce them. He advanced his 'minimum effects' theory which said that voters already have their own preconceptions and ideas and these act as a barrier to any message received from the media. The media may 'firm up' previously held views, but they do not create or mould them. Hence the alternative label sometimes used, 'reinforcement theory'. Birch later adopted a similar approach, suggesting that 'people expose themselves mainly to communications with which they are predisposed to agree, and tend to remember the content only of those items with which they are in agreement'.

For a long while, people believed this idea of reinforcement. But in the 1970s GUMG began to stress the importance of agenda-setting by television and newspapers. This suggests that the media influence the electorate by more subtle means, by determining what is seen and heard. The media may not determine what people think, but they do determine what they think about. GUMG went further and argued that the hidden bias resulted from the background and outlook of those who worked as journalists (often white, male, middle class and middle aged). Their outlook and the way in which they present the news tends to make us more sympathetically disposed towards moderate attitudes and policies and critical of those who challenge society's ideas, such as strikers, protesters and others portrayed as militants or extremists.

Many writers now support the independent effects theory. Life has moved on since Lazarsfeld wrote. Television is watched for so long and by so many people that common sense suggests it must influence us. Saturation coverage of politics at election time means that we cannot escape the barrage of news and views. This must have some effect, even if we cannot be sure what it is. At the very least, television especially expands our knowledge; we should know more than our parents and grandparents could ever find out. Over a long period, all of this viewing probably has some influence over our thinking. The effects may be

Activities

1 Look at copies of the *Daily Telegraph* and/or *Daily Mail*, and copies of the *Guardian* and/or Daily *Mirror*. From the choice of headlines, selection of stories and the way in which they are treated, do you detect any leanings towards one party rather than another?

2 'Television sets the agenda for much of our political discussion'. In the same evening, listen to a news bulletin on the BBC, ITV and Sky News. Compare the top five stories. Is there agreement on the main news stories? Do you notice any differences or bias in the coverage?

3 If you were a Labour politician today, do you think you should worry about the treatment your party might get from the tabloids?

4 Write down the things that you like and dislike about coverage of political stories and events in broadcasting and the press.

Key term

Political consultants are professional advisers and they have increasingly been used by the parties over the last 30 years. Most of them specialise in some aspect of election campaigning, e.g. fund-raising, polling or handling the media. Media advisers understand how television operates and what the candidate needs to do to create a good impression.

Spin doctors are specialist party consultants whose task it is to change the way the public perceives an issue/event and encourage favourable media coverage for the party and its leader.

Activities

1. Write a couple of paragraphs to explain which of the theories of media influence you find the most convincing and why.

2. In what ways do you think the media influence the conduct of elections and electioneering?

different on different people, some being passive spectators who take little notice of what they see, others being much more involved and open to persuasion. Above all, because voting behaviour is today more volatile than in the past, many voters' long-held allegiances to one or other party have broken down. What they see or hear may matter more.

If the effects of media influence are not immediately apparent in the short term, it is likely that over a longer period cumulative exposure may make a more lasting impression. There has been no major long-term study of the impact of broadcasting or newspapers on public opinion and voting. In truth, it would be very difficult and costly to organise. If such a survey could be conducted, it may at the very least reveal slow and subtle changes over a period of years.

One final consideration. The parties' **political consultants** clearly think that television has a significant impact. They place much emphasis on ensuring that the campaign is appropriate for the medium, carefully packaging the product and portraying the candidates in their best light. Before 1997, New Labour set out to establish good links with the press in opposition, the hope being that they could persuade editors to support their cause. New owners and editors of national tabloids were often warmly welcomed by the party leadership, particularly if they were seen as being susceptible to influence. New Labour also developed an increasingly systematic and professional approach to media management. As with politicians of other parties, its **spin doctors** were convinced that the media do matter in shaping the opinions of the electorate. Hence their concern to ensure that they received fair treatment and their willingness to complain loudly when they felt that they were getting unfavourable treatment.

Summary questions

1. Do you think that television is in any way biased towards one party or another?

2. Does media bias matter?

3. In your view, do the media have a significant impact on voting behaviour?

6 Age, gender and ethnicity

Learning objectives:

- How does voting behaviour vary across the age ranges?

- Why have women in general leaned towards Labour in recent elections?

- What factors might make some women abandon their support for the Labour party in the next election?

- How do members of ethnic minorities use their vote?

- Why have ethnic minorities traditionally favoured Labour?

Apart from social class, psephologists have often pointed to the association of other social and demographic characteristics with voting behaviour. Some of these, such as education or housing, are clearly linked to social class, whereas age and gender are not, and ethnicity may not be.

Age

In 2005, the 'progressive' parties, Labour and the Liberal Democrats, again fared better among young people, the Conservatives only having a lead among those who are over 55 Labour scored well among the 35–44 age group which might be most involved with family. Most early voting surveys suggested that young people (especially 18–24-year-olds) were more inclined to vote Labour, whilst older people (especially the over-55s) were more likely to vote Conservative. In a major analysis conducted in the 1960s, Butler and Stokes (1969) wrote of 'senescent Conservatism', the idea that the more senile you become, the more likely you are to be a Conservative.

The usual explanation given for this tendency was that young people tended to be more idealistic in their thinking, wanting a better and more peaceful world with more social justice and a genuine attempt to tackle world poverty. They favoured policies involving more public spending on domestic and international policies, not least because the burden of the necessary taxation would not fall upon them. As they become older, people have a more realistic and perhaps more cynical view of what can be achieved by way of social change at home and abroad. They have mortgages to pay and other costs associated with family responsibilities, and would be alarmed by high taxation to finance generous or reckless public spending. Once they are more soundly financially established in their fifties and sixties, they are particularly likely to be affronted by having to pay more to finance the education of young students and other groups who are reliant on government handouts.

Another influence was the era in which a person was brought up, each generation being influenced by the issues and circumstances of the day. Any person who was 80 in 1960 would have been brought up in an era when there was no national Labour party, formative influences therefore being Conservative or Liberal.

In Labour's landslide 1997 win, it did better than the Conservatives among all age groups other than the over-65s. In 2005, the 'progressive' parties, Labour and the Liberal Democrats, again fared better among young people. Labour scored well among the 35–44 age group which might be most involved with family responsibilities. The third party did especially well with those under 34. Labour's policy on tuition fees was widely believed to have troubled many voters in constituencies that had a university. The more students in a constituency, the greater the fall in the Labour vote and the rise in the Liberal Democrat vote.

Gender

In early surveys, women were usually found to be strongly more pro Conservative than men across all the social classes. According to Pulzer

Activities

Here is a table showing what happened to the share of the vote in constituencies where there was a significant Muslim vote in the last election:

Table 8 *Impact of the Muslim vote on main parties in 2005*

Muslim voters	Con.	Lab.	Lib Dem
Up to 1%	+0.4	–4.8	+3.1
1–5%	+0.4	–6.4	+4.1
5–10%	–0.1	–8.1	+6.1
More than 10%	–1.8	–10.6	+8.8

1 Suggest reasons for the strong performance of the Liberal Democrats, as recorded in the table.

2 To what extent did the Conservative party benefit from Labour's difficulties in the seats in which there was a substantial Muslim population? Explain your answer.

(1967), women were 'overwhelmingly' more pro Conservative. The following explanations for this fact were given:

- Women often stayed at home and were protected from bad working conditions and from the influence of trade union membership.
- When women did go out to work, they tended to be in cleaner and more pleasant environments such as offices.
- Women had a greater commitment to the traditional values of family and religion.
- Women were naturally more cautious in their attitude to social change.

In the 1980s, there was evidence that this gender gap was being reversed and women were becoming more inclined to vote Labour, perhaps attracted by its less harsh outlook on issues such as immigration and by its commitment to family matters such as education and health. In 1997, the swing to Labour was greater among women than men, although in both groups there was a strong pro-Labour lead. In 2005, as in 2001, women were more likely than men to vote Labour, although Labour had lost some female support.

Ethnicity

Members of the ethnic minorities have traditionally been more likely to vote Labour than Conservative. The tendency has been most marked among Afro-Caribbeans, slightly less so among Asians. Across all ethnic minorities the turnout of voters is relatively low.

Saggar's findings (2000), based on data derived from the 1997 election, suggested that of those who voted, 89% of black and 81% of Asians opted for Labour. As several within these categories would have been working class living in poorer areas of large cities, their association with Labour was perhaps unsurprising. Traditionally tough, more restrictive Conservative attitudes on immigration and race relations made the trend even more understandable. Successful middle-class professionals and businessmen, many of them Asian, may also have viewed Labour as the party that was more committed to social justice.

In 2005, turnout was again lower in seats where there was a substantial ethnic minority population. Labour lost a lot of ground in constituencies with large Muslim populations, seats where the Liberal Democrats made their strongest advances. The Iraq war is thought to account for this withdrawal of support from Labour.

Fig. 4 *Muslim voters, Bethnal Green, 2005*

Summary questions

1 How could more members of ethnic minority families be encouraged to vote?

2 Why might female voters still prefer Labour?

7 Voting patterns in second-order elections

Learning objectives:

- What are second-order elections?

- In what ways does voting behaviour differ in second-order elections as opposed to general elections?

- What are the main characteristics of voting behaviour in local, devolved, and European elections?

Second-order elections are contests other than general elections, for example local and regional ones. Some voters take the view that second-order elections are less important than first-order ones because they do not determine which party is in government. Therefore they take the opportunity to punish the current governing parties. Their protest may be registered by abstention or voting for different (often minor) parties. Elections to the European parliament are considered to be second-order national elections. Voters may use their choice of representative to the Strasbourg body to send a signal to their national government.

Voters differentiate between the levels and types of elections according to the importance they attach to the body being elected. This determines whether or not they choose to vote. Turnout is notably lower in local elections than general elections unless both happen to be held on the same day as happened in 2005. The usual characteristics of second-order elections are low turnout, an anti-government swing and a relatively high level of support for small parties.

By-elections

A by-election is an election held between general elections to fill a seat that has become vacant because of the resignation, expulsion or death of an elected representative. There is a long history of volatility in by-election voting that stretches back to the 1960s. Many popular, newly elected MPs fade from view at the next general election. Their victory is often founded on the apathy of government supporters who may not have turned out to vote or may have flirted with one of the Opposition parties.

Over the years, governments have suffered some stunning defeats in by-elections but have gone on to win the general election – the only battle that really makes a difference to them. For voters, there is a vast difference between a general election and a by-election. They do not treat them in the same way. In a by-election, they know that they are not choosing a government and feel free to give ministers a timely reminder of their dissatisfaction and to prod them into action on their behalf. The fate of the government does not usually depend on the result, and mid- or even late-term protest voting is seen as a safe outlet.

Key term

Tactical voting occurs when an elector votes not for their favoured candidate but for another candidate who has a better chance of winning. This is usually done to prevent the election of a candidate representing the most disliked party. (In 1997, many Lib Dem and Labour voters voted tactically to get sitting Conservative MPs out.)

Factors of greater relevance in by-elections include a wider choice of candidates, including some representing small and/or unusual parties, lower turnouts, more emphasis on the personality and performance of the candidate, and more **tactical voting** to get the incumbent out.

Because voting behaviour is different in by-elections, it is dangerous to attach too much significance to the outcome. But when a government has a small majority or no majority at all, just one result can be altogether more significant. At other times, a series of by-election setbacks may be enough to send ministers a message.

Local elections

Local councils have steadily lost powers to central government over recent decades and many voters think that the outcome of local elections will not make much difference to their everyday lives. Because of this, they are less likely to vote. If they do vote, in many cases they do not look at local elections in isolation, but more as a reflection of national politics. Many people cast their vote according to national rather than to local issues. In 2007, voters took the opportunity to express one last – and adverse – verdict on the New Labour administration of Tony Blair. Of course, in some areas there may be a particular local issue that attracts publicity and controversy. This may influence how voters react.

Elections for local councils typically have a turnout of around 30%, a little higher in the case of the more prestigious office of the Mayor of London (see p261).

Activities

Here is the result of the by-election held in Bromley and Chislehurst in May 2006:

Table 9 *By-election results*

Party	Vote (%)	+ or – (based on 2005 result)
Con.	40.0	–11.1
Lib Dem	37.8	+17.5
UKIP	8.1	+4.9
Labour	6.6	–15.6
Green	2.8	–0.4
National Front	1.6	N/a
Ind.	1.5	N/a
English Democrats	0.7	N/a
Monster Raving Loonies	0.5	N/a
Ind.	0.2	N/a
Money Reform	0.1	N/a

N/a: not applicable

Turnout 40.8% (64.8% in 2005)

1. What share of the vote was won by parties other than the Conservatives and Labour?

2. What evidence is there of tactical voting in this contest?

3. To what extent does this by-election support the view that second-order elections are usually characterised by 'low turnout, an anti-government swing and a relatively high level of support for small parties'?

4. 'An astonishing rebuff to the two main parties'. Is this a fair overall description of the result?

5. What reasons for optimism might the Conservatives have about their prospects in this seat at the next election?

Devolved elections

The Scottish parliament is more powerful than the Welsh National Assembly, and perhaps because of this it attracts a higher turnout of voters. In 1999, turnout was 58% (Scotland) as against 46% (Wales), in 2003 it was 49% as against 38%, and in 2007 it was 51.8% as against 43.7%. Of course the figures are well below those expected in a general election for Westminster's parliament.

In all three elections, a variety of parties stood, but the three main British parties and the nationalist Scottish National party (SNP)/Plaid Cymru were the most successful. However, the use of a semi-proportional electoral system (see Chapter 3) has ensured that minority parties gain representation. Nationalists have done well. Many voters in Scotland vote for the SNP as the more 'Scottish' party and as the preferred alternative to Labour rather than because they want independence. In 2003, voters in Scotland elected 27 nationalists, seven Green **MSPs**, six Scottish Socialists, one member of the Scottish Senior Citizens Unity party and five Independents. In 2007, SNP leader Alex Salmond urged Scottish voters to give 'one last kicking' to Tony Blair before he left office, a reflection of the fact that even as a Scotsman he saw UK-wide issues (especially policy on Iraq) as an issue which might influence how people cast their vote.

The use of an electoral system with an element of proportionality (see p50 for details of Additional Member System (AMS)) means that in casting their two votes, voters can react differently in their choices for the constituency and party list contests. In 2003, between them the two main parties (Labour and the SNP) obtained 1,109,355 votes in the constituency vote and 961,038 in the list vote, suggesting that nearly 150,000 either abstained in the list contest or felt free to vote for one of the smaller parties. The Greens do not even contest the constituency element in which they are unlikely to gain success, but they do put up a list enabling voters to vote them in this more proportional list component.

> **Key term**
>
> **MSPs**: members of the Scottish parliament.

Fig. 5 *Alex Salmond, MP for Banff and Buchan, SNP leader and First Minister in Scotland since 2007*

European elections

The role played by European elections in the British political process is very similar to that assumed by local elections. The electorate does not look on European elections in isolation, but more as an opportunity to cast a vote on the performance of the national parties or to show their general antipathy to the European Union (EU). This is true not just of Britain but also of the rest of the EU, where in 2004 there was evidence that the movement of votes had much to do with a general disillusionment with governing parties. The Liberal Democrats campaigned strongly on the war in Iraq, portraying the election as a chance for the voters to deliver their verdict on Blairite backing for George W Bush. As the most obviously pro-European party for several years, the party had little to say about the British role in Europe or support for the euro. Only the United Kingdom Independence party (UKIP) campaigned mainly on European issues.

Turnout in European elections in Britain is usually low – in 1999 less than 24% of people voted. In 2004 this increased to nearly 39%. Labour's decision to create a 'Super Thursday' on which voters could vote in local and London Assembly/Mayoralty elections at the same time as the European contests helped to create more interest in the outcome.

Again, using a list electoral system (see Chapter 3) which is highly proportional, voters were able to cast their vote for a range of parties. UKIP, the Greens and the Nationalists in Scotland and Wales all gained representation in the European parliament.

Why is turnout low in European elections?

- Voters are uninformed about the **Strasbourg parliament** and have little idea of what it can do.
- As with by-elections, there is no prospect of a change of administration (no government is formed out of the Strasbourg parliament), so polling creates little excitement or interest.
- Campaigns are essentially national contests, but only of a secondary variety – the 'big names' in the major parties play little role in them, perhaps on the governing side wishing to play down the mid-term protest that voters might choose to make.
- There is little media interest in the campaign and outcome.

Not a great deal seems to be at stake in any of the second-order elections mentioned. The main parties tend to campaign less vigorously and the media are not very enthusiastic. Many voters either treat the elections with indifference, as an opportunity to express their protest at the way things are going, or as an opportunity to vote for parties that they would not normally think of supporting. By contrast, in general elections, the parties engage in extensive national and local campaigning, the media give them saturation coverage and the voters are more interested in who wins. These are 'first-order' elections in which voters are more willing to vote and more likely to do so according to their preferred allegiance.

Key term

The **Strasbourg parliament** is a reference to the European parliament (see p103 and pp297–298).

Activity

Look at the results of the local, devolved and European elections, on p37–8. What do they tell you about the performance of smaller parties as compared with what happens in general elections? Explain the difference.

Further reading

R Gibson, W Lusoli and S Ward, 'The Internet and Political Campaigning: The New Media Comes of Age', *Representation* 39:3, 2003.

D Butler and D Kavanagh, **The British General Election of 2005**, Palgrave, 2005.

A Geddes and J Tonge (eds), **Britain Decides: The UK General Election 2005**, Palgrave, 2005.

✓ Summary questions

1. Should governments take much note of lost by-elections?
2. Why do people vote differently in by-elections from general elections?
3. Why do you think that voters show less interest in local, devolved and European elections than they do in general elections?

AQA Examination-style questions

1 ☑ Read the extract and answer questions (a) to (c) which follow.

Politics and democracy

Politics is about how people are governed. It concerns the ways in which decisions are made about government, state and public affairs; where power lies; how governments and states work; and different theories and practices such as democracy, equality, tyranny and violence. In ancient Athens, every qualified citizen had the opportunity to participate in political decision making. This was direct democracy in action. In today's large industrialised societies, it is not practical for people to gather and vote on issues. People elect representatives to act on their behalf. This is representative democracy.

Source: adapted from Chapter 1 of this textbook

(a) Briefly explain the term politics as it is used in the extract. *(5 marks)*

(b) Using your own knowledge as well as the extract, outline two differences between direct and representative democracy. *(10 marks)*

(c) 'Citizen participation is basic to democracy.' Discuss. *(25 marks)*

2 Read the extract and answer questions (a) to (c) which follow.

Issue-based voting

Political scientists have suggested that issues are becoming increasingly important in influencing which party voters support at election time. Now that the electorate have become more dealigned and open to media influence, voters are more likely to base their votes upon a judgement, a one-off assessment of parties' politics and reputations. In an era of judgemental voting, party image has become more significant than ever before.

Source: adapted from Chapter 2 of this textbook

(a) Briefly explain the term party image used in the extract. *(5 marks)*

(b) Using your own knowledge as well as the extract, briefly consider the impact of dealignment on patterns of Labour and Conservative support. *(10 marks)*

(c) Assess the impact of issue voting on the outcomes of recent general elections. *(25 marks)*

3 The role of elections in a democracy

1 Elections in Britain

Learning objectives:

■ Why are elections central to democracy?

■ What types of election are held in the UK?

Key terms

Disenfranchised millions relates to the vast number of black South Africans who were denied the vote before majority rule was introduced.

In **multi-party systems** several parties compete for political power, but no single party is likely to emerge with an overall majority of seats in the legislature.

Elections are central to democracy. As Farrell points out, they are 'the cogs which keep the wheels of democracy properly functioning'. The existence of free, competitive elections in which there is a meaningful choice of candidates is an essential criterion for any state claiming to be a democracy. Only a government that is elected has a claim to legitimacy.

In the last quarter of the 20th century, millions of people acquired the right to vote for the first time. In 1994, South Africa held its first free election in which the previously **disenfranchised millions** were entitled to vote. On the African continent, elections providing a choice of candidates and **multi-party systems** are now the norm. In the newly-emergent Eastern European democracies, there is free and open competition. Even countries such as communist North Korea allow for a narrow range of candidates, although they belong to the same party.

Elections in established democracies are generally free and fair, in that they enable the will of the majority of voters to be expressed, freely, clearly, knowledgeably and in secret. Today, more countries hold elections that meet these criteria than ever before. Yet even in countries with dubious democratic credentials, elections are still recognised by the ruling authorities as being useful, in that they convey the impression that the government represents the people's wishes.

The value of elections

Elections allow for popular participation. Hence they are not only a means of filling public offices, but they confer legitimacy on the government. In Britain, we may only get a vote in a general election every few years, but at least there is a genuine opportunity to express an opinion about those who have presided over our fortunes and to indicate whether we think it is time for a change.

Elections are the principal means by which British citizens participate in the political process, and for many this is their only form of involvement. Elections give them a peaceful way to show what they think about the government and the direction of public policy. The voters have a say in determining the policies of the government and the personnel who implement them. In this

Fig. 1 *A purple-fingered Iraqi citizen indicates that she has voted in the country's first parliamentary election, 2005*

way, elections ensure that governments are ultimately accountable to the electorate because during the brief period of an election campaign, the voters are the masters, deciding the fate of those who rule over them.

Types of election in Britain

When considering British elections, many people think of the general elections that are held every four or five years. In addition, there has been an elected system of local government in operation since the 19th century. But the range of British elections has increased in recent years and we now have:

Fig. 2 *The votes are counted*

- **General elections**, to elect members of the House of Commons.
- **Local elections**, to elect members of local councils at various levels (in local elections, voters in London can also vote for a mayor and assembly; some other local authorities also now have an elected mayor).
- **European elections**, to elect members of the European parliament.
- **Elections in Scotland, Wales and Northern Ireland**, to elect members of the devolved assemblies in those areas.
- **Other elections**: beyond government, there are now also other opportunities to vote by secret ballot, for example the elections held to choose trade union officials and to decide whether or not to take industrial action.

In addition, there are occasional **by-elections** to fill vacancies that may arise when an elected representative dies or resigns during his term of elected office. For instance, when an MP dies, loses his or her seat through disqualification or quits whilst in office, an election will be held in the individual constituency affected. By-elections are also held when there are vacancies for elected representatives on local councils and in some circumstances in devolved assemblies or the European parliament (normally the vacancy is filled by the next person on the party list of the representative who has died or retired, but if the list has been exhausted or the person was an Independent an election is necessary).

Summary questions

1. Why does voting matter to people living in new democracies?
2. What is the point of elections?

41

2 Types of electoral system and where they are employed

Learning objectives:

- What is the difference between plurality/majoritarian and proportional electoral systems?
- What makes a good electoral system?
- Does it matter which electoral system is used?

Key terms

Majoritarian systems use single-member constituencies in which only one representative is elected to serve the area. The candidate that gets a majority (more than half of the votes cast) or plurality (more votes than any other candidate) is elected.

Proportional systems (often known as PR or proportional representation systems) use multi-member constituencies in which a number of representatives are elected to serve a very large area. These are designed to ensure that the seats a party obtains in the legislature broadly reflect its share of the vote.

The popular vote relates to the total number of votes received by a party across the nation.

Many different electoral systems exist around the world and several different ones are used for elections held within the UK.

Broadly speaking, there are two categories of electoral system: those which are not proportional and those which are. Within both groups there are many potential variations. Moreover, it is possible to combine elements of the two categories.

1 Plurality or **majoritarian systems** are based on the idea of one elected representative per constituency; they are not designed to provide a proportional result in which parties gain seats in relation to the votes they obtain, although some varieties are less unproportional than others. They are designed to produce a clear winner. Their supporters attach importance to having a government with a clear majority of support in the legislature. They believe that governmental stability is more important than proportionality.

There is a distinction between plurality and majoritarian systems. In plurality systems, the candidate who gets a plurality of the votes is elected, i.e. they get more votes than any other candidate. In majority ones, the candidate who gets a majority of the votes is elected, i.e. they get more than half the votes cast. Plurality/majoritarian systems include First Past the Post (FPTP), the Double Ballot (used in French elections), the Alternative Vote and the Supplementary Vote. Non-proportional systems are the simplest to explain and to operate. The key point about them is that parties are not rewarded strictly according to the share of votes they obtain.

2 **Proportional systems** make use of multi-member constituencies or districts, in which several representatives are elected. They are designed to achieve far greater proportionality than plurality/majoritarian systems. The number of seats that a party gets in the legislature fairly accurately reflects its share of **the popular vote** across the country. In a perfectly proportional system, every party would receive the same share of seats as votes, e.g. 40 per cent of the votes would mean 40 per cent of the seats. In practice, although the mechanics are designed with that goal in mind, most systems are not exactly proportional and tend to offer some modest bonus to the largest party. But the guiding principle is that there should be a close relationship between the numbers of seats and votes.

Proportional systems can be divided into three groups: list systems, mixed systems, or hybrid systems with a proportional element and the single transferable vote (STV). They are more complex to understand than non-proportional ones. Also, the final result of the election is not immediately apparent after the first count of the votes so there may be some delay before a government can be formed.

The criteria of a good electoral system

There are different views about the criteria necessary for a good electoral system. Former Labour Home Secretary Jack Straw set out four useful criteria for the Jenkins inquiry that was set up by the Blair government to examine the most appropriate way of electing our MPs. The inquiry reported in 1998. Its brief was to:

observe the requirement for broad proportionality, the need for stable government, an extension of voter choice and the maintenance of a link between honourable members and geographical constituencies.

These were not absolute conditions. Indeed, in some respects the interpretation of the four 'guidelines' is unclear. On proportionality there is no difficulty as a concept may be deemed as 'broad' without too many problems of definition; to have asked for 'strict' proportionality would have tied the hands of those involved by limiting the range of systems that they could recommend. 'Stable government' is another general phrase that has different meanings. Also, the words 'a link' might have seemed to imply that the existing bonds between an MP and his or her constituency had to be maintained in their present form. As for 'voter choice', this also sounded important, but the term is capable of different explanations.

Does the choice of electoral system really matter?

The choice of electoral system is important. It raises issues about the nature of **representative government** and the purpose of elections. To a considerable degree, it shapes how the body politic operates. It determines the nature of party systems, the fate of individual parties, the formation of governments and the **politics of coalition**. Indeed, one report on the subject noted that: 'There can be nothing more fundamental in a democracy than proposals to change an electoral system'.

Representative government is based on the idea that the elected legislature represents the will of the people. For some people, it is crucial that the chamber elected should mathematically reflect the voters' wishes and be sensitive to every shade of opinion, thereby catering for minority views. Out of that chamber, a government will be formed. For other people, it is less important to have a system that arithmetically reflects the way electors vote. In their view, an election very broadly represents the swing in the public mood, so that in Britain in 1997 few would doubt that the country wanted a change of government, even if the scale of the Labour victory was exaggerated. According to this view, it is important to find a system that produces strong government, based upon an effective parliamentary majority. This enables those in power to develop coherent and consistent policies without facing the risk of regular defeats in the legislature.

Key terms

Representative government is a political system in which an assembly is elected to represent the people's wishes.

The **politics of coalition** refers to the situation that arises when no single party has an overall majority in the legislature, necessitating discussion and compromise in order to form a government of more than one party.

Summary questions

1. Can there be a perfect electoral system that commands general approval?

2. Does Britain have too many electoral systems?

3 How we elect MPs to Westminster: first past the post

Learning objectives:

- How do we elect MPs to the House of Commons?
- What are the advantages of the British FPTP electoral system?
- What are its disadvantages?
- How did the system work in 2005?

All elections to the House of Commons are held under the relative (or simple) majority system, although often it is referred to as the First Past the Post method and sometimes as 'winner takes all'. Voting takes place in 646 single-member constituencies. The same method is used in the US and various countries of the British Commonwealth such as Bangladesh, Canada and India. FPTP is unknown in democratic western Europe, where varieties of proportional representation exist. All UK elections to the Commons have been held on this basis since 1950.

Under our FPTP method, the candidate in each constituency who has the largest number of votes is elected, even though it may be that he or she has less than half of the votes cast. The party that has secured the most votes nationally usually forms the government, though this has not always happened. Sometimes, a party has won an election having obtained less votes than its closest rival. To form a government, a party needs to win a majority of the seats in the House of Commons.

The FPTP system over-represents at least one of the two main parties (giving them a higher proportion of seats than their number of votes merits) and under-represents others, a point to which we will return. As a result of this 'rough justice', 19 out of 23 of the elections held since 1922 have yielded an absolute majority of seats for one party. In only three of these has the majority been very small (in 1950, 1964 and October 1974). Otherwise majorities have ranged from 179 in 1997 down to a barely adequate 17 for the Conservatives in 1951.

The advantages of FPTP

There are many strong supporters of our present system who think that on the whole the system has worked well. They are primarily in the Conservative and Labour parties that have for much of their existence benefited from the system. The following points have been made in its favour:

1 **We know who is to form the government immediately after the election is over**. There is no need for private deals to be done by politicians who make bargains in secret, removed from public attention. It is the voters directly who choose which party is in office. This is not true of coalitions.

2 **It usually provides strong, stable, single-party governments with an overall majority**. Coalition government – other than in times of emergency – is virtually unknown. Such administrations can provide effective leadership for the nation. This might be more important than achieving a proportional result. Democracy does not depend on arithmetic, but it does benefit from the clear accountability of governments to the governed. FPTP usually gives one party a decisive victory and that party forms the government. In office, it has clear responsibility for what is done well or badly. The public can vote accordingly at the next election, directly punishing a party it believes to be blameworthy for policy failures.

3 **It provides 'rough justice'**. The result may be distorted, but usually it broadly reflects the tide of popular opinion. In 1945, 1964, 1979 and 1997, it reflected the public desire for a change of direction.

4 **Because we have single-member constituencies, there is a close relationship between the MP and his/her constituency**. Once elected, the MP represents all who live in the area, not just those who voted for one particular party. All citizens know who to approach if they have a problem or grievance with which they need help.

5 **The system is easy to understand**, especially for the voter who marks an X on the ballot paper. It is simple and familiar. This consideration has often been played down by commentators, but its importance was underlined by what can happen when other systems are employed. See p54 for further information of what happened in the Scottish parliament elections in 2007.

These are, in the words of the Jenkins inquiry, 'by no means negligible merits'. Moreover, an examination of alternative electoral systems may yield another factor in favour of FPTP, the negative defence that all of the other systems have their disadvantages. In particular, they tend to encourage minor parties to stand for election and make it more difficult for any one party to emerge victorious; they often result in coalition governments; and to some degree they always break the link of an elected member to their constituency.

The case against FPTP

In recent years, the trend has been for countries to move away from the FPTP method of voting. Within the Commonwealth, New Zealand and South Africa have abandoned it in favour of more proportional systems, and none of the 'new democracies' of southern, central or eastern Europe has chosen to use it. In Britain, discussion of the case for **electoral reform** has taken place over many years, although it has been mainly confined to **members of the 'chattering' classes** and close observers of the political scene. Over many years, the call to abandon FPTP in Britain has been led by the Liberals/Liberal Democrats and the Electoral Reform Society.

Critics of FPTP point to the decline in support for the two main parties and the increased support for third parties over the last generation. They argue that the backing given to the centre parties shows that the public favours a less confrontational form of politics that places more emphasis on cooperation than on conflict. They suggest that in a three-party situation, FPTP produces seemingly bizarre outcomes that are a travesty of democracy.

Specific criticisms of FPTP are that:

1 **Election results do not reflect the views of the electorate as a whole**. For instance:

   a The number of seats won by the parties does not reflect the number of votes cast for each of them. It can be the case that the party winning the election has fewer votes nationally than its rival, as in February 1974.

   b Always, the effect of the system is to over-represent the winning party that gets more seats than its support justifies. In 1983, the Conservatives' 42.4 per cent of the votes gave them a hefty 61 per cent of the MPs elected. In 1997, Labour's 43.2 per cent gave it a landslide victory, its 63.6 per cent of the seats providing the party with a majority of 179 in the House of Commons.

   c Often, in recent years, the second party has benefited from the system, winning a higher percentage of seats than votes, as in 1950, 1964, 1970, February and October 1974, 1979, 1983, 1987 and

Key terms

Electoral reform means different things in different countries depending on the system of election currently in use and what the alternatives under consideration might be. 'Reform' means change for the better, so electoral reform means something different and better than what we now have. In other words, for Westminster elections it would involve a move away from FPTP.

Members of the 'chattering' classes are those members of the educated sections of society who enjoy discussion of politics, social and cultural issues. In politics, they are sometimes known as political anoraks.

1992. If it does not, it knows that it will benefit the next time it wins power, because the victorious party always does well out of the system. (NB: The Conservatives have actually suffered badly from the workings of the system in recent elections.)

  d The over-exaggeration of the result of the winning party is such that in no election since 1945 has it won a majority of the votes cast (i.e. at least 50.1 per cent).

2 **The system is very harsh on small parties that are usually under-represented.** The support of the nationalist parties is at least concentrated in particular regions, whereas Liberal/Liberal Democrat votes have traditionally been more thinly spread throughout England, Scotland and Wales, with no very great area of strength. The party has been able to come a close runner-up and build up a useful tally of votes, but winning seats is what matters.

3 **FPTP encourages the under-representation of 'minority' groups.** In multi-member constituencies, parties might be willing to run candidates from all backgrounds, classes and colours. The tendency is now to play it safe, and the result is that the House of Commons is overwhelmingly white, male and middle class.

The outcome in May 2005

In May 2005:

  9,556,183 people voted Labour, fewer than in any other post-war election since 1983, an election that has gone down in history as a never-again disaster for the party.

  No administration since 1929 has been elected by as few voters as the one elected in 2005.

  The composition of the present House of Commons is a distortion of the way people actually voted.

Table 1 *The outcome in 2005*

	Votes obtained (%)	No. of seats obtained	Seats obtained (%)
Labour	35.22	356	55.10
Conservatives	32.33	197	30.49
Liberal Democrats	22.05	62	9.59
Others	10.42	30	4.64

The anomalies (oddities) that can arise under the British FPTP system were again clear in 2005. Among them were the following:

1 **There was a clear discrepancy between the proportion of total votes gained by the parties and the seats they won.** Labour, the winning party, benefited from the system and ended up massively over-represented. Its exaggerated victory was based on the support of just over 35 per cent of those who voted, less than 22 per cent of the 44 million electorate. Labour's lead over the Conservatives was barely 3 per cent, yet it obtained 159 more seats. As a result, Labour still dominates the House of Commons.

2 **As in 1997 and 2001, the second party, the Conservatives, did not benefit from the workings of the FPTP system.** They ended up slightly under-represented, 208 being the number they would have ended up with if they had gained seats exactly in proportion to

the votes cast. The recent bias in the electoral system has been brought about by a combination of Labour having many sparsely-populated inner city seats, the fact that English constituencies are historically larger than those in Scotland and Wales where Labour does better, and the effects of anti-Conservative tactical voting. This worked against the Conservatives and, although they gained 50,000 more votes than Labour in England, they won 92 fewer victories.

3 **Third parties suffered**. Although the Liberal Democrats improved their overall position, they ended up with far fewer seats than their performance justified. An exactly proportional outcome would have left them with 142 seats. Other small parties fared badly – UKIP, the Greens and the BNP failed to win any seats. Overall, it took only 26,877 votes to elect a Labour MP, 44,521 to elect a Conservative and 96,378 to elect a Liberal Democrat. (The calculation is, of course, impossible for the others as they had no MPs elected.)

4 **The 'electoral deserts' noted by the Jenkins inquiry (areas in which a party fails to gain any reward for the votes it receives) were once more in evidence**. Conservative voters were effectively disenfranchised in much of Scotland and northern England. Labour supporters across whole swathes of the South were left unrepresented. Although more than 235,000 votes were cast for the Liberal Democrats and Labour in Surrey, the Conservatives control every constituency in the county.

5 **More MPs than ever before (some 65%) failed to win majority support**, in other words they received less than 50 per cent of the support of their local electorate. Notably, George Galloway, who won Bethnal Green and Bow standing for Respect (an anti-war coalition party) against Labour's Oona King, was not the preferred choice of 64.1 per cent of the voters in that constituency.

Fig. 3 *George Galloway, one of the 65% of MPs voted in without majority support (more than 50% of the vote) in May 2005*

Summary questions

1 Can you defend FPTP after the experience of the 2005 election?

2 How much importance do you attach to the need for strong, single-party government?

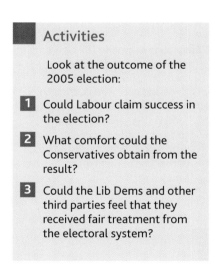

Activities

Look at the outcome of the 2005 election:

1 Could Labour claim success in the election?

2 What comfort could the Conservatives obtain from the result?

3 Could the Lib Dems and other third parties feel that they received fair treatment from the electoral system?

4 Proportional and hybrid UK systems

Learning objectives:

- What are the main majoritarian alternatives to FPTP?
- What are the main proportional alternatives to FPTP?
- What are the main hybrid alternatives to FPTP?

Key terms

Plant Report (1993): the outcome of an enquiry set up to consider the most appropriate electoral systems for Labour's proposed Scottish parliament, regional assemblies, reformed House of Lords, the House of Commons and local government. It was chaired by Professor Raymond Plant.

Supplementary vote (SV) is a simple variation of Alternative Vote, used to elect London's Mayor. If no candidate wins outright in the single-member constituency contest, the second preference votes of all other candidates are distributed between the top two, so that one of them ultimately has a majority.

Hint

You may be required to write 2–3 advantages and disadvantages of any particular alternative electoral system. As you tackle each one, compare it with the three specific criticisms listed for FPTP on p45. Think carefully about whether a different system would remedy these alleged defects.

Non-proportional majoritarian: supplementary vote (SV)

Labour's **Plant Report** (1993) surprisingly recommended the **supplementary vote (SV)** for use in British general elections. The system was unknown to most students of electoral systems at the time. Used in London Mayoral elections, it is a cross between the **alternative vote** and the French **double ballot**, neither of which is used in the UK. If used at Westminster, it would retain the 646 single-member constituencies and allow the voter to express a second choice. If no candidate obtained an overall majority, second preferences would be counted. In this case, all but the top two candidates would be eliminated and the votes redistributed to those remaining in the contest.

Advantages claimed by its supporters are that:

- It is likely to lead to majority governments.
- It retains the single-member–constituency link.
- It avoids the counting of 'weak' preferences as only a first and second choice is recorded in the ballot box.

But:

- It is not proportional; it would provide a more 'fair' result to the Liberal Democrats and others, but not complete arithmetical justice.
- Like FPTP, it would also tend to reward parties that have concentrated areas of support.

Proportional: closed list system

The most common method of achieving the goal of proportionality is the list system, by which an elector votes for several party candidates rather than just a single candidate. The number of votes won by the party determines how many candidates are elected from that party's list.

Of the lists used on the continent, a few are open list systems, the majority are closed ones. In open list systems, used in countries such as Austria, Finland and Sweden, there is a degree of voter choice so that the voters have some say in deciding which candidates are elected. In closed list systems (used in Portugal, Spain and the UK in the European elections, 1999) the voter chooses one party and has no control over which of its candidates are successful. In both systems, the larger the constituency the more proportional the result. At the most extreme end, Israel treats the whole country as one giant, multi-membered constituency. The outcome is very 'fair', and even very small parties are likely to win seats.

For the British European elections, the country is divided into 75 multi-member constituencies (e.g. Scotland is one giant constituency with seven members). Voters have one vote, cast for a party list rather than an individual candidate. Seats are divided between parties according to the share of the vote that each has gained. They are allocated to individuals according to their placing on the party list. In 2004, the three main parties won a slightly higher percentage of seats than their votes entitled them to, but the big winners were UKIP who won 12 seats for 16.1 per cent of the vote.

Advantages claimed by the supporters of the closed list system are that:

- There is usually a strong connection between the votes won and the seats obtained.
- It is fairer to small parties and in situations where there are minorities in the population.
- It is likely to produce coalitions, which have some advantages (see p59).
- It is good at securing the representation of more women and members of minority groups in the legislature.

But:

- Closed lists place power in the hands of the party managers who can position troublesome candidates near the bottom of the list and so reduce their chances of election.
- Closed lists deny the voters a choice of candidates.
- They makes coalitions more likely, with all their possible disadvantages (see p59).
- There is no clear link between the MP and his or her constituency.

Proportional: Single Transferable Vote (STV)

Within the UK, the Single Transferable Vote (STV) is used for local, devolved and European elections in Northern Ireland. It is the option favoured by the Electoral Reform Society and the Liberal Democrats. Voters list candidates in the multi-member constituency in order of preference, and can choose contenders from more than one party. **To get elected, a candidate needs to obtain a quota determined by a mathematical formula**. In effect, this means that in a five-seat constituency, around 20 per cent of the votes might be required. Normally, on the first count one candidate will be elected. Any 'surplus' votes (more than the quota requires) for that successful candidate are redistributed according to the second preferences on his or her ballot papers, a process that might lead to another candidate or two achieving the quota. Then, there is a step-by-step elimination of candidates from the bottom up, their votes being transferred to the remaining candidates on the basis of the second preferences – a process that continues until all seats are filled.

Advantages claimed by its supporters are that:

- There is a good connection between votes and seats.
- It is fairer to small parties and particularly good where there are significant minorities in the population, as in Northern Ireland.
- It allows the voter to choose between candidates of the same party.
- It is likely to produce coalitions, which have some advantages (see p59).
- It is good at securing the election of more women and minority groups to the legislature.

But:

- It is a more complex system than the others considered here, although the difficulty is for the Returning Officers rather than for the voters; it is likely to delay the publication of the final result.

Key term

Alternative vote: the voter simply marks the candidates in order of preference. If a candidate gets an overall majority, he/she is elected. If no one does, the bottom candidate is eliminated and the votes of his/her supporters are redistributed to the others based on the second choice. The process continues until one person emerges with a majority.

Double ballot under this run-off system, the polling is split into two parts, with perhaps a fortnight between the two election days. If one candidate achieves a majority in the first ballot, then he/she is elected. If not, all but the top two withdraw for the second round. The person chosen is then a majority choice.

The **quota** is determined by the outcome of the formula, calculated by dividing the total number of votes cast by the number of seats plus one.

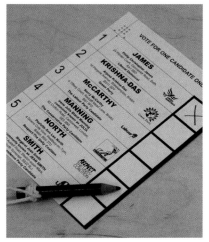

Fig. 4 *A party list ballot paper as used in the 2004 elections*

Table 2 *Results if party lists or STV used in 2005 election*

	Seats won: party lists*	Seats won: STV
Labour	227	263
Conservative	209	200
Lib Dems	142	147
SNP/Plaid	14	13
Others	54	23

*Calculated on the basis of treating country as one constituency, for which each party submits one list – the most accurate reflection of the way people actually voted.

Source: Figures taken from The UK general election of 5th May 2005: report and analysis, *published by the Electoral Reform Society. It offers this cautionary warning: 'Modelling alternative electoral systems is a highly artificial exercise that cannot give precise results and certainly cannot replicate all the effects of introducing a new electoral system. It is, however, indicative of the properties of alternative electoral systems'*

Activities

1 What is the key difference between SV and party lists?

2 In 2005, if we had used party lists or STV in the general election for the House of Commons, the outcome would have been as shown in Table 2.

  a Would the result have been fairer if either system had been in use in 2005?

  b Think about the figures given on p46 for the percentages of votes actually won by the three largest parties. Work out approximately how many seats would have been won by each party if the voting system had been exactly proportional. What do you deduce about the relative proportionality of the two 'proportional' systems?

It makes coalitions more likely, with all their possible disadvantages (see p59).

There is no close link between the MP and his or her constituency.

Mixed/hybrid: Additional Member System (AMS)

Hybrid systems combine elements that are designed to increase proportionality with features of FPTP such as single-member constituencies. Germany has such a scheme and the voter has two votes, one for the party and one for the candidate in the individual constituency (the list votes for the party are used to share seats proportionally between the parties). Again, there are considerable variations in the possible schemes available, which is why various titles are used such as the 'Mixed Member Proportional' or 'Additional Member' systems. Several of the newer central and Eastern European democracies (e.g. Hungary) have opted for these 'mixed' systems, which are also used in Taiwan and New Zealand. Most varieties involve the voter in making two choices, but in other respects there is scope for variety. The degree of proportionality will depend upon the split between the constituency and the top-up list element. In Germany, it is a 50:50 split, in Italy 75:25.

Because it has some characteristics in common with FPTP, the Additional Member System has been more favourably received in Britain than some other alternative systems. It is currently used in the elections for the Scottish parliament, the Welsh Assembly and the London Assembly. Scottish devolved elections are based upon the seven European constituencies, the split in the 129-strong chamber being 73 FPTP members as against 56 elected on a list basis as additional members. Voters have two votes, voting for an MSP to represent their single-member constituency and for a party list from which the additional members will be chosen in proportion to the votes cast for each party. The second vote therefore provides a mechanism to ensure greater justice for parties that would be under-represented under FPTP. The SNP dislikes the scheme, favouring a more directly proportional one. In Wales, the split is 40:20. For details of how it worked in the 2007 election, see p37.

Advantages claimed by its supporters are that:

It produces fairly proportional results.

It is fairer to small parties.

It retains to some degree the MP–constituency link.

It makes coalitions more likely, with all their possible advantages.

It is good at securing the election of more women and minority groups to the legislature.

But:

There are doubts about the status of top-up members relating to who they represent and whether or not they are viewed as second-class representatives.

It is not as proportional as PR systems such as party lists and STV.

It makes coalitions more likely, with all their possible disadvantages.

Activities

1. Why do you think that many people in all three main parties find AMS acceptable for use in devolved elections in Scotland and Wales? Why does the SNP dislike it?

2. If the system had been in use in the UK general election of 2005, the outcome would have been as shown in Table 3.

Table 3 *Results if AMS had been used in 2005 election*

	No. of seats
Labour	242
Conservative	208
Lib Dems	144
SNP/Plaid	16
Others	36

Do you think this is a fair result?

3. Why might the status of a top-up member elected under the proportional element of AMS be more questionable than one elected under the constituency element?

Table 4 *Summary of electoral systems currently used in the UK, by country (no. in brackets)*

England (4)	Scotland (4)	Wales (3)	Northern Ireland (2)
General/local – FPTP	General – FPTP	General/local – FPTP	General – FPTP
European parliament – closed list	European parliament – closed list	European parliament – closed list	European parliament/ Devolved/local } STV
London Mayoralty – SV	Devolved – AMS	Devolved – AMS	
London Assembly – AMS	Local – STV		

Summary questions

1. Which is the best electoral system that we have described? Why?

2. Does it matter if the electoral system fails to produce a single-party government?

5 Electoral systems and the party system

Learning objectives:

- Does the use of a proportional voting system encourage the growth and success of small parties?

- What evidence of this is provided by the use of AMS in Scotland and Wales?

- What evidence is provided by the use of party lists in European elections?

- What evidence is provided by the use of STV in Northern Ireland?

Key term

Weimar Germany was the era before Hitler gained power in Germany. Government was based upon a highly democratic constitution which included the use of a proportional electoral system.

For many years, when students studied alternative electoral systems they had to rely on a few overseas examples to substantiate their case. Since the late 1990s, proportional and mixed systems have been used in the UK. Therefore there is some recent and more local evidence to consider. As you assess these recent methods of election, it is important to examine their impact on the fate of British parties. Ask yourself how the parties have fared under a proportional system, not just the main ones but the smaller parties as well. This will help you decide whether the use of proportional representation (PR) encourages the representation of small parties and by so doing makes it more difficult for any party to gain an overall majority in the legislature.

Does the use of PR encourage small parties?

Among the comments often made about schemes of proportional representation, a common allegation is that PR encourages a proliferation of minor parties. Some of these have a chance of gaining representation in the legislature and their successes come at the expense of larger parties, making it more difficult for any one party to gain an overall majority.

Critics of PR can point to past and present examples to show that any system that gives small parties a chance of success makes it more difficult for any one party to win enough seats to govern on its own. In other words, coalition government becomes more likely.

- In **Weimar Germany**, prior to the rise of Hitler, 24 parties contested the 1930 election, held under a highly proportional electoral system. This made it difficult for any one party to form a strong ministry that had a chance of survival. Because of this, there were weak and unstable coalition governments, the existence of which made it more likely that German people would be impressed by Hitler's Nazi party that promised firm leadership.

- In Israel and the Irish Republic today, individuals and small parties have been able to gain representation, again making it more difficult to form stable administrations. Many other countries that employ some variant of PR also have more parties than Britain does. Such examples are often quoted to illustrate the truth of the observation made several decades ago by Duverger (1962), a famous writer on political parties: 'The simple majority, single ballot system favours the two party system; the simple majority system with second ballot and proportional representation favours multipartyism'.

This link between the nature of the electoral and party systems is often asserted, but it is not entirely clear that it is actually a causal relationship. It is too easy to conclude that because countries with proportional electoral systems tend to have multi-party systems, the latter must be the result of the former. For two reasons, the case may not be convincing:

1 **Some examples do not fit the argument**. For instance, Malta uses the single transferable vote but has a solid two-party system. The

movement towards multi-partyism in Austria has been a recent phenomenon, but the country has used PR for several decades. In the late 20th century Italy changed to a considerably less proportional system; its supporters hoped this would weaken the tendency to multi-partyism, but this has not happened.

2 **There are other factors besides electoral systems that shape party systems**. Historical, social and personal factors may all encourage the existence of several parties. Electoral systems are a factor in determining the nature of the party system, but they are not the only one (see Chapter 5).

Experience of the use of PR in the UK

We can concentrate on the evidence provided by the use of three alternative systems to FPTP:

1 The devolved elections in Scotland and Wales, held under AMS.
2 The European elections, held under a closed party list system.
3 The experience of Northern Ireland that has long used the single transferable vote for local and European elections, and now uses them for its devolved ones.

The devolved elections (held in 1999, 2003 and 2007)

The first two elections in Scotland delivered a parliament that was representative of the people. There was a shift towards small parties and independents, and away from the two largest parties (Labour and the Scottish Nationalists (SNP)) on both the first (constituency) and second (party) votes. In the first session, six different parties were represented plus two independents. The 2003 election saw another new party – the Scottish Senior Citizens Unity party – take its place in the parliament, along with another independent. This was truly a 'rainbow parliament' in which many shades of political opinion were represented. In both cases, the outcome was a Labour–Liberal Democrat coalition.

Voters see more point in voting for a small party in devolved elections (particularly for their second party vote), because it means that their vote may not be a wasted one. The party has a chance of gaining success. It does pick up seats from the list element of AMS to get a more proportional result than it would achieve under the constituency element held under FPTP. A party such as the Greens – which suffers under the FPTP system used for Westminster elections – won seven seats in Scotland in 2003, all under the list element.

In Wales, the three main parties and Plaid Cymru all won seats in 1999 and 2003, Plaid winning 17 and 12 respectively. Its success and the fairer representation of the Conservatives and Liberal Democrats denied Labour the dominance it had always achieved in general elections. The outcome varied between a Labour administration with a small majority, a minority Labour administration and a Labour–Liberal Democrat coalition.

NB: AMS is also used for London Assembly elections. In 2003, five of the 25 seats were won by Liberal Democrats and two each by the Greens and UKIP.

Table 5 *Scottish devolved (2007) and European (2004) election results*

	Devolved	European
	Votes (%) Seats (%) (number in brackets)	Votes (%) Seats (%)
Conservative	13.9	26.7
	13.2 (17)	36.0
Labour	29.2	22.6
	35.7 (46)	25.3
Lib Dems	11.3	14.9
	12.4 (16)	16.0
SNP	31.0	19.7
	36.4 (47)	28.6
Greens	4.0	6.3
	1.6 (2)	2.7

Activities

Table 5. shows the results of the Scottish devolved (2007) and European (2004) elections.

NB: for devolved elections, the percentages are those for the regional rather than the constituency contests. The Greens made little effort to win constituency seats. For the European elections, the SNP figure relates to percentage of Scottish votes and seats.

Consider the position of the Liberal Democrats and the Greens:

1 Compare their results to those achieved in the 2005 election.

2 Under which of the two systems above do they fare best?

Look at Table 5 to see the outcome of the devolved elections in Scotland, in 2007. Note that on this occasion, the trend to small party representation was halted; five parties and one independent gained seats.

In depth

Voter confusion in the elections to the Scottish parliament, 2007

In May 2007, Scottish voters were electing members of their parliament and of local councils on the same day. There were several complications for these elections:

1 Different voting systems were being used in each case, AMS and STV respectively. The two ballot papers had a different design and of course on one they were marking an X and on the other they were using numbers.

2 In the parliament elections, for the first time:

a the constituencies used to elect the 73 constituency MSPs were not the same as those used in the previous (2005) general election, and

b the ballot papers for the constituency elections were combined with those for the regional lists.

3 New scanners were used to electronically count the paper ballots for both sets of elections.

Alarm had previously been expressed about the way in which the changes were being introduced, with everything happening on the same day. The procedures were bound to be unfamiliar to the voters. As the voting got underway, it was obvious that the worst fears had been realised. There were reports of voter confusion over how they should fill in their ballot papers for the parliamentary election. Many of them had misunderstood the instructions at the top of the poorly-designed paper, which indicated 'have two votes'. In a large number of cases, they thought that they could use both votes to choose from the regional list.

The outcome was that 142,000 votes (or 7 per cent of the total) were rejected in the counting process. The situation was made worse because in some constituencies the majority for the winning candidate was less than the number of rejected votes. There was talk of legal challenges to a few of the results, particularly in Cunninghame North where the SNP beat Labour by just 48 votes.

The European elections (held in 1999, 2004)

In the more recent of the two elections held under the list system of PR, Labour fared badly (obtaining its worst result in terms of the popular vote since 1918 in a national election, winning 19 seats) and the Conservatives were badly down on 1999, with 27 seats. The Liberal Democrats and UKIP each won 12/75 mainland seats, the Greens won two and the nationalists in Scotland and Wales won two and one respectively.

If we take the experience of Northern Ireland, which used STV for these same 2004 elections, the two unionist parties each won one seat, as did the nationalist Sinn Fein party. The divide of seats between loyalist unionists and republican nationalists has usually been in the ratio of 2:1, a reflection of the larger number of Protestants in Northern Ireland. (In a country with a history of religious strife, the STV variety of PR ensures that both communities gain representation.)

What can we learn from these results?

On the mainland, in devolved and European elections, the nationalist parties in Scotland and Wales (the SNP and Plaid Cymru) gain fair representation. In Scotland, they do better than they would under FPTP. FPTP has never been as harsh on Plaid in Westminster elections because support for Plaid has traditionally been geographically concentrated in five mainly Welsh-speaking constituencies.

The experience of elections using PR or the hybrid AMS is that in the UK they do benefit small parties at the expense of the traditional choices, Labour and the Conservatives. By contrast, FPTP in Westminster elections has been good for the two parties for most of their existence, which is why neither campaigns to change the system. It has been harsh on the Liberal Democrats, and minor parties have usually failed to gain representation, except in special circumstances such as the election of the anti-war George Galloway for Respect, in 2005.

In Scotland and Wales, a more proportional system has produced an assembly in which all or most shades of opinion are represented. If smaller or third parties fare well, these gains can only come at the expense of the large parties. This has resulted in eight years of coalition and now **minority government** in Scotland since the Scottish parliament was created. In Wales, there have been single-party, coalition and minority administrations.

Fig. 5 *Support for Plaid Cymru. The party has performed well in both devolved and European elections*

Key term

Minority government means a government made up of a party or parties whose members do not command a majority of seats in parliament.

Summary questions

1 Why do proportional electoral systems often encourage the representation of small parties?

2 Is it a good thing to have a large number of political parties represented in the legislature? Give reasons for your answer.

6 Single-party (majority), minority and coalition governments

Learning objectives:

- What are the advantages of single-party government?
- What are the possible forms of coalition government?
- What are the advantages and disadvantages of coalitions?

In countries that use FPTP it is more likely that the election will result in the formation of **single-party governments** with an overall majority of seats (see Table 6); minority or coalition government other than in times of emergency is rare and virtually unknown in Britain.

Further information

Party majorities in UK governments

Table 6 *Party majorities*

Year	Party	Majority of seats in the House of Commons
1987	Conservative	101
1992	Conservative	21
1997	Labour	178
2001	Labour	165
2005	Labour	66

NB: Since 1945 the UK has had only three governments with a majority of less than 20 or no majority at all (1950–51, 1964–66 and 1974–79).

Single-party government

Single-party government is said to have certain advantages:

- **It pinpoints political responsibility**. The voters know which party to praise or blame when things go right or wrong. The party in office cannot seek to blame a coalition partner for its failings.

- **It is associated with the formation of strong, stable and durable administrations** capable of providing effective leadership for the nation. Governments can pursue the programmes for which they receive a **mandate** in the election. They can tackle problems directly rather than spend time searching for agreement. Their proposals are less liable to be delayed or diluted as a result of some politically messy compromise with their coalition partners.

- **In Britain, we usually know immediately after the election which party will form the government**. There is no need for private deals to be done by politicians away from the public gaze; the voters directly choose which party is in office.

- **Coalitions have clear disadvantages**. They are by comparison weak and unstable, incapable of providing strong leadership. Moreover, in Britain they might hand disproportionate power to a third party such as the Liberal Democrats.

Key terms

A **mandate** is the authority of the government (as granted by the voters) to carry out its programme according to the promises of the manifesto.

A **single-party government** is a government made up of members of only one party (e.g. the Labour administrations of Tony Blair).

56

Can governments claim a mandate for their policies?

In a situation of single-party government, an electoral mandate is claimed by the winning party in a general election. On forming a government it claims to have the right to implement its programme as was set out in the election **manifesto**.

In practice, mandate theory is undermined in several ways:

No one can be sure why people supported a party in the last election. It was not necessarily because they approved of every aspect of its programme; it is more likely that they broadly approved of its general performance and outlook.

Manifestos are often vague, so that when people vote for the party they are not anticipating some of the very specific measures that governments introduce after the election. For example, they might know that it is going to take a strong stance against international terrorism but not realise that the measures introduced may involve serious curbs on civil liberties.

Governments have to make decisions on issues that arise during the lifetime of an administration, about which nothing would have been said in the manifesto. It is part of the responsibility of government.

Post-war governments – most obviously that elected in 2005 – have not received the backing of a majority of those who voted. Labour's mandate rests on the support of only 35.2 per cent of the voters.

Coalition government

As we have seen from UK experience, the use of proportional electoral systems makes coalitions more likely. There are several forms of coalition, including:

The grand coalition, a government including representatives of the two main parties such as the one led by Angela Merkel in Germany since November 2005.

The multi-party coalition, involving perhaps three or four parties in a country that lacks two predominant groupings, such as Austria, Italy and the Netherlands.

Fig. 6 *Andrea Merkel, right, leader of the grand coalition in Germany*

■ **The coalition of one major and one minor party which may itself be a significant 'third force'.** In the past, West Germany had several such administrations, usually involving the relatively small Free Democrats. In Britain, the Liberal Democrats would be the most likely partner for one of the two main parties in the event of a 'hung parliament'. Scotland was governed by this type of coalition between 1999 and 2007

■ Some general points about coalitions

The main worry of those who oppose any abandonment of FPTP for Westminster elections is that it would greatly increase the likelihood of perpetual coalition government. A third force (probably the Liberal Democrats) would gain a greater share of influence, and this would be at the expense of the two main parties. Bearing in mind that in no election since 1945 has the winning party won at least 50 per cent of the popular vote even under FPTP, coalition government could well become a reality.

The pros and cons of coalition government are highly relevant in any discussion of electoral systems. However, there is a danger of over-generalising about its alleged strengths or deficiencies. The danger is all the greater because of the tendency to use examples selectively. From supporters and opponents, the case tends to be over-stated or over-simplified. Coalitions can be strong or weak, successful or unsuccessful. Much depends on the nature of the country involved and its political system. However, some points are worth stressing:

1 **In Europe, where proportional electoral systems are used, coalition governments are common.** In many European countries, there is no tradition of a two-party system where voters know that the party they vote for will be able to put their programme into effect. At best, their party will be part of a governing coalition, able only to carry out the parts of its policy that its partners agree upon.

2 **The idea of coalition arrangements (with bargains and deals over policy after the election) is alien to British tradition.** This may not matter but it has to be appreciated. The voters know that after a general election, the winning party will be largely able to carry out its programme, so that an election is a choice of a party and set of policies to govern. (But do not disregard Scottish experience in the devolved elections; Scottish voters are now familiar with coalitions.)

3 **Coalitions and PR may be associated with greater instability of government, but not all countries experience this.** Under the Weimar Republic, Germany did, but the country was then facing acute problems; post-Nazi Germany has had coalitions and stable government. As we have seen already, we can now draw on the experience of Scotland's devolved government. The Executive was governed by a Labour–Liberal Democrat coalition for eight years from 1999. The arrangement proved to be a stable one, with ministers capable of implementing an agreed programme.

4 **Where coalitions have not lasted nearly as well, as in France's 4th Republic to 1958 or Italy more recently, it is possible to overstate the instability.** Governments have often collapsed and a game of musical chairs has been played with ministerial positions, but there has often been much continuity of policy and considerable economic development has still taken place. So coalition does not always paralyse economic and social progress because of the failure to agree on specific policies.

5 Sometimes, coalitions have taken a few days to form, often longer.
In pre-1958 France, one coalition took a month, and in late 1988
Israel experienced very prolonged bargaining. However, if stable
administrations are formed that can last a few years, then the
wait may seem worthwhile. At least, the changes made by such a
government will be agreed ones, backed by a group of parties who have
more electoral support than a British government normally has.

Table 7 *The pros and cons of coalition government: some points to consider*

For	Against
FPTP may produce strong government, but that is not always a good thing. Governments with a large majority can ride roughshod over parliament and be over-bearing.	Forming coalitions can be difficult and slow. Once formed, they may not prove durable because one of the partners may wish to withdraw over some policy disagreement.
Coalitions provide more stability and continuity of government as there are not the lurches from left to right that can occur when Labour replaces the Conservatives or vice versa. These make it difficult for businessmen and others to plan ahead (e.g. taxation levels for industry are liable to fluctuate).	In the formation of coalitions, behind-the-scenes bargaining will occur, over both the allocation of government positions and over policy issues. On policy, what may result is a compromise, in which the policies of the main party are toned down. People vote for a party in the expectation that its policies will be carried out by its leadership. No one votes for a coalition.
The third party – in Britain, probably the Liberal Democrats – has a moderating effect, keeping extremist tendencies in check and making for more consensal, middle-of-the-road government.	Major policy decisions may be shelved if it is difficult to reach agreement on a controversial issue. The French had a word for this, *'immobilisme'*. It was easier to do nothing than to do something.
Policies would be based upon the support of a greater percentage of the population. Following the 2005 election, the majority Labour administration has been able to introduce policies, despite having been backed by only 35.2% of the voters. Coalition governments are more broadly based.	Policies that result may be widely appealing to middle-of-the-road opinion, to moderates of the left and right. But they may be fuzzy, consensual ones. Yet at times there is a need for a radical departure from existing policy, some would say of the type that occurred in 1979 when Margaret Thatcher became PM.
Coalitions are about parties working together in a spirit of compromise for the good of the country, whereas FPTP produces a sharp conflict between two main parties who each behave in a partisan manner and tend to oppose what the other does or says.	The third party may be in office for much of the time; in Britain, the Liberals/Liberal Democrats would probably have been a partner in many of the post-1945 governments. The small party might seem to be having some influence that is out of proportion to its size, a party with 50 or 60 MPs being able to stop its much larger partner from carrying out its legislative wishes.

 Summary questions

1 Supporters of FPTP claim Britain has effective, single-party, strong government, based on a parliamentary majority. Has this been to Britain's advantage?

2 Would coalitions work in Westminster today?

Further reading

C Robinson, *Elections and Voting in the UK*, Edinburgh University Press, 2008.

J Curtice and M Steed, 'And Now for the Commons? Lessons from Britain's First Experience with Proportional Representation', *Politics Review*, September 2000.

D Denver, 'Whatever happened to Electoral Reform?', *Politics Review*, September 2003.

I Davenport, 'Electoral Reform', *Talking Politics*, September 2004.

4 The nature of representation

1 Direct and indirect democracy

Learning objectives:

- Why has direct democracy as practised in ancient Athens been seen as generally impractical in recent centuries?

- What are the characteristics of representative democracy?

- What do we mean by representation?

- What are the modern forms of direct democracy?

Key terms

Pericles was born around 495 BC. He was a prominent and influential statesman, orator and general of Athens in the city's Golden Age.

Representation is a form of indirect democracy in which those elected represent the views, interests or social composition of the electorate. They make decisions on behalf of the mass of citizens who only directly participate at election time.

Fig. 1 *The orators' stand in the Pnyx, the meeting ground where the great struggles of Athenian democracy were conducted and speeches were delivered by men such as Pericles but also less exalted citizens*

In Chapter 1, we saw that the Ancient Greeks were the first people to develop democratic ideas. Athenian democracy was practised in a small city-state or *polis* comprising some 40,000 citizens. Any citizen aged over 20 could attend the Ekklesia (People's Assembly) sessions and speak to his peers. The assembly met some 40 times a year to discuss issues that came before it. The participation involved could develop both the citizen and the community. As **Pericles** observed: 'Our constitution is named a democracy, because it is in the hands not of the few but of the many'. Democracy then involved the direct involvement of the citizenry in making decisions. At that time, it was possible for all citizens to come together and play an active role.

After the decline of the Greek states, the term 'democracy' went out of fashion for several centuries. For many rulers, any idea of people power conjured up worrying images of the possible tyranny of the masses. It was not until the late eighteenth century that ideas of democracy began to emerge once more, largely in the writings of political thinkers. When it did so, it bore little relation to the practice of Ancient Athens.

Thomas Paine, a radical late 18th-century thinker and writer, published his work *Common sense* in 1776. In it, he noted that in a small colony, where it was possible for all to come together and participate directly in government, Athenian-type democracy could exist. But in a large area, with increased populations, representatives would be needed. The Americans were influenced by his ideas when they developed their constitution at Philadelphia in 1787. Four years later, in *The Rights of Man*, Paine (1791) took the view that the US political system was **representation** grafted onto democracy. Paine explained the evolution of democracy in this way:

> The original simple democracy . . . is incapable of extension, not from its principle, but from the inconvenience of its form. Simple democracy was society governing itself without the aid of secondary means. By ingrafting representation upon democracy, we arrive at a system of government capable of embracing and confederating all the various interests and every extent of territory and population.

By the time of the French Revolution in 1789, writers were then discussing two main forms of democracy: direct democracy and indirect or representative democracy. Today, as we have seen, democracy is recognised as a desirable system in many parts of the world. But the contrast between the original Athenian form and democracies of the 21st century is startling. Circumstances have changed dramatically. What we now have is indirect or representative democracy, a situation in which representatives of the people, freely elected, make decisions subject to popular control.

Regular and free elections are central to representative democracy, the people being consigned to the role of deciding who will decide. Via methods of direct democracy, people can decide issues for themselves.

Direct democracy

Direct democracy involves people power or the self-government of the people. It is not practical to practise it today in the way that it was carried out in ancient Greece, but elements of it survive even in some modern societies. The US still has town meetings in parts of New England. In several US states and a number of other countries, referendums and initiatives allow for direct popular involvement in decision making. Switzerland provides perhaps the closest approximation to the Greek model. Its very decentralised structure allows the public to vote regularly on political issues and policies.

Some commentators argue that even in modern industrial states it is possible to break down governing structures in such a way that people see themselves as belonging to small units. According to this view, more decisions could be made at the local level by voters in their communities. However, this idea has little chance of ever being implemented as national political leaders are unlikely to surrender their powers of decision making. Another possibility in the future would be the development of direct personal involvement by the voters via internet websites, interactive television and mobile phones.

In depth

The town meetings of New England: direct democracy in action

In New England, town meetings have operated ever since the first British settlements. Of Maine's 493 incorporated municipalities, 440 have a town meeting form of government. Residents attend for a morning or a day to chart the direction of public policy on local issues. Topics debated range widely, from same-sex marriages to nuts-and-bolts issues concerning local facilities.

Town meetings are not without their critics and there are problems with the way they function today. In particular:

- Meetings are often not well attended. Rarely do more than 10 per cent of registered voters turn out to participate, the trend being consistently downwards in recent years.

- Those who can attend are often self-employed, retired or otherwise not working at regular daytime jobs and therefore cannot accurately reflect the opinions of local citizens. An article in a local newspaper in Maine carried a report that in Kingfield '65 people are calling the shots for the entire town'.

Even at the level of a small New England town, society is now too large and complex for direct democracy to be a complete success. Towns used to be less populated, with more of a sense of community. Today, urbanisation has affected New England. Also, people are busy, often travelling some distance to work; meetings take too long for those with little time available. People have the means to spend their spare time on various – and perhaps more interesting – forms of entertainment.

Indirect or representative democracy

The Greek model of direct democracy has an obvious appeal. It provided for a high degree of public participation in the political process. It is markedly distinct from the democracy practised in modern times, often in large countries with huge populations:

Fig. 2 *The Scottish parliament: an example of a representative assembly*

- Citizenship was then an elite status denied to many people, whereas now it has been extended to the majority of the adult population: only 40,000 Athenians could vote, compared with the 44 million entitled to do so in Britain today.

- Today's democracies are representative, the democratic principle no longer meaning self-government but government conducted on our behalf by elected representatives.

In representative democracies, government must be derived from the people, answerable to them via representatives gathered in the popularly elected legislature. Britain has a system of representative democracy. The House of Commons, the elected element in parliament, has the key representative role. There are 646 MPs there to represent the people of Britain. They represent the people because they have been chosen by them. In western democracies, it is the manner of choice – free elections – which is seen as the key component of representative government. As such, the House of Commons – and its equivalent in other countries – is the institution that forms the basis of representative democracy.

Britain has a system of representative democracy in which the elected few represent the many. When we say that our MPs are the elected representatives of the people, what do we mean by the term 'represent'? There are three meanings. It might mean that:

- **They have been freely elected by their constituents whose needs they should represent** (they are at Westminster to act on behalf of all of them, even those who did not give them their vote).

- **They represent the interests of the voters as they understand them, rather than acting as a delegate for any particular organisation or group of voters**.

- **They are socially representative of those whom they represent**, i.e. typical of a class or group. The membership of the House of Commons is not socially representative of the people, because it is overwhelmingly more white, male, middle class and middle aged than the bulk of the population. In other words, it does not mirror or reflect the characteristics of the community as a whole.

> ### Key term
>
> A **delegate** is a person chosen to act on behalf of others, in effect conveying their views.

Fig. 3 *Edmund Burke: Anglo-Irish statesman, author, orator, political theorist and philosopher, often seen as the father of the Conservative party*

Are our MPs representatives or delegates?

The proper role of an MP has been much debated. The classic case for allowing an MP to act as an individual, once elected, was set out in 1774 by a well-known political theorist of the day, Edmund Burke, who had just been elected for Bristol. In a famous, much-quoted letter to his new constituents, he informed them that MPs should not be considered to be merely delegates or agents of the voters in the area for which they had been elected. Rather, they should be considered firstly as Members of parliament, representing the one interest of the nation. They must define this according to their own judgement of the issues to be decided by parliament:

> Your representative owes you, not his industry only, but his judgement: and he betrays, instead of serving you, if he sacrifices it to your opinion.

Burke was of course writing before the development of organised parties and **party discipline** in the House of Commons which now have a major impact on the way MPs react. But many members would still argue that on issues of private morality, they have a duty to seek out information, listen to the speeches in the House and then make up their mind in the light of what they hear and not vote under the pressure of their constituency postbag.

So there are two views about the way that MPs should interpret the meaning of representation. In his Bristol speech, Burke made it clear that elected representatives should act and speak on behalf of those they represent. By this, he meant that having heard the arguments and facts in debate, they should use their discretion when deciding how to vote. They are not merely a mouthpiece for others. The alternative view is that MPs are delegates who are expected to advance the views of those whom they represent, irrespective of their own inclinations. This means taking note of and acting upon constituency feeling because according to this view they are there to safeguard and promote constituents' interests.

Barristers, commercial travellers and overseas ambassadors are representatives in this sense of the term. So too are the spokespersons for pressure groups such as the British Medical Association and the National Union of Teachers, who respectively speak up for the doctors and teachers who voted for them. Trade unionists expect that when consulting with government their leaders will convey their views and make it clear what their membership will not stand. Unlike the situation until the 1980s, all union leaders are subjected to periodic re-election. But as elected power holders, they are expected to act as they are instructed or mandated to do.

Summary questions

1 What do we mean by saying that our MPs are representatives?

2 Should MPs be representatives or delegates?

Key term

Party discipline is the system via which MPs are expected to 'toe the party line' by voting with their parties in the House of Commons.

Activity

Here is the rest of the relevant text from Burke's Bristol speech:

He betrays instead of serving you if he sacrifices [his judgement] to your opinion . . . authoritative instructions arise from a fundamental mistake of the whole order and tenor of our constitution. parliament is not a congress of ambassadors from different and hostile interests . . . [it] is a deliberative assembly of one nation, with one interest, that of the whole . . . You choose a member indeed; but when you have chosen him, he is not a member of Bristol, but he is a Member of parliament.

Argue the case that your MP should listen to his conscience when voting on a controversial issue such as abortion or capital punishment rather than listen to the weight of constituency opinion.

2 Referendums and initiatives as forms of direct democracy

Learning objectives:

- In what parts of the world and for what sorts of issues are referendums used?

- Why have referendums become more popular worldwide and in the UK?

- In what circumstances have they been used in the UK?

Key terms

Demagogues are political agitators who seek to win support by playing upon and inflaming the prejudices and passions of the mob.

Legislature is a type of representative assembly with the power to make or adopt laws.

The European Union (EU) is an organisation of 27 states with both economic and political aims. (See chapter 17.)

Referendums, initiatives and the recall are methods of direct democracy, enabling voters to decide issues for themselves. In parts of the US some or all forms of direct democracy are practised, but in Britain we have only made use of the referendum.

The worldwide use of referendums

A referendum involves a public vote on some single issue of public policy. It is a means of presenting a question of importance for popular consideration and decision.

Usually then known as plebiscites, referendums were employed by some twentieth-century dictators such as Hitler and Mussolini. They used the trappings of democracy to conceal their real intentions which were to boost their authority by creating an impression of legitimacy for the policies they intended to carry out. Because plebiscites became associated with undemocratic regimes, Clement Attlee (British Prime Minister 1945–51) was dismissive of them. He described them as 'devices alien to our traditions', the instruments of '**demagogues** and dictators'.

Plebiscites have also featured in some democratic regimes with authoritarian overtones, such as the Fifth French Republic in the days of Charles de Gaulle. However, such unfortunate associations have largely disappeared. **Referendums – as they are known today – are now used with increasing regularity in countries and states that have strong democratic credentials**.

In recent years referendums have been much more widely employed in most parts of the world. In Europe, most referendums have been held to decide questions considered too difficult or too crucial for the **legislature** to70 decide on its own (perhaps because they involve decisions on abortion or divorce or because they impact upon the constitution). This has been the case especially when an issue appears likely to split ruling parties or when governments wish to protect themselves from any negative electoral effects it might have on them. For instance, three European countries (Austria, Sweden and Italy) resorted to referendums on the divisive matter of the civil use of nuclear power. Similarly, the UK's surprise announcement in 2004 that it would hold a referendum on the proposed **European Union (EU)** constitution fell into this category. In the event, it was never needed, because by rejecting the Constitutional Treaty in their own referendums the voters of France and the Netherlands effectively stopped it from being introduced anywhere in its existing form.

Some Member States of the EU have used referendums to confirm their membership or to ratify some important constitutional development. In Austria, Denmark, Estonia and six other countries, there is a constitutional requirement that a vote will take place before a new treaty can be approved. In Sweden, referendums can be held if they seem appropriate on any particular issue. Their status is advisory only, meaning that the people's verdict does not have to be translated into law. The Swedish government ignored the public vote in 1955, when the people voted to continue driving on the left and ministers of the day decided to change to driving on the right. Ministers were also slow to follow the voters' wishes expressed in 1980 to decommission nuclear power stations; the process did not begin for 20 years! In Switzerland, a non-EU state, single-issue votes are built into the regular machinery of government and held on a three-monthly basis. They are binding rather than advisory. In 2003, the voters were asked nine questions resulting – among other things – in the decision to ban car use on four Sundays every year.

In Britain, with its commitment to the idea of **parliamentary sovereignty**, only parliament can cast a decisive vote on any issue, but it is unlikely that a majority of MPs would make a habit of casting their parliamentary vote in defiance of the popular will as expressed in a referendum. British governments have accepted that to consult and then to ignore the verdict is worse than not seeking an opinion. In 1975, Prime Minister Wilson accepted that a majority of even a single vote against the UK remaining in the European Community would mean that it would have to leave. In other words, both governments and MPs accept that they should treat the popular verdict as mandatory in the sense that it is morally and politically binding.

Activities

Using the internet to assist, find out:

1. Details of the latest referendums held in Switzerland.

2. Which US states use referendums and/or initiatives? See if you can find some examples of such votes held at the time of the November 2006 presidential or November 2008 congressional elections.

Experience of referendums in Britain

Britain has until recently had very little experience of voting on a single issue, even though the case has often been canvassed in the 20th century. The Conservatives held a referendum on the border issue in Northern Ireland in 1973, and Labour allowed the Scots and the Welsh to vote on whether they wanted **devolution** in 1979. Yet the only occasion when all of the voters have been allowed to vote on a key national issue was four years earlier, when they were asked whether or not they wished the country to remain in the **European Economic Community** (see Table on p66).

Since May 1997, referendums have been used to resolve the issue of devolution and the future shape of London's government. Also, in votes held on the same day, the voters of the **six counties** and of the Irish Republic signified their approval of the **Good Friday Agreement**. In the early Blair years, ministers suggested the possibility of a vote on electoral reform and membership of the single currency if it was decided that Britain would join the **eurozone**. But neither has materialised, nor do they seem likely to do so in the near future.

Key terms

Parliamentary sovereignty is the concept that parliament has absolute sovereignty (complete power), making it supreme over all other government institutions and able to introduce, change or repeal legislation as it wishes. (See chapter 11).

Devolution is the statutory granting of powers from the central government to government at regional or local level.

European Economic Community was the name for the organisation set up by the Treaty of Rome in 1957. It later became known as the European Community before becoming the European Union in late 1993.

The **six counties** relates to the province of Northern Ireland, comprising six out of the nine counties of Ulster.

The **Good Friday** (or Belfast) **Agreement** (1998) reached between the British and Irish governments and endorsed by most Northern Ireland political parties was a major political development in the Northern Ireland peace process. (See Chapter 16).

The **eurozone** is the area of the European Union that includes the 13 Member States that have adopted the euro as their currency.

Hint

Examiners will be impressed if you can quote actual and recent examples of overseas referendums in your answers.

Table 1 *National referendums in the UK, 1973–2008*

Year	Topic	Turnout (%)	Outcome
1973	Border poll in Northern Ireland: electorate asked if they wished to remain a part of the UK or join the Republic of Ireland	61.0	Massive majority to remain in the UK
1975	UK's membership of the EEC: electorate asked if they wished to stay in the Community or withdraw from it	64.0	64% (two-thirds) majority to stay in (43% of the whole electorate)
1979	Devolution to Scotland and Wales: each electorate was asked if it wanted a devolved assembly	62.8 58.3	Scotland: narrow majority in favour Wales: majority against
1997	Devolution to Scotland and Wales: each electorate was asked if it wanted a devolved assembly	60.1 50.1	Scotland: strong majority in favour Wales: very narrow majority in favour
1998	Good Friday Agreement on Northern Ireland: voters north (and south) of the border were asked to endorse the package	81.0	Overwhelming majority in favour

NB: In the case of the 1979 referendums, there was a requirement that a certain percentage of votes (a threshold) should be reached, before devolution came into effect. Although the majority of Scots wanted a devolved assembly, the 'yes' campaign did not achieve the required backing of at least 40 per cent of the whole electorate.

There have been local referendums on the future status of schools and the ownership of council estates, as well as in a few cases on the issue of whether to cut the level of Council Tax or to cut services provided. More than 30 local authorities held referendums a few years ago to decide on whether there should be an elected mayor in their area. In Wales the issue of 'local option' (the Sunday opening of pubs) used to be decided in this way.

Why have referendums become more popular in Britain?

Referendums have become more popular across the world. In Britain, they have secured an established place in our constitutional arrangements. This was confirmed by the fact that regulation of their conduct was a task granted to the new Electoral Commission, established under the terms of the Political Parties, Elections and Referendums Act 2000. Their increased popularity reflects some recognition by governments of the growing desire of some people to participate in between general elections and express their views on the decisions that immediately shape their lives.

Governments have found referendums helpful in resolving controversial issues that cut across the party divide. They tend to be held because ministers want to get the public to express a view on difficult and contentious matters, rather than make the final decision themselves. Labour is most clearly associated with the use of referendums. It has taken the view that the device is a democratic one in that it gives people a direct voice in decision making, so that any decision made acquires legitimacy because it has popular approval. Three referendums were held in the last period of Labour ascendancy (1974–79). Others have been discussed or held since 1997. There have been key constitutional issues to decide on devolution, the Good Friday Agreement in Northern Ireland, and Europe.

3 Arguments for and against the greater use of referendums

Learning objective:

- What are the merits and disadvantages of referendums?

There is disagreement among academics, commentators and politicians over the respective merits of the referendum. For some, it is the ultimate means of achieving direct democracy, having the benefit of increasing people's understanding of issues of public policy. For others, it has undesirable side effects, notably that it hands power to special interests such as the European Community or big business that can deploy their considerable wealth to influence the outcome. More progressive observers worry about the repercussions of such votes for minority groups; there is some evidence in the US that gays and immigrants have tended to suffer when a specific issue affecting them is put to the test of public opinion. But of course in Britain the referendums held have not been about matters of social policy, but ones of constitutional significance.

Referendums are a good thing!

Supporters of referendums believe that they encourage participation, act as an important educational device and mobilise the people. For Bogdanor, they might 'improve the quality of the relationship between government and people: and that constitutes the central argument in favour of [their] wider use'.

Specifically, referendums:

- **Are not just democratic, but are a means of saving democracy with which some people have become disenchanted**. There has been widespread disillusion with the behaviour of politicians in recent years and trust has seriously declined. If politicians and parties seem distant from the people and unwilling to listen to them, referendums are a means of restoring their faith in the democratic process, allowing the will of the people to be expressed on an issue in the clearest possible manner. They have a direct say on issues that affect their lives. Indeed, there is arguably scope for referendum democracy to be developed in the future. With devices such as digital television, computers and mobile phones it has become technically feasible to consult the people more regularly and easily.

- **Encourage participation in the political process**. In a country in which participation for many people is limited to election day, the greater use of referendums would stimulate involvement and lead to more public discussion of important issues. In Denmark and Switzerland, supporters of referendums claim that they have significantly advanced citizen understanding of issues under consideration.

- **Make the electorate better informed on individual issues**. There is a thorough airing of the topics involved, and literature is produced to make the case for and against the proposal. In some US states, a weighty document (sometimes more than one) is produced, setting out the arguments and financial costs involved. Past experience in Britain and elsewhere seems to show that referendums increase people's understanding of the issues and provide an education for those who participate in them.

- **Are better than general elections**, because in an election the people are voting on a range of issues whereas they can specify their views on a particular issue in a referendum. When people vote for a party manifesto in an election, it is not clear exactly which policies are favoured and which are not.

■ **Strengthen the hand of the government** in dealing with difficult issues. They can be used to resolve an impasse, especially when ministers are divided over what to do. For Harold Wilson in 1975, it was useful to be able to hand the issue of 'Britain in or out of Europe' over to the public and therefore avoid upsetting some of his party. In the vivid phrase of Hague and Harrop: 'Like a plumber's drainrods, referendums resolve blockages'.

■ **Are good for tackling issues which cut across party lines**, on which the nation is divided. Europe and devolution in the 1970s were not issues on which there was a simple Conservative v Labour argument.

■ **Resolve issues in such a way that there is a final or at least long-term solution**. The 1979 referendums resolved the devolution issue for 20 years and the 1975 referendum resolved the European issue for considerably longer. Following the latter vote, a leading anti-EEC campaigner, Tony Benn, explicitly made this point: 'I read the message loud and clear. When the British people speak, everyone – including ourselves – should tremble before their decisions'.

■ When the initiative and recall are allowed, votes on a single issue allow aggrieved citizens to raise matters and criticisms that might otherwise go unheard.

The *Guardian* (4 March 1993) summed up the case for referendums:

> Britain suffers from an enormous democratic deficit and imaginative means have to be sought to redress the imbalance . . . referendums would generate urgent civic discussion which will never take place with such purpose in any other way.

■ Oh no they are not!

Opponents of referendums dismiss the democratic argument. They point out that Britain is a representative democracy rather than a direct one. In representative democracies, the idea is that politicians give a lead and produce policies that the public can then accept or reject in a general election. Before they vote on a bill in the House of Commons, MPs hear the arguments and become knowledgeable about the facts and figures; they are therefore in the best position to decide on complex issues. If they pass the decision to the voters, then they shirk the responsibility for which they were elected.

Critics of referendums have other arguments besides the central one outlined above. They point out that:

■ **Referendums are complex devices for the electorate**: it is all very well to ask whether Britain should stay in the European Community (now the European Union). It is very different to ask a technical question as to whether the country should be in the eurozone. There are important constitutional implications in a decision as to whether to adopt the euro, but there are also difficult economic effects to try and gauge.

■ Although referendums are supposed to keep government in line with popular opinion, **they only tell you the state of public feeling at a particular time**. If government is to be continuously responsible, then the logic is to have continuous referendums on the same topic. This is not practical, it might bore the electorate to the extent that they would not turn out to vote, and it would be costly to organise.

Activities

1 In light of the points set out above, consider the arguments for and against holding a referendum on whether:

a Britain should join the eurozone

b Britain should leave the European Union.

2 In Europe, outside Switzerland, referendums on moral and social issues are uncommon. Why do you think they are rarely used?

3 Bale (2005) argues that 'referendums are not a "silver bullet" that can revivify ailing democracies'. Could they do just that?

Much depends on the question asked. By framing a question in a particular way, it may be possible to get an outcome that does not really represent public opinion. The experience of some dictatorships suggests that the referendum can be abused in this way. In Chile, the notorious **General Pinochet** gained 75 per cent acquiescence for a proposition that offered no meaningful choice, because the voter was in effect being asked either to be loyal or disloyal to his country:

> In the face of international aggression unleashed against the government of the fatherland, I support President Pinochet in his defence of the dignity of Chile.

(NB: In a democracy it should be possible to ensure that clarity and fairness prevail, particularly since the Electoral Commission now has responsibility for approving the wording of any question asked of the voters.)

Referendums have their use for resolving constitutional issues, but as a means of deciding social ones they are not very satisfactory. On matters like immigration and crime, on which public opinion can be liable to bouts of emotion, referendums are especially unsuitable. Penal reform – in particular the abolition of capital punishment – would never have come about if the public had its way. Surely it is up to ministers to lead the public.

People might vote 'for the wrong reasons'. The choice they make can be muddied by other, irrelevant considerations. In 1979, in the failed attempt to introduce devolution, it may be that the voters were really expressing their judgement on a government that they did not really like after five years of 'hard Labour'. Similarly in the French referendum of 2005 on the proposed EU constitutional treaty – among the majority that registered a 'no' vote there were people of many shades of opinion. It was widely felt that voters were expressing their disapproval of the government's economic record, the way in which EU social policy was evolving, and immigration, among other things.

Campaigns can be expensive and therefore advantageous to well-funded groups. Money is too dominant in the process. Business interests have far more scope to influence the outcome in order to advance their own economic interests. In 1975, the major manufacturing organisations spent heavily on the pro-European side.

Key term

General Pinochet (1915–2006) was a Chilean general and statesman who presided over a dictatorial regime between 1973 and 1990 and was best known in Europe for his brutal treatment of political opponents.

Fig. 5 *General Pinochet*

Further reading

D Watts, 'The Growing Attractions of Direct Democracy', *Talking Politics*, September 1997.

M Rathbone, 'Referendums in Britain', *Talking Politics*, September 1999.

A Batchelor, 'Direct Democracy', *Talking Politics*, January 2002.

AQA Examination-style questions

1 ☑ Read the extract and answer questions (a) to (c) which follow.

First past the post

The principal advantage of the First Past the Post electoral system is that it almost always provides strong, stable, single-party government with an overall *parliamentary majority*. Other than in times of emergency, coalition government is virtually unknown. Minority government is also very rare. Because First Past the Post has single-member constituencies, there is also the advantage of close relationships between MPs and their constituents.

Source: adapted from Chapter 3 of this textbook

(a) Briefly explain the term *parliamentary majority* used in the extract. *(5 marks)*

(b) Using your own knowledge as well as the extract, distinguish between coalition government and minority government. *(10 marks)*

(c) 'Under First Past the Post election results do not reflect the views of the electorate.' Discuss. *(25 marks)*

2 Read the extract and answer questions (a) to (c) which follow.

Direct democracy

Until recently, Britain had very little experience of voting on a single issue. The Conservatives held a *referendum* on the border issue in Northern Ireland in 1973, and Labour allowed the Scots and Welsh to vote on whether they wanted devolution in 1979. Yet the only occasion when all of the voters have been allowed to vote on a key national issue was four years earlier, when they were asked whether or not they wished to remain in the European Economic Community. But since 1997, referendums have been used to resolve the issue of devolution in Scotland and Wales and the future of Northern Ireland. In London, as well as up and down the country, the creation of directly elected mayors has been decided by referendums.

Source: adapted from Chapter 4 of this textbook

(a) Briefly explain the term *referendum* as it is used in the extract. *(5 marks)*

(b) Using your own knowledge as well as the extract, assess the extent to which referendums increase participation. *(10 marks)*

(c) 'Whilst referendums may be useful for resolving constitutional issues, they are an unsatisfactory means of deciding social issues.' Discuss. *(25 marks)*

5 Parties and the party system

1 Political parties and the need for them

Learning objectives:

- What are political parties?
- Why are parties important to democracy?
- What are the different types of party systems?
- Is it correct to describe Britain as having a two-party system?
- What are the benefits and disadvantages of two-party systems?

Key terms

Political parties are organisations of broadly like-minded men and women that seek to win elections in order that they can then assume responsibility for controlling the apparatus of government with a view to implementing their policies.

Party whips are the officials who manage the supporters of their party in the House of Commons and are responsible for maintaining discipline and unity. In British politics, the chief whip is assisted by between eight and 10 assistant whips, all members of parliament.

Links

For more on 'Campaigns' see p26, Chapter 2, 'Election campaigns and their impact'.

Western liberal democracy is unthinkable without competition between **political parties**. They bring together a variety of different interests in society. Via the electoral process, they determine the shape of governments. European, US and other democracies are party democracies. Parties have played a significant role in British politics for more than 200 years. They influence all aspects of government and politics. Their primary purpose is to win elections. This is the main feature that distinguishes them from pressure groups which may try to influence elections but do not usually put up candidates for office (see Chapters 7 and 8).

Parties fulfil several functions:

- **They sift ideas and organise opinion**. They take on board the ideas of individuals and groups and aggregate (put together) and simplify them into a package of policies. In this way, they clarify the political process for the voter who is confronted with a choice of alternative proposals, programmes and leaders. The voter is then able to choose the party that most resembles his or her own policy preferences.

- **They are a source of political knowledge**. Even for voters who lack any strong party ties, their ideas and outlook are likely to be influenced by the information that parties offer and by their perception of what the parties support.

- **They act as a link between the individual and the political system**. Most people rely on various political interests to represent their concerns and demands. Parties formulate, aggregate and communicate a package of such demands, and if they win power they attempt to implement them. In this way, parties act as bridge organisations, mediators between the conflicting interests of government and the electorate.

- **They mobilise and recruit activists**. Parties offer a structure into which individuals can channel their interests. They provide contact with other individuals and groups and an opportunity to become political foot soldiers or local or national politicians. In many democracies including Britain, the recruitment, selection and training of parliamentary candidates is a key task. Parties offer candidates support during election campaigns and are responsible for local and national campaigning.

- **They provide an organisational structure via which to coordinate the actions of government, encouraging those who belong to them to work towards shared objectives**. Leaders and their colleagues (including **party whips**) seek to persuade members of the legislature to vote for their policies. Where necessary they do coalition deals to secure a majority for particular programmes.

- **They serve as a source of opposition**. The parties not in government provide explicit, organised opposition. In Britain there is a fully institutionalised party known as Her Majesty's Loyal Opposition, with its own shadow ministerial team.

Activities

1 Identify reasons why use of FPTP encourages the development of a two-party system.

2 Using the internet for research, write down the names of the two major parties in the US and briefly describe what they stand for. Can you work out which of the two is more like the British Conservative party in approach and policies?

■ Party systems: the two-party system in Britain

In the same way that in international football the World Cup requires teams representing many countries, a **party system** usually requires the interaction of several parties. The term refers to the network of relationships between parties that determines how the political system functions.

Just as national soccer teams learn from each other and borrow successful tactics, political parties draw conclusions from the experiences of one another. They compete with each other, modernising and improving their outlook, policies, fund-raising and organisation to enable them to cope with the challenge presented by their rivals. As we have seen, in a bid to win power, **party competition** is basic to any democracy. The pattern of that competition tends to persist over a period of time. In Britain and the US, this involves the main parties being engaged in a permanent contest for power.

The most usual means of distinguishing between different types of party system is by reference to the number of parties involved. There are four categories of party systems:

1 **One-party systems**. Mostly associated with authoritarian regimes in which a single party enjoys a monopoly of power, e.g. in remaining communist regimes such as China and North Korea, no effective opposition is officially tolerated.

2 **Two-party systems**. In these systems, as in Britain and the US, there are two major parties, each of which has a strong chance of obtaining a majority of seats in the legislature and winning political power. There may be other parties – some sizeable – but they do not compete for office with any hope of winning. Two-party systems tend to flourish where the FPTP electoral system is used. Indeed, it is this that helps them to survive. In cases where there has been a shift away from the plurality method (FPTP) (e.g. New Zealand), the two-party system has come under pressure.

3 **Dominant party systems**. These exist in a country where there is free competition between parties, but only one party is likely to achieve an absolute majority of the votes cast and dominate governmental office. Before black majority rule, the Nationalist party in South Africa was in this position, as today is the African National Congress. In the 1980s, commentators noted that Britain had one-party dominance in a traditionally two-party system.

4 **Multi-party systems**. These are the norm in European countries, such as Belgium, Finland, Holland and Italy, and are common in most parts of the democratic world. Government tends to be based on coalitions of more than one party, maybe three or four. Under this type of party system, there is not usually a clear distinction between government and opposition as many of the broadly centrist parties tend to be members of most administrations. Such systems are common where proportional representation is employed.

■ Britain – historically a two-party system

Britain has had a two-party system for most of the last 200 years, Labour and the Conservatives being the dominant parties since the 1930s. Only once since 1945 has one of the major parties failed to win an outright Commons majority. The peak of the two-party system was in 1951 when between them Labour and the Conservatives won 98.6 per cent of the votes and 96.8 per cent of the seats. Since then, the two-party system has generally been resilient, although the rise in third-party support since the mid-1970s has made the picture more confused. The two main parties have lost electoral support and their overwhelming dominance in parliamentary seats.

The election of 2005 provided confusing evidence as to whether we still have a two-party system. The two main parties won just over two-thirds of the vote, yet between them gained 554 seats at Westminster. Their joint share of the parliamentary seats was the lowest in any post-war election (85.6 per cent), with the Liberal Democrats winning 62 seats (the strongest performance by a third party since 1923). In view of the strength of this third party, some commentators would refer to the UK as having a two-and-a-half party system, or a two-party system and three-party politics.

In fact, the situation is more complex than this. In 2005, no fewer than six parties (and two independents) won seats in Great Britain and another four parties won seats in Northern Ireland. Moreover, in recent elections, there have been national and regional variations that make the two-party system primarily an English phenomenon. Leaving aside Northern Ireland which has a distinctive political system, Scotland and Wales both have a strong nationalist party. In general elections, Labour is the largest of the four parties in both countries, so that in effect there is one-party dominance but four-party politics.

Key term

Catch-all parties are umbrella or 'broker' parties that seek to maximise their voter appeal by reaching out to as many groups as possible, rather than representing specific class, regional or partisan interests.

In depth

Conditions which have helped to create and sustain the British two-party system

- **The natural tendency for opinion on issues to divide into a 'for' and 'against' position**, which often follows the basic division between those who generally favour the status quo (the Conservatives) and those who wish to see innovation and a faster rate of change (Labour).

- **The electoral system**. The FPTP simple majority system used in Britain means that the candidate with the most votes wins, whether or not he or she actually obtained a majority of all the votes cast. This discourages parties from splintering and restricts the growth of new parties. Broadly, as we saw in Chapter 3, more proportional voting systems are likely to be associated with multi-party systems.

- **The existence of broad catch-all parties that aim to win backing from all sections of the electorate**. The two main parties try to reach out to a broad range of opinion, which generally keeps them moderate and middle-of-the-road. As such, there is little scope for a third party to establish itself and become electorally successful.

- **The emphasis on being in government or opposition**. Whereas continental legislatures have semi-circular seating arrangements, allowing shades of political opinion to be expressed, in Britain the rectangular House of Commons forces MPs to choose. Either they are for the government of the day, or against it.

- **The traditional absence of deep ethnic, linguistic, religious and sectional differences within the population**. In Britain, most members of ethnic groups have not felt it necessary to create new parties to represent their interests.

- **The problems faced by third or other parties.** Lack of finance and other resources, the difficulty of establishing a distinct identity and the danger of being squeezed out by the two main rivals all make life hard for a new party trying to establish itself.

Activities

1 Below are the figures for the combined percentages of votes received and seats won by the two main parties in post-1945 general elections. Work out the average for each set of figures:

   a in the eight elections of the period from 1945 to 1970, and

   b in the nine elections from February 1974 to 2005. What do your findings tell you about the state of Britain's two-party system since 1945?

2 Make a list of all of the political parties represented in the present House of Commons. Use the internet to help you if necessary.

Table 1 *Post-1945 elections, votes received and seats won by the two main parties*

Year	Combined Lab. + Con. votes (%)	Combined Lab. + Con. seats (%)
1945	87.6	94.7
1950	89.6	98.1
1951	96.8	98.6
1955	96.1	98.6
1959	93.2	98.9
1964	87.5	98.6
1966	89.8	97.8
1970	89.4	98.0
1974 (Feb.)	75.0	94.2
1974 (Oct.)	75.0	93.8
1979	80.8	95.8
1983	70.0	93.0
1987	73.2	93.0
1992	76.2	93.2
1997	73.9	88.4
2001	72.4	87.7
2005	67.6	85.6

The advantages of Britain's two-party system

1 **It promotes effective, stable and strong government**. The success of the British political system has often been attributed to the fact that there have been two strong parties, either of which wins a clear majority and is usually capable of forming a government on its own. Stability is promoted because a government can carry out its policies relieved of the possible fear that it will be suddenly overthrown by a coalition of the minority parties. By contrast, multi-party systems result in coalition governments that are often said to give too much power to politicians to indulge in secret **horse-trading** and make bargains that do not reflect the wishes of the voters.

2 **It simplifies voter choice**, because only two parties are viable as governing bodies. Accordingly, the people can in effect vote directly for or against an outgoing government, not merely for a party.

3 **The government is clearly accountable to the electorate**. The voters know who to praise or blame for the policies in operation, whereas in a coalition situation responsibility is less clear-cut. Governments can govern, but there is another one in waiting should they fail.

4 **Moderation is encouraged**. If an opposition party knows that its turn will come, this encourages it to be constructive and pose as an alternative government, and not to lapse into extremism that would probably alienate the majority of people in the political centre. There is therefore a strong incentive for both parties to try and hold the middle ground. Indeed, they need to do so to win a general election.

The disadvantages of the British two-party system

1 **It restricts voter choice**. This matters less when the main parties are popular and command majority support, but is more serious when many voters feel alienated. Many voters have seemed to be increasingly disenchanted with Labour and the Conservatives, as their declining combined levels of voter support in recent elections indicate.

2 **Far from promoting moderation, it can sometimes be characterised by** adversary politics, with an emphasis on conflict and argument rather than consensus and compromise. Governments sometimes come in and undo the work of their predecessors. Although complete reversals in direction are uncommon, the detail of policies can be significantly changed.

3 **There is growing dissatisfaction with the performance of the main parties**. Especially in Britain in recent years, all has not been well with the two-party system. Governments have not always delivered the goods and the main opposition party has not necessarily been appealing. Support for third parties, in particular the Liberal Democrats and Nationalists, has been growing. In European elections, voters have been willing to vote for a party with a clear alternative message, the United Kingdom Independence party (UKIP).

Activities

1 Using the internet to help you, find out and record the main aims and policies of any two minor parties represented in the present House of Commons. What are their prospects over the coming years?

2 Reflect on whether it would be a good thing if we had strong parties specifically designed to represent the interests of different ethnic groups within the community.

Key terms

Horse-trading is making shrewd bargains or deals that are of benefit to those who make them.

Adversary politics relate to a period in which there is fundamental disagreement between the parties on the political issues of the day. 'Adversarial politics' are characterised by ideological antagonism (a fierce clash of ideas and outlook) as part of an ongoing electoral battle between the major parties.

Summary questions

1 Distinguish between the different types of party system.

2 Does the experience of the years since 1979 suggest that Britain really has a two-party system with one-party dominance (a 'two-and-a-half party system') or a straightforward two-party system?

3 From what you have found out so far, do you think that on balance Britain benefits or suffers from broadly having a two-party system?

2 The party spectrum: Left and Right

Learning objectives:

- What is meant by an ideology?

- What are party families?

- What is meant by the Left-Right spectrum?

- What are the main differences between supporters of the Left and of the Right?

Key terms

Ideologues are people strongly committed to one body of ideas.

A **political spectrum** is a convenient means of visualising different political positions, stretching from the far left parties that want radical or even revolutionary change, through more moderate groups of left, centre and right, to far right extremists such as neo (born-again) fascists and neo-Nazis.

Parties are created around broad principles. Although most of their members are not strict **ideologues**, these broad ideologies provide recognition and mean something to many people. Budge *et al.* (2005) describe ideology as 'a theory about the world and about society, and of the place of you and your group within it'. These ideologies are important 'not only in telling leaders what to do but in telling their supporters who they are and thus making them receptive to leaders' diagnoses of the political situation'. Ideologies change and develop over time, their supporters often belong to different schools of thought which disagree over their vision, tactics and the timing of how their goals might be achieved.

In an interesting essay entitled 'The End of History', Fukuyama (1989) has suggested that political ideology has lost much of its relevance today. For with the downfall of the Soviet Union and its satellites, and the establishment of 'new democracies', the battle for ideas has been won. In his view, liberal democracy has triumphed over its rivals.

The main political ideologies found in Europe

The terms 'Left-Right politics' or the 'Left-Right **political spectrum**' are commonly used as a means of classifying political ideologies and political positions. The words were originally used to describe the attitudes adopted by different groups in the French Estates-General in 1789. The moderate royalists seated themselves on the right side of the chamber, whilst those wanting reform sat on the left. In effect, this meant that being a member of 'the Right' implied support for aristocratic, royal or clerical interests, whereas being a member of 'the Left' implied opposition to the *ancien regime* (the old order).

LEFT   Communism ⟵ Socialism ⟵ Liberalism ⟶ Conservatism ⟶ Fascism   RIGHT

Fig. 1 *A spectrum of political ideas*

Key terms

Socialism: socialists believe that unrestrained capitalism or free enterprise is responsible for a variety of social evils, such as the exploitation of working people and the pursuit of greed and selfishness. They favour cooperative values, which emphasise the values of community, equality and justice, and state action to promote these values.

Liberalism is a term which came into use in the 19th century, although liberal theory dates back much further. It is associated with the values of individualism, liberty, rationalism (reason) and political and legal equality, ideas which have influenced all parties to some degree. In economic and social terms, classical liberals supported laissez-faire policies, involving the minimum of government intervention and regulation.

Conservatism is a creed that generally opposes innovation and change, and advocates preserving the best of the established order in society.

Fascism was the political creed and movement associated with the regime of Benito Mussolini in Italy between the two World Wars. It is usually regarded as authoritarian, militaristic and in practice extremely right wing.

Marxian socialism is a variety of socialist thinking associated with the ideas of the left-wing German political thinker, Karl Marx, which has a strong economic as well as an ethical dimension.

The terms are still employed today. Broadly, those on the Left – traditionally identified with the interests of the masses – support an increase in governmental activity. They want to create a more just society in which economic and social problems can be addressed. Accordingly, they favour political, economic and social change, and want to promote greater equality. Those on the Right – traditionally identified with preservation of the interests of the established, propertied classes – broadly oppose the type of change favoured by the Left. They are more wary of state intervention and seek to limit the scope of government as much as possible. They place more emphasis on personal responsibility and individual enterprise.

A linear spectrum of political ideas is shown in Fig. 1.

Party families in Europe

Parties in many countries tend to employ similar names, so that across the continent words such as Christian, Conservative, Democrat, Green, Labour, Liberal and Socialist are in regular use. This suggests that they have assumptions and ideas that are similar. These common values and beliefs help us to interpret events and policies more clearly. In particular, many European voters still subscribe in some degree to causes such as socialism, in its various forms. However, even those parties within the socialist family can differ sharply over their vision of end goals and the tactics to be pursued in attaining them. **Marxian socialism** is probably the most developed and influential ideology because many groups have been formed to argue for it, debate what it means or react against it. Some socialists are fundamentalists who wish to stick to the ideas of Marx as they see them. Others are revisionists who wish to place the ideas in the context of today's society that has changed dramatically since the time in which Marx wrote.

Further information

European party families

■ Party families are parties in different countries that share a similar ideology, having similar beliefs, policies and often support groups.

Examples are:

■ Christian Democratic parties

■ communist parties

■ conservative parties

■ liberal/reform parties

■ regional autonomist parties

■ socialist/social democratic parties.

In Britain, Labour falls into the general 'family' of socialist/social democratic parties, whereas the Greens resemble many other ecologically-minded parties.

Left and Right in British politics

In Britain as in other parts of democratic Europe, the essential Left-Right battle over ideas and policies has been between socialism and conservatism. However, liberal thinking has spread through the attitudes and approaches of all three main parties because they share a commitment to representative democracy and its core values.

When people talk about party politics in Britain, they still often speak of the Left, Right and Centre. Parties and their leading members are often described as left wing or right wing, although these labels can be misleading and confusing. People who seem left wing on one issue may adopt a right-wing stance on another. More seriously, the division of Left and Right has become somewhat blurred because over recent years supporters of New Labour have increasingly employed terminology and adopted approaches traditionally associated with the British Conservative party. Nonetheless, the terms remain a convenient shorthand by which to summarise different attitudes on important political, economic and social questions.

Traditionally:

- **A left-wing person** challenges traditional attitudes and practices, and wants to see reform. This involves a more active role for government in bringing about desirable change. A left-winger may also believe in higher levels of taxation to pay for increased welfare; some redistribution of wealth from the better-off to the least well-off; and movement towards a more equal and less class-bound society. Some are keen to see more state control over basic industries, believing that private ownership is unsuitable as a means of running the railways and other essential services. They talk in terms of progress, reform and rights. They are more likely to be internationalists (in other words, they see issues affecting Britain in world terms).

- **A right-wing person** is more likely to support the status quo, keeping things as they are unless there is a very strong case for change; is unlikely to favour extensive government regulation; favours private enterprise over state ownership; likes to think that people are left in freedom to run their own lives; and will probably favour lower levels of taxation, good rewards for effort and enterprise, and freedom more than equality. An unequal society is accepted as inevitable, even desirable. Right-wingers tend to have a strong belief in authority, duties, order and tradition, as well as seeing issues from a national rather than an international point of view.

Fig. 2 *Karl Marx (1818–83), German scholar and political activist, whose ideas were highly influential in the evolution of socialist thinking*

In recent years, the broad Left-Right ideological divide of the past has become less clear-cut. New Labour has shed its nominal socialism and positioned itself firmly in the political centre, seeking to maximise its appeal to moderates of the Left and Right as part of a 'big tent' approach. As the Liberal Democrats inhabit similar territory, it means that the middle ground is very crowded. People in the centre of the political spectrum tend to support a mixed economy:

- They accept the marketplace as the best means of running the economy.
- They believe that it is the duty of the government to take action to ensure that vulnerable members of society are not exploited.
- They exhibit tolerance towards ethnic and other minorities.
- They uphold the cause of constitutional change, especially provision for personal rights.

Activities

1. Write down how the attitudes and ideas of an orthodox left-winger and an orthodox right-winger conflict on:

   a ownership of industry

   b equality, and

   c the role of Britain in the world.

2. Within the parties, some politicians are described as being 'of the Left' or 'of the Right'. Find examples of current politicians who may be described as being 'Left' and 'Right' in the two main parties. Why might the people concerned be so described?

The party leaderships are aware of the need to attract and maintain support from a wide variety of interests and from people with a wide range of political beliefs. To some extent, as is common in most two-party systems, Labour and the Conservatives are catch-all parties, in both cases having their own left and right wing whose members advance a range of views on the issues of the day. However, members and supporters of both main parties share a number of distinctive ideas and philosophies, as described below.

Summary questions

1. How applicable is the use of the terms 'Left' and 'Right' to describe the positions of Labour and the Conservatives today?

2. How do left- and right-wing parties differ in their approaches to equality of outcome?

3 The Labour party

Learning objectives:

- What is socialism?

- In what ways has Clause Four been changed?

- How is Blairism different from earlier Labour attitudes and beliefs?

- How did Labour fare in the 2005 general election?

- What are the main strengths and weaknesses of Labour's position today?

Origins and early history

The Labour party emerged out of the Labour Representation Committee (LRC) which was formed in 1900 as a federation of groups representing various reforming traditions. There were among them radicals from the Independent Labour party (ILP) and moderates such as the Fabians. Supporters of the ILP wanted to achieve their socialist goals quickly, although they were committed to doing so via parliamentary elections. They saw the need for a separate party to further working-class aims. Members of the Fabian Society were willing to work more gradually to gain acceptance for their ideas, being willing in the short term to work with members of other parties. Besides these and other socialist societies, the key element in the formation of the Labour party was the trade unions. They were to retain an important position for much of the 20th century.

The LRC became a fully fledged political party in 1906, when it adopted its present name. It grew steadily both inside and outside parliament and by the end of the First World War it was in a position to challenge the ailing Liberal party. Between the wars (1918–39), there were two minority Labour administrations whose existence proved that Labour was capable of being a recognised party of government. But it was not until 1945 that the party won a landslide victory under the leadership of **Clement Attlee** and was able to govern on its own.

Differing ideas about socialism within the party

In its 1918 constitution, Labour committed itself to socialism. Socialism is not a precise term and different party thinkers and leaders have given it their own slant. However, many early socialists in the party saw the creed in terms of **Clause Four of their Constitution**:

> To secure for the workers by hand or by brain the full fruits of their industry and the most equitable distribution thereof that may be possible upon the basis of the common ownership of the means of production, distribution and exchange.

Clause Four was for many years a 'sacred cow' (a belief beyond challenge) of the Labour Movement and the Left of the party acted as its guardian. Traditionalists wanted to preserve it intact and continued to see socialism in terms of public ownership of key industries (more usually known as 'nationalisation').

In depth

Strands of socialist thinking

'Socialism' is a term that lacks a clear meaning. It developed as a radical or revolutionary ideology in response to the rise of industrial capitalism. It has several strands, including:

- The ethical socialism of **Robert Owen**.
- The Christian socialism which sought to draw parallels between what they saw as the **egalitarian** and anti-establishment message of Jesus and contemporary varieties of socialism.
- The Marxian socialism of the late 19th century which was sharply different from the earlier '**utopian**' varieties, in that it was primarily about economics.

The supporters of Karl Marx were revolutionary socialists who wanted to bring about the total overthrow of the existing economic and political system.

Several British socialist movements had a different character to their European counterparts. European socialists were either revolutionaries or supporters of more moderate social democracy who were willing to work through the ballot box. British enthusiasts formed a party that did not use the term socialism within its name, the Labour party. It was committed to retaining the democratic system of government, promoting the interests of the working classes and achieving radical social change through elections.

With the fall of the Berlin Wall in 1989 and the subsequent collapse of communist rule in Eastern Europe, far left-wing ideas have gone out of fashion in recent years. In addition, the success of Thatcherism in winning support for economic policies based on the free market and competition, helped to undermine the credibility of the traditional Left. In these circumstances, left-wing politicians have had to rethink many of their traditional attitudes. They have tended to shed their old 'tax-and-spend' approaches and instead placed increasing importance on ideas such as community, social partnership and 'stakeholder economics'.

Fig. 3 *Following a massive defeat on a leftwing programme in the 1983 election, Neil Kinnock tried to modernise the party's image, organisation and policies*

Fig. 4 *Bill Clinton: US Democrat politician, President 1993–2001; responsible for an overhaul of the party's image designed to broaden its appeal*

Key term

The **privatisation programme** is the policy of transferring of ownership of industries and utilities from the public sector to the private sector, as pursued by the Thatcher (Conservative) government in the 1980s.

After World War Two, some leaders such as **Gaitskell** tried to get Clause Four rewritten. He and most moderate, right-of-centre Labour MPs saw socialism less in terms of nationalisation and more in terms of the pursuit of greater equality, working towards a more just and fair society. The welfare state embraced many Labour ideas about the importance of society, brotherhood and care for each other.

The party moved to the left in the early 1980s and its policies seemed out of touch with the needs of ordinary Labour voters. Then, under **Neil Kinnock**, it shed some of the more extreme policies (wide-scale nationalisation, abandonment of the British nuclear deterrent and withdrawal from the European Community). But it was Tony Blair who set out to re-invent the party as New Labour after 1994 when he became leader. He boldly tackled the party's Constitution and re-wrote Clause Four (see below) so that it now stresses community values such as equality of power, tolerance and respect, and rights and duties, the emphasis being upon society. He modernised the party, along similar lines to the way in which **Bill Clinton** had overhauled and updated the US Democrats. Its values were tougher in some areas and on some groups who traditionally looked to Labour to protect them (such as trade unions and the poor to whom Tony Blair wished to give 'a hand-up rather than a hand-out').

In depth

Tony Blair and Clause Four

Clause Four in its Blairite form is a long statement of more than 300 words. It states that Labour:

> is a democratic socialist party. It believes that by the strength of our common endeavour we achieve more than we achieve alone so as to create for each of us the means to realise our true potential and for all of us a community in which power, wealth and opportunity are in the hands of the many not the few.

Two distinctive elements are:

- the prominence given to enterprise, competition and the free market
- the moral dimension, evident in references to personal responsibility, the family and our duty to care for each other.

The Blair leadership

As leader from 1994 to 2007, Tony Blair adopted some terminology more associated with the Conservatives. He used terms such as 'the market', 'achievement', 'opportunity' and 'aspirations', his whole approach representing an attempt to broaden Labour's appeal so that the party might be in tune with the supposed wishes of Middle England. Some of his policies echoed Thatcherite ideas – his administrations did not reverse the **privatisation programme** of earlier Conservative governments, they accepted the free market and made controversial use of public–private partnerships in building new schools and hospitals.

In the process of pursuing New Labour, Tony Blair's ideas and policies upset many traditional Labour voters who felt that he made the party too pro-business. Yet he also introduced policies that the Conservatives strongly opposed at the time – constitutional reform, a national

Fig. 5 *Tony Blair: Labour MP 1983–2007, leader 1994–2007, Prime Minister 1997–2007*

minimum wage, a massive injection of funds into the NHS (largely financed by increases in National Insurance contributions), as well as adopting a more positive approach towards the European Union. His broad approach was to advance the case that it was possible, indeed necessary, to combine economic efficiency with social justice.

Tony Blair was willing to draw upon aspects of not only the socialist and social democratic tradition, but also other ideologies such as the **New Liberalism** of the early 20th century and even **One Nation Conservatism**, as he searched for a **Third Way** between old-style socialism and the unrestrained free market aspirations of the Thatcherites. His approach delivered Labour two electoral landslides and a third substantial victory in 2005, the only time in history that Labour has won three successive elections.

Tony Blair and socialism

The Blair approach was a long way from traditional socialism. Some on the Left saw it as little more than Thatcherism with a human face. Even many on the Right of the party regretted the downgrading of **equality of outcome** and its replacement by an emphasis on **equality of opportunity**. There was less emphasis on levelling-down and more on creating opportunities for people to make the most of their talents.

Significantly, Tony Blair rarely used the word 'socialism' in his public statements. Occasionally he labelled himself as 'social democratic', but more often talked of governing from the 'radical centre'. In as much as he is a socialist, he is an ethical socialist rather than an economic one. As leader, he talked of 'old ideas in a modern setting'.

> New Labour is very much what I believe in. It's very much my own creation.

Tony Blair, interviewed on Panorama, 7 April 1999

Fig. 6 *Gordon Brown: Labour MP from 1983, party leader and Prime Minister from 2007*

Labour and the 2005 election: the need to regain lost voters

Tony Blair's announcement prior to the 2005 election that he would not serve a full third term led many Labour MPs to contemplate life after Blair. Blairites were concerned to entrench Blairism and fought the 2005 election on an 'unremittingly New Labour' manifesto.

Labour's share of the vote in 2005 compared unfavourably with its support in previous elections. Back in 1955, it won 46.4 per cent in a contest that it lost. In 1979, it lost with 36.9 per cent. In 1992, it did little worse in winning votes than in 2005 (34.5 per cent, as against 35.2 per cent). In 2005, only 21.6 per cent of the whole electorate of 44.4 million cast a vote for Labour, its lowest total in any post-1945 election other than in 1983. This was the lowest percentage for any governing party since 1832.

The 2005 result highlighted dissatisfaction with particular policies pursued by New Labour in office. Several measures introduced in the second term alienated sections of the electorate:

- The top-up tuition fees for those seeking higher education antagonised students and some middle-class parents.
- The willingness to use the private sector to support state provision of health and education upset many middle-class progressives.
- Above all, the Iraq war antagonised Muslims (the Labour vote fell on average by 10.6 per cent and 8.1 per cent in heavily Muslim and Muslim-influenced constituencies), middle-class progressives, university lecturers and students, and a core section of Labour's working-class support.

Labour propagandists inevitably tended to concentrate on the historic nature of their win rather than on its relatively flimsy popular backing. The majority remained a good one, sufficient to enable the government to continue its work. Had Labour succeeded in 1997 with a majority of 'just 66', many people in the party would have been well satisfied. Nonetheless, the 2005 result was a bitter-sweet verdict from the electorate. Whilst giving Labour another four or five years, the voters delivered a clear warning that if it wanted to hold onto its share of the progressive vote, it must repair aspects of its fraying coalition of support and maybe show greater sensitivity to the views of some who are naturally inclined to vote Labour. It must pay heed to its lost supporters, seeking to win back many of the very different groups of former voters who went elsewhere.

Many Labour supporters, whilst recognising the electoral success that Tony Blair delivered, did not share his enthusiasm for free-market solutions in health and education, and lamented the lack of a stronger bid to tackle inequality. It remains to be seen whether – and how much – under Gordon Brown, Labour policy will move in a different direction. He has been a central figure in the New Labour project and there are clear lines of continuity between some of his early statements and the policies of his predecessor. But he has tried to dissociate himself with some of the more unpopular aspects of the Blairite leadership. Moreover, his roots belong to a more traditional Labour background and, if nothing else, the language by which he expresses himself is different.

Activity

Go to the Labour website (www. labour.org.uk). Seek out the Labour manifesto (2005) or other information on party policy. List five current policies of the party.

Summary questions

1. What are the similarities and differences between Old and New Labour?
2. What are the different strands of thinking to be found in the Labour party today?
3. 'New Labour is committed to a more just and more equal society'. Is this a fair assessment?
4. Discuss the view that Labour has ceased to be a socialist party or never has been one.
5. In *The Alistair Campbell Diaries*, Tony Blair is quoted as saying 'what gives me real edge as a politician is that I'm not as Labour as you lot'. What do you think he meant by this? Was he a successful party leader?

4   The Conservative party

Learning objectives:

- What does Conservatism stand for as an ideology?

- What are the main ideas associated with the modern Conservative party?

- What is the difference between a One Nation and a Thatcherite Conservative?

- What particular slant has David Cameron given to Conservative party thinking?

- What are the problems and prospects of the Conservatives today?

Key term

The **French Revolution** (1789–99) was a period of prolonged political and social upheaval in the political history of France and Europe as a whole, during which French governmental structure and society underwent radical change.

As its name suggests, Conservatism is associated with keeping things as they are as opposed to working for change and reform. Conservatives of the early 19th century were suspicious of the doctrines associated with the **French Revolution**, such as freedom, equality and fraternity (brotherhood), which they saw as dangerous to established society. However, as the century progressed, more thoughtful Conservatives recognised the need to maintain a broad appeal. They emphasised that they were concerned for the interests of the whole nation because there were ties of interdependence between all elements within the country. Rather than seek to put the clock back, they were willing to accept worthwhile change when it had already been introduced. Conservatives of any variety have always supported national institutions and traditions. They also believe in firm government, seeing it as necessary to maintain law and order and restrain antisocial behaviour.

British Conservatism has a long history. It embraces a broad spectrum of ideas about the nature of man, society and political change. It is a right-wing creed that emphasises preserving the best of the past (the traditions and institutions of the country) and allowing society to develop gradually, adapting only where change is proved necessary. At different times, the Conservative party has placed more or less emphasis on conserving the past and on reform.

The Conservative party was astonishingly successful in elections in the 20th century, being in office on its own or in coalition for some 66 years. Part of this success was because of the willingness of more thoughtful leaders to adapt their party to changing circumstances. Unlike some continental right-wing parties primarily representing the middle and upper classes, the party never allowed itself to be in the position of opposing all progress just to preserve their self-interest. Under moderate leaders, it reached out to working-class voters and was able to attract the support of a considerable number of them. Without working-class

Key enduring themes for Conservatives

- Cautious approach to change.
- Distrust of 'big government'.
- Emphasis on law and order.
- 'Britishness'.
- Preference for liberty over equality.
- Preference for private enterprise.

Key terms

Pragmatic means practical, non-ideological, capable of being adjusted to meet the needs of the day.

The **New Right** relates to a strand of thinking that describes the beliefs of many Thatcherite Conservatives of the 1980s. It was a blend of some traditional conservative elements (strong government, with an emphasis on leadership, defence, law and order, family values and patriotism) and some neo-liberal attitudes (support for free markets, individualism and minimal state intervention). The free market is seen as the cornerstone of economic and political freedom.

support, it would never have won as many elections in an age of mass franchise.

The party has always recognised the importance of electoral success. In the words of one writer, 'the primary and abiding aim of the [Conservative] party is the achievement of power'. This has mattered more than being too preoccupied with ideas. Indeed, an excess of ideological baggage is seen as a barrier to success. When it comes to ideology, the Conservative (in Sir Ian Gilmour's words) 'travels light'.

The post-war years to the mid-1970s

During the early decades after 1945, the one-nation approach influenced all Conservative leaders and Prime Ministers. One-nation Conservatives embraced a positive role for the state and the need for government intervention and regulation in the economy. They were concerned to protect the most vulnerable members of society. They accepted the Welfare State and the NHS, realising that they were services that were popular within the country. Party policies were seen as **pragmatic**, based on practical experience.

By contrast, another strand of Conservatism that is embraced by many of the businessmen within the party was committed to economic liberalism. It was associated with a belief in minimal government intervention to tackle economic and social issues. Supporters felt that human beings should be left to pursue their own self-interest through free market forces. In the 1970s and 1980s, there was a resurgence of this emphasis on minimal state intervention and much talk of 'rolling back the frontiers of the state' by supporters of the **New Right**.

Fig. 7 *Margaret Thatcher, the only woman to be PM or leader of a major British political party and the longest-serving British PM of the 20th century*

In the Thatcher era, there was a clear break with post-war one-nation Conservatism. Under her leadership, there was support for the free market and competition, combined with strong support for more traditional **authoritarian and nationalist attitudes**.

Margaret Thatcher was committed to traditional party policies such as a firm stand on law and order, and promoting the idea of 'Great Britain'. But she scorned the timid 'wets' (Conservative moderates) of the post-war era and wanted clearer, more distinctive Conservative policies. She was strongly pro-free enterprise, market forces, lower taxes and more consumer choice, and anti trade union power. **Thatcherism** stressed individual effort, wanted people to solve their own problems, admired perseverance and self-reliance and felt that it should be rewarded. This more right-wing Conservatism endured after her retirement. The bulk of the party continues to want less government and lower taxes, and to be wary of the European Union, as she was.

Post-Thatcherite Conservatism

As we have seen, the strength of Conservatism has in the past been its pragmatism, its ability to adapt to changing circumstances. After her departure in 1990, Lady Thatcher used her influence against candidates for the leadership who might have changed the party's direction towards a more traditional one-nation, moderately pro-European stance. She backed those thought more likely to protect her legacy: **John Major**, **William Hague**, **Iain Duncan Smith** and **Michael Howard** would all claim to be in some respects inheritors of the Thatcherite vision and approach.

All of these leaders have found difficulty in trying to adjust modern Conservatism to the demands of a more diverse electorate and make Conservatism socially, as well as economically, liberal. Their task was made the more difficult because several long-term Conservative enemies that had for years united the party now seemed either weakened or dead. Trade union power had been weakened, the fear of communism in the form of the Soviet Union had been removed, and the Labour party under Tony Blair could no longer convincingly be labelled as dangerously left-wing. Indeed, New Labour was often employing Conservative rhetoric and talking about the free market rather than public ownership, duties as well as rights.

The Cameron approach

David Cameron describes himself as a 'modern **compassionate Conservative**'. He claims to be 'certainly a big Thatcher fan, but I don't know whether that makes me a Thatcherite'. He has also claimed to be a 'liberal Conservative', and 'not a deeply ideological person'. Indeed, some journalists claim that he described himself to journalists at a dinner during the leadership contest as the natural 'heir to Blair'.

Cameron is in many ways distinctive from his predecessors. He has consciously tried to reposition his party, distancing his leadership from some of the attitudes and policies that its members previously expressed. He is socially liberal on gay issues, exhibits a concern for minority groups in general, does not adopt tough/harsh language when speaking of asylum seekers, stresses the need to think about the causes of crime as well as the manifestations of criminal behaviour and regularly emphasises quality-of-life concerns. He has focused on quality-of-life issues such as the work–life balance and the environment. He also emphasises the improvement of government services (most prominently the National Health Service and the Home Office); schools; and international development – issues not recently seen as priorities for the post-Thatcher Conservative party.

Key terms

Margaret Thatcher (born 1925) was a Conservative MP 1959–92, leader 1975–90 and Prime Minister 1979–90. She has been a peer since 1992.

Authoritarian attitudes included toughness on law and order, opposition to liberal and progressive educational and moral thinking, emphasis on the traditional family, strong defence of the rights of property owners, support for established institutions such as the Church of England and House of Lords, and a belief in the centralised state.

Nationalist attitudes included preservation of the Union of the UK, opposition to handing over power to the European Union, opposition to immigration, wariness about asylum seeking, support for strong defence and a powerful British influence on world affairs.

Thatcherism is the creed associated with Margaret Thatcher, involving a market-based economic system, and emphasising competition, free enterprise, lower taxes and curbs on trade union power. The Prime Minister was a strong believer in family values and the so-called 'Victorian virtues' of hard work,

Fig. 8 *William Hague: the youngest post-war leader of the party. Since surrendering the leadership, he has gained public attention because of his skilful and witty performances as a debater in the House of Commons and his hosting of the satirical television programme* Have I Got News For You

Key terms

John Major (born 1943) was Conservative MP 1983–2001, leader and Prime Minister 1990–97.

William Hague (born 1961) has been a Conservative MP since 1989 and was leader 1997–2001.

Iain Duncan Smith (born 1954) has been a Conservative MP since 1992 and was leader 2001–2003.

Michael Howard (born 1941) has been a Conservative MP since 1983 and was leader 2003–05.

Compassionate Conservatives stress the use of traditionally Conservative techniques and concepts in order to improve the general welfare of society. They believe that conservatism and compassion complement each other, arguing that they can find better answers to social problems than their opponents. The idea was popularised by George W Bush in his 2000 presidential election campaign.

Activity

Go to the Conservative website (www.conservatives.com). Find the party manifesto (2005) or other information on party policy. List five current policies of the party.

All of this is part of an attempt to move the party back into the centre ground. Some critics are unhappy with this attempted rebranding and repositioning of the party, and with David Cameron's interest in presentation. They see it as too reminiscent of the political style of the early years of the Blair leadership.

Fig. 9 *David Cameron: MP since 2000, leader since 2005. The most inexperienced parliamentarian to take the leadership of a major British political party since William Pitt the Younger, although he was active in politics before becoming an MP*

Defeat in 2005 and the problems of renewal

For the Conservatives, 2005 was a bad result. Although they won the popular vote in England (35.7 per cent to 35.5 per cent) and generally improved upon their performance in 2001, they did not significantly increase their share of the vote in Great Britain as a whole (it was up by about 0.5 per cent only). They still face a massive task to rekindle popular support.

In the eyes of many observers, the Conservatives in 2005 continued to talk mainly to the already-converted, the long-term party supporters. The temptation was to rely on anti-crime, anti-immigration/asylum seekers rhetoric. Some commentators felt that the programme seemed more like a collection of whinges, things Conservative enthusiasts disliked about modern Britain, rather than a carefully thought-out programme for government. There was no 'big idea'. The party failed to reach out to newer groups of potential voters, the young and the minorities, be they ethnic, gay or any other group. Iraq might have been fertile ground for a convincing attack, but Conservatives were compromised in their criticisms because under Iain Duncan Smith and Michael Howard the leadership broadly approved of the war, whatever its doubts about the handling of particular aspects.

The Conservatives have for several years found it hard to compete with a New Labour government, which has established itself firmly in the centre ground. They are a more united force than they were in the late 1990s when Europe split the party asunder. But within their midst there are still differences between more elderly and socially authoritarian Conservatives who prefer the party's past outlook and policies on issues such as asylum seekers and gay rights, and social liberals who see the need to modernise and widen its appeal.

Further information

Ageing Conservatives

Seyd and others have highlighted the ageing nature of Conservative membership.

1992:

- average age 62
- 5 per cent under 35.

Today:

- average age 65
- 3 per cent under 35.

The research points to a serious imbalance in the membership, with a lack of new and younger recruits to replace the elderly (who are less able to participate) and those who have died.

In these circumstances, should the party seek to defeat Labour on the centre ground, hoping that by the next election it will seem a more competent alternative to what the government can offer? Or would it do better to move to the Right and distance itself from the positions advanced by ministers on issues such as crime, immigration and Europe? David Cameron has concluded that he must establish his party firmly in the political mainstream and not be tempted to give way to party pressure to advance more right-wing Conservative policies.

Summary questions

1. Prior to the leadership of Margaret Thatcher, it was sometimes said that the Conservatives were not an ideological party but one more committed to the pursuit of power. Is this true today?

2. In what ways did Margaret Thatcher modify the direction of post-war Conservative thinking and policies?

3. Why has the party found it difficult to win general elections in the period since 1997?

4. Why are Cameronian policies worrying or even unpalatable to traditional Conservatives?

5. Are the Conservatives now a viable party of government?

5 British third and minor parties

Learning objectives:

- What are 'third' and 'minor' parties?

- What role do they play in the political system?

- How do the Liberal Democrats fit into the party spectrum?

- Which are the other parties that put up a substantial number of candidates in elections?

By a third party, we usually mean one that is capable of gathering a sizeable percentage of popular support and regularly gains seats in the legislature, e.g. the British Liberal Democrat party. On occasion, it may win – or threaten to win – sufficient support to influence the outcome of an election.

By a minor party, we mean one that gains only a tiny percentage of popular support and almost never gains representation in the legislature, e.g. the British National party.

The role and value of third and minor parties

They take up particular causes neglected by the other parties, such as the Pro-Life Alliance in Britain, in the 1997 and 2001 elections. Similarly, the Greens in many countries give special emphasis to environmental policies.

They air certain grievances not being taken up by traditional parties – as in the case of the Scottish National party (SNP) and Plaid Cymru, both of which long argued for more attention to be paid to the needs of Scotland and Wales, respectively. The same could be said of Far Right policies such as the British National party, which thrives on unease over immigration and race relations.

Key term

The **Lib-Lab Pact** was an agreement between Labour and the Liberal party that operated between 1976 and 1978. Liberal spokespersons had the right to be consulted by ministers on policy issues before legislation was introduced. This was the nearest the Liberals had been to political power for many years.

Equidistance is the strategy of placing the Liberal Democrats in the political centre, in between the positions of Left and Right.

Further information

Some ideas of modern liberalism

Modern liberal thinking, combining the views of classical and new liberalism, is noted for the following beliefs:

- individual freedom
- equality of opportunity
- promoting social justice
- encouraging political participation, e.g. voting
- protection of individual rights
- dispersal of power
- improvements to the quality of life.

Fig. 10 *Charles Kennedy: born 1959, Liberal Democrat MP since 1983, leader 1999–2006*

- **They can act as a haven for protest voters**. The Liberals and their successors have often fulfilled this role in British politics. Such protest can act as a spur to the traditional parties, saving them from apathy and indifference.
- **At times, they may affect the outcome of elections**. In the British system, in which the government is dependent on majority support in the legislature, there may be times when a third party can maintain a government in power, e.g. the Liberals in the late 1970s maintained the Callaghan administration in office, having agreed a **Lib-Lab Pact**.

The Liberal Democrats

In depth

Liberalism and the Liberal/Liberal Democrat parties

Liberalism as a creed has been highly significant, several of the ideas of both classical and new liberalism having been adopted by other movements and parties. Some of the values of classical liberalism are basic to democracy, including belief in the importance of government by popular consent, the emphasis on liberty and personal rights, and tolerance of other attitudes and ideas. Indeed, the word 'liberal' derives from the Latin *liber*, and is usually translated as 'free' or 'generous', characteristics associated with the democratic way of life.

In the early 20th century, Labour adopted much of the radical tradition of reforming liberals who were prepared to tackle social injustices. The introduction of the welfare state was a development of New Liberal ideas. It became commonplace to believe that state action to reduce such evils as unemployment and poverty would provide greater freedom. One-nation Conservatives between the 1950s and the 1970s were also generally willing to accept such thinking. On the other hand, supporters of the New Right of the late 20th century were attracted by classical liberal ideas, such as a reduced role for the state, an interest in free markets and an emphasis on personal responsibility.

In other words, the ideas of liberalism have been influential in British politics in the 20th and 21st centuries. Conservatives and socialists have taken on board some of its core beliefs. But for much of the post-war era the Liberal party has not been a significant force in British politics. Particularly in the early decades after 1945, it struggled to establish a distinctive identity. One important Liberal party policy of the previous century had by then already been achieved – the commitment to extension of the franchise (i.e. the right to vote) to all adults.

The Liberal Democrats were formed as a result of a merger between the old British Liberal party and the Social Democrats, a breakaway element from the Labour right. The new party soon established its own identity, but the past commitment to pro-Europeanism, racial justice and tolerance was preserved. Under Paddy Ashdown's leadership (1988–99), the party moved nearer to the Opposition Labour party, abandoning its former **equidistance**. Labour and the Liberal Democrats cooperated on constitutional proposals before the 1997 election.

Under the leadership of Charles Kennedy, the Liberal Democrats distanced themselves from ministerial policies, especially as Labour ran into trouble. He and other Liberal Democrats criticised the timidness of the Prime Minister in not giving a clear lead in favour of Britain's early membership of the eurozone. They reserved their strongest criticism for the conduct of events leading to the Iraq war; they were deeply uneasy about the decision to embark on hostilities.

In electoral terms, the Liberal Democrats have fared well in recent elections. In 2005, they won nearly 6 million votes (22 per cent), and had 62 MPs – more than at any time since 1923. Yet many observers thought that with the lack of enthusiasm for the two main parties, the party might have expected to do better.

Post 2005

Differing views over the direction of the party developed following its rather disappointing performance in the 2005 election. There were various options available to the Liberal Democrats:

- **To move more to the right** and further embrace market principles, individual choice and responsibility – an approach which might help them fend off any Conservative recovery, particularly in the seats they hold in which they are vulnerable to a Conservative challenge.

- **To move to the left**, promoting their radical credentials. This would position the party to the left of New Labour on socio-economic policy, and maintain its distinctiveness on matters such as civil liberties and the environment. This might help it fend off the Labour challenge in seats they had won from Labour in 2005, but might alarm potential Conservative voters.

Fig. 11 *Menzies (Ming) Campbell: born 1941, Liberal Democrat MP since 1987, leader 2006–2007*

- **To be pragmatic** and adopt a 'middle way' approach – neither left nor right – which might find favour with disaffected Labour and Conservative supporters and leave the leadership free to adjust policy and seize opportunities as they arise. Such a policy requires the party to retain its distinctiveness on issues that are traditionally associated with it. Under the leadership of Menzies Campbell, it has adopted this strategy.

Other parties

Whereas the Liberal Democrats are a third force to be reckoned with, having substantial parliamentary representation, the other UK-wide parties have much less popular support and rarely gain any representation. Yet they do articulate the thinking of a section of the voters, and even the more distasteful ones serve as an outlet for the views of an extremist minority. Denied such an outlet, their supporters might turn to more violent forms of protest to get their views across.

One of the fast-growing parties in Britain is the **UK Independence party (UKIP)**, committed to outright withdrawal from the European Union. Since 1994, it has put up a candidate in every parliamentary by-election and the party gained a strong result in the 2004 European elections. None of its 496 candidates in 2005 were elected.

Activity

Which of these traditional Liberal ideas do you now associate with the Labour and/or the Conservative parties?

Activity

Using the internet to help you, find out and write a couple of paragraphs about the main policies put forward by the Liberal Democrats at the last election.

Consider the truth of this quotation as it applies today:

Some people consider voting for them because they seem to be a comfortable middle option . . . roughly midway between Labour and the Conservatives. Nothing could be further from the truth . . . they have become a radical left-wing party committed to threatening policies.

Brian Mawhinney, Conservative party chairman, 1996

Activity

These factors may help to explain why third and minor parties make little headway at election time:

- Few influential financial backers.
- No reliable body of support within the electorate.
- No distinctive identity.
- Voters' fear of wasting their vote.
- Few opportunities to get message across.

For each of the third and minor parties listed, how important is each of these five factors? You might answer in table form.

Further reading

R Garner and R Kelly, *British Political Parties Today*, MUP, 2003.

R Hefferman, 'Political Parties and the Party System', in P Dunleavy *et al.* (eds), *Developments in British Politics 7*, Palgrave, 2003.

N Jackson, 'Two, Two and a Half and Three Party Politics', *Talking Politics*, January 2004.

N McNaughton, 'The Changing Nature of UK Political Parties', *Talking Politics*, April 2003.

P Norton, 'The Conservative Party: Is There Anyone Out There?', in A King (ed.), *Britain at the Polls, 2001*, Chatham House, 2002.

R Tillson, 'Is the Party Over for the Conservatives?', *Talking Politics*, April 2005.

Of the other parties, the nationalists are by far the most important. The **Scottish Nationalist party (SNP)** is a separatist party, wanting independence from Great Britain. In the 2007 devolved elections, it became the largest party in the Scottish parliament and forms a minority government. It does not emphasise the usual cultural nationalism of parties of the nationalist type. By contrast, **Plaid Cymru** has always been a more traditional nationalist party, speaking up for the culture and language of Wales. This has tended to limit its appeal to Welsh-speaking areas, although there are signs in the Welsh National Assembly elections that the party is now extending its support into the southern valleys.

Both the SNP and Plaid Cymru are pro European and have contested European elections keenly. They have been helped in European and devolved elections because both use more proportional voting systems than the FPTP which – particularly in the case of the SNP – limits progress at Westminster.

The **British National party (BNP)** is the most prominent far-right political party in the UK. It has a number of councillors in local government, but lacks representation in parliament. According to its constitution the BNP 'stands for the preservation of the national and ethnic character of the British people and is wholly opposed to any form of racial integration between British and non-European peoples'.

The Greens are primarily an ecological party, concerned with promoting a sustainable way of life, conservation of the earth's capital and increasing reliance on resources that can be renewed or recycled. But they have in recent years tried to broaden their appeal by taking up other policy issues, offering a comprehensive manifesto that is broadly left wing in tone. They have won representation in the Scottish and European parliaments in recent years, as well as several seats on local councils.

Respect (The Unity Coalition) is a left-wing political party in England and Wales founded in 2004 in London. Its name is an acronym for Respect, Equality, Socialism, Peace, Environmentalism, Community, and Trade Unionism. Many mainstream commentators present Respect as a single-issue party focusing on its opposition to the war in Iraq. However, it claims to 'provide a broad-based and inclusive alternative to the parties of privatisation, war, and occupation' and have a wide-ranging progressive agenda.

✔ Summary questions

1. 'On the party spectrum, Labour was traditionally on the Left, the Conservatives on the Right and the Liberals/Liberal Democrats in the middle.' Is this still an appropriate categorisation?

2. Do the Liberal Democrats have a significant influence in British politics?

3. 'Minor parties are a useful outlet for people's thinking, even if few people share their views.' Is this true?

6 Membership, finance and organisation

1 Party membership and finance

Learning objectives:

- Why is party membership in decline in the UK?
- Why do parties need finance?
- Where do the main British parties get their funds from?
- What problems have beset the issue of party funding in recent years?
- What are the arguments for and against further state funding of parties?

Party membership has been declining in most of Europe over the last few decades, but as the figures below indicate, they are particularly low in the UK.

Table 1 *Party membership figures*

1990–2000: membership as percentage of electorate		Party Membership in Britain, December 2006	
Austria	18	Conservatives	250,000
Finland	10	Labour	200,000
Norway	7	Lib Dems	73,000
Germany	3	SNP	12,000
UK	2	Plaid Cymru	8,000

Commentators often portray declining membership as an indication of a lessening of enthusiasm for and interest in political parties. They point to the loss of members by established parties and compare it to the growth in pressure group activity. The low figures quoted may also reflect the fact that parties today spend less time recruiting than in the past, because they once needed activists to engage in voluntary work and rally the local voters to turn out in support of their candidate (nowadays, in an age when much campaigning is done via television, there is more emphasis on the whereabouts of party leaders and their senior colleagues). Finally, there may be too many other things that people can do with their time. For many people, politics has a very low priority in their lives. For others, it is now a lower priority than it was, perhaps because many of the big issues of world peace and hunger have been less significant than they were in the early post-1945 years.

Although changing methods of election campaigning may provide an explanation, parties would be foolish to allow this to deter them from seeking to revive their membership. New Labour enthusiasts initially saw it as essential to create a mass membership at a time when its trade union links were being downplayed.

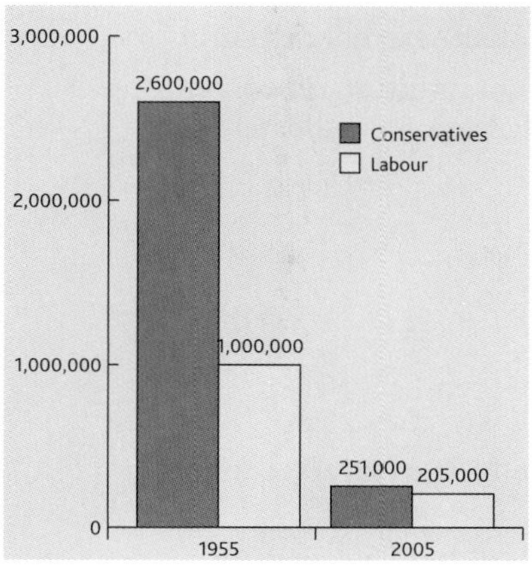

Finance

The role of money in political life is an issue of daily debate in old and new democracies alike. It is the driving force for modern competitive political systems, a point recognised some decades ago by a Californian politician, Jesse Unruh, who described it as 'the mother's milk of politics'.

Party financing is a vital aspect of modern party politics. The ways in which parties get access to money can influence the outcome of elections, determine the relationship between party leaders and members, and have

Fig. 1 *Party membership, 1955–2005: declining fortunes*

Activities

1 Using the internet to help you, try and find out what the benefits are of membership of:

a the Conservative party

b the Labour party.

NB: Full membership of the Conservative party costs £25 per year, and membership of the Labour party costs £36 per year.

2 Again using the internet, find out how some other countries fund their political parties.

Further information

Sources of money

Labour:

- Union/other affiliation fees: 25.1 per cent
- Donations/fundraising: 36.8 per cent
- Subscriptions 12.8 per cent
- Commercial enterprises: 11.6 per cent
- Interest, legacies, etc.: 13.7 per cent
- Total = £26,940,000

Conservatives:

- Donations/fundraising: 56.1 per cent
- Subscriptions: 5.8 per cent
- Grants: 30.4 per cent
- Interest, legacies, etc.: 7.7 per cent
- Total = £13,619,000

(Source: Electoral Commission, year to 31 December 2003)

---

a bearing upon the level of public trust as a whole. Parties everywhere are finding it difficult to raise sufficient income to meet increased costs.

The widespread fall in figures for party membership has implications for party finances. But in many European countries, the decline in income from membership has been compensated for by the establishment of some form of state funding of party activity. Such aid is normally unconditional, being dependent upon the support achieved in the previous election. German parties receive generous subsidies that often constitute well over a quarter of their income. Australia, Canada and the US have seen state funding as a necessity to bridge the gap between the expenditure that is necessary for political purposes and the funds raised from voluntary donations to parties and candidates.

Other than public subsidies, parties receive funding from three main sources:

- Subscriptions from individual party members.
- Donations, either from companies or from individuals (sometimes these are one-off sums from generous benefactors or they take the form of bequests).
- Contributions from associated bodies, such as affiliated trade unions.

Many people feel uneasy about huge contributions from wealthy businessmen, particularly those who reside outside the country concerned. However, it is the income from business organisations and trade unions that causes the most anxiety. There is a common perception that 'he who pays the piper calls the tune'. Money may be given not just because an organisation shares the broad outlook of the party it is backing, but in the hope and anticipation that decisions made by ministers will be favourable to it.

The finance of British parties

Money is needed for four types of expense:

1 **Maintaining party headquarters**: this involves personnel and equipment, as well as much educational and research work, producing pamphlets and publicity materials.

2 **Maintaining a reserve fund**: for sudden emergencies, such as a new roof at party headquarters or other major capital repairs.

3 **Campaign costs**: in particular the costs of political advertising, and fighting general elections and also local and European elections. Occasional referendums have to be financed, and in Scotland and Wales there are the parliament/National Assembly elections too.

4 **Local constituencies' expenses**: maintaining an office, printing leaflets and meeting the costs of the election candidates.

In depth

Campaign costs

Modern campaigns are very costly.

In 1997:

- The Conservatives spent around £20m (over £13m on advertising).
- Labour spent £15m (nearly half of it on advertising).
- The Liberal Democrats spent £3.5m.

NB: There was then no legal limit on national campaign spending. A cap was put in place for the 2001 election.

In 2005:

- The Conservatives spent £17,852,240 (£8.2m on advertising).
- Labour spent £17,939,617 (£5.3m on advertising).
- The Liberal Democrats spent £4,324,574 (£1.5m on advertising).

There is a legal limit on constituency election campaigning of around £6,000. The law also regulates the financial relationship of trade unions to the Labour party. There are no such requirements on companies to disclose how much they contribute to political parties, but they do have to declare to their shareholders donations of more than £200. There are ways in which, by using overseas accounts and foreign associate companies, the need for such declarations can be evaded.

Until recently, parties have not had to make their accounts public in an open, accessible and intelligible form. The Conservative party has traditionally been secretive about its sources of income, but in advance of legal changes it opted under William Hague for greater transparency.

The three main parties have all had financial problems in recent years and have found themselves in debt. Today, Labour finds itself heavily reliant on gifts from corporations and wealthy individuals. The Conservatives have a small number of affluent donors who substantially fund their election campaigns. They all need money from sources that do not undermine the integrity of the political process. Party funding is an issue that has moved up the political agenda.

State funding of parties?

Many UK academics and commentators have drawn attention to methods of state funding of political parties in other countries. In most cases, the procedures seem to have been acceptable to the parties and to the voters, although in Italy the idea was dropped in 1993 following corruption scandals. Generally, it has been seen as preferable to have state subsidy rather than to rely on business or other institutional backers.

Fig. 2 *Lord Sainsbury: billionaire supermarket businessman, politician and life peer of the Labour party*

In Britain, the principle of state support is not entirely new:

1 Help is given to opposition parties to assist them in their parliamentary work, to meet travel and associated expenses and fund policy research (the **'Short' money**). It was recognised as far back as 1975 that the government of the day has an advantage over the Opposition, in that it can rely on the work of the regular civil service, paid special advisers and appointed committees of enquiry. The grant was meant to counter this advantage. It amounted to more than £7m in the 2006–07 parliamentary session.

2 At election time, various facilities are made freely available, such as a free mailing of election literature and free air time for party election broadcasts.

Key term

The **'Short' money** is a subsidy designed to help opposition parties perform their parliamentary duties. Named after the leader of the House of Commons who introduced it in 1975, the amount payable to any party is calculated according to the number of seats and votes won at the previous election.

Activities

1 Look at the website of the Electoral Commission (www. electoralcommission.org. uk) or alternatively the party websites. In the latest year for which figures are available, see if you can find out where the three parties received their income from. What did they spend most of their money on?

2 Why do you think that the trades unions give money to the Labour party? What do they hope to get in return?

Arguments in favour of state aid for political parties

- **The central argument is that party activity is essential to democratic government**. It depends on parties competing for power and engaging in the process of public education. Parties would be better able to carry out these functions if they were better funded. In other words, investing in parties is really investing in democracy.

- **It would help reduce party dependence on backers** such as unions and big business.

- **Parties of the centre-left suffer a disadvantage**, lacking the means to compete with better-off parties such as the Conservatives whose traditional strength lies in middle-class, more affluent, residential areas, and whose supporters can afford to give generously of their time and money, staging garden parties and fêtes, etc. The Conservatives can almost always afford to outspend the other parties at election time, and in an age when image and marketing are so important this can be a significant factor.

- **Party difficulties over funding are aggravated now that there are so many elections and referendums**. In 1997, there was a general election and local elections, and later in the year two referendums on devolution were held. There has not been a similar conjunction of election dates subsequently, but this is likely to happen occasionally in the future.

Arguments against state aid for political parties

- **There is nothing wrong with institutional backing** and nothing sinister in parties gaining financial support from interests with whom there is some similarity of outlook – as long as the process is open.

- **Politics is a voluntary activity** and no one should find their money being used, via taxation, to finance a party they do not favour. If necessary, parties should raise money by other means, such as boosting membership and staging fund-raising events. If any party cannot, this suggests that there is a lack of enthusiasm for its ideas and performance.

- **At a time of much public disillusionment with politicians, the public cannot be expected to bail out parties**. Indeed, a scheme of aid might worsen such feelings. Voters might think the money was going on glossy brochures which do not tell the whole truth.

- **Support for state funding seems to be greater when there is evidence of abuse and corruption**: any scheme for state funding might not end this but actually open up new opportunities for illegal payments and other improprieties. France, Germany and Spain have had such cases in recent decades.

- **The time is not ripe**, we cannot afford it when other needs are more pressing.

Recent developments

The award of honours by Tony Blair drew attention to the issue of party funding. A recent quirk of electoral law in the UK meant that although anyone donating even small sums of money to a political party had to declare this as a matter of public record, those *loaning* money, even for an indefinite period, did not have to make a public declaration. 'Loans for peerages' was the name given by some in the media to the political scandal of 2006–07 concerning the connection between political donations and the granting of life peerages (see below for further details).

Since the scandal was unveiled, Labour has had to repay some of these loans and is now in considerable debt. As a result of the issues uncovered, since September 2006 the Electoral Commission has been required to gather and publish the details of loans received by the parties, as they have done for donations.

In depth

The 'loans for peerages' scandal

- It concerned the alleged connection between political donations and the awarding of life peerages.

- The issue of cash for peerages has arisen in previous premierships. During John Major's premiership, allegations were made that those who contributed generously to the party were granted political honours.

- In March 2006, several people nominated for life peerages by Tony Blair were rejected by the House of Lords Appointments Commission. It was later revealed that they had loaned large amounts of money to the governing Labour party, at the suggestion of Labour fundraiser Lord Levy.

- Suspicion was aroused that the peerages were given in exchange for the loans.

- The incident was referred to the Metropolitan Police who investigated whether the Honours (Prevention of Abuses) Act 1925 or the Political Parties, Elections and Referendums Act 2000 had been breached.

- Subsequently, various members of the Labour, Conservative and Liberal Democrat parties were questioned and Labour's Lord Levy and Ruth Turner (a key Downing Street aide) were arrested and released on bail.

- A dossier of evidence was placed before the Crown Prosecutions Service (CPS) which after a long review reported in July 2007 that it would not bring any charges against any of the individuals involved. The reputations of those under suspicion were cleared as the CPS could not find any direct evidence of a prior agreement that a peerage would be granted in return for any loan given, therefore making a successful prosecution highly unlikely.

Fig. 3 *Lord Levy, at the heart of the 'loans for peerage' scandal*

A radical overhaul of the way British politics is financed was proposed by Sir Hayden Phillips in March 2007 in a report commissioned by Tony Blair. In *Strengthening Democracy: Fair and Sustainable Party Funding of Political Parties*, he suggested that there should be:

- a £50,000 limit on donations from individuals or organisations

- a cap on spending by the largest parties between elections, with permanent controls on spending at constituency level

- new measures to prevent the breach of regulations on donations

- strengthened controls on expenditure by third parties

Activity

Consider the information about the loans for peerages scandal of 2006–07. Why do you think it is relevant to the issue of party finances? Does it convince you of the need for state funding?

- public access to better, clearer information about the sources of party income
- new powers for the Electoral Commission watchdog to oversee the new system
- an increase in state funding by £25m a year (eligible parties should receive 50p each year for every vote cast for them in the most recent general election and 25p for every vote in the most recent Scottish, Welsh and European elections).

Summary questions

1. Can/should British parties seek to build larger mass memberships?
2. Do you favour state funding of political parties? Give reasons for your answer.

2 Party organisation

Learning objectives:

- Why did parties develop national and local organisations?
- By what techniques do parties seek to win the support of the electorate?
- In what ways do the origins of the two main British parties impact upon their organisation?
- How do parties choose their parliamentary candidates?
- What is the role and value of party conferences?

With the development of a universal franchise, parties in most democracies saw the need to create national and local organisations to ensure that they were in a position to maximise their support. Among other things, they needed to raise funds, organise canvassing and provide opportunities for the new voters to become involved. Usually the organisation operated on a top-down basis. National organisations were created and given the task of supervising the activities of local branches established throughout the country. Decisions were made at party headquarters, and policy statements and lists of likely candidates were handed down to the local associations where much of the day-to-day voluntary work of mobilising the voters was carried out.

This pattern has not been as true in recent years. Older parties have had to adapt to changing conditions. The arrival of television has made local organisation less essential; indeed, some party associations and clubs have lapsed to such an extent that they have effectively disappeared, only to be briefly resurrected at election time. In Britain, Labour has been concerned to modernise its image and organisation, and since its defeat in 1997 the Conservative party has engaged in an overhaul of its traditional approach, streamlining the party and making it more open in its operations. In both cases there has been a new emphasis on making the party more democratic. An attempt has been made to give members a greater say in how the party functions, whilst at the same time ensuring that the leadership retains key powers to act to keep out dissidents who might bring discredit on the organisation.

Across Europe and the US, existing parties have recognised the importance of employing new techniques to galvanise the electorate via mass mailings and other devices. In particular, they are keen to appeal to new voters. More recently-formed parties are wary of formal party organisation, seeing it as a means of stifling dissent or ignoring the views of party supporters. They have been more democratic in their workings from the beginning.

Green parties in most countries have tended to shun the central control associated with established parties, and they often operate more informally via a network of informal local organisations. In as much as they need leadership, they have sometimes been willing to experiment with new forms, such as having two or three leaders/decision makers. The emphasis has been on democratic consultation with the membership rather than on strong leadership that manipulates the rules to keep decision making effectively in its own hands.

The organisation of British political parties

In studying party organisation, the key issue is where power resides. The two main British parties are organised very differently, reflecting their different origins. The Conservatives developed as a party at Westminster in the early 19th century, before the extension of the vote to working people. Once the franchise was extended, they needed to ensure that their MPs were supported by a network of local associations to organise support within the constituencies. They developed a Central Office to act as the professional headquarters of the party.

Central Office controls the activities of the provincial areas and the constituency agents. But such organisation – local, regional and national – was there to serve the parliamentary party and the leadership. The leader's influence over the party machine has always been strong, its role being seen as helping the occupant pursue his or her desired goals and prepare the party for election success.

In depth

The Conservatives and plebiscitary democracy

In recent years, the Conservatives have frequently put key issues to a vote of the membership. This is a form of referendum that some would see as a supplement to representative institutions, whilst others would see it as a means – open to manipulation – of enhancing the power of the leadership. Examples are:

- giving the membership a voice in the leadership election
- under William Hague, the votes to gain backing for the stance on Europe and his organisational reforms (more a case of looking for popular support than offering a genuine choice of party direction).

NB: Labour held a similar vote on the rewriting of Clause Four in 1998.

Key terms

Plebiscitary democracy relates to a direct vote on a single issue (a referendum), in this case by the party membership.

Labour originated outside parliament, and developed out of the wish of trade unions, early socialist societies and others to get working people elected into parliament. Its 1918 Constitution made provision for the control of the party by the elements beyond Westminster. In other words, the party in parliament was made responsible to the party outside. Labour was therefore keen to avoid a focus on the figure of the party leader. The affiliated organisations, the Constituency Labour Parties (CLPs) and the parliamentary party (PLP) are all important elements in what is a federal structure.

Both parties have several tiers in which people can be active – local, regional and national. They may join the local party organisation as fee-paying members and participate in the political and social activities within the constituency, ranging from fund-raising to canvassing and distributing party literature. Labour associations have affiliated organisations, including trade unions, socialist societies and young socialists.

Party members have a voice in the selection of the constituency candidate when a vacancy occurs. Periodically they will also have a chance to take part in a leadership election, when there is a contest for the top position. One of the attractions for a limited number of grass-roots members is the opportunity to attend the annual party conference.

Gordon Brown is interested in finding new ways of involving individuals in party affairs. This might be done by establishing policy forums in every constituency, issuing regular questionnaires to members and establishing 'citizens' forums' designed to improve Labour's campaigning edge and engage local people outside the party.

Fig. 4 *Adam Rickitt: once an actor on Coronation Street, now an actor cum Conservative politician*

Choosing the parliamentary candidate

Local Conservative associations have always jealously protected their right to choose the parliamentary candidate of their choice. Sometimes, this has caused a headache for the party leadership when those chosen pose a threat to the image of the party and may reduce its appeal to various sections of the electorate.

Conservative Central Office has kept a national list of candidates who are professionally screened, and there is a right of veto over unsuitable candidates. Constituencies seeking a candidate draw up a shortlist that may include people who have put their own names forward and are not on the party list. At the final selection stage, there is an interview before a selection panel.

David Cameron has modified the process. He has been keen to change the party's image and promote greater diversity among Conservative candidates. He came up with the idea of an 'A List' of prospective candidates that included several successful women, members of ethnic minorities and celebrities. The list has been attacked by members of his party, partly because many men felt that it was unfair, but also because some of the names on it seemed to have only a limited acquaintance with Conservative policies. It was also noted that there were more people from Kensington and Chelsea than from Yorkshire and Lancashire combined. The 'A List' policy has now been discontinued in favour of gender-balanced final shortlists.

When a vacancy arises in the Labour party, individuals do not put their own names forward – they have to be nominated. Traditionally, the management in constituency parties then had considerable discretion to choose their preferred candidate, although there were some ways by which national headquarters could intervene to veto candidates thought to be unsuitable. The selection process tended to be dominated either by the trade unions or by cliques of activists who were sometimes unrepresentative of the party membership.

As part of a bid to dilute the power of activists, the party introduced a system of 'one person, one vote' (OMOV) in 1992 for the choice of candidate. This was a more open and fair system. However, the leadership wanted to see an improved system of screening candidates, to avoid 'undesirables' being chosen and then going on to become troublesome Labour MPs. This move was viewed with suspicion by the left of the party. They saw it as a further attempt by Tony Blair and his associates to enhance the control of the leadership and ensure that party MPs were sufficiently docile that they would not involve themselves in back-bench rebellions.

One other feature of the Labour process has been the attempt to secure a diverse range of candidates, with more women and members of ethnic minorities having a chance of selection. This was initially achieved by the use of all-women shortlists, but the system has now been replaced by selection lists in which there is an equal balance of men and women.

Party conferences in Britain

In both parties, conferences are now heavily stage-managed. The leaderships are conscious of the television coverage they receive and speeches are seen as a chance to communicate directly with the public as well as a chance to address an audience at the conference venue, usually in Blackpool or Bournemouth.

The annual party conference is the most important annual gathering of the Conservatives. It provides the main forum for the expression of opinion by all sections of the party. It serves as a rally of the faithful who enjoy the opportunity to vent their feelings and urge the party forward. Representatives of the constituency associations have complete freedom to speak and vote as they choose. They are not delegates committed to act in a certain way.

The agenda is carefully controlled and only rarely are formal votes taken at the conclusion of a debate. Many debates lack passion and impact, being only advisory and having no binding effect on the people at the top. Revolts can occur over sensitive issues such as Europe, immigration and law and order. In recent years, there have been more revolts than in the past and there has been a stronger expression of feeling. But this has been combined with a strong sense of respect for the leader. Overall, in its discussion of key issues, the conference sets a mood and a wise leader will recognise what that mood is and take it into account.

By contrast, the Labour conference was given the supreme function of directing and controlling the affairs of the party. The 1918 Constitution established that party policy is the responsibility of conference and that decisions made by a two-thirds majority are supposed to be regarded as sacrosanct and included in the next manifesto. However, although opposition leaders pay greater respect to the sanctity of such decisions (not least because the union block vote gave trade unions considerable power in their making), Labour Prime Ministers have often treated them in a more cavalier manner.

The role and significance of the Labour conference has long been a matter of controversy and academic debate. Strong leaders, even in opposition, can override its decisions if they have the backing of the National Executive Committee (the administrative authority of the party that acts as the guardian of

Fig. 5 *Labour uses strong-arm tactics against hecklers at the 2005 conference: 82-year-old Walter Wolfgang (a party member for 60 years) is forcibly removed after shouting 'nonsense' during a speech by the then Foreign Secretary, Jack Straw*

Key term

The **National Policy Forum (NPF)** comprises 184 members representing key elements in the Labour party, e.g. trade unions and constituency representatives. It is responsible for overseeing policy development. Labour critics allege that it lacks sufficient influence and that the leadership still has the final say on policy issues. It tends to use the Forum to sell already-formulated policy to the assembled gathering, rather than genuinely involve members in policy making.

conference decisions). As the unions have lost much of their former status in the party and the Left has been effectively sidelined in recent years, the conference has lost much of its former status. It has a diminished role because the modernisation since the late 1990s has seen the development of alternative sources of power and influence, such as the **National Policy Forum**. In particular, the centralisation of the party structure around the leader, his office and entourage, has concentrated media attention on the person at the helm. Prior to the 1997 election, when there was a scent of victory in the air, delegates were reluctant to rock the party boat in front of the television cameras. From time to time, the conference tries to reassert its authority, but more generally the tendency is to listen to and applaud appearances by the key party figures.

In depth

The Labour Annual Conference

The conference is formally the supreme decision-making body in the Labour party.

Who attends the conference?

Delegates to the conference are elected by Constituency Labour Parties, affiliated trade unions and socialist societies. Currently, affiliates hold 50 per cent of the votes at the conference, as opposed to 80 per cent in the era before Tony Blair. Some 40 per cent of the votes are wielded by the four largest trade unions (Amicus, TGWU, GMB and UNISON).

About 1,000 attend each year.

How democratic is the conference?

Critics argue that the conference has become less democratic in recent years, more akin to the US party conventions, which are mass rallies in which party enthusiasts let off steam amidst great hullabaloo. They say that:

- the agenda is fixed, with contentious issues often not being debated
- controversial voices are not heard, because party managers stifle genuine debate (see fig. 5 p99).

Defenders say that:

- the Labour conference is more democratic than that of the rival Conservative party. Conservative conferences have traditionally shunned voting and have no effective say in policy-making. It has been recognised that divisions in a party are unpopular electorally, so it has been thought wise to keep dissent under wraps and air disputes behind closed doors.

Power in the parties

Much of the research and writing on political parties has highlighted the fact that, in general, authority flows downwards from the top rather than upwards from the bottom. What tends to happen in many European parties is that the leaders – who are the face of the party most well known to the public – have a key role in determining the direction of party policies and strategies. This was noted almost 100 years ago by

Michels (1911) who developed an '**iron law of oligarchy**'. He argued that parties that claimed to be democratic were in reality usually run by a ruling clique of leaders and officials who possessed well-developed organisational skills and an understanding of what was necessary to keep the party – and themselves – in power. Ordinary members were usually prepared to accept this as they were keen to see the party prosper in and between elections.

In a study published amore than 50 years ago, McKenzie (1955) claimed that final authority did lie in the hands of the parliamentary leadership. Many insiders in the Labour movement questioned his thesis and stressed the importance of party conference as the guardian of party policy. However, experience over recent decades has suggested that the role of conference has been downgraded. Labour Prime Ministers have been willing to ignore resolutions that were passed by a clear majority.

In particular, recent experience tends to confirm this analysis. The Kinnock- and Blair-led Labour party were dominated by a strong leadership that tended to impose its will and policies. In opposition, Tony Blair was able to introduce major changes (e.g. over Clause Four), because – however reluctantly – many members agreed that they must remain disciplined and united as part of a bid for electoral victory. During the period when he was Prime Minister (1997–2007), members sometimes felt that their views were invited or quoted when they might provide backing for the line the leaders wished to pursue, but disregarded when they did not coincide with what was being proposed.

Starved of office for several years, many Conservative party members have been prepared to at least go along with the policies and broad thrust of the Cameron leadership, believing that his approach offers the most favourable chance of the party attaining power.

Key term

The **iron law of oligarchy** states that mass organisations cannot, by their very nature, be democratic. They are – and always will be – in reality controlled by a ruling elite. Leaders of political parties, possessed with expert knowledge, specialist skills and a desire to enhance their prospects of retaining power, dominate the organisations they lead.

In depth

Party organisation in the Labour and Conservative parties: common features

Both parties have:

- local organisations based on parliamentary constituencies
- traditionally used these organisations for campaigning and fund-raising. Today, the mass party has become less important with the development of the media. Parties now use television to convince voters rather than local meetings and door-to-door canvassing; they use the telephone, e-mail and texting to reach the electorate
- tried to recruit a mass membership – but are finding it difficult to achieve this
- established avenues that claim to give members an opportunity to help determine the way in which the party is run. The Conservatives have adopted Labour's idea of policy forums, which allow ordinary members to be consulted on policy issues
- to choose their parliamentary candidates locally, though Labour headquarters retains a strong influence
- to allow members to have a say in the choice of leader
- modernised their organisations in recent years (especially under Tony Blair and William Hague) in a way that centralises effective control. Labour is keen to weed out potential dissidents in the

parliamentary ranks, just as the Conservatives seek to stop potentially embarrassing candidates from being selected

■ as a result of recent changes, on the one hand empowered local members and on the other hand ensured that the party leadership has a dominant influence over the direction of the party

■ an association with European groupings, both in the European parliament and more widely.

■ A note on British parties and European organisations

Political parties are usually viewed as national organisations which have local and regional branches. However, they may also have an international dimension. Given its immense size, the European Union provides opportunities for like-minded parties in the Member States to cooperate in order to pursue their aims.

In Europe today, **Social Democracy** is the main ideology of the Left and **Christian Democracy** the main inspiration of the Right. These two positions dominate party politics within the 27 Member States. The two main transnational parties are the left-wing party of European Socialists (PES) and the right-wing European People's party (EPP). Labour is a full member of the PES. The British Conservatives have a loose association with the EPP, the largest political force on the continent. However, they are uneasy about the idea of a federal Europe to which it is committed and are contemplating ending their ties with the party.

British national political parties are involved in the affairs of the European Union in two ways:

■ at the transnational level
■ via the political groupings in the European parliament.

Transnational parties

Transnational parties are loose confederations of national parties. They bring together in one organisation broadly like-minded parties from Member States. Their development was given further impetus as a consequence of the introduction of direct elections to the European parliament in 1979. Since then, transnational parties have played a growing role in EU affairs. Those involved recognise that there are benefits in mutual cooperation and the exchange of information, when party leaders from across Europe meet together. However, transnational parties do not yet provide opportunities for individual membership. No British person can become a full member of the EPP or PES, though there are associations for certain categories of people, such as women and young people.

Party groupings in the European parliament: the PES and EPP

Better known than the transnational federations are the party blocs which have developed in the European parliament and which share the same name as the bodies already described. Their activities have a specific focus – the assembly itself – and they can and do play an important role in its organisation and operations. These party groupings at Strasbourg

Key terms

Social Democracy is a significant ideology of the Left which is concerned with the promotion of equality and social well-being via state intervention in the economy and welfare policies.

Christian Democracy is a significant centre-right movement which in Europe tends to be conservative on moral and cultural issues but progressive on social issues such as workers' conditions and tackling poverty.

are then a part of the wider transnational parties, but, because they have a more definite role, they are much more significant.

Fig. 6 *The European parliament in session*

The organisation of the European parliament emphasises its **supranational** leanings. Members do not sit or associate as national groups but as members of a variety of political groupings based on ideological similarity. The PES and EPP provide mutual assistance at election time, creating propaganda and campaigning material based on an agreed manifesto. In the chamber, the groups have more influence than individuals or small national groupings would have and they receive financial support from parliament for administrative and research purposes (depending on their size). They are a recognised feature of the workings of the assembly. The drafting of the agenda, committee chairmanships, speaking rights, and other duties and facilities are allocated on a group basis.

Key term

Supranational literally means 'above nations or states', so the tendency is for decisions to be made by institutions largely independent of national government.

Activities

Find out more about the PES and the EPP on the internet:

1. See what they stand for and how they operate in the European parliament.

2. Why are the Conservatives uneasy about the EPP?

3. In what ways can membership of transnational parties and the party groupings in the European parliament benefit the main British parties?

Summary questions

1. Make a list of the things about the organisation of the Labour and Conservative parties that seem to be: (a) democratic and (b) undemocratic.

2. What are the main differences in the organisation of the two main parties?

3   The party leaders

Learning objectives:

- Why is the leader of a main political party in Britain so influential?

- How does the power of Conservative and Labour leaders compare?

- Which party gives the leader greater security of power?

- How do the parties choose their leaders? Is the mechanism democratic?

Key terms

Autocracy relates to rule by an individual who has unrestricted authority.

The **1922 Committee** is the collective name for all back-bench Conservative members of parliament. When the party is in opposition, frontbench MPs other than the party leader also usually attend its meetings.

Any leader of a main political party in a two-party system is either an actual or potential Prime Minister. As such, he or she is bound to have great authority as either now or in the future there will be a chance to distribute ministerial offices and make or break the careers of rivals.

The opposition leader is a key figure. Traditionally, he or she has been more powerful in the Conservative party, although the experience of recent years points the other way. Neil Kinnock and Tony Blair both operated a highly centralised system of control, whereas Conservative leaders from Hague to Howard had difficulties in establishing their undisputed authority. In either case, if the party can scent victory in the next election, it tends to be willing to grant the leader wide discretion to make the changes in policy and organisation that he or she considers necessary. If the leader becomes Prime Minister, he or she becomes so powerful that writers describe Britain as having 'government by Prime Minister' (see Chapter 13).

At face value the Conservative leader has enormous power. Many years ago, Robert McKenzie described the incumbent as possessing greater authority and being subject to less restraint than his or her counterpart in any other democratic country. The leadership was once described by the US writer, Austin Ranney, as 'one of **autocracy** tempered by advice and information'.

> Historically, one of the most conspicuous aspects of the internal politics of the Conservative party has been the amount of autonomy and discretion allowed to the leader, but the emphasis given to leadership places a premium on electoral success . . .
>
> The traditional Conservative party has frequently celebrated strong leadership, creating icons of Winston Churchill, Harold Macmillan and Margaret Thatcher.

Gillian Peele, Governing the UK, Blackwell, 2004

In particular, the leader:

- has exclusive responsibility for writing the election manifesto and formulating party policy
- does not have to attend meetings of the **1922 Committee** of Conservative back-bench MPs
- has enormous control over the activities of Central Office and the party machine
- appoints (and dismisses) the party chairman, vice-chairman and treasurer
- chooses the cabinet or shadow cabinet.

This is an important package of powers, recognition of the fact that the party embraces the idea of strong leadership, having grown up as a party within the House of Commons and wanting to see a powerful leader who could espouse the party cause and dominate the chamber.

Yet the position is one of leadership by consent. On several occasions, that consent has been withdrawn and power has melted away. This is particularly the case when the party is in opposition, although the experiences of Margaret Thatcher (challenged in 1989 and 1990 and forced out of office) and John Major (challenged in 1995) suggest that even a Prime Minister is not as secure as a formal reading of the leader's powers would suggest.

The Conservative party thrives on – and for much of the twentieth century attained – electoral success. When that success proves elusive – for example, when the party has been defeated in an election or appears to be making little electoral headway – it can act harshly against its leaders and make them scapegoats for failure. Several leaders have lost the support of MPs and been under pressure to go, including William Hague following the 2001 defeat and Iain Duncan Smith who never even had the opportunity to lead his party into an election. After the 2005 defeat, Michael Howard soon announced that he would be standing down (on grounds of age).

Labour originally had a Chairman of the Labour MPs in the House of Commons, but no leader. It only appointed a leader when it became a party large enough to mount a significant electoral challenge to the Conservatives and Liberals. The way the party developed and a bad experience of excessive leadership power in 1931 combined to make party members reluctant to recognise the supremacy of the leader over the Labour movement. They have always wanted to ensure that the leader is accountable.

Accordingly, the 1918 Constitution imposed restrictions on the power of the leader, in order to ensure his subservience to the party in parliament and to the mass organisation outside. In opposition, leaders have to:

- attend back-bench meetings of the **parliamentary Labour party (PLP)**
- work with a shadow cabinet the membership of which has been elected by MPs
- implement policies in line with conference decisions
- attend the conference
- give an annual report of their stewardship.

They also lack the control over the affairs of the party organisation that Conservative leaders possess.

Yet in recent years, Labour leaders have become markedly more dominant than this portrayal suggests and the leadership has accumulated ever-greater power. The process gathered pace under Neil Kinnock who did much to weaken internal opposition. In the Blair era, the leadership maintained an iron grip, so that dissident voices were weeded out, the union ties loosened and power concentrated in the leader's hands. Starved of victory for many years, many Labour members seemed willing to give Blair a remarkably free hand, although when he was perceived as being more out of touch with grass-roots opinion many members lamented this centralisation of power. Party loyalty was strained by many of the policies that he adopted.

The Labour party has been less severe on its leaders than the Conservatives, many of them enjoying a lengthy period of service. It shows less brutality to those who lead it, so that although there were often mutterings about the performance of Neil Kinnock in the House and real doubts about whether he was an electoral asset, talk of a replacement was infrequent. He easily survived a challenge to his position in 1988.

Since 1945, the Conservatives have had 11 different leaders; Labour have had only nine. Recent experience suggests that the Conservatives

Activity

Why do you think that the leaders in the era from William Hague to Michael Howard would have found it difficult to continue in their position, even if they had wanted to?

Key term

The **parliamentary Labour party (PLP)** is the name for Labour MPs as a collective body. Like the 1922 Committee of the Conservatives, it meets regularly to make its general views known to the leadership.

have found it difficult to find a strong figure who can unite the party, impart vigour to its performance and achieve electoral success. Generally speaking, parties accept strong leaders when they are delivering electoral success or at least the prospect of it. If that strength shows signs of becoming too overbearing, and particularly when electoral success is proving elusive, supporters begin to have doubts about their suitability for the role. Leaders then need to watch their backs.

Key term

Parliamentary Private Secretaries are MPs appointed by a minister to be the minister's unpaid assistant.

Fig. 7 *Tony Blair leaves 10 Downing Street for the last time as Prime Minister*

Activity

Write a couple of paragraphs to explain where power lies in the Labour party.

In depth

The departure of Tony Blair

- Tony Blair announced in 2004 that he would not fight a fourth general election as Labour leader, but would serve a full third term.
- After much sniping against his leadership, in early September, a letter was circulated among Labour MPs demanding that he should resign 'sooner rather than later'.
- The letter was followed by a series of resignations of **parliamentary Private Secretaries**.
- These tactics by Blairite critics increased the pressure on Tony Blair to resign immediately or to name a timetable for a handover.
- He survived and eventually determined the timing of his departure, ensuring that he had completed a decade as Prime Minister.
- He is one of the few premiers to have stepped down at a time of his choosing, Baldwin and Wilson being two 20th-century examples. He served 12 years 11 months as leader of the party.

How the main parties choose their leaders

There have been changes to the way in which both main parties choose their leader in recent years. Labour reformed its selection process in 1981, as did the Conservatives 20 years later. In both cases, the membership now has a say in the choice and there is provision to rid the party of an unwanted incumbent. At election time, the contest enables the party to resolve issues of personality as well as party policy and direction.

The two main parties adopt different approaches to choosing their leaders. Labour was first to involve party members in the choice back in the early 1980s, but its arrangements are more complex because it has affiliated bodies such as trade unions to consider. After much pressure from within the party to adopt a more democratic method, the Conservatives under William Hague devised a new procedure. In both parties, the candidates are already sitting MPs. The present arrangements are set out below.

The Conservatives

The sitting leader can be challenged if 15 per cent of the parliamentary party express no confidence in the leader (at least 25 MPs at present). They would need to sign an open letter to the chairman of the back-bench 1922 Committee. The sitting leader needs to win 50 per cent + one in a secret ballot on a motion of confidence in his leadership. Should he/she fail, then he/she is excluded from the contest. At this stage, other candidates step forward. The parliamentary party holds as many rounds as it takes to choose two candidates, with the worst-performing MP eliminated from each ballot. Then, the 250,000 or so party members vote and the candidate with the most votes wins.

If a vacancy occurs because of the resignation or death of the incumbent, then the parliamentary party moves straight into a series of ballots of MPs. When all but two candidates have been eliminated, the choice is then made by party members. The procedure was first used in 2001 to elect Iain Duncan Smith. In 2003, when he failed to secure enough votes in a leadership challenge, there was not a contest. Michael Howard was the undisputed candidate for the job. Following his resignation in 2005, David Cameron was chosen under the same system as that used in 2001.

Candidate	Round 1 (vote of MPs)	Round 2 (vote of MPs)	Round 3 (vote of party members)
Cameron	56	90	67.6%
Clarke	38		
Davis	62	57	32.4%
Fox	42	51	

Table 2 *The Conservative choice of leader in 2005*

Labour

Labour uses an **Electoral College** to choose its leader. It includes a 33 per cent share for each of the parliamentary Labour party, the party members and the trade unions.

Those MPs who wish to become leader need 12.5 per cent of Labour MPs to back them if there is a vacancy, or 20 per cent if there is a challenge to a sitting leader. To be elected, a candidate needs to receive an absolute majority of the votes cast. If no one achieves this, then further ballots are held on an elimination basis. To avoid repeated balloting, voters are asked to express second and third preferences.

In 1994, the procedure worked relatively smoothly to elect Tony Blair who won a majority in each of the three elements of the party vote. He received 57 per cent of the vote overall, out of 952,109 votes cast. The election was widely seen as the biggest democratic exercise in European party politics, giving the winner what his admirers called 'a million vote mandate'. Nonetheless, some people within the party would like to see the College abandoned in favour of a more straightforward system of 'one person, one vote', in which each vote counted equally.

In 2007, Gordon Brown was unopposed in his bid for the leadership. No rival could obtain the necessary 42 nominations needed to mount a challenge once he had received the 308th nomination from a Labour MP. Without submitting to any form of electoral contest, he became Prime Minister. Some people felt that he should have called an early general election to confirm his right to lead. But in a parliamentary system such as ours, a person automatically becomes PM by becoming the leader of the majority party. The premiership is not an elected post.

Key term

An **Electoral College** is a party mechanism for electing someone to an office, its members being selected or elected to represent different parts of the party.

Activities

1 Using the internet to assist you, find out who the leaders of the nationalist parties in Scotland and Wales are. See if you can find out how they were chosen.

2 Write down what can be said for and against the way in which Gordon Brown was chosen as Labour leader.

Key terms

A **levy-payer** is someone who in addition to paying his union dues also pays a political levy. This goes into the political fund of the union, which is in most cases used to support the Labour party.

The **levy-plus** is the political levy and an extra sum that qualifies the person paying it as an individual member of the Labour party.

The systems compared

The Conservatives traditionally took the view that MPs alone were best able to judge the merits of the candidates. They feared that giving a say to the party outside parliament could lead to a person being imposed on them in whom they did not have confidence and whose views did not accord with their own. Accordingly, until recently, the membership of the party played no formal part in the process, though it could put pressure on their sitting MP to use his/her vote in a particular way when a contest arose.

Today, the new Conservative system has several advantages. There is still provision for MPs to have a say, enabling them to demonstrate who they feel they can work with and support. But more positively, 'one person one vote' provides the opportunity for party members to exercise their choice.

Labour's procedure has for a long time recognised the need for a wider involvement than that of MPs alone. In its present form, the scheme has some sound democratic credentials, but there are anomalies. 'One man one vote' is applied to each of the three individual elements within the party, so that each union **levy-payer** is entitled to vote within the contest staged by the union. But some Labour supporters may belong to more than one union or to a socialist society as well as a local association in the constituency where they reside and the one they represent. Hence Neil Kinnock was able to cast seven votes in 1994.

This is probably not the ultimate Labour scheme: that would be for all members of the Labour party, either those who pay the **levy-plus** through their union or who join the party directly, to have a vote on the choice of leader. There would be no Electoral College but there would be a large mass party with an increased membership. That would be a genuine 'one person, one vote' approach.

Summary questions

1 How do leaders of the two main parties obtain, retain and lose power?

2 Assuming there is a contest, which party has the better system for choosing its leader?

4 Do parties matter any more?

Learning objectives:

- What evidence is there that political parties are in long-term decline?
- Why have traditional parties lost support?
- Do parties still have an important role?
- Has the importance of ideology in politics declined?
- What was meant by consensus politics?
- Is there still a consensus?
- How have the policies of the main two parties differed in recent years?

Further information

What parties do

Bale's 'job description for parties' includes:

- representing significant interests
- recruiting/selecting/supporting candidates/elected representatives
- structuring the choices available to voters
- facilitating the formation of governments
- mediating between citizen and state
- ensuring that no one group gains disproportionate power over government.

Activity

Look at Bale's job description for parties. Write a paragraph to argue that parties still have a worthwhile role and one to oppose this viewpoint.

Some writers point to a crisis in party politics, suggesting that parties are in long-term decline. In the US, there has been a debate over the last few decades as to whether America's parties – historically weak – are now even weaker. As David Broder put it back in 1972, 'The party's over'. Of parties in general, the suggestion has been made that perhaps they were merely a stage that democracy passed through in the modern era. Perhaps they are now in danger of becoming what Tim Bale (2005) calls 'hollow hulks or dinosaurs destined to extinction as the citizens of post-modern, post-industrial Europe turn to other more direct or more digital ways of doing politics – or simply turn away from politics altogether'.

Those who take this view note the decline in party membership, increasing partisan dealignment and the rise of extremist parties. Parties such as those of the Far Right in many parts of Europe are sometimes labelled 'anti-party parties', in that they aim to subvert traditional party politics, rejecting parliamentary compromise and emphasising popular mobilisation.

Established parties in several countries are finding their task more difficult. They have been the victims of public disillusion as voters compare the promise and performance of parties in government. They have also lost support because many young people feel that they do not talk about issues that matter to them. Their ideas seem less relevant to a post-materialist society. On topics such as animal rights, gender, nuclear power and the environment, pressure groups express popular feeling more successfully than parties.

Why have traditional parties lost some of their support?

- **Single-issue protest politics seem more relevant and exciting**, particularly to young people. The young seem to prefer more loosely organised, less authoritarian and centralised parties, compared with the oligarchical established parties whose membership is often inactive or engaged in dull, routine tasks. Pressure groups and especially new social movements (see p119) are seen as better at expressing the direct material or identity needs of those who support them.

- **Traditional parties having served in office – and the politicians who represent them – have been tainted by power and lost their freshness and appeal.** They are seen as sleazy, jaded failures, sometimes prone to lapses of financial probity. They have often been unable to make their performance match up to the promises once made and have lost respect.

- **Perhaps countries are more difficult to govern today.** People have high expectations which politicians find hard to match because often their capacity to influence events in an age of globalisation is strictly limited.

- **The media have played a role in undermining trust in politicians, helping to spread cynicism about the way they operate.** In particular, in an age of 24-hour news, politicians and their actions are subject to a degree of scrutiny that can make it difficult for them to function and over the long term maintain a positive image.

For all of the signs of weakness and fatigue in existing parties, parties are unlikely to become extinct. If the bonds are tenuous, they remain as the main mechanism that links the voters and those who rule them. They continue to perform useful tasks that can be summarised as:

- **Recruiting representatives** for national legislatures and thereby at least influencing – in the British case determining – the choice of those who serve in government.
- Acting as the **best way of ensuring competitive elections** in which there is a meaningful choice of candidates.
- **Educating the electorate** by developing, elaborating and promoting policies, thereby offering a reasonably predictable set of responses to new and traditional problems.
- **Offering an opportunity for popular participation** in the political process, even if in many cases this opportunity is shunned by the majority of voters.

Even in the US, where party organisation is weaker and more decentralised, there are signs of party renewal as parties have adapted to changing circumstances and made use of new technology to keep in touch with the voters. Today, most Americans still think of politics in terms of the Democrat-Republican divide, and elected representatives are almost entirely elected according to their party label. In Britain and much of Europe, parties have been traditionally stronger, more organised and underpinned with a stronger ideological basis. Politicians and voters still think in party terms, even if the dominance of the two main parties has been challenged in recent years. Parties matter.

Parties in Europe: a retreat from ideology?

Much has been written in recent years about the demise of ideology. According to US sociologist Daniel Bell, 'the end of ideology' came about soon after the end of the Second World War, with the collapse of fascism in Italy and of Nazism in Germany, and the decline of communism in the developed West. Francis Fukuyama's more recent work *The End of History* (1989) was written against the background of the collapse of communism in Eastern Europe, which he portrayed as the decline of Marxism as a doctrine of world-historical significance.

The suggestion is that ideological questions have become increasingly irrelevant in the post-1945 era. There is no longer the major clash of democracy versus dictatorship that characterised much of the 20th century because there is now a broad acceptance of democratic values across many parts of the globe. In Western societies of the last few decades, party competition has been less about the traditional struggle between socialism and capitalism, and more about how parties can best deliver economic growth and material well-being. What Bell was suggesting back in 1960 was that there was a broad ideological **consensus** amongst major parties in support of 'welfare capitalism'. In Britain, commentators have labelled the post-war years as ones of 'consensus politics'.

Key terms

Consensus implies a wide measure of agreement. In political life, it refers to a circumstance where a large proportion of the population and of the political community is broadly agreed upon certain values, even if there is some disagreement on matters of emphasis or detail.

Mixed economy is an economy in which there is a significant role for both private and public ownership, as existed in Britain between the late 1940s and the 1980s, before Margaret Thatcher introduced a programme of privatisation of major utilities.

Parties in Britain since 1945: the pursuit of consensus?

In spite of fierce electoral competition and strong theoretical disagreements over the role of the state, private or public ownership of industry and the pursuit of greater social equality, between 1951 and 1979 there was broad agreement between the parties over key economic and social policies. Some commentators portrayed elections as a contest to decide which team of politicians would administer the policies on which everyone was substantially agreed. Robert McKenzie (1955) portrayed a situation in which the two parties conducted 'furious arguments about the comparatively minor issues that separate them'.

Not all observers have seen the era of consensus politics in the same light. Ben Pimlott (1989) saw the consensus as 'a mirage, an illusion that rapidly fades the closer one gets to it'. In his view, the 'era of consensus' was in no way one of all-pervasive sweet reason and compromise; at times there were bitter party clashes. He noted that the word consensus was little used before the 1980s and that it was then used to distinguish Thatcherism from the period that preceded it. His point was that it was much easier to detect consensus in retrospect than it was at the time.

1979–97

The period of so-called consensus came under threat in the mid–late 1970s, as the Conservatives under the leadership of Margaret Thatcher began to embark upon a radical overhaul of their post-war thinking and approach. Instead of following one-nation Conservative policies, her governments took a more radical, New Right stance quite distinctive from that of previous Conservative administrations. Labour initially responded to its defeat in 1979 by moving sharply to the left, so that in 1983 there was a polarised contest between a right-wing Conservative administration and a left-wing Labour opposition. However, in response to successive further defeats between 1983 and 1992 and defections to the breakaway Social Democratic party, Labour moved back towards the centre ground. By 1997, this process had gone so far that Labour had become New Labour and discarded many of its traditional policies.

Margaret Thatcher had succeeded in moving the battleground of political debate to the Right. Her approach to taxation, trade unions, the free market economy and privatisation had influenced the policy agenda of the Labour party. Tony Blair accepted a greater role for the market, embraced Conservative rhetoric on competition and did not seek to reverse privatisation or significantly restore trade union power. Critics in his own party felt that he had been too willing to employ Conservative rhetoric and policies in his bid to make the Labour party electable.

1997–2007

If by the late 1980s there were signs of a 'new consensus' around Thatcherite ideas, this has been refined since 1997. Tony Blair tried to create broad agreement based around his own version of firm but fair policies, combining free market economics with a not-too-generous dash of compassion. As he put it, New Labour was intent on showing that economic efficiency and social justice can and must go hand in hand.

By seeking to create a 'big tent' under which all moderates of goodwill could shelter, Tony Blair went a long way to removing ideology from political debate. He attempted to isolate the Conservatives as being beyond the mainstream, sticking to social attitudes and policies that no

Key term

Bureaucracy relates to government by non-elected salaried administrative officers. Such officials conduct the detailed business of public administration and advise on and apply ministerial decisions. In Britain, it is more usual to speak of the civil service.

longer represented the Britain of today. For several years it worked as an electoral ploy, enabling him to win again in 2001 and 2005 without facing a strong challenge. Yet his command of the centre ground also meant that there was no clear choice in British politics. The parties seemed to be offering variations of the same theme. David Cameron has gone some way towards restoring Conservative fortunes, but he too has tried to position his party in the middle territory.

Significant differences do emerge between the main parties from time to time. In the late 20th century, Labour's commitment to reform of the UK constitution, greater spending on education and health, and its greater pro-Europeanism opened up such a divide. But often the conflict is not so much about ends to be pursued, but about how they can be attained. For example, both parties want better public services, but there is disagreement about how they should be funded and the detail of policies. Each party attempts to show that they could manage public services more effectively.

There is not a sharp Left–Right divide in British politics today. But neither is there the consensus of the 1950s–70s. Circumstances have changed. In those years, two large parties and their ideas dominated the political system. In the 21st century, there are new causes that were not around or were little noticed a few decades ago, environmentalism and feminism amongst them. The force of Scottish and to a lesser extent Welsh nationalism (and the parties that represent them) have become factors in our political life. So too has the 'third force', the Liberal Democrats.

Table 3 *Party priorities: the 2005 manifestos*

Labour	Conservatives
Strong economy	Lower taxes through savings on bureaucracy
Higher living standards	Tougher school discipline
Faster NHS treatment	More school choice
Better results at school	Cleaner hospitals
Tougher border protection	Shorter waiting lists
Safer communities	Immigration controls
More family leave and childcare	More police
More aid for Africa	More prisons

Do British parties offer a real alternative?

The beliefs and philosophies of the two main parties have been explained on pp90–98. Programmes and policies put forward in an election campaign reflect those broad principles. But support for ideas such as community, equality of opportunity or free enterprise does not provide a clear indication of what actual policy will emerge at any given time.

Policy has to be created to suit the needs of the moment amidst a range of competing pressures. In office, those pressures include those coming from international organisations such as the European Union and NATO, world trade and globalisation. Government ministers do not have an entirely free hand in pursuing the solutions that they instinctively favour. They have to respond to events, both within and beyond Britain.

Table 4 *Policies in the 2005 manifestos*

Issue	Labour	Conservatives
Economy	No rise in basic tax rates More help for working families More help for pensioners Raise **stamp duty** threshold	£4bn in tax cuts £1.3bn cuts in Council Tax for pensioners Boost to pensions savings Abolish stamp duty on houses under £250,000
Asylum and immigration	Reduce number of asylum seekers Tougher rules on settlement and more deportations Skills-based points system for permanent immigrants	Annual refugee and immigrant quotas Compulsory health checks Offshore asylum processing centres Quit UN refugee convention
Education	Parents to be able to select specialist schools 200 new City Academies University top-up fees up to £3,000; grants for poorest	More new school places to boost choice Allow good schools to expand Heads to be able to expel disruptive pupils No student fees, charge interest on loans
Equal rights	Create new equality commission Civil unions for gay couples Strengthen race relations Ban incitement to religious hatred	Reservations over equalities commission 'red tape' Oppose politically correct human rights laws No legislation on incitement to religious hatred
Law and order	Dedicated policing teams in every area 25,000 more community support officers 1,300 more prison places Double cash for drug treatment	40,000 extra police officers 10-fold increase in drug rehab places Tougher enforcement of ASBOs 20,000 more prison places, less early releases
Europe	Support proposed new EU constitution Support joining single currency, subject to five key economic tests UK to be at heart of reformed Europe	Oppose EU constitution Allow other nations to cooperate more closely, but UK not to be more fully involved Claw back powers over fishing, oppose euro

As a result, the basic philosophies that have inspired party supporters over generations do not tell the full story of the actual policies that parties introduce when in office.

Neither party offers a radically different vision of the good society. But a study of the manifestos in 2005 indicates some of the priorities and preferences that separate Labour and the Conservatives at the present time.

 Summary questions

1 'Anti-traditional party feeling and electoral apathy suggest that "parties have had their day"; they are in long-term decline'. Can you answer this allegation?

2 Are parties beneficial to British democracy?

3 Do you think that ideology is still a useful factor in establishing the identity and direction of the main parties?

4 Did we ever have consensus politics? Do we have consensus politics today?

Further reading

R Garner and R Kelly, **British Political Parties Today**, MUP, 2003.

 Key term

Stamp Duty is a tax payable by buyers when purchasing a house.

Activities

1 List three pieces of evidence to say that parties have become less significant than they were a few decades ago and three to say that they still retain their significance.

2 Examine the tables and consider what the two main parties were offering the voters in 2005. Were there any significant differences between them?

3 Write a short speech to address the rest of your group on either:

   a the case for the Conservatives in the next election, or

   b the case for Labour.

AQA Examination-style questions

1 ☑ Read the extract below and answer questions (a) to (c) which follow.

Ideology and political party

Parties are created around broad principles or *ideologies*. The terms 'Left' and 'Right' are commonly used as a means of classifying the position of ideologies on a political spectrum. Broadly, those on the Left – traditionally identified with the interests of the masses – support an increase in governmental activity. Those on the Right – traditionally identified with preservation of the interests of the established, propertied classes – broadly oppose the type of change favoured by the Left. They are more wary of state intervention and seek to limit the scope of government as much as possible.

Source: adapted from Chapter 5 of this textbook

(a) Briefly explain the term *ideology* as it is used in the extract. *(5 marks)*

(b) Using your own knowledge as well as the extract, discuss two distinctive values associated with either the Left or the Right. *(10 marks)*

(c) Assess the extent to which the contemporary Conservative and Labour parties reflect distinctive political principles. *(25 marks)*

2 Read the extract below and answer questions (a) to (c) which follow.

Party origins

The two main parties are organised very differently, reflecting their differing origins. The Conservatives developed as a party at Westminster before the extension of the vote to working people. Once the franchise was extended, they needed to ensure that their MPs were supported by a network of local organisations to organise support within the *constituencies*. Labour originated outside Parliament, and developed out of the wish of trade unions, early socialist societies and others to get working people elected into Parliament. Some grass-roots members from both parties have the opportunity to attend the annual party conference.

Source: adapted from Chapter 6 of this textbook

(a) Briefly explain the term *constituencies* used in the extract. *(5 marks)*

(b) Using your own knowledge as well as the extract, assess the importance of the annual conference within the Conservative and Labour parties. *(10 marks)*

(c) Analyse the view that the Labour and Conservative parties are dominated by their respective leaders. *(25 marks)*

7 The world of pressure groups

1 The diversity and extent of group activity

Learning objectives:

- What are pressure groups?
- Why do people join groups?
- What is civil society and why do you think that it is important in a democracy?
- Why has the number of groups dramatically increased?

Key terms

Defensive groups are those which seek to defend the interests of people or categories of people in society.

Campaigning groups are those that seek to advance particular causes and ideas not of immediate benefit to themselves.

Alexis de Tocqueville (1805–59) was a liberal French aristocrat and politician, who visited the US, was impressed and wrote a classic book on the workings of the US political system, *Democracy in America*.

Civil society is that arena of social life 'above' the personal realm of the family but 'beneath' the state. It comprises mainly voluntary organisations and civil associations that allow individuals to work together in groups, freely and independently of state regulation.

Trade unions are organisations that represent groups of workers in order to defend their interests and work for better pay and conditions.

There is a vast range of groups in modern society. Some of these groups are long-lived, others are transient; some are national, others local. They range from the well-known ones recognised by their initials (the BMA (British Medical Association) and the TUC (Trades Union Congress)) to the much less high-profile British Toilet Association and English Collective of Prostitutes. They cover the whole spectrum of policy issues.

They are formed for an infinite variety of purposes. Many exist primarily to benefit the interests of members or to advance some specific cause. When such groups are formed to influence public policy, they are known as pressure groups. Some 34,000 organisations are recognised by the *Directory of British Associations*, but there are many more that operate at the local level. In addition to a huge number of **defensive** and **campaigning groups**, there are more than half a million voluntary bodies.

Why people join groups

Today, most people belong to at least one voluntary association, be it a church, a social or sports club or an organisation concerned to promote civil liberties or rights. Minorities and women have been active in organising themselves to demand access to the social and political benefits long denied to them. Women have also spoken out on important issues associated with human reproduction.

Human beings are essentially social creatures and it is natural for people to form groups. But there is also another sound motivation for joining together with other people. On their own, individuals are rarely influential enough to influence policy and decisions that affect their lives. Therefore, they act together to secure the introduction, prevention, continuation or abolition of whatever measures they feel are important to them. After visiting the US in the 1830s, **Alexis de Tocqueville** was impressed by the way in which 'Americans of all ages, all conditions, and all dispositions constantly form associations'. These had in his view become a 'powerful instrument of action'. Their existence was to be celebrated as an indication – indeed a bastion – of a healthy democracy.

This associative tendency (the tendency of people to group together) constitutes a country's **civil society**, a term often used but seldom clearly defined. It includes those public groups that are above the personal realm of the family but beneath the state. It covers a variety of bodies such as registered charities, non-governmental organisations concerned with trade and development, community groups, women's organisations, faith-based organisations, professional associations, **trade unions**, self-help groups, social movements, business associations and advocacy groups. These are areas of social life – the domestic world, the economic sphere, cultural activities and political interaction – which are organised by voluntary arrangements between individuals and groups, outside and beyond the direct control of the state.

Activities

1 Using a broadsheet and/or a tabloid newspaper, identify stories concerned with the activities of pressure groups. You may see some pictures or reports about meetings of protesters. You could also try looking through the local paper.

2 Identify the groups to which members of your family belong. Do you belong to any yourself? If so, why?

Why pressure groups have grown in number in the modern age

Pressure group activity has a long history, although the increase in the number and range of organisations has been dramatic in recent decades. There are several reasons for this:

1 **The growth in the extent and scope of governmental activity in the second half of the 20th century**, in the areas of national economic management and social services. Governments have become increasingly involved in issues such as education, health and housing. Many people want to see more and better facilities and benefits. A range of groups has emerged to articulate the views of the poor, the homeless, the old and the mentally and physically handicapped, among many others.

2 **The growing complexity and specialism of modern life**. People belong to many sub-groups, not least those based on their occupation. For instance, those working in the medical field may belong to one main union of health-sector workers and also to more specialised associations such as those for ambulance drivers and paramedics.

3 **There has been a surge of interest in single-issue campaigning**, on subjects from gay rights to the export of live animals to the continent, from gun control to the siting of a motorway or other public amenity. Since the 1980s, the number of pressure groups has soared.

Fig. 1 *Protesters block the line just outside Heiligendamm, Germany, the venue of the 2007 G8 summit*

4 **The development since the middle of the 20th century of a multi-ethnic and multicultural society**. This has encouraged the formation of a variety of groups to represent particular minorities, including bodies such as the British Sikh Federation, the Forum of British Hindus and the Muslim Council of Britain. As well as these groups working to promote and defend the interests of sections of the community, other groups have emerged to counter discrimination and combat racism, such as the Anti-Nazi League.

5 **The emergence of new issues and the onset of post-materialism**. Whereas many voters were once primarily concerned with bread-and-butter matters affecting their lifestyle – their home, their work, their income – in recent decades ideas such as **ecology**, feminism and gender equality have come onto the political agenda. Many younger, better-educated voters share post-materialist attitudes and want to express their views about a better environment, the future of nuclear energy and the need for social and political empowerment.

6 **Improvements in communication have facilitated the trend towards association and organisation** and further stimulated group development – as with the use of e-mails and other such innovations by those protesting against globalisation.

Fig. 2 *Demonstrators call for greater protection for the people of Darfur, western Sudan*

Key terms

Multi-ethnic relates to the diverse range of ethnic groups that makes up society.

Multicultural relates to the diverse range of cultures that makes up society. Multiculturalists argue that all people of goodwill – whatever their background – can live together and celebrate diversity, with each community preserving its culture whilst respecting that of others.

Post-materialism is a theory that explains the nature of political concerns and values in terms of levels of economic development. In today's conditions of relative prosperity and wealth, post-materialists are more concerned with the search for a better quality of life. They are interested in issues such as animal rights, environmentalism and world peace.

Ecology is the study of the relationships between living organisms and their environment. As a political doctrine, ecologists have a 'deep green', anti-materialist and anti-technological stance. They wish to change society's present direction because they fundamentally question its values. Many British ecologists belong to Greenpeace UK.

Summary questions

1 What is the difference between civil society and the state or government?

2 Based on your reading of this section, do you think that pressure groups are a good thing? If so, in what ways? If not, why not?

2 Pressure groups, political parties and movements

Learning objectives:

- How do pressure groups differ from political parties?

- What do they have in common?

- What are the main characteristics of the new social movements (NSMs) that have developed since the 1960s? How do these NSMs differ from pressure groups?

Hint

There is no agreed terminology to cater for pressure group activity. The Americans talk of interest groups and lobbying. In Britain, the tendency is to use the term 'pressure groups' and then to classify them into different categories. 'Pressure' usually amounts to influence/persuasion rather than intimidation. Because of the negative connotation of 'pressure', some campaigning voluntary groups (e.g. Cafod and Oxfam) now tend to describe themselves as **non-governmental organisations** (NGOs).

Key term

Non-governmental organisations are non-profit making voluntary sector bodies, such as the Red Cross and Medecins Sans Frontieres, an international medical and humanitarian aid organisation. Many pressure groups that promote a cause tend to think of themselves as NGOs, finding the term 'pressure' troublesome.

Pressure groups are organised bodies that seek to influence government and the development of public policy by defending their common interest or promoting a cause.

Pressure groups and political parties: their similarities and differences

There is some overlap between parties and pressure groups. Both are vehicles through which opinions can be expressed and serve as outlets for popular participation. Both have a role in the workings of government, in the case of parties by forming or opposing an administration, in the case of groups by providing information and assisting in governmental enquiries. There is also an overlap between their activities. For example:

- **There may be a close relationship between pressure groups and particular political parties**. Fifteen trade unions are actually affiliated to the Labour party and form part of the wider Labour movement in the country. The same broadly 'progressive' people may be active in 'social' pressure groups and in the ranks of the Labour or Liberal Democrat parties.

- **Within the parties there are groups that seek to influence party thinking**, such as the Tory Reform Club and the Bruges Group in the Conservative party and the Tribune Group in the Labour party. These **tendencies or factions may be thought of as pressure groups within a party**.

- **Some think tanks act alongside the political parties**. Members share the broad outlook of the party, but act independently and seek to have an impact on the general thrust of public policy. The Institute for Public Policy Research (IPPR) operates on the moderate Left, the Centre for Policy Studies operates on the Right.

- **Some groups actually put up candidates in an election**, as did the Pro-Life Alliance in 1997 and 2001.

However, pressure groups differ from political parties. They do not seek to win elections to gain political office, rather they wish to influence those in office. Indeed, they do not usually contest elections, and if they do, it is mainly to draw attention to some matter of national concern or to gain publicity. Also, their goals are narrower in that they do not attempt to advance ideas covering the whole range of public policy. Some of their aspirations may be non-political.

Pressure groups and movements: the politics of protest

Movements are different to pressure groups, although there is a close relationship between them and they may adopt similar tactics. A movement is a large body of people who are interested in a common theme that is of continuing significance. The Women's Movement is made up of various individuals and groups, all of which are concerned in some way or other to advance the position of women in society. Those who belong to it may have their own specific interests and differing views about the strategies they should adopt. Some will focus on the provision of child care, others on equal pay or the protection of part-time employees, some on abortion rights, etc.

In recent decades there has been an explosion in pressure and protest politics. **Social movements** have a long history. Social movements in the 19th century were concerned with issues such as harsh working conditions. They wanted improvements in workers' rights and urged governments to introduce changes. **New social movements** (NSMs) have emerged since the 1960s. NSMs are different in that they deal with a new range of issues and are much less willing to be absorbed into the established political system. Members often provide a radical critique of society and institutions. They are interested in finding different ways of organising political activity. They want fundamental change to the status quo and the dominant values in society. By contrast, members of pressure groups may want to see substantial changes in public policy, but broadly they are more likely to support the existing political and social framework in society, and the dominant values that underpin it.

NSMs are less structured and cohesive than pressure groups. They tend to have a core group that provides general direction and a loosely organised network of widespread supporters. Often, their activities arise at grass-roots level, before later evolving into national crusades. They are broadly united around a central idea, issue or concern whose goal is to change attitudes or institutions, as well as policies. Characteristic concerns include equality for women and ethnic minorities, the environment and animal rights, globalisation and international peace.

Key terms

Think tanks are groups formed to research and develop policy proposals. They are sometimes influential with the parties with which they share a broad affinity (e.g. Demos and the Labour party).

Social movements are made up of large bodies of people united around a central idea of continuing significance whose goal is to change attitudes or institutions, not just policies. The Women's Movement has a long history in Britain and the US.

New social movements are movements that have emerged since the 1960s in order to influence public policy on issues such as the environment, nuclear energy, peace and women's rights. They aim to bring about fundamental change in society.

Summary questions

1. Outline two similarities and two differences between pressure groups and political parties.

2. Why do you think that many young people find involvement in new social movements more appealing than belonging to political parties?

3 Classifying pressure groups

Learning objectives:

■ What is the difference between protective and promotional groups?

■ Which are usually more powerful?

■ What are the difficulties about this classification?

■ What is the difference between insider and outsider groups?

■ What are the problems with this classification?

Key terms

Peak or umbrella organisations coordinate and represent the broad activities and interests of business or labour, such as the CBI and TUC. Their members are not individuals, they are other bodies such as firms, trade associations or labour unions.

The **British Retail Consortium** is the main trade association representing the whole range of retailers, from large department stores to out-of-town or rural outlets. The BRC works closely with government on all campaigning and policy issues, and has established a good relationship with several governmental departments, regulatory agencies and non-governmental organisations (NGOs).

Early studies of pressure groups sometimes distinguished between groups involved in different areas of activity, for instance the 'labour lobby', 'civic' groups, and 'educational, recreational and cultural' ones. However, there are two more usual ways of classifying them. The first describes them according to what and whom they represent, the second in terms of their relationship with government and the way in which they operate:

■ Protective (interest) and promotional (cause) groups

The distinction originally made by Stewart (1958) and subsequently employed by many others divided groups into:

■ **protective, defensive, interest or sectional groups**, those which seek to cater for the needs and defend the rights of persons or categories of persons in society and

■ **promotional, propaganda, cause or ideas groups**, those which seek to advance particular causes and ideas not of immediate benefit to themselves.

Protective groups are primarily self-interested bodies that seek selective benefits for and offer services to their members. Business interests are among the most powerful and well known. Many of them are represented in **peak or umbrella organisations**, which bring together within one organisation a whole range of other bodies and coordinate their activity and speak on their behalf (e.g. the **British Retail Consortium** represents the interests of 11,000 stores). Business groups are usually well organised and financed.

Trade unions are probably the best-known protective or interest groups. They exist to represent the interests of organised working people by defending and improving their wages and working conditions. They have a closed membership as only those who work in an industry or possess a particular skill are eligible to join them. Individual unions often belong to an umbrella organisation; in Britain 66 (including the largest, the 2 million-strong Unite) are affiliated to the Trades Union Congress (TUC).

Among other sectors, the National Farmers Union has long been considered to be one of the most effective protective groups, representing as it does a clear majority of British farmers. Its views are listened to with respect in Whitehall. Other highly significant protective groups cover the interests of those engaged in the professions, doctors, lawyers and teachers among them. Because they represent clear occupational interests, protective associations are often well established, well connected and well resourced.

Promotional groups seek to advance ideas and causes which are not of benefit to their membership other than in a most general sense. They are selfless rather than self-interested in their concerns. They are also open to people from all sections of the community who share the same values, whereas members of interest groups have a shared experience. Again, unlike the many interest groups that have been in existence for several decades, many promotional ones have a short life span, disappearing once their cause has been appropriately tackled.

Further information

The RSPB

The RSPB was founded in 1889 and has grown into Europe's largest wildlife conservation charity with more than a million members. Its initial stance was against the trade in wild birds' plumage, but it now tackles a vast range of issues. It is much involved with environmental developments, researching wildlife problems and promoting practical solutions. It shares its specialist knowledge with decision makers in government.

Fig. 3 *Protesters against the plume trade: the RSPB was formed in 1860 to counter the trade in 'grebe fur'*

Further information

The British Retail Consortium is an example of a group with very close links to many aspects of government and government related agencies. These include:

- Cabinet office
- Department For education and Skills (DFES)
- Department for Environment, Food and Rural Affairs (Defra)
- Department of Health (DH)
- Department of Trade and Industry (DTI)
- Department for Transport (DfT)
- Department for Work and Pensions (DWP)
- Food Standards Agency (FSA)
- Foreign and Commonwealth Office (FCO)
- HM Revenue and Customs
- HM Treasury
- Home Office

Promotional groups are defined by the cause or idea they represent. The Royal Society for the Prevention of Cruelty to Animals (RSPCA) is concerned with the welfare of animals, Friends of the Earth (FoE) urges greater environmental awareness, and Amnesty International campaigns on behalf of political prisoners. Many cause groups are today **single issue** ones. In Britain, Snowdrop had a brief existence. It lobbied effectively for a ban on handguns and when the goal was attained, its *raison d'être* (reason to exist) no longer existed.

Protective associations are traditionally stronger than promotional ones, they are better organised and resourced. Many promotional groups operate with limited funds and few, if any, full-time staff. They have a tendency to split into rival factions. They usually have less access to government.

In addition, there are some hybrid groups. The Royal Association for Disability and Rehabilitation (**Radar**) defends the interests of its members who are disabled, but works for the general betterment of all disabled people. Of course, many other interest groups directly pursue causes. The British Medical Association (BMA) engages in campaigning on general health issues such as diet and smoking, although it primarily exists to defend the interest of professionals.

Insider and outsider groups

Groups may also be classified by an alternative **typology** originally developed in the 1980s by Wyn Grant. His ideas appeared in articles and lectures and then became a book in 2000. He finds the protective versus promotional distinction unsatisfactory because along with it there tends to be the assumption that protective groups are more influential than promotional groups because they represent powerful interests. Also, it is easy to assume that promotional groups are of greater benefit to society than protective ones because they are more concerned with the general good rather than personal advantage.

Grant's preferred approach is based on the relationship of groups with the central decision makers in government. For him, the key issues are whether any particular group wants to gain acceptance by government and – if it does – whether or not it achieves that status. In his words: 'The principle on which such a typology is based is that in order to understand pressure groups, one needs to look not just at the behaviour of the groups but also at the behaviour of government.'

Grant divides groups into:

- insider groups that are regularly consulted by government, having good access to the corridors of power, and
- outsider groups that either do not want such access or are unable to attain recognition.

Many but not all protective groups are insider ones and have consultative status. Similarly, in most cases promotional groups are outsider ones. However, there are significant exceptions, such as the Howard League for Penal Reform and the Royal Society for the Protection of Birds, both of which are promotional groups which are in frequent touch with representatives of government.

Hint

Beware of confusion when categorising some groups that contain words like 'protect' or 'save' in the title. The Campaign to Protect Rural England campaigns for a sustainable future for the English countryside. Although it is concerned to 'protect' the countryside, it is a promotional group. It promotes the idea of protecting the countryside. Members of a protective group belong for the sake of defending their own interests, not to advance a cause.

Key terms

Single issue groups concentrate their attention on the achievement of one specific objective, such as banning abortions.

Radar is a national network of disability organisations and disabled people.

Typology is the study of types.

Activities

1. List any five examples of:
   a protective groups
   b promotional groups
   c insider groups
   d outsider groups.

2. On the internet look up some well-known groups and find out more about the issues with which they are concerned. Note the size of their membership.

The Grant typology has itself been criticised. It has been pointed out that:

- **The distinction is not clear-cut, as some groups pursue insider and outsider strategies at the same time**. Over the years, Friends of the Earth has shifted towards more dialogue with government and business, whilst maintaining direct action activities that attract money and popular support. Tactics such as peaceful public demonstrations and letter-writing campaigns are compatible with insider status, although more violent direct action is not.

- **More groups have insider status than Grant originally suggested**. Many groups are consulted by government but their influence may be marginal. Some 200 bodies are on the list for consultation on issues relating to motor cycles, so that consultation is hardly a special privilege reflecting insider status.

- **The distinction is less valid today because new forms of politics have arisen in the 1990s and subsequently**. Pressure-group politics has changed, with more middle-class involvement in issues such as animal welfare and anti-roads protests. Also, there are more arenas than before, most obviously the European Union. Some groups concentrate much of the time on Brussels where key decisions are made. In matters relating to agriculture and animal welfare, access to the corridors of power in Whitehall is less desirable than access to the policy makers in the EU.

Summary questions

1. Label each of the following groups as protective or promotional, insider or outsider. In some cases, you might need to make an informed guess for the insider/outsider categorisation:

a BLESMA	c NFU	e BAAS	g RSPCA
b CBI	d RSPB	f FoE	h TUC

2. Which classification of groups do you find to be the more helpful, and why?

4 The methods employed by pressure groups

Learning objectives:

- What are the main access points that British pressure groups target?

- Why do protective groups tend to concentrate on operating in Whitehall?

- How do the government and protective groups benefit from close cooperation?

- What are the main advantages and disadvantages of **lobbying** the legislature?

- Why is the House of Lords an increasingly important focus for group activity?

- Why do some groups now also **lobby** the devolved institutions and the EU?

Key terms

A **lobby** is a group of people who represent a particular interest or cause, e.g. the environment lobby. The lobby (a term often used in the US to describe group activity) normally refers to all of those groups that seek to influence public policy.

Lobbying is the practice of meeting with elected representatives to persuade them of the merits of the case you wish to advance.

Lobbyists are therefore employees of associations who try to influence policy decisions, especially in the Executive and legislative branches of government.

In any free society there are access points, formal parts of the governmental structure that are accessible to group influence. Where the emphasis is placed will vary from democracy to democracy. In Britain, the most obvious ones are:

- The Executive (ministers and civil servants).
- The Legislature (MPs individually and as members of their party).
- Public opinion and the media.

In Britain, the approach adopted depends on the type of group involved. Large, powerful protective groups tend to focus on where the power lies. In a highly centralised country such as Britain, this is in Whitehall as key decisions are made in government departments. They may also have contacts in Westminster, and in the case of the unions have close links with MPs. By contrast, many promotional groups will have very infrequent contact and little influence in Whitehall, unless they are an insider group such as the RSPB. They may have some spasmodic support at Westminster but will try to persuade public opinion in their favour in the hope that the press and MPs will then take up the cause if it proves to be one of much concern.

Pressure groups and government

Protective or interest groups target the Executive branch of government. Sometimes, they deal with ministers directly. More often, **lobbyists** – who are interested in the details of policy – have contact with senior officials in the various departments. Higher civil servants make decisions on many routine, technical and less important decisions, which are nonetheless of vital concern to interest groups. On major issues they offer advice to the Secretary of State, the political head of a government department. Civil servants and ministers find the network of groups with whom they are in dialogue very helpful. They can get technical information and advice, and maybe assistance in carrying out a policy. In return, the groups learn the department's current thinking and hope to influence its decisions and get bills drawn up in line with their recommendations.

Consultation between government representatives and groups is a constant process and the range of dialogue is immense. In some cases, it is statutory, a particular measure laying down the interests that ministers are obliged to consult. More often, it is discretionary, although once any group has been asked for its views it tends to assume that this will be the forerunner of similar contacts in the future. If ministers feel that high-quality and specialist advice and assistance are available, that the leadership of the group is representative of its members, and that the organisation has wide support within the sector in which it operates, they are likely to want to see any initial consultation as a precedent for further consultation.

Contact between group spokespersons and government takes place in various ways. They serve on government-established committees, benefit from the circulation of government documents and are involved in widespread formal and informal consultation in various ways.

The National Farmers Union (NFU) and those employed at the lower end of senior policy grades in the Department for Environment, Food and Rural Affairs (Defra) are in frequent communication. The NFU values its consultative status in Whitehall and likes to operate in a quiet, behind-the-scenes way that avoids too much publicity. Only when a row breaks out will it turn to more open public methods.

Pressure groups and the legislature

Groups often voice their views through the legislature. Powerful British groups prefer contact with the Executive, but MPs are much lobbied by them as well as by promotional groups. Both types of group have shown increasing interest in lobbying the European parliament, its MEPs and committees, particularly so as parliament's powers have increased.

British groups lobby parliament because it can influence public policy, although the strong system of party discipline means that MPs are likely to be less responsive to group persuasion. In Michael Rush's study (1990), 75 per cent of groups claimed to be in regular or frequent contact with MPs and more than half also maintained contact with the House of Lords. They might rank its influence below that of the Executive branch, but the trend since the 1980s has been towards more lobbying of the legislature. This has been partly because of the growth of the select committee system as another target for influence, but also because the Thatcher, Major and to some extent the Blair governments have had some reservations about pressure group influence. In addition, the existence of governments with large majorities means that it is sometimes more productive for groups to work on back-benchers in the hope of persuading them to oppose what ministers are trying to steamroller through the House.

Elected representatives may be willing to put forward a Private Member's Bill (see p190 for further details). MPs who draw a high position in the annual ballot early in each session of parliament, soon find themselves contacted by campaigners who hope to persuade them to introduce a measure relating to their cause. For example, if they find someone interested in introducing a bill restricting abortions, pro-life campaigners would probably have ready draft proposals that can easily be turned into legislation.

In lobbying parliament, groups hope to:

- amend or sponsor legislation in a direction favourable to them
- influence the climate of discussion on relevant issues of public interest and limit any potential damage to their own interests
- gain parliamentary backing for causes that may have first been raised outside the chamber.

In depth

Lobbying the House of Lords

Since the 1980s, the reputation of the upper house has significantly improved and its contribution to the working of parliament is now more highly rated than two or three decades ago. Campaigners have come to see the benefits to be gained from lobbying the upper chamber that has become an important new focus of group activity.

The role of the Lords in scrutinising legislation has sometimes created considerable difficulties for recent governments, for example over controversial bills involving civil liberties (e.g. the legislation on freedom of information, the detention of alleged terrorists, asylum seekers and ID cards). Campaigners have been active in contacting peers to strengthen their resolve in thwarting or improving government proposals. Similarly, in the case of disadvantaged groups varying from the disabled to students threatened with the prospect of payment of tuition fees, campaigners have been willing to work with cross-bench and opposition peers in a bid to defeat ministers. The amendments that the Lords can make to bills are more likely to be accepted by the Commons when they are broadly in line with government thinking and more concerned with detail than fundamental principle.

In its campaign against the abolition of foxhunting, the Countryside Alliance made extensive use of contacts in the Lords as a large number of peers shared its broad approach. They made use of circulars to and meetings with peers who sympathised with their cause.

The appeal to the public

Groups try to influence the public who, after all, are the voters in the next election. Aims for Freedom and Enterprise, an established organisation that crusades against nationalisation, employs **background campaigns** to create a favourable impression for a cause over a period of time. They keep up a steady flow of information, and become more prominent at election time. A dramatic **fire brigade campaign** may quickly rally support and get MPs and government ministers to take notice. The Snowdrop campaign in 1996–97 used this blitz approach, as do local action groups set up to achieve a particular goal such as keeping open a local park as an open space. They disband when the issue is resolved.

Whereas lobbying at the public level often seemed unrewarding a few decades ago, its importance has increased in recent years. Television has provided opportunities for publicity and some organisations now recognise the value of this medium. By persuading voters to take an issue on board, they hope to generate public interest and raise awareness. Environmental groups have grown rapidly since the 1990s. They have consciously sought to mobilise support through the use of television images and discussions.

For those groups that employ **direct action**, television can provide valuable publicity. The prolonged Greenham Common anti-Cruise missile protest of the early 1980s attracted some attention, and the campaigns against the M3 extension at Twyford Down and against the Newbury bypass a decade or so later gained extensive coverage. More recently, the campaigning activities of **Fathers4Justice** and **Plane Stupid** have been publicised.

Other outlets

The courts are another focus for the attention of lobbyists. As yet, British groups have made less use of the legal route than their US counterparts, although bodies such as the Equal Opportunities Commission and Greenpeace have won considerable victories

Fig. 4 *Plane Stupid protestors, Heathrow, 2007*

Key terms

Background campaigns are designed to present a favourable image for some cause or interest over a period of time.

A **fire brigade campaign** is a dramatic type of group campaign designed to rally support quickly.

Direct action is any action beyond the usual constitutional and legal framework, such as obstructing access to a building or the building of a motorway. Terrorism is an extreme form. Essentially, it is an attempt to coerce those in authority into doing something they would not otherwise do.

Fathers4Justice is a direct action fathers' rights group, formed to campaign on behalf of fathers who claim to have suffered injustice in the quagmire of divorce proceedings and feel that the legal system is stacked against them.

Plane Stupid is a direct action climate group that has emerged from the new wave of radical green activism seen in Britain recently. Actions carried out by the group include the grounding of planes through the establishment of a 'climate camp' on an airport taxiway and the occupation of offices belonging to airport operators, e.g. BAA and Easyjet.

■ **Activity**

Look at the website of the Fathers4Justice organisation (www.fathers-4-justice.org) to find out how a direct action group campaigns. You might also look at the site for Plane Stupid (www.planestupid.com).

■ Key terms

Multi-level governance relates to the multiple layering of government and describes the way in which the British political system operates today. There are various tiers of government, with the EU at the top, then the UK government, devolved bodies and local administration, plus many unelected bodies that exercise considerable power.

Nimby groups are local action groups whose members wish to protect their own lifestyle. Often, they campaign against developments that will impact adversely on the view from and value of their own house or land, but are less concerned about developments affecting other people and areas.

■ Key term

G8, the Group of Eight, comprises eight advanced industrial countries whose heads of state meet in an annual summit, as at Gleneagles (Scotland) in 2005, to discuss trade and development issues.

in the courts. The Countryside Alliance used the judicial route in an attempt to delay the implementation of the ban on fox-hunting, claiming that it was a denial of members' rights under the European Convention.

Other than by direct approaches to the three tiers of government and the public, groups can be effective in other ways such as lobbying other pressure groups and companies and using the mass media to create a favourable climate of opinion for their action. There are also other layers of government that provide access, at the local, devolved and European levels. Many groups have become increasingly sophisticated in their understanding of the appropriate outlets for their campaigning. The well-resourced RSPCA has become familiar with the new world of **multi-level governance**, its main UK operations being complemented by the activities of the Scottish SPCA and its European department.

■ The local level

Lobbying at local authority level has increased in recent years. Some councils have encouraged participation via consultative exercises, creating forums and joint committees or holding public meetings to enable individuals and groups to put their cases. National legislation on issues such as the existence of grammar schools and moves to enable housing authorities to take over council estates have also encouraged group involvement.

Many local action organisations have been formed, often **Nimby** ('not in my back yard') **groups**. They have mushroomed and regularly use media-oriented tactics in their campaigning to try to block some development of which they disapprove, e.g. moves to build a housing estate on green-belt land or to fell an ancient tree in the name of progress.

■ The devolved level

The advent of devolution in the UK has created new opportunities for pressure-group activity. Before the creation of the Scottish parliament, there were interest groups operating north of the border. However, since 1999 their range and number have significantly increased and they now concentrate much of their attention on the Scottish parliament and Executive. Moreover, several UK groups have developed separate Scottish branches in order to lobby more effectively. Those groups that regularly come into contact with the Edinburgh machinery generally appear to have a positive view of the process.

From the beginning, the Executive has encouraged groups and individuals to become involved in the process of consultation. The presence of Labour and the Liberal Democrats in office between 1999 and 2009 may have encouraged a close relationship because there is some movement of personnel between social group activists and the two broadly progressive parties. MSPs have also encouraged campaigners to petition parliament and liaise with its committees. Committees engage in consultations in a bid to discover public opinion on a wide range of issues prior to proposed legislation.

■ The European level

NB: For a fuller discussion of the European Union and its institutions, see Chapter 17.

Many British groups are involved in lobbying at the international level. In particular, those concerned with trade and overseas development issues may be in contact with the United Nations, UN-related bodies such as the World Bank and the **G8**, as well as representatives of overseas governments. However, it is the European Union that has become the main target beyond British shores.

From the time the UK joined the European Community in 1973, some groups saw the need to lobby its institutions. The larger manufacturing interests and organisations such as the National Farmers' Union were first off the mark. Since then, many others – including bodies such as Friends of the Earth and Greenpeace in the environmental field, and the British Veterinary Association and the RSPCA operating in the topical area of animal welfare – have seen the need to adapt their campaigning approach to allow for British membership of the EU.

Many decisions affecting key areas of our national life are now made in Brussels. Many of our laws derive from **regulations** and **directives** of the **European Commission**, so that in some sectors the bulk of new regulatory activity now takes place not in Whitehall but in Brussels. On topics ranging from food hygiene to the movement of live animals, from fishing to the outbreak of **Bovine Spongiform Encephalopathy (BSE)** a few years ago, the actions of British governments are much affected by what is laid down by the Commission. The passage of the Single European Act in 1986 that paved the way for the creation of a **single market** was of concern to many group campaigners.

For a long time the European Commission was the key target of lobbyists. It is a relatively open bureaucracy and it considers the views of various 'interests' in the early stages of draft legislation. As the **European parliament** has acquired more power, it too has become a popular focus for lobbying. **MEPs** and their party groupings, and committees of the Strasbourg parliament, also attract the attention of campaigners. Some groups have made use of the **European Court of Justice**.

Not surprisingly, the number of groups involved in EU affairs has increased dramatically since the 1970s. But the growing importance of EU lobbying is not merely a matter of volume but also of quality, as group activity becomes more professional and sophisticated. Three avenues are open to groups that wish to engage with the European machinery:

1   **Placing pressure on the national government**. Many groups try to influence the stance adopted by their governments in the **Council of Ministers** and to make their views known on the implementation of EU decisions. They can do this by entering into discussions with ministers and senior civil servants in the relevant Whitehall ministry. Some groups prefer to operate via the British government rather than make a direct approach to the Union.

2   **Operating through Eurogroups**. Many groups feel that in addition to utilising their contact with their own governments, they wish to exert pressure via a European-level federation of national groups. For instance, the TUC is a member of ETUC, a **Eurogroup** that currently represents 81 national organisations from 36 countries.

3   **Direct lobbying**. Direct contacts with union institutions are becoming increasingly important for many groups. A few large organisations have established offices in Brussels as a means of closely monitoring European legislation (the Confederation of British Industry (CBI)) and also as an outlet that can offer protection for members working in the EU (the Law Society). More usually, contact takes other forms, such as working via MEPs, approaching a Commissioner formally or informally, or writing letters to/phoning union institutions.

Summary questions

1 List six different methods used by pressure groups to get their ideas across.

2 Which level of government would you lobby if you were seeking to persuade the government to introduce legislation on the following?

a abortion
b animal welfare
c increasing the size of the overseas aid budget.

Further information

Access points available to British groups: a summary

International level:
- United Nations
- UN-related bodies such as the World Bank
- G8
- Overseas governments.

European Union level:
- Council of Ministers
- Commission
- Parliament
- Court of Justice.

UK national government:
- Executive
- Parliament (both chambers)
- Courts
- Devolved machinery
- Local authorities.

Miscellaneous:
- Public
- Other pressure groups
- Private companies
- Public corporations
- Media.

5   Pressure group resources and success

Learning objectives:

- What factors make success more likely for any group?

- What are the key resources that help groups achieve success?

- Why might a good relationship with decision makers improve the chances of success?

- How can the media be helpful to any group in advancing its ideas?

- In what ways does success vary according to the political circumstances of the time?

Group influence not only varies from country to country, but even within the same state. Groups experience varying degrees of success at different times. Success may be interpreted as gaining access to a centre of decision making and exerting influence over the development of policy. Inevitably, some groups exert more influence than others. In part this may reflect their ability to exploit opportunities for influence available to them, but a more likely explanation must lie in the nature and underlying strength of the groups themselves.

Three general considerations require further discussion:

1 The resources of the pressure group.
2 The ability to get the message across to decision makers and those who influence them.
3 The political circumstances and the climate of the times in which the group is operating.

Group resources

Individual pressure groups have very different levels of resources. Their behaviour in particular circumstances often depends on the resources that are available and their calculation of the costs and benefits associated with employing a particular mix of them. The resources that are relevant can therefore differ according to the situation, but they include such things as membership, leadership and staffing, esteem, funding, organisation, public support and the capacity for social disruption.

A group's political resources include such things as:

- **Membership**: the extent of a group's membership, its density (does it speak for most people in the industry or profession?) and more especially the size of its activist base.
- **Leadership and staffing**: successful organisations tend to be those that are well led, with charismatic, creative and energetic leaders being supported by an efficient staff.
- **Esteem**: professional groups generally have a high social status. Doctors are less criticised than unions. NACRO (representing ex-offenders) and Release (representing drug addicts) lack strong public appeal.
- **Funding**: money helps groups organise internally and exercise influence externally. It enables expenditure on quality leadership, the creation of a favourable image and generous office/staffing provision.
- **Organisation**: protective groups can afford generous staffing and office space. Promotional groups, including some of the most vulnerable sections of society, cannot. But they can be well-run by a small, highly centralised and professional command structure. The RSPB is very highly organised.
- **Public support**: groups whose campaigns are in tune with the popular mood have a considerable advantage. Governments are sensitive to the views of the electorate particularly near election time.
- **The ability to make strategic alliances**: some groups supplement their own resources by forming alliances. In opposing identity cards, libertarian campaigners cooperated with activists from groups representing asylum seekers and immigrants who feared that they would be the victims of endless requests to prove that they have a right to be in Britain.

The ability to get the message across to decision makers and those who influence them

Many groups have strong connections with the Executive. Insider groups – business, labour and professions among them – are in a better position than outsider groups to claim decisive or exclusive expertise. Decision makers and legislators may have their own views on issues of broad community benefit (e.g. rights for lone parents and gay people), but on matters involving technical understanding and help in the implementation of policy, they may be reliant on the advice and assistance of well-resourced groups. They may receive detailed assistance in drafting legislation from a well-informed group. **Shelter** was actively involved in drawing up the Homelessness Act 2002.

The BMA, the NFU and the RSPB all command an audience among decision makers because of their specialist knowledge. They offer policy makers in Whitehall valuable information, which is helpful because ministers and officials cannot be familiar with all the technical detail in business, professional and environmental practices. They offer consent as officials know that it is prudent to be seen to have consulted affected interests, and finally they may occasionally offer active help in administering decisions.

> **Key term**
>
> **Shelter** is a national charity that campaigns to end homelessness and bad housing.

Contacts with the Executive and parliament are invaluable, but in recent years many groups have been also aimed to influence public opinion. In attempting to do so, they increasingly rely on the media (see p155).

In depth

British Medical Association (BMA)

The British Medical Association represents doctors from all branches of medicine in the UK. It is a voluntary association with 130,000 members, some 80 per cent of practising doctors. It speaks up for the interests of doctors at home and abroad, provides a range of services for its members and engages in scientific research. This involves lobbying not only the British government but also the European Union.

Given the wealth of its members, the BMA can commit substantial amounts of money to influence policy makers directly or to finance public information campaigns. Its members command respect from politicians because of the doctors' high status and standing, and the recognition that their work involves the delivery of a vital public service, health care.

The BMA is one of the most influential and effective protective, insider groups. It has a specialist parliamentary Affairs team in London (and in Scotland, Wales and Northern Ireland) which briefs politicians and advises its members on how to lobby ministers and senior civil servants. It also has a number of professional committees including the Board of Science, Medical Ethics Committee and International Committee. These undertake a range of activities which include supporting public health initiatives such as a ban on smoking in public places, responding on behalf of doctors to consultations by national public bodies and the government, and promoting the views and reputation of doctors in different arenas.

Like many protective groups, the BMA is also involved in campaigning on aspects of the NHS that it sees as being in need of improvement. It is also a major publisher, the *British Medical Journal* having a reputation for airing medical controversies as well as conveying important scientific developments.

In the past, some GPs felt that it represented the interests of consultants rather than their own and formed a breakaway group. The National Association of Sessional GPs (NASGP) was founded in January 1997 by a group of enthusiastic GPs who campaigned energetically to improve their status and representation via a handbook, regular newsletters, national conference, code of good practice, local groups, practice induction pack, website and the media. There is also another body for consultants. The Hospital Consultants and Specialists Association (HCSA) is specifically designed for senior hospital doctors.

Activities

1. In this chapter, you have been presented with information about the BMA and RSPB. For each one, make a list of the ingredients of its success as a pressure group. Bear in mind the three factors listed on the first page of this sub-topic and the information about group resources.

2. Choose a pressure group that you know and write a few sentences to explain its aims, its approach to lobbying, its resources and its effectiveness. Do you think that on balance it operates in a self-interested way, or for the greater good of the whole community?

The political circumstances and climate

The attitude of ministers is crucial to the prospects for group success. Some have goals that are compatible with the aims and outlook of the ruling party, in the way that a Labour administration was traditionally expected to be sympathetic to union pressure and a Conservative one to approaches from big business.

The governmental response may be affected by the size of the parliamentary majority. Governments in the 1970s – especially the Labour ones from 1974 to 1979 – lacked the dominance of subsequent administrations. Two out of three of each of the Thatcher and Blair election victories left ministers in an overwhelmingly dominant position in the House of Commons, so that they were able to pass much of their legislation through the lower chamber with little difficulty. This may have made them less interested in consultation, although arguably it was more the general attitude of ministers to the role and value of pressure groups that made it hard for them to achieve the influence they wanted. In both cases, there was what Baggott (2000) describes as an 'anti-group philosophy' within the government, as illustrated by the Blair observation relating to anti-GM campaigners: 'we should resist the tyranny of pressure groups'.

In the case of any group, timing is all important. Governments are more willing to make tough decisions and ride roughshod over opposition to their policies in the period after an election victory. In the last year or so in office and with an election looming, ministers are likely to be more sensitive to group and public pressure and more susceptible to influence. This is especially true if the cause seems to have popular support. Having delayed taking decisive action over the abolition of hunting with hounds in the first few years in power, ministers – and certainly Labour MPs – seemed more willing to resolve the issue in 2004–05. They understood the need to enthuse their demoralised supporters by giving them a good rallying issue on which to campaign.

Some groups that once had a very powerful position in the economy find that opinion has moved against them. Miners were in a very strong bargaining position in the 1970s when oil supplies were in short demand following the quintupling of prices by the **OPEC** countries. A decade later, when the Thatcher government confronted them in the Miners Strike of 1984–85, ministers were prepared and oil stocks were ample. This seriously weakened the position of the NUM and its leaders. Their industrial action posed less of a threat to power supplies.

Of course, the homeless cannot think about withdrawing cooperation or going on strike. Neither can lone parents or ex-prisoners.

✓ Summary questions

1. What do we mean by 'pressure group success'?

2. Why are protective groups generally more successful than promotional ones?

3. How do the media help pressure groups get their messages across?

4. It used to be said that 'more noise equals least success'. Is it still true that the most effective groups are those that can put their case across quietly in Whitehall?

Key term

OPEC (Oil Producing and Exporting Countries) is a permanent intergovernmental organisation created in 1960. It aims to coordinate policy on the production and distribution of petroleum among its members and ensure stability of prices.

Further reading

Useful articles:

N Jackson, 'Pressure group politics', *Politics Review*, September 2004.

D Watts, 'Lobbying Europe: an update', *Talking Politics*, September 2004.

D Watts, 'Pressure Group Activity in Post-Devolution Scotland', *Talking Politics*, January 2006.

Useful books:

R Baggott, **Pressure groups today**, MUP, 1995.

B Coxall, **Pressure Groups in British Politics**, Pearson, 2001.

W Grant, **Pressure Groups and British Politics**, Palgrave, 2000.

J Greenwood, **Representing Interests in the European Union**, Macmillan, 1997.

D Watts, **Pressure Groups**, EUP, 2007

8 Pressure group behaviour

1 Perspectives on pressure group activity

Learning objectives:

- What is meant by pluralism and pluralists?
- What is corporatism?
- How did British tripartism differ from continental corporatism?
- Why is the New Right wary of pressure group activity?
- Why do Marxists see pressure groups as ultimately irrelevant?

Key terms

Pluralists believe that there is a political marketplace in which ideas can be traded and group activity can flourish. Groups are viewed as a natural and desirable feature of political life, in a democracy in which power is dispersed.

Corporatists are those who believe in corporatism, the idea of bringing organised interests into the process of government.

Heterogeneous population is a diverse population in which many different ethnic groups are represented.

Countervailing groups are groups formed to oppose the views of and compete with the dominant group in any particular sector. The result is that any one group is likely to be counterbalanced by a group hostile to its viewpoint, the influence of the one cancelling out the influence of the other.

Governments are elected by the people and are answerable to them for their deeds. They alone are ultimately responsible for determining the shape, direction and detail of policy. But in almost every democracy the role of groups in the processes of policy formation and implementation is greater than such a view implies.

There are four theories that help us to understand the operations of pressure groups and their importance in political life more clearly. In particular, they help to explain how peak organisations such as those representing employers and employees (e.g. the CBI and TUC) perform a role in government alongside that of the state. All bar one of the theories outlined see groups as being significant. However, the theories differ considerably in how they view group activity in the political system; in their view of the balance of power between groups; and on whether or not groups enhance or undermine democratic life.

Two theories have dominated investigations into the relationship of government and groups and group behaviour: those advanced by **pluralists** and those advanced by **corporatists**. However, two more are worth mentioning: the views of the New Right and of Marxists.

The pluralist approach

Group theory was for a long time dominated by the pluralist model that was originally developed in the US by David Truman in 1951. He and subsequent pluralists believed that groups were an entirely natural and healthy feature of political life. They benefited the political system in various ways:

- Their concerns reflected those of ordinary people who were entitled to air their views.
- They provided informed views and specialist expertise to government.
- They allowed minority voices to be clearly advanced, helping to achieve a necessary balance in a democracy between minority and majority rights.
- They catered for the representation of a **heterogeneous population**, allowing the diverse views of ethnic and other groups to organise and be heard
- They prevented any single group from exercising disproportionate influence because there were opportunities for **countervailing groups** to form and compete with them. In the marketplace for ideas, all shades of opinion can be aired. Often, one side will not get everything that it wants because other groups can prevent it from riding roughshod over their interests.

The essence of the pluralist case is that power should be dispersed in society and that diversity should be encouraged. It stresses that there are no barriers to the formation of groups and no single group monopolises political resources. Access to the political system is open to everyone;

all can put forward their case without significant difficulty. The government may take – indeed, sometimes rely upon – advice from groups in making and carrying out their policies. However, groups are recognised as having sectional interests and are granted no special favours. Numerous groups compete for influence over a responsible government that holds the ring, 'more umpire than player'.

For all of the reasons outlined, pluralist writers portray pressure groups as having a beneficial impact on the political system. Far from posing any sort of threat, they contribute to our democracy.

> Politics is seen as 'a competition between a multitude of freely organised interest groups . . . as new interests emerge, groups form to represent them. In pluralism, politics is a competitive market with few barriers to entry.

R Hague and M Harrop, *Comparative Government and Politics: An Introduction*, Palgrave, 2004

The corporatist approach

As a theory, **corporatism** is a means of bringing organised interests into the process of government. Corporatists place greater emphasis on the close links that exist between certain types of groups and the state in industrialised countries, enabling manufacturing groups to have access to the government and assist in shaping and implementing policy.

Corporatism is difficult to describe for the term is used differently by many of those who use it. Its meaning can range from the institutionalised involvement of interest groups with the state to a much weaker version involving bargaining between the state, employers and employees about the conduct of economic and social policy, often known as **tripartism**.

Corporatism was practised in several European countries, often in a very advanced form involving close links between industry and government. In the 1960s and 1970s, governments in Britain sought to achieve agreement between employers and employees on a prices and incomes policy. The British version lasted through the period of the Wilson (Labour) government (1966–70) and the Heath (Conservative) administration (1970–74) to the era of Wilson/Callaghan (Labour) rule (1974–79).

Further information

Countervailing groups: the case of hunting

The pro-hunting Countryside Alliance was supported by the Association of Masters of Harriers and Beagles, the British Field Sports Society and the Country Land and Business Association. Ranged against it was the organisation Campaigning to Protect Hunted Animals which incorporated bodies such as the League Against Cruel Sports and the RSPCA.

Key terms

Corporatism is a system of policy making in which major economic interests work closely together within the formal structures of government to devise and carry out public policies. See tripartism below.

Tripartism or neo-corporatism is a loose, less centralised form of corporatism of the type operated under administrations of both British parties in the 1960s and 1970s. It is weaker than the continental form of corporatism in which corporatist decision making has often been institutionalised (built into the system of government).

Fig. 1 *Harold Wilson, Edward Heath and James Callaghan*

Critics regard corporatism as unhealthy, a threat to representative democracy. They dislike the way that decisions are made behind closed doors, beyond the means of public scrutiny and democratic accountability. They prefer more open governing arrangements and see parliament as the place where conflicts about the allocation of national resources should ultimately be debated and resolved.

The pluralist versus corporatist debate is central to democratic politics for it sets out the framework for discussion of the relationship between society and the state. Hague and Harrop put it clearly: 'Pluralists see society dominating the state: corporatists view the state as leading society'.

The New Right approach

In the late 1970s and 1980s, the New Right developed a different view of group activity. Its supporters questioned the value of groups in democratic life, portraying them as sectional bodies primarily concerned with advancing their own interests rather than those of society at large. In particular, they expressed alarm about the role and power of some groups. They noted the dominance of producer interests (employers and employees) and their easy access to government. In comparison, the viewpoint of consumers, taxpayers and promotional groups was neglected.

Followers of the New Right were more doubtful as to whether groups were an influence for good. They saw them as distorting the proper role of the Executive and legislature. Their influence over both branches of government made it more difficult for ministers and officials to resist the demands of consulted groups and to act in the general good. It also made it more difficult for MPs to represent all viewpoints among their constituents.

The Marxist approach

A very different analysis has been provided by members of the radical Left. They see real control in society as being exercised by the ruling economic group that makes decisions to serve its own interests. As the owners of productive wealth, they control the levers of political power. Whether the system of group activity is described as pluralist or corporatist, the dominant ruling group in the power structure will prevail.

Marxists draw attention to the unequal distribution of power between employers and employees, pointing out that business interests exercise excessive influence. They control economic resources and possess status and access to government. Workers' organisations do not have such power, status and access.

Activity

Copy the table below. Then, having checked the sections on pluralism and corporatism, identify five features about them to enable you to fill in the spaces. This will help remind you of the key information.

Table 1 *Plural/corporatist approaches*

	The pluralist approach	The corporatist approach
i		
ii		
iii		
iv		
v		

Key term

Marxists are those who subscribe to the set of political ideas associated with the German thinker, Karl Marx. Modern communism is based on his ideas.

Summary questions

1. Why do some writers and politicians worry about the influence of pressure groups?

2. What were the merits of corporatism and in what ways might its use be desirable today?

3. Which of the four perspectives appear to be the most convincing? Does your view differ when you think of a large interest group such as the TUC and the promotional RSPB?

2 The relationship of pressure groups to government

Learning objectives:

■ Why do powerful interest groups seek a close relationship with government?

■ In what ways might they closely cooperate with government?

■ What does government get out of the close relationship?

■ Why has corporatism gone out of fashion in recent years?

■ What is the difference between policy communities and issue networks?

Fig. 2 *Arthur Scargill, leader of the National Union of Mineworkers, is arrested during the 1984/5 miners strikes. The NUM were very influential prior to these actions. Most major protective groups identify the importance of a close relationship with the government.*

In almost all countries, major protective groups – particularly those representing employers and employees – seek a close relationship with government. Sometimes, they deal with ministers directly, but elected politicians mainly deal with the broad contours of policy rather than the specific details. More often, lobbyists – who are interested in the small print of policy – have contact with senior officials in the various departments of state, such as the British Treasury or Department of Trade and Industry. Group representatives want to obtain access to the seat of power. It is in the departments that decisions are made and the details of legislation finalised. In Britain, this means that most leading British protective groups have close contacts in Whitehall.

Ministers and civil servants find spokespersons of groups such as the CBI, TUC, BMA and the NFU useful to them. This is because governing large, industrialised societies is a complex business in which there are many choices to be made and competing demands to reconcile. Governments therefore consult widely, dealing with representatives of all significant groups in society. Such consultation is valuable to them because:

■ **It is a means of obtaining the views of members of the group**, in the case of protective groups, employers, employees, doctors and farmers. This may be valuable in helping ministers develop plans for legislation and monitor the success of measures that have passed into law.

■ **They can get technical information and advice**, based on the knowledge and practical experience that members possess.

■ **They may obtain assistance in carrying out policy**. From the BMA they may find out about the incidence of any infectious diseases that GPs are coming across, and also gain the support of doctors in any programme of mass or localised vaccination. The same is true of farmers who are in a position to help ministers handle outbreaks such as BSE and foot-and-mouth disease.

■ **Finally, ministers can use such contacts as a means of passing information to the people who will be most interested**, so that groups become important avenues for communication between government and members of affected interests.

In the case of insider promotional groups such as the RSPB and the RSPCA, they are valued in Whitehall for the knowledge and expertise they can provide. Other campaigners may be contacted where their specialism might be useful to decision makers in Whitehall, especially if their cases are well argued and their methods of campaigning are non-provocative and responsible.

Of course, groups benefit in return. They get to know about the department's current thinking and they try to influence its decisions and get legislation drawn up in line with their recommendations.

Contact with government can be formal and/or informal. It can involve serving on government-established committees of enquiry and receiving government documents on which comment is invited. On the other hand, it might involve being in touch by phone or e-mail or having a discussion over lunch.

Government meeting with employers and employees: corporatism or tripartism in practice

Business groups tend to be in regular contact with government. They have an advantage at this level because they play a pivotal role in the economy as producers and employers. In the 1960s and 1970s (the age of corporatism or tripartism in its looser form), it became fashionable for leading bodies such as business/trade organisations and trade unions to work with representatives of government in the management of the economy. Each side contributed its views and ministers sought to get agreement about what the economy could afford by way of price rises and wage increases. It was a means of making the process of government more **consensual**, i.e. open conflict was avoided and harmony was fostered among the competitive interests in a market economy.

In the discussions, the interests represented agreed to certain deals, making trade-offs that gave them some of what their members wanted. The underlying idea was that all those involved were seeking to elevate the national interests above purely sectional concerns. Union leaders were prepared to exhibit restraint in wage demands in return for employers doing their best to maintain employment and keep the prices of their goods down. The government was there to represent the national interest, doing its best to create a stable economic atmosphere for the benefit of everyone, which would encourage the other elements to pursue unselfish policies. Granted such influence, the **social partners** were willing to seek and encourage the cooperation of their members.

Such corporatism has gone out of fashion since the 1980s, although it is still practised in some European countries. Since that time, governments have increasingly moved to free market competition, with greater use of competition and deregulation. Margaret Thatcher was very hostile to the influence of entrenched interests. She was unwilling to accept the power of organised labour and was unwilling to bargain with its leaders. Heads of big business organisations also detected a change in their status, the CBI being distanced from government. The Thatcher approach was based upon vigorous competition and more open markets, with government unwilling to step in and assist companies experiencing trading difficulties.

Today, there is dialogue between ministers and representatives of manufacturing and the workers. But it is much less close, organised and regular than it was in the past. In spite of its links with the trades unions, New Labour in office has not been willing to grant them any special favours and their leaders have often seemed disillusioned with the responses of ministers to their demands.

Policy making in British government: who is involved?

The concept of **policy networks** has attracted much attention in recent years. They describe the different kinds of relationships between groups and government and the range of players (organised groups, national and European civil servants, regulators and academics) that exist in any particular sector. Each sector has its own policy network involving decision makers and group lobbyists working together to do something that may be of benefit to them both or at least prevent them from developing attitudes and adopting policies that damage one side or the

Key terms

Consensual means existing by consent; seeking the maximum degree of agreement before any action is taken.

Social partners relates to the trade unions and the employers (or their representative organisations) engaged in social dialogue. The idea of social partnership is strongly founded in European models of industrial relations and is now adopted across the EU.

Activities

1. Write down a list of reasons why ministers might want to hear the views of a body such as the RSPB or the RSPCA.

2. Margaret Thatcher was not keen on meetings with CBI and TUC leaders. Of the business groups, she was more sympathetic to the Institute of Directors (IoD). Look it up on the internet (www.iod.com) and think why she might have approved of it.

other. The relationships within these sectoral groupings may be either close and continual (**policy communities**) or loose and wide (**issue networks**).

When it was put forward, the idea of policy communities fitted in well with Grant's classification of insider and outsider groups, the former having close involvement in decision making. In Britain, policy communities were formed around subjects such as food and drink policy, technical education and water privatisation. In all cases, the dialogue between the groups and government was close and regular. Both sides attached importance to mutual and largely secret cooperation.

Since the 1980s, the dominance of such communities has given way to broader consultation and discussion in issue networks. In addition to government and the lobbyists, others are involved in any negotiations of a policy area. These include the research institutes and the media. Media scrutiny and the attentions of consumer protest groups – for instance in the food and drinks sector – have led to a more probing analysis of policy-making processes, so that secret deals and mutual back-scratching are now less frequent or effective. The impact of any particular group (for instance, academics or the consumers) may vary from time to time or issue to issue, partly depending on the expertise it possesses in any given case.

Key terms

Policy networks are the different kinds of relationships that can apply between government, pressure groups and the range of other players involved in policy making in a particular sector. Policy communities and issue networks are subsections of policy networks.

Policy communities are small, stable and consensual groupings of government officials and group leaders involved in decision making in a particular policy area.

Issue networks are large, flexible and open networks of particular individuals in any policy area. They are wider than policy communities and involve more people.

Further information

An issue network in practice: agricultural policy

Past

Policy was made in the corridors of Whitehall between representatives of the NFU and the Ministry of Agriculture.

Present

DEFRA will meet with:

- European civil servants
- the NFU
- other interested pressure groups (e.g. environment groups such as Friends of the Earth)
- food manufacturers
- academic and research specialists
- consumer organisations.

Activity

Think of any sectors of policy other than agriculture and list the representatives that might meet together to discuss policy. You might start by considering policy on fishing.

Summary questions

1. Is it:

   a inevitable and
   b desirable

   that 'big business' should be close to government?

2. Are there dangers in the traditionally close cooperation between the NFU and the Ministry of Agriculture, now Defra?

3. What is the difference between consulting with a group and negotiating with it? Might negotiation seem improper?

3 Mobilising public concern

Learning objectives:

- What do groups hope to gain from creating a favourable climate of public opinion?

- Why might direct action promotional groups like to summon a media presence at their protests?

- How can the media assist pressure groups?

- Why do groups sometimes target the media?

Key terms

Farmers for Action (FFA) was set up in May 2000 by a group of farmers who wished to safeguard the long-term future of British agriculture and the British countryside. It aims to secure a sustainable level of income for farmers and growers.

Make Poverty History was a campaign based upon a coalition of charities, religious groups, trade unions, campaigning groups and celebrities who mobilised in 2005 to increase awareness and pressure governments into taking action to relieve absolute poverty.

GM foods: genetic modification is a special set of technologies that alters the genetic makeup of such living organisms as animals, plants or bacteria. A genetically modified (GM) food is a food product that contains some quantity of any genetically modified organism.

In the early studies of pressure group activity, the view was often expressed that 'least noise equals most success'. In other words, the groups that were really influential were the large protective groups that operated behind the scenes in meetings in government departments. Groups such as the NFU only decided to go public if they were becoming frustrated in their negotiations with ministers. The views of noisy campaigners involved in protest demonstrations carried little weight, having very little influence with ministers. For any significant group, it was not really worth operating at the public level if access to departmental officials was available.

Since the 1980s this has no longer been the case. Much more attention has been paid by pressure group activists to mobilising public support. Many members of the NFU are now aware of such possibilities. They also belong to the more activist **Farmers for Action**, so that they get the advantages of applying insider and outsider pressure.

Campaigns are often expensive, time-consuming to organise and unpredictable in their outcome, but the development of modern mailshots, advertising and marketing techniques has made them more appealing. In addition, television provides opportunities for publicity and some organisations now campaign via the medium. By persuading voters to take an issue on board, they hope to generate public interest and raise awareness. Environmental groups and those concerned with world poverty have grown rapidly since the late 1990s. Their leaders have consciously sought to mobilise support through the use of television images and discussions.

Fig. 3 *The Make Poverty History campaign*

The role of the media

Over recent decades, the media have become an increasingly acknowledged part of group activity in all democracies. Many British promotional groups have taken up public campaigns – sometimes involving direct action (see pp141–144) – in the knowledge that the media can provide information and publicity for their cause and help to create a more favourable climate of opinion. Campaigners are becoming more media savvy. Often, they use well-known personalities to gain attention.

Insider groups have also used the media. Well-resourced bodies such as the BMA may be able to fund poster advertisements and press advertising. For most groups of whatever type, these would be an enormous drain on finances. But there are other opportunities to convey their work and achievements. If they can attract the curiosity of journalists by the inherent interest of their campaigns and the vivid images conveyed, the cause may receive much coverage. **Make Poverty History** was able to draw attention to the plight of the world's poor and the African continent in particular in its crusade in 2004–05. The ability to use the mass media and arouse public indignation has at various times been particularly significant over emotive issues such as the export of live animals, **GM foods**, hunting and the war in Iraq.

Groups are becoming more media savvy. Often, they use well-known personalities to gain attention.

Fig. 4 *Surfers Against Sewage*

Baggott (1995) quotes an interesting example of use of the media – that concerning Surfers Against Sewage. The group has been successful in 'highlighting the pollution of beaches and coastal waters by attracting media attention'. He notes its use of strong visuals, with activists clad in wetsuits and gas masks surfing in sewage-ridden waters and riding in brown inflatable dinghies: 'The spectacle has attracted the attention of the media and even resulted in a television documentary about the issue of sewage pollution which examined the activities of the group'.

New technologies, particularly the development of computerised targeted and personalised mass mailing, have increased the reach of pressure groups. Targeting has been used to contact people likely to share a common concern, such as members of environmental groups. Key figures in Friends of the Earth have had a close association with the media, some having at one time worked in television or the newspaper industry.

Occasionally, newspapers, television, radio stations and advertising bodies are themselves the target for group activity. They help to set the political and social agenda, so that those who wish to see a cause obtain

Activities

1. Use the internet (e.g. www.makepovertyhistory. org), to find out about the campaigning methods of a group, including its use of the media and direct action.

2. Use the internet (e.g. www. sas.org.uk) to find out about the goals and campaigning methods of Surfers Against Sewage. Is it a protective or promotional group, an insider or an outsider?

3. List the ways in which the Save the Valley campaign used the media to its advantage.

a higher or lower profile are naturally attracted to the broadcasting authorities. Grant (2000) refers to the interesting example of the popular BBC Radio Four serial, *The Archers*, whose writers and producers have regularly been the object of campaigners concerned about alleged moral decline and farming practices in the fictional village of Ambridge. Media-watch UK maintains pressure on the television authorities to explain their policies on standards of taste and decency. It regularly monitors the use of bad language and levels of violence in soaps and other popular programmes such as *Big Brother* and *Celebrity Love Island*.

An example of media influence: the Save the Valley campaign

In the 1980s, the media were used by campaigners seeking to save the Valley as the football ground of Charlton Athletic FC. After serious financial problems, the club no longer owned its ground, which was in need of substantial and costly renovation. However, its decision to share facilities with Crystal Palace at Selhurst Park never won the backing of many supporters who disliked the idea of driving 10 miles across London to see a home game. For two seasons they maintained a weekly chant: 'We should have stayed at the Valley'. In 1987 the directors decided to return to their home area and repurchased the Valley with a view to building a new ground there. They even formed a political party, the Valley party, which fought a full-scale election campaign through the ballot box at the local elections.

Canvassers used door-stepping and leaflets to publicise the cause. Above all, what the campaigners needed in order to persuade the Labour-controlled council to back their return, was attention from the media. The local paper was fully behind the venture. An extensive poster campaign was undertaken and 35 sites were booked for most of the month before the April 1990 election.

Media coverage was an important part of the success. Although funds were limited, the Valley party was able to attract national coverage of what was a local issue, both at the press conference to launch the campaign and in items on *Thames News*, *Newsnight* and LBC and Capital Radio. Articles in the *Guardian* were also seen as helpful. Above all, however, advertising was at the heart of an effective campaign. It was the advertising that generated the powerful media coverage and helped to recruit 60 citizens who in the space of a couple of months became a potential political force in the Borough.

Summary questions

1. Which kinds of group are likely to win a sympathetic response from the public and which are not?

2. Can you think of any high-profile campaigns that have mobilised the media to create a sympathetic public response? With what success?

3. Use a local newspaper to identify a neighbourhood campaign and identify how it is using the media to put across its views.

4 The role of direct action

Learning objectives:

■ What is direct action?

■ Why has direct action become more popular in recent years?

■ What are the main characteristics of new popular movements? How does their activity differ from that of traditional pressure groups?

As we have mentioned, those groups that employ direct action find that television in particular is a useful means of gaining valuable publicity.

Direct action is not a new phenomenon. For many centuries marches and demonstrations have been used by those wishing to protest against their living and working conditions. Trade unions have employed industrial action as a weapon with which to persuade reluctant employers to meet their demands over the last 200 years or more. But in the last few decades there has been a remarkable upsurge in the growth of forms of direct action by individuals and groups. Forms range from demonstrations and 'sit-in' protests to squatting and striking, from interrupting televised events and non-payment of taxation to the invasion of institutions in which the activities conducted cause offence. Groups committed to opposing hunting or other forms of alleged mistreatment of animals have often been willing to resort to forms of direct action to voice their protest.

■ What do we mean by direct action?

By direct action we mean doing for yourself what the government has refused to do. This may mean that homeless people find a home by living in unoccupied property. The term has been used more widely to allude to any attempt to coerce those in authority into changing their viewpoint – for example, the homeless might occupy a council office until they are housed. These activities invariably involve law breaking, which may be passive (e.g. obstruction, trespass) or violent (e.g. if a person is threatened or furniture is broken).

Today, the usual meaning of the term direct action is 'action taken outside the constitutional and legal framework'. In Baggott's words (1995), it describes a situation when a group 'takes matters into its own hands, rather than relying on established methods of decision making, to resolve a problem'.

Direct action does not have to be violent. It can be **militant** without being violent. If violence is used it may be against property rather than against a person. Non-payment of a portion of taxation by Quakers who disapprove of any governmental defence policy based on the willingness to use force, is non-violent but illegal. So was the willingness of those seeking the vote for women at the beginning of the 20th century, who organised themselves into the Tax Resistance League (their cry was 'no taxation without representation').

Campaigns of direct action may start off as peaceful protests but can easily become violent. Many people might choose to engage in an orderly demonstration against some motorway development or the export of live animals to the continent. They might find that as passions become inflamed, so disorder creeps in. Protest marches have often turned out to be occasions when violence erupts, and the demonstrators confront the police who are seeking to maintain law and order. Of course, this does not necessarily happen, and the right to peaceful protest is one that civil libertarians strongly defend.

Operating at the extreme end of the spectrum of forms of direct action, hijackers and terrorists among others have shown how effective

Key term

Militant means aggressive or forceful in support of a cause.

Activities

1 Use national or local newspapers to find recent examples of direct action. Note down the methods of direct action that were employed.

2 Look up Friends of the Earth (www.foe.co.uk) or Greenpeace (www. greenpeace.org.uk) to find out about their campaigning methods and any instances of direct action in which they have been involved.

Key term

Ecotage is direct action in the environmental field, including acts of sabotage on buildings and equipment; similar to eco-terrorism. An eco-terrorist is an extremist who is prepared to carry out terrorist acts against companies, industries and other workplaces and their personnel if he or she feels that unnecessary damage to the environment is being caused.

Hint

It will be beneficial in your examination if you can refer to good and recent specific examples when answering questions. When talking about direct action, give examples and show that you are aware of the different forms it can take.

techniques of law-breaking can be. Fortunately, few groups are willing to resort to such tactics in order to obtain their desired goals. Because they operate beyond the realms of democratic politics, many would consider that they cannot be included within the scope of any study of direct action.

The growing popularity of direct action: why has it come about?

In recent years, a number of promotional groups have decided to use direct action as an additional means of persuading the government to follow their ideas. They get publicity as the television cameras are likely to be present at a mass protest or demonstration. Many local action and promotional groups have used direct action as an additional tool. Members of Nimby groups have often used this approach in their bid to block the building of housing estates on green-belt land, or to stop the felling of some ancient tree in the name of progress. Local papers regularly reveal the activities of groups who seek to gain publicity by some dramatic gesture.

Various reasons for the growth in direct action have been put forward:

- The growing recognition that protest is an effective means of getting concerns placed on the national agenda.
- Since the 1980s, there has been a huge increase in interest and concern for the environment. This has triggered a mass of activity (local, national and international), much of it informal, loosely organised and characterised by willingness to resort to less traditional methods of campaigning. Friends of the Earth has provided help and training to concerned individuals and groups. Some environmentalist organisations such as Earth First! have been willing to resort to **ecotage**.
- In the Conservative years (1979–97), there were often limited opportunities for consultation, with previously powerful groups such as trade unions finding themselves distanced.
- Developing disillusion on the part of many campaigners with the performance of the Labour government. Public campaigning may have increased since 1997 because of the widespread expectations that had been unleashed by the arrival in office of a 'progressive government' and the subsequent disappointment when it failed to carry out the policies favoured by protest campaigners. Environmentalists and civil libertarians are among the ranks of the disillusioned.
- More recently, the ease of organising protest via the world wide web, e-mail and mobile phones. Technology has assisted protesters and also journalists, who have become ever more alive to the opportunities for identifying themselves with causes, the publicising of which might help to establish their own careers.

The merits of direct action: alternative viewpoints

I was one of those imprisoned for protesting at Twyford Down. Sometimes, when the shady avenues of bureaucracy have been exhausted, there is no choice but to throw yourself in front of the digger.

Twyford campaigner

Direct action doesn't just highlight issues; it simplifies highly complex subjects. It cuts through the jargon, mystery and bureaucracy, and it demands a straight answer.

Peter Melchett, formerly prominent in Greenpeace

Violence as a means for obtaining social change has several flaws: it often causes suffering; it abdicates moral superiority and alienates potential support. It requires secrecy and hence leads to undemocratic decision making; and, if successful, it tends to lead towards a violent and authoritarian new ruling elite. Non-violent action as a policy and as a technique avoids these problems; its means reflect its ends. With non-violent action, energy is aimed at policies or structures, and not their supporters.

Brian Martin, an Australian Friends of the Earth activist

Direct action should be used sparingly; the more it is used, the less effective it becomes. It should follow every possible effort to persuade by reason and reflect total frustration at the obstinacy, unfairness, and possibly the brutality of the system, rather than be a self-indulgent expression of the impatience of protesters.

Des Wilson, a longstanding campaigner on behalf of British promotional groups

The increased use of popular protests in recent years

Much of the protest of recent years has not been carried out by individuals or groups operating on their own. The trend has been towards their involvement in wider populist movements that have benefited from communications technology and careful use of the media. In some cases these movements plan a programme of activities over many months (e.g. Make Poverty History and the Countryside Alliance), but often they erupt onto the political scene, as in the case of the fuel protests of 2000 and 2005. In this latter case and many others, a single issue captures the public imagination and galvanises people into action.

There are common factors in the outlook and behaviour of some of the recent popular movements. They tend to:

- emerge abruptly, maybe ignited by a spark (e.g. the rapid increase in petrol prices on garage forecourts)
- be based on issues which arouse an emotional response, perhaps fuelled by a tabloid campaign and accompanying television coverage
- use direct action to draw attention to their demands
- get a swift – if carefully managed – governmental response, to head off the escalating protest.

Rather than relying on persuasion and rational argument and operating through the conventional pressure group methods of lobbying the Executive, the legislature, participating in enquiries, etc., popular movements rely on the implied threat that the government will lose votes in the next election. Such activity does not fall easily into the classic typologies of pressure group activity. Movements cannot easily be described as protective or promotional. They have features of both sectional and cause groups. On the one hand they represent the private interest of those whose lifestyle or livelihood has been threatened or

Activities

1. Can you think of any Nimby groups at work in your neighbourhood or nearest town or city?
2. Look up and list three current campaigns of Earth First! (www.earthfirst.org.uk).
3. Try to find out what happened in the protests at Twyford Down.

Activities

1. Look up the Countryside Alliance (www.countryside-alliance.org) and the League Against Cruel Sports (www.league.org.uk) and compare and contrast the methods they have employed to get their messages across. Why do you think that the League was on the winning side and the Countryside Alliance was on the losing side of the issue of hunting in England and Wales?
2. List the ways in which the campaigning of popular movements is different from that of traditional pressure groups.

damaged (rural interests and parents in the case of the Countryside March and Snowdrop). Yet their campaigning quickly develops into a wider crusade for action supported by many people not immediately involved and with no personal interest at stake.

Opinions vary about the contribution that such popular movements make to democracy. It can be viewed as positive, in that they mobilise the interest and encourage the participation of many people who would otherwise remain uninvolved in the political process. They illustrate that ordinary people can have an impact on government and force those who govern to be responsive to public concerns. But on the other hand, their behaviour is coercive in that there is an implied threat that if their grievances are not addressed there will be serious consequences for those in authority, possibly mass punishment at the ballot box.

Fig. 5 *The Countryside Alliance protest against the ban on hunting with dogs*

Summary questions

1. Can direct action be worthwhile, even beneficial?

2. Is there a valid distinction between the use of peaceful direct action and violent protest?

3. Under what circumstances can non-violent but militant direct action be justified?

4. Can the use of physical force to obtain a political objective ever be appropriate?

5. Can the use of direct action can be an engine of social progress? Give examples.

5 Do pressure groups benefit British democracy?

Learning objectives:

- Why is it difficult to reach a conclusion on whether groups are good or otherwise for democracy?

- Why might they be considered beneficial for our democracy?

- Why might they be considered damaging to our democracy?

It is now time to consider the role of groups in British democracy, whether they enhance or diminish the quality of our democratic political system. In so doing, we face the difficulty that we are dealing with thousands of organisations whose aims, composition and methods vary significantly. Some may be guilty of the charges often laid against group activity, others are not. Some may serve the public good for much of the time, others have only a marginal benefit. We can only make generalised comments that do not apply to all groups in all circumstances, but here are some arguments to consider.

Yes! Groups are good for British democracy

In a democracy such as ours, pressure groups are an inevitable feature. The chance to freely voice a viewpoint is basic to a democratic system. The group system has mushroomed in recent years and this growth is unlikely to be reversed. More specifically:

- **They allow people to band together and express their views**. In a pluralist society, in which power is dispersed in many different locations, pressure groups are seen as being at the heart of the democratic process. The existence of groups allows individuals to associate with one another and proclaim their views – essential rights in any democracy. They provide a safety valve enabling anyone with a grievance to feel that they are able to vent their disenchantment.

- **They act as a defence for minority interests, especially those connected with parties not in government**. This function is particularly important in the case of ethnic and gender minorities and other disadvantaged groups. It allows them to express their distinctive point of view, providing an opportunity to express any resentment about their treatment and to outline any ideas that would help overcome obstacles that prevent them from fulfilling their potential.

- **They encourage wider participation in public life and the decision-making process**. They allow participation in decision making by ordinary individuals. Many people otherwise only participate in political life at election time, effectively only every four or five years. They do not have a chance to express their preference on individual issues. Via groups, people can play a part in and make a contribution to the workings of democracy, thereby having the chance to influence the decisions of public bodies. Via such activity, some might develop their political skills to such an extent that it might encourage them to serve as officers of their group or even stand as candidates for election.

- **They act as a better link between the people and those who govern them than political parties**. Groups provide an outlet for people with little interest in party politics who may find themselves galvanised into action over an issue that is directly of concern to them. Sometimes, traditional party attitudes seem irrelevant to their lives, whereas via group activity they feel that they have a chance to achieve their goals. Groups counter the monopoly of the political process by political parties, sometimes raising items for discussion that fall outside the realm of party ideas and policy, and which do not tend to get into the manifestos. They made the running in the environmental arena well before the parties took up ecological issues.

Activity

Reflect on whether or not you think that the views of ethnic and gender minorities are adequately represented through pressure groups. Can you think of any examples of groups operating in either field?

Activities

1. Think of any examples in which pressure groups were able to (a) embarrass or (b) assist the Blair governments. You might think of examples in the area of civil liberties.

2. Consider what are the advantages of pressure groups over parties as vehicles for dealing with the issues of concern to ordinary people.

3. Look up the CBI website (www.cbi.org.uk) and that of the NFU (www.nfuonline.com). See if you can find examples of any issues on which they are having dealings with government and contributing their expertise.

4. Using the BMA, CBI and NFU as examples, how would you describe these groups?

   a Exclusively self-interested.
   b Self-interested but responsible.
   c Strongly concerned for the public interest most of the time.

Fig. 6 *Outside NFU HQ in the Sixties the message about foot and mouth is clear. The NFU have been protecting farmers interests since 1908*

They act as a valuable check upon those who exercise political power. Groups can help to keep a government in check, helping to expose information that would otherwise remain secret. Even governments with a large majority, as in 1997 and 2001, can be vulnerable to the probing activities of lobbyists who publicise/leak information and highlight governmental lapses or attempted cover-ups. They can also highlight any potential abuses of civil liberty in proposed legislation.

They provide valuable information to government departments based upon their specialist knowledge of their field. In some cases, this is backed by cooperation in administering a particular policy and monitoring its effectiveness. They are indispensable to governmental decision making because they are available for regular consultation. Indeed, this may be on a very frequent basis, there being continuing dialogue between a government department and a key interest group such as the CBI or the BMA. The government knows that a group of this type represents the bulk of people in that particular sector. Most farmers are in the NFU, and therefore its voice is representative.

No! Groups endanger British democracy

They are a sectional interest. A pressure group by definition represents a number of broadly like-minded citizens in society. In other words it is a 'sectional' interest, in the way that the NFU represents farmers and the NUM miners. Governments have to govern in the 'national interest', and consider the views/needs of all sections of the community, not the voice only of the powerful large interests. For instance, the TUC still represents a substantial proportion of working people, but by no means all workers; the nurses may arguably have a strong case for better pay, but the rest of society may be asked to pay more in taxation to finance it.

The better resourced and organised sections of the community are at an advantage. Not all sections of the community are equally capable of exerting influence, though virtually everyone is free to join a group. There is not a level playing field for influence. Some, especially ideas groups, are much less likely to be acknowledged. Campaigners can point to the failure of the Child Poverty Action Group (CPAG) and other welfare groups to prevent Labour from cutting benefits to one-parent families and the disabled. Of the interest groups, the voice less frequently heard (other than via the ballot box) is that of consumers who are difficult to organise. By contrast, the producer groups, the unions and – particularly in the Tory years – the industrialists and businessmen, have easier access to Whitehall.

Too much goes on in secret, with lobbying carried out behind closed doors. Some people worry about the circumstances under which bargains between interest groups and Whitehall departments are made – hence Finer's plea many years ago for 'Light, more light'. Also, they fear that too many MPs are beholden to outside groups and business commitments.

Groups are often oligarchic in tendency, their leadership being unrepresentative of the views of the membership. Leaders may achieve their domination as a result of their experience and longstanding involvement, many members not having the time or inclination to get more fully involved. This was the case with a number of unions before a change in the law forced them to hold elections for the post of General Secretary. It is important that any government knows that people it talks to do genuinely reflect their members' wishes, and that deals made with leaders will stick because they have the backing of group supporters.

In depth

The representativeness or otherwise of group leadership

Many small private organisations represent the views of a few activists at their head rather than the bulk of their members. They may be run by a handful or less of professional officers. Some downplay the influence of sections of the population, such as women and minorities, not allowing or encouraging the expression of their viewpoints. These considerations cast doubt on the representativeness of their leadership.

Few groups have well-developed electoral arrangements to link the rank and file to those who lead them. But in any case, representative leadership is not necessarily guaranteed by ensuring that leaders are elected. Turnouts in trade union elections are often low.

Furthermore, as we have seen in the case of farmers, many members of the NFU also belong to the breakaway Farmers for Action. In speaking to NFU leaders, Defra ministers and officials might not therefore be hearing a representative statement of the views of the farming community. In any case, within large and influential bodies such as the BMA and the AA, it would be unwise to assume that the leadership speaks for all doctors and motorists respectively. There may be splits or groupings within a group that has doubts about the direction in which the leadership is heading.

Finally, we might recall Michels' 'iron law of oligarchy' (1911) (see p101), which states that even bodies with democratic pretensions tend to become controlled by a ruling oligarchy. His claim was that in modern life (1911, when he wrote) there was a need for large-scale organisations such as trade unions, other pressure groups and churches, but that inevitably they would fall into the hands of a small elite because:

- The leaders better understood the means of internal communication and usually possessed greater skills than the membership.
- Few members had much knowledge of the details of policy or felt the urge to turn up at meetings; they actually wanted the 'direction and guidance' of the leadership.
- Michels argued that the longer the leaders remained in power, the more their own interests and goals might tend to depart from those of the members.

Activities

1. Look up the CPAG website (www.childpoverty.org.uk/campaigns) and find out what it does. On what specific issues is it currently campaigning?

2. What do you think Finer meant by urging 'Light, more light' when talking about the relationship between protective interest groups and Whitehall departments?

3. If you were a government minister, think about whether or not you would be concerned to discover whether a group with which you were dealing was genuinely representative of the supporters it claimed to represent. Does it really matter?

Threatening methods. The very word 'pressure' conjures up an image of threats and coercion, which is why some NGOs dislike it to describe their organisations. Via their unions, certain categories of workers have had the ability to 'hold the country to ransom'. By

Hint

Obviously it is desirable to understand as much as possible about the case for and against groups, but in arguing the case it is always worth ensuring that you have a clear knowledge of and can elaborate (with examples) upon three or four good points on either side.

Further reading

Useful articles:

N Jackson, 'Pressure group politics', *Politics Review*, September 2004.

D Watts, 'Lobbying Europe: an update', *Talking Politics*, September 2004.

D Watts, 'Pressure Group Activity in Post-Devolution Scotland', *Talking Politics*, January 2006.

Useful books:

R Baggott, ***Pressure groups today***, MUP, 1995.

B Coxall, P***ressure Groups in British Politics***, Pearson, 2001.

W Grant, ***Pressure Groups and British Politics***, Palgrave, 2000.

J Greenwood, ***Representing Interests in the European Union***, Macmillan, 1997.

D Watts, ***Pressure Groups***, EUP, 2007.

Useful websites: most individual pressure groups have their own sites that cover such aspects as the history, objectives and organisation of organisations. Some are listed below:

www.cbi.org.uk. Confederation of British Industry.

www.countryside-alliance.org. Countryside Alliance

www.greenpeace.org.uk. Greenpeace.

www.ippr.org.uk IPPR

www.cps.org.uk Centre for Policy Studies

www.demos.co.uk DEMOS

withdrawing their labour, they can disrupt industry or cause havoc in hospitals or schools. Any failure to attend calls by members of the fire service could have appalling repercussions.

Slowing down decision making and acting as a barrier to social progress. Governments can be very critical of group activity, especially when relevant groups are finding out and publicising information that is damaging to their cause. As Home Secretary, David Blunkett, Charles Clarke and John Reid have all at times felt frustrated by the way in which the civil liberties' lobby has been a thorn in their flesh as they tried to introduce legislation on asylum seekers and the prevention of terrorism. They felt that their policies were needed for the protection of society and that campaigners often seemed out of touch with the real concerns of members of the public. Moreover, those groups that oppose developments such as new roads, industrial installations and wind farms may be preventing policies that will be of general benefit to the community. It was for such reasons that a Conservative Home secretary, Douglas Hurd, attacked groups as 'strangling serpents' which created unnecessary work for ministers and made it difficult for them reach decisions in the public interest.

Contrasting views of pressure group activity

The views which pressure groups convey are legitimate interests . . . Modern democracy would not exist without [them]. As a channel of communication, they are as legitimate as the ballot box.

R Baggott (1995)

Militant pressure groups . . . rush to judgement exaggerating their case and in expressing themselves in simplistic terms designed for easy headlines, they undermine both balanced decision-making and parliamentary democracy.

M Dobbs, *The Times*, 13 September 1995

Summary questions

1 On balance, do pressure groups enhance or undermine democracy? Does it make a difference as to whether we are considering a peak group such as the CBI and the TUC or a promotional group such as the National Trust and the RSPB?

2 Is dialogue between pressure groups and government desirable? Is it more acceptable when it concerns a promotional group such as the RSPCA rather than a business or labour interest group?

AQA Examination-style questions

1.   ☑ Read the extract below and answer questions (a) to (c) which follow.

New social movements

In recent decades there has been an explosion in *pressure-group politics*. New social movements have emerged since the 1970s. They tend to have a core group that provides general direction and a loosely organised network of widespread supporters. Often their activities arise at grass-roots level before later evolving into national crusades. They are broadly united around a central idea, issue or concern whose goal is to change attitudes or institutions as well as policies. Characteristic concerns include equality for women and ethnic minorities, the environment and animal rights, globalisation and international peace.

Source: adapted from Chapter 7 of this textbook

(a)	Briefly explain the term *pressure group politics* used in the extract.	*(5 marks)*
(b)	Using your own knowledge as well as the extract, consider the main ways in which new social movements differ from pressure groups.	*(10 marks)*
(c)	'Despite involving mass participation, new social movements have had little political impact'. Discuss.	*(25 marks)*

2.   Read the extract below and answer questions (a) to (c) which follow.

Pressure groups and the media

Insider groups have also used the media to mobilise public support. Well-resourced bodies such as the British Medical Association may be able to fund poster advertisements and press advertising. For most groups of whatever type, these would be an enormous drain on finances. But there are other opportunities to convey their work and achievement. If they can attract the curiosity of journalists by the inherent interest of their campaigns and the vivid images conveyed, the group's cause may receive much media coverage.

Source: adapted from Chapter 8 of this textbook

(a)	Briefly explain the term *insider groups* used in the extract.	*(5 marks)*
(b)	Using your own knowledge as well as the extract, consider the importance of two pressure-group resources other than media exposure.	*(10 marks)*
(c)	'Influential pressure groups prefer to operate in situations where their dealings are concluded in private rather than in the spotlight of media attention.' Discuss.	*(25 marks)*

9 The British Constitution

1 What is a constitution?

Learning objectives:

- What is a constitution?
- Why do countries need constitutions?

Key term

A **constitution** is 'The system or body of fundamental principles according to which a nation state or body politic is constituted and governed' (*OED*).

Fig. 1 *A key document of revolutionary France: the Declaration of the Rights of Man and Citizen 1789*

A **constitution** establishes the rules and principles that govern an organisation. Constitutions are found in many political organisations, in government at several levels, in political parties, pressure groups and trade unions. Non-political bodies such as companies and voluntary organisations may also have constitutions.

In the case of countries, the term refers specifically to a national constitution defining the fundamental political principles, and establishing the structure, procedures, powers and duties, of a government. Every country has a constitution of some kind. When we think of constitutions, we normally have in mind the documents of countries such as France and the US. But countries that do not possess such a single, authoritative statement still possess a constitution. Most national constitutions also include a statement of the rights of the individual.

Specifically, constitutions set out:

- The division of governmental activities, outlining which structures will perform which tasks.
- The power relationships between the various institutions, showing how each is dependent upon or independent of the operations of the others.
- The limitations upon the powers of rulers and guarantees of the rights of the ruled: an explanation of the constraints on the state's authority and a listing of the freedoms of the individual citizen and the benefits to which he or she is entitled from the state.

The purpose and content of constitutions

Constitutions tend to come about as a result of some major internal dissension or upheaval over a period of years, be it civil war or revolution, or defeat in war. Following the dismantling of a governmental structure, those charged with writing a new constitution have to think about how the political system should be organised.

Constitutions have several functions, including to:

- Provide legitimacy to those in power: even non-democratic states have them because their existence gives the appearance of legality.
- Protect freedom: they restrain the behaviour of those in office as they set out what those in authority can do and define the limits of their power.

Key term

Federal countries such as that of the US divide power between a central (federal) government and a number of state or provincial governments, according to a written constitution.

Further information

The standard format of constitutions

- Preamble: often a stirring declaration of principle, perhaps the aims of the state (see p152).
- Organisational section: describing the main institutions of government.
- Bill of rights: a statement of individual freedoms and rights.
- Amendment: the procedure for bringing about constitutional change.

- Encourage governmental stability: they introduce a degree of order and predictability into governmental arrangements, enabling everyone to understand the rules of the political game.
- Draw attention to the goals and values that characterise a particular state. They proclaim a commitment. The 1958 French Constitution solemnly proclaimed 'its attachment to the Rights of Man . . . as defined by the Declaration of 1789, confirmed and completed by the preamble to the Constitution of 1946'.
- Set out the respective spheres of influence of the central and regional/provincial tiers in **federal** countries, such as the US. Each of the US states has its own constitution.
- Create a fresh start, especially after a period of long-term upheaval. The US Constitution followed the War of Independence, just as the West German documents followed defeat of the Hitler dictatorship in World War Two.

Summary questions

1. Why do countries need constitutions?
2. Have they any value?

---

2 Characteristics of the British Constitution

Learning objectives:

- What is the difference between codified and uncodified, flexible and rigid, and unitary and federal constitutions?

- Does Britain have a written constitution?

- What are the main characteristics of the British Constitution?

Constitutions are often classified according to their characteristics. They may be:

1. **Written or unwritten.** The terms are unclear as most of the UK Constitution is written down somewhere, so that it is not technically unwritten. Back in 1963, Kenneth Wheare stressed that rather than having an unwritten constitution, Britain lacked a written one. Given the confusion of terms, it is probably more useful to distinguish between:

   a codified constitutions, in which all the main provisions are brought together in a single document and

   b uncodified constitutions, such as the British one, which exist where many of the constitutional rules are written down but have not been gathered together.

2. **Flexible or rigid.** Flexible constitutions are rare. They can be altered via the law-making process (i.e. by a simple majority in the legislature), as in New Zealand and the UK. In other words, no laws are regarded as fundamental and there is no formal process for constitutional amendment. In rigid constitutions, the principles and institutions assume the character of fundamental law. The procedure

Key terms

The **Executive** is the branch of government responsible for directing the nation's affairs and the initiation and execution of laws and policies, e.g. the UK government.

The **Legislature** is the branch of government responsible for discussing and passing laws (legislation) and acting as a watchdog over the government, e.g. the UK parliament.

Separation of powers is the doctrine that political power should be divided between the Executive, Legislature and Judiciary, in order to prevent an undue concentration of power.

Further information

The separation of powers

The doctrine was first advanced in the 18th century by the French thinker, Baron de Montesquieu.

He identified three branches of power in the government of a country: legislative power (the need for a law-making assembly), executive power (the need for a decision-making body) and judicial power (the need to adjudicate on any violation of the law).

for amendment is therefore deliberately made difficult, so that no change can be made without due consideration and discussion.

3 **Unitary or federal constitutions.** Unitary systems are to be found in countries ranging from Britain to Israel, from France to Ireland. They tend to be especially suitable in smaller countries and in those where there are no significant ethnic, linguistic or religious differences. In unitary systems, all power is concentrated in the hands of the central government, whereas in federal systems there is a division between a federal (central) government and various regional units that may be called states (in the US), lander (in Germany) or provinces (in Belgium). In federal countries the powers and functions of the central authority and the regional unit are clearly defined in a written constitution.

4 Other characteristics that distinguish constitutions are that:

a Some are monarchical, others republican. Today this is not a key distinction as monarchy in democratic states takes the constitutional form. In Britain, Belgium, Denmark, Holland, Norway and Sweden, the monarch reigns by hereditary right; absolute monarchies, in which the rulers' powers are unlimited, are very rare. Republics have no hereditary head of state, but rather someone who is either elected by the people or their elected representatives.

b Some are presidential, others parliamentary – a distinction that informs us about the relationship between the **Executive** and **Legislature**. In presidential constitutions, the two branches of government function independently on the basis of the **separation of powers**, e.g. in the US, the President is elected separately from Congress. In parliamentary systems such as that of the UK, the Executive is chosen from and accountable to the legislature.

c Some are based on the sovereignty of parliament, others on the sovereignty of the people. Britain provides an example of the former, with parliament formally possessing supreme power. The US provides an example of the latter, its constitution opening with the words: 'We the people of the US . . . do ordain and establish this Constitution'. This is in line with Lincoln's definition of democracy (see p3), which refers to government 'of the people'.

Fig. 3 *Baron de Montesquieu*

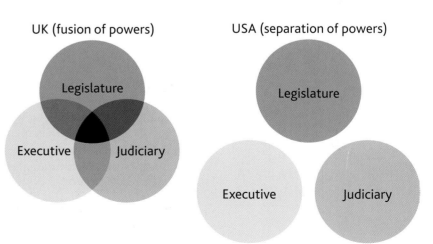

Fig. 2 *The fusion and separation of powers*

152

The constitution of the UK

The UK Constitution comprises an accumulation over many centuries of traditions, customs, conventions, precedents and Acts of parliament that serve as a complex framework within which those who exercise power must operate. It is old by any standards – the oldest constitution in the world – for its origins can be traced back at least to the period after the Norman Conquest in 1066. Constitutional developments have come about gradually.

As we have seen, the UK does not have a written constitution in the sense of a single written document, though substantial elements of it are written in various places. It is largely because of its ancient origins that the British Constitution is so unsystematic. No attempt has been made to collate it and codify the various rules and conventions that are part of it. Yet those who are involved in operating the Constitution generally understand the key issues involved.

Aspects of the UK Constitution: a summary of its key elements

The British Constitution is:

- **uncodified**, there being no single document in which most of the rules concerning the government of the country are brought together
- **unitary** rather than a federal. Parliament at Westminster makes laws for all parts of the UK. Parts of the UK may have powers devolved to them, nonetheless all parts of the UK are subject to the legislative supremacy of parliament
- **flexible**. The Constitution can be amended easily. Even drastic changes can be made by passing an Act of parliament, though there is a developing custom that fundamental changes would probably require a referendum if they have not already been submitted to the electorate in a general election.

The basic elements of the Constitution rest on three major constitutional principles:

1 The sovereignty of parliament: the idea that parliament theoretically possesses and exercises unlimited authority. Parliamentary Sovereignty has traditionally been viewed as a key element of the British Constitution. Constitutional experts such as AV Dicey have proclaimed that parliament has legal sovereignty (absolute and unlimited authority), in that it is the supreme law-making body in Great Britain. Only parliament can make, amend and unmake law, and no other institution can override its decisions. No one parliament can bind its successor; for example, decisions made in the parliament elected in 2005 can be reversed or amended by the one elected in the election that follows.

2 The rule of law: the principle that no one is above the law; that ministers, public authorities and individuals are subject to it. AV Dicey, the foremost constitutional lawyer of the late 19th century, was the person who most clearly articulated the doctrine. He saw it as the cardinal principle of government in a democratic system, one which seeks to equate law and justice. He discerned three ideas in the concept:

   a Equality before the law, with disputes resolved in the courts: people of any class, gender or race are universally subject to one law administered by the courts, whether they are ordinary citizens or servants of the state.

Activity

List any advantages and disadvantages that Britain has from having an uncodified constitution.

■ Key term

Walter Bagehot (1826–77) was a 19th-century essayist, journalist, one-time editor of *The Economist* and author of the classic study, *The English Constitution* (1867).

b The belief that no person should be punished except for a breach of the law, just as no person should be viewed as 'above the law'; laws are clearly published and accessible, so that everyone is capable of knowing what they are.

c The laws of the constitution, especially essential liberties, derive from judicial decisions based on common law. Unlike rules set out in a written constitution, they cannot be removed. (Of course, many liberties are now covered by the Human Rights Act 1998, see p178.)

3 The fusion (rather than the complete separation) of powers: government ministers who head executive departments sit as members of the legislature and are responsible to it. **Walter Bagehot** observed that the key to the success of our constitutional system lay in this fusion of power. The Cabinet makes decisions, but it is derived from parliament. Such an overlap enables power to be coordinated and government to be carried on effectively.

Summary questions

1 What is meant by saying that Britain has a unitary system of government?

2 What are the main principles underlying the British Constitution?

3 The sources of the UK Constitution

Learning objectives:

■ How did the Constitution develop?

■ Where can we look for the Constitution?

■ What impact has membership of European bodies had on the Constitution?

■ Key term

Common law is a body of rules that has evolved over a long period of time. Non-statutory law reflects precedent deriving from centuries of judgments by working judges.

A judicial precedent is a decision of a court of law which is quoted as an authority for future decision making when deciding a case involving a similar set of facts; in other words, it serves as authority for the legal principle embodied in its decision.

Although many of our national institutions have a long history, the role they play is constantly undergoing change. That is why Hanson and Walles have written of the British habit of placing 'new wine in old bottles'.

Because of the way in which our political system has evolved over time, there are many sources that can be consulted in order to locate the elusive Constitution. These include:

■ Major constitutional documents that express important constitutional principles. The Magna Carta (1215) asserted the view that a monarch could and should be controlled by their subjects. It influenced **common law** and documents (such as the US Constitution and the 1689 **Bill of Rights**) and is considered one of the most important legal documents in the history of democracy.

■ Major texts and commentaries by eminent experts on the Constitution that have been so influential in their interpretation of the constitution that they are seen as part of the constitution itself. Bagehot's *The English Constitution* (originally published in 1867) is most noted for distinguishing between the 'dignified' and 'efficient' parts of the Constitution. Bagehot, a Victorian journalist, argued that the genius of the Constitution lay in its ability to combine the gradualism of continuity with the capacity for adaptation.

Major statutes (Acts of parliament) that have an impact on the constitutional structure, in that they have changed the way we are governed or the relationships within the state. For example, the Wales Act 1998 established the Welsh National Assembly. The nature and operation of UK electoral systems and the structures and powers of local government are both matters covered primarily in statutes.

The prerogative powers of the Crown. The Royal Prerogative comprises a number of powers or privileges performed in the past by the monarch, but now performed in his or her name by ministers. Their authority derives from the Crown rather than from parliament, so that parliamentary authority is not required by the Executive as it conducts these tasks. Prerogative powers are exercised by ministers individually or collectively. They include the rights to exercise mercy (a prerogative of the Home Secretary), to declare war and make treaties, and dispense honours (duties performed by the Prime Minister and his colleagues).

The law and customs of parliament, the rules relating to the procedures of the House and the privileges of its members. These are set out in a book sometimes consulted by the **Speaker of the House of Commons**, Erskine May's *Treatise on the Law, Privileges, Proceedings and Usages of Parliament* (originally published in 1844). The analysis is regarded as the authoritative commentary on the interpretation of parliamentary rules, a sort of parliamentary bible.

Common and case (judge-made) law. In common-law legal systems, judges have the authority and duty to decide what the law is in the absence of any other authoritative statement. Common law is a body of rules that has evolved over a long period of time. It is the traditional basis in Britain of the right to free speech and free assembly, which have over time been implemented by judges. Judicial decisions have been important in establishing individual rights in relation to those in authority.

Judges have for centuries had an important role in deciding how any law, whether common or statute, should apply in a particular case. A body of case law has been developed over the years, until eventually a new statute tidies up areas of uncertainty. The growing use of **judicial review** (see pp173–174) in recent decades has enabled judges to make important decisions on the justice and fairness of particular laws, and thereby to influence government policy. The importance of judges in our constitutional arrangements has been further increased by the passage of the **Human Rights Act 1998**.

Constitutional conventions. **Conventions** are unwritten rules that guide our constitutional behaviour, customs of political practice that are usually accepted and observed. Examples include the general recognition that the choice of Prime Minister should be made from the House of Commons and that the proceedings of the Cabinet should be kept secret; the concepts of individual and collective cabinet responsibility (see p221), both of which have been modified in recent years; and the formal requirement that the sovereign will always give consent to any bill that has passed through its parliamentary stages (no bill has been rejected by the monarch since 1707).

European Union law. By joining the European Community (now the European Union) in 1973, the UK agreed to accept a body of constitutional law that had already been passed on the creation of the EC. It continues to be bound by European law. This includes primary legislation (as found in the **Treaty of Rome** and the other treaties) and secondary law (as found in EU **regulations** and

Key terms

The Bill of Rights 1689 is an Act of parliament which has become a basic document of English constitutional law. It is largely a statement of certain positive rights which its authors considered that citizens living under a constitutional monarchy ought to possess.

The **Speaker of the House of Commons** is the non-partisan officer of the House of Commons who presides over its debates, determines which members may speak and is responsible for maintaining order during debate.

Judicial review is the power of the courts to overturn executive or legislative actions they hold to be illegal or unconstitutional. The UK has a weak form; the courts can review executive actions, deciding whether the Executive has acted *ultra vires* (beyond its powers), unfairly or without reference to relevant facts.

The **Human Rights Act 1998** is the statute which incorporated most of the rights contained in the European Convention on Human Rights into UK law. It provides a remedy in UK courts for any breach of a Convention right, without the need for the complainant to go to the European Court of Human Rights in Strasbourg.

Conventions are unwritten rules which govern political conduct. They are traditionally regarded as binding, but have no legal force.

Treaty of Rome (1957) is the agreement signed by six western European countries to establish the European Economic Community, now known as the European Union (EU).

Regulations are a type of European law which is binding on all Member States of the EU without the need for any national legislation.

Key terms

Directives are a type of European law which is binding on all EU Member States as to the result to be achieved, but can be implemented as best suits the needs of individual countries.

The **Factortame** case was a landmark constitutional case (involving a fishing dispute) in the UK, which confirmed the primacy of EU law over UK law.

Activity

Using the internet to assist you, look up the details of the following statutes which all have an impact on the Constitution. Write a brief paragraph about two of them:

- The Life Peerages Act 1958.
- The European Communities Act 1972.
- The Human Rights Act 1998.
- The Scotland Act 1998.
- The Freedom of Information Act 2000.

directives). European law takes precedence over UK law, is binding on the UK and applicable by UK courts. In several cases, pieces of European economic and social legislation have conferred important rights on British workers, as in the area of equal pay. The impact of membership was made very apparent in the **Factortame** case (*Factortame Ltd & Ors* v *Secretary of State for Transport*, ECJ case C-213/89, ECJ decision 19 June 1990) which illustrated how the courts can overrule parliamentary legislation which conflicts with Community law.

The UK Constitution is a model that has been followed by many other countries, and peoples in other countries who have long been denied their rights have seen Britain as an inspiration. As Wade and Phillips (1998) put it, the Constitution 'embraces laws, customs and conventions hammered out, as it were, on the anvil of experience'. The British approach has been empirical (based on practical experience), making adjustments as necessary. No attempt has been made to bring together the various constitutional laws and rulings.

Summary questions

1 Where can we look for the UK Constitution?

2 What is meant by judicial review? Does the UK have it?

4 The UK Constitution in flux: constitutional change, theory and practice

Learning objectives:

- Why have several countries revised or rewritten their constitutions?

- Why did many academics and commentators think that the UK Constitution should be reformed?

- What measures of constitutional reform have the Labour government introduced?

■ The worldwide growth of interest in constitutional revision

Constitutions are solemn and binding documents that are meant to last. They have a certain timeless quality about them and are seemingly eternal features of the political scene. However, they are liable to undergo fundamental change. Indeed, most European constitutions are 20th-century creations. The Swiss version is now the oldest on the continent, dating from 1874.

In recent decades, interest in constitutions and constitutional matters has developed in many parts of the world. Some constitutions have been rewritten, others revised. More than two-thirds of those now in existence have been drawn up since the end of the Second World War. The purpose of this writing and revising of constitutions has been the same in most cases, i.e. to bring the formal documents up to date and make them more in tune with the country's governing arrangements.

Doubts about the UK Constitution: the case for constitutional renewal

From the 1960s, many thinkers and writers began to urge the cause of 'constitutional reform'. It became a fashionable topic for discussion among the chattering classes. It has been on the political agenda ever since. There were specific concerns such as the case for devolution of power to Scotland and Wales in the 1970s and 1980s, but subsequent concern has been more wide ranging.

Those who favoured constitutional change suggested that:

- Whereas in the past the flexibility of the Constitution had been regarded as an asset, the basis of good government, from the 1970s there were increasing doubts about the effectiveness of some institutions. The political system seemed less successful in 'delivering the goods' than it had been. In particular, there were serious problems at the periphery with the rise of **nationalism** in Scotland and Wales, serious disruption in Northern Ireland, a stagnant economy, poor industrial relations and other signs of political discontent. Commentators began to wonder if constitutional malaise was at the root of many problems.

- The UK's Constitution was in any case undergoing change. By signing up to the European Convention on Human Rights (especially by allowing individuals to appeal to Strasbourg), ministers were acknowledging that decisions made in Europe had an impact on the fate of political events in Britain. It was a matter for the UK government whether or not to accept the judgments of the European Court of Human Rights. Membership of the European Community/Union after 1973 had a more direct impact on the Constitution. European Community law took, and still takes, precedence over British law, thus undermining the traditional doctrine of the sovereignty of parliament.

Key terms

Nationalism is the desire of a nation to be recognised as a state, e.g. Scottish nationalists want Scotland to be governed by the Scots.

Quangos are publicly funded bodies that operate at arm's length from a government department and carry out executive and advisory functions. Their members are not elected and therefore are not accountable to the voters.

In depth

Quangos

The acronym stands for Quasi Autonomous Non-governmental Organisations.

Examples connected to the Department of Health include:

- Advisory Committee on Novel Foods and Processes.
- Advisory Committee on the Microbiological Safety of Food.
- Committee on Toxicity of Chemicals in Food, Consumer Products and the Environment.
- Expert Group on Vitamins and Minerals.
- Human Tissue Authority.
- National Blood Authority.
- UK Transplant.

In the autumn of 2007, the Economic Research Council found that:

- there were 883 quangos in existence
- two hundred had been created in the previous two years, among them the School Food Trust
- collectively they spent £170bn in 2005–06.

The report criticised the number, cost, secrecy and unaccountability of quangos.

Government in the UK was becoming increasingly powerful and undemocratic. After 1979, in particular, some academics worried about the increasing centralisation of government, a process being intensified by the era of one-party (Conservative) dominance. Prime Minister Thatcher developed a very personal style of leadership; other agencies such as the Cabinet and the civil service lost power. Some pointed to the steady erosion of the functions and powers of local government, the increased number of quangos and the limitations on human rights. Given such dangers, if a fully fledged written constitution was not a priority, we certainly needed measures to reform the House of Lords, increase personal rights, bring in freedom of information legislation and other things which might shift power from Whitehall in favour of the citizen. As it was, the state was becoming too powerful, with too few checks and balances.

Attitudes to change: the debate for and against

Radical reformers took the view that fundamental change was required. In their view, the balance of the constitution had been undermined by the era of prolonged Conservative rule (1979–97). They wanted to address important issues of centralisation, accountability and human rights. Many of them, including the pressure group **Charter 88**, urged the introduction of a package of constitutional measures ranging from a written constitution to a reformed, democratic second chamber, and from a Bill of Rights to an independent, reformed **judiciary**.

By contrast, moderate reformers such as Philip Norton conceded that there was a need for change, but their purpose was 'to strengthen the existing framework, not destroy it'. Norton argued for the strengthening of parliament, the abolition or reduction of quangos and the devolving of more power to citizens at the local level. In the *Observer*, the academic and writer Andrew Adonis (later to be a Blairite adviser (and then a minister) on educational policy) outlined the case for more moderate change:

> Ardent reformers claim that Britain is appallingly governed and barely democratic . . . In reality, Britain is seriously democratic and comparatively well governed. For all its shortcomings, I am hard put to name countries of a similar size or larger which on any long view have been better, more democratically governed. Germany is the only contender, though for less than fifty years . . . The case for reform is not that Britain's governance is chronically bad, but that it could be so much better. It could be so if Westminster revived its once proud tradition of incremental reform to adapt Britain's governing institutions to the times . . . since the First World War, inflexibility has been the rule.

Most Conservatives did not embrace the case for constitutional change. They saw little scope for substantial improvement in our constitutional arrangements. In their 1997 manifesto, they stressed the importance of the 'strength and stability of our Constitution – the institutions, laws and traditions that bind us together as a nation'. They feared that 'radical changes' might endanger 'the whole character of our constitutional balance' and 'unravel what generations of our predecessors have created'. In other words, the Constitution is a delicate flower and to tamper with something that has grown so organically could imperil the whole.

Most of the interest in reform came from the Centre-Left. Labour and the Liberal Democrats held joint discussions on the issue of constitutional reform for several months prior to the 1997 election. In its 1997

Key terms

Charter 88 is a campaigning pressure group set up 300 years after the Glorious Revolution to urge the case for constitutional and electoral reform. The Glorious Revolution (1688) was the overthrow of King James II of England in 1688 by a combination of parliamentarians and Prince William of Orange, aka the 'bloodless revolution'.

The **judiciary** is the branch of government responsible for interpreting and applying the laws in particular cases, e.g. the British judges.

manifesto, Labour criticised British government as 'centralised, inefficient and bureaucratic'. It wanted 'measured and sensible reform' to open up government, improve the quality of our democracy and decentralise power. To remedy this situation, it outlined a series of proposed reforms along the lines of the package agreed with the Liberal Democrats.

Governmental action since 1997

Following Labour's victory in 1997, constitutional reform was introduced at a remarkable pace. Three measures stand out as having a particularly high profile – the removal of most of the hereditary peers from the Lords, the passing of the Human Rights Act 1998 and the creation of devolved machinery in Scotland and Wales, all of which are discussed in the appropriate sections of this book.

Other governmental action on constitutional reform

In addition to those mentioned immediately above, a number of other changes have been introduced since 1997:

- The Freedom of Information Act, operative from 2005 (citizens have been given a right to view information held about them and much internal detail relating to the work of government has been made accessible).
- The creation of the office of an elected London Mayor and Greater London Assembly via a referendum: other cities have been given the opportunity to have city mayors.
- The use of proportional representation for elections to devolved bodies in the UK, European parliament and London Assembly and the establishment of the Jenkins enquiry to examine the system used for Westminster elections.
- Changes to modernise the House of Commons, such as the creation of more reasonable hours and the payment of Select Committee chairpersons.

Fig. 4 *The new building of the Supreme Court, the Middlesex Guildhall*

Key term

The **Supreme Court** is the body created to act as the final court of appeal in all matters under English, Welsh and Northern Irish law, from 2009. In effect, it takes over the judicial functions of the House of Lords.

- The creation of regional machinery: voters in the North East were given the chance to opt for the establishment of an elected assembly in their region (they overwhelmingly rejected the idea).

- The principle of referendums to determine constitutional change has been more widely embraced and legislation passed in 2000 to set out the terms for such votes.

Finally, the Constitutional Reform Act 2005 has been passed. This is the most important shake up in relations between the Executive and the judiciary for many years. It provides for the creation of a new **Supreme Court** to take over the judicial work of the House of Lords and a reduced role for the Lord Chancellor. In future, appointments to the judiciary will be made by a new Judicial Appointments Commission.

5 Assessment of the changes since 1997

Learning objectives:

- What are the merits of the Labour government's programme of constitutional renewal?

- Does the UK need a written constitution?

In favour

The general case for the package of reform is that the Constitution was in need of repair, the subject having been neglected over the years. It was time to tackle some of the criticisms that had been levelled against it for many years. What the Labour government has done amounts to a major and unprecedented constitutional change, with several key bills having been passed into law. Of course, there are gaps and things that might have been done differently, but nonetheless little or none of this package would have been achieved if Labour had not been in power. No 20th-century government has attempted so much in the constitutional arena. This is in marked contrast to constitutional change in the past, which has always evolved slowly and over a long period of time.

The changes have come about without too much controversy, partly because of Labour's majority but also because Labour has learned from the difficulties of earlier administrations, e.g. it held referendums prior to the parliamentary passage of devolution, thereby allowing the public to settle the substantive issue and parliament to fill in the details. Similarly, it has adopted a gradualist, step-by-step approach over the House of Lords, getting rid of the hereditaries before embarking on discussion of the alternatives (a much more contentious matter). Tony Blair had written in the *Guardian* (1995) of the need to carry people with him: 'there is a very great danger that groups like Charter 88 and other constitutional enthusiasts get so far ahead of where the public is that you fail to take them along'.

The changes can also be defended by reference to the merits of specific changes, such as the legislation on human rights and freedom of information.

Against

From the political Right, the general attack might be that a package of change was unnecessary, unwanted and undesirable. There was little interest among the public on constitutional matters because it is a subject of concern only to academics, political anoraks and groups like Charter 88. Moreover, there were dangers in interfering with a structure that has evolved over the years, because in tackling one problem you may cause another. Some Conservatives also point out that for all the talk of decentralisation, Tony Blair acquired more personal power.

From the Centre-Left, the attack (or rather, the sense of disappointment) might be that some changes have not gone far enough. As Labour got nearer to power, so it became more timid. Government ministers tend to be more timid than shadow ministers, knowing that constitutional changes can create difficulties for themselves.

Other criticisms are that:

- Labour in office has been determined to strengthen its strategic hold on government and policy making, so that in spite of the changes introduced there has been more personalised and centralised government with too much power in the hands of the Prime Minister and centred on 10 Downing Street.
- This wish to control has been evident in the House of Commons where there has been an attempt to impose very strict **party discipline** and management that has undermined any attempts made to improve parliament's ability to act as a watchdog over the Executive.
- Many of the reforms have been piecemeal, responding to particular problems. There has not been an overall theme, consistently applied. For instance, in seeking to reform the electoral system, we have ended up with several different ones in use for different levels of election.

Of course, the proposals can also be criticised on a more specific basis. Each individual measure is open to scrutiny. In some cases, reforms have either not worked as well as might have been hoped or have created their own difficulties.

A written constitution for the UK?

There has been much debate about whether the UK should have a written constitution. In a number of public addresses (e.g. the Hamlyn Lectures of Lord Scarman in 1974, the pronouncements by politicians and judges, and publications by bodies such as Charter 88) there have been calls for a fresh start on the Constitution to provide a more clear-cut statement of our constitutional arrangements.

Does the UK need a written constitution?

Yes, it does!

- Because the Constitution has evolved over centuries and is uncodified, there is nowhere where it can easily be seen. It has been added to from time to time and new sources have arisen such as the EU. A written document would provide a clear statement of what is constitutional, removing the uncertainty of such things as the role of the Monarch in the event of a **hung parliament** after an election. This is perhaps even more desirable in an era of constitutional change as bodies such as the EU are now so important.

Key terms

Party discipline is the system of maintaining order within the parliamentary parties. MPs are expected to 'toe the party line' by voting in favour of their parties' proposals in the House of Commons.

A **hung parliament** is a parliament in which no single party has sufficient support to form an administration by itself, creating a situation where a coalition or minority government has to be formed.

Key terms

Elective dictatorship is the term coined by Lord Hailsham to describe the constitutional imbalance in which executive power has increased and parliamentary power diminished. His argument was that a government armed with a strong majority in the House of Commons, assisted by strong party discipline, could drive its programme through the chamber.

Question Time is the daily opportunity for back-benchers in parliament to ask questions of government ministers, which they are obliged to answer. Question Time originated in the Westminster system of the UK, but it also occurs in several other countries as well. Questions to the British Prime Minister take place every Wednesday, 12–12.30pm.

- There has been a strong tendency to executive dominance in British government, hence the complaint about Britain having an 'elective dictatorship' or Prime Ministerial (or even presidential) government (see pp236–238). The government of the day can change the rules in its own interests. Tony Blair was able to remove one session of Prime Minister's **Question Time** in the House of Commons, without any consultation with other parties, just as his government changed the electoral system and the composition of the House of Lords. Governments with a strong majority can pass even the most controversial measures.

- It would provide an up-to-date statement of our rights, more relevant to our age than the European Convention which is now more than 50 years old.

- Key provisions would be entrenched (i.e. firmly established and difficult to amend).

- It would be easier for the courts to interpret what is lawful behaviour and uphold the Constitution.

- It would have an educative value, highlighting the values of the political system. It would also encourage politicians to ensure that in taking action and making decisions they were careful not to exceed the bounds of constitutional behaviour.

No, it doesn't!

- The Constitution seems to work generally well, having survived over several hundred years and provided the country with liberty and stability.

- There is no widespread demand for or interest in change.

- The flexibility of British arrangements enables us to make adjustments as needs demand so that the constitution evolves according to circumstances – 'new wine in old bottles'.

- The protection of rights has generally been good; there may be occasional blemishes, but compared to many countries Britain has a strong record in respecting individual liberty. In contrast, the existence of a written constitution in the former Soviet Union did not guarantee respect for personal freedom, neither does the Zimbabwean one today. Even in a democracy such as the US, the voting rights of black Americans were long denied.

The negative defence includes the following:

- the difficulty in devising a new constitution which commands general approval, particularly as the present arrangements are contained in such a variety of sources

- the fact that written constitutions can be inflexible

- the suggestion that even with a written constitution, there is no absolute guarantee of rights

- the fact that written constitutions do not necessarily prove durable (France has had more than a dozen since 1789; in Europe only a few countries such as Switzerland have constitutions pre-dating 1914).

Further reading

Two short articles provide a brief but useful assessment of recent developments:

N Smith, 'New Labour and constitutional reform', *Talking Politics*, September 2001.

A Granath, 'Constitutional reform: a work in progress', *Talking Politics*, April 2002.

Two more detailed, analytical studies are offered by:

D Beetham, P Ngan and S Weir, 'Democratic audit: Labour's record so far', *Parliamentary Affairs*, 54, 2001.

R Hazell, R Masterman, M Sandord, B Seyd and J Croft, 'The Constitution: coming in from the cold', *Parliamentary Affairs*, 54, 2002.

Books include:

A Lansley and R Wilson, ***Conservatives and the Constitution***, Conservative 2000 Foundation, 1997.

R Blackburn and R Plant (ed.), ***Constitutional Reform: the Labour Government's Constitutional Reform Agenda***, Longman, 1999.

N Forman, ***Constitutional Change in the UK***, Routledge, 2002.

A King, ***Does the UK Still Have a Constitution?***, Sweet and Maxwell, 2001.

J Morrison, *Reforming Britain: **New Labour, New Constitution?***, Reuters/Pearson Educational, 2001.

K Harrison and T Boyd, ***The Changing Constitution***, EUP, 2006.

Websites:

Charter 88 offers a pro-reform look at constitutional issues at www. charter88.org.uk.

The Constitution Unit provides an academic analysis of the changes made and contemplated at www.ucl.ac.uk/constitution-unit.

Summary questions

1. Has Labour's programme of constitutional reform been a success?

2. 'The UK needs a written constitution'. Consider the pros and cons of such a document.

3. Do you agree with the following statement made by Menzies Campbell in the *Guardian* (6 September 2007)?

   A written constitution is essential to ensure that the sovereignty of the citizen is established . . . We propose a constitutional convention, at least 50% of which would be composed of members of the public drawn by a lot. This will put the political process on a real jury trial . . . People need to be involved, not just consulted.

10 The judiciary

1 The judiciary and its independence

Learning objectives:

- What is the judiciary?
- What is the role of judges?
- Why is the independence of the judiciary important?
- How is it secured in Britain?

The judiciary is the branch of government responsible for the adjudication of law and the arbitration between parties in any legal dispute. The term includes those individuals and bodies (primarily judges and the courts) involved in administering and interpreting the meaning of laws. In democratic countries, it is expected that the judicial system will be able to function freely without any interference from the government of the day.

The roles of judges and their increasing political significance

Judges are involved in the interpretation of the constitution and – in countries with judicial review – in ensuring that laws passed are in accordance with its wording and spirit. But their political role goes beyond this. The meaning of other laws may be unclear and this ambiguity may have political implications. Sometimes legislation is vague because it has emerged as a result of bargaining between competing parties and groups. In these circumstances, judges interpret what the law means and set out how it should be applied in particular cases. In so doing, they sometimes go beyond mere interpretation and actually modify the law. Therefore, they can play an important political role as the third branch of government.

Around the world, judges are taking a more active political role and have become increasingly significant actors in the political system. The traditional dividing line between politics and the law has become blurred. Many people trust their judgement and expertise, regarding them as an independent and incorruptible source of experience and wisdom. However, their greater willingness to step into the political arena and concern themselves with issues affecting public policy has created unease among some elected politicians who see their policy-making role as being under threat.

Judges perform several functions:

- **They preside over criminal trials for serious offences**, being responsible for all matters of **criminal law** (determining what it means and how it applies in changing circumstances) and making sure that all of the rules of procedure are properly applied.
- **They deliver sentences**, giving what they believe to be an appropriate sentence – maybe imprisonment or, in cases where the guilty person presents no obvious danger, a community punishment.
- **They peacefully resolve civil disputes between individuals**, adjudicating (giving a decision) in controversies within the limits of the **civil law** and awarding compensation or making a legally binding order for the parties to behave in a particular way.
- **They uphold the will of the legislature**, acting as guardians of the law, taking responsibility for applying its rules without fear or favour,

as well as securing the liberties of the person and ensuring that governments and people comply with the spirit of the constitution.

- Particularly in states with a codified constitution, **they have responsibility for judicial review** of particular laws and administrative actions.
- In the case of senior judges, **they may be asked to chair enquiries**, e.g. the Hutton enquiry in the aftermath of the invasion of Iraq.
- If they are Law Lords, **they sit in parliament**, contributing to its debates on public policy and sharing in the various tasks performed by the House of Lords. Under the terms of the Constitutional Reform Act (CRA), from 2009 they will instead operate in the new Supreme Court.

The role of the courts is tending to widen for several reasons:

- **The expanding role of government**, with more legislation on which to adjudicate.
- **The increasing complexity of governmental machinery, which means that there is more likelihood of conflict between branches and levels of government**, especially in federal countries or where new supranational machinery has been created (as with the European Union, see pp297–298).
- **An increasing emphasis on the rule of law and the rights of citizens** which may be written down in a bill or charter of rights, e.g. the Human Rights Act 1998 in Britain.
- **An increasing willingness on the part of groups and individuals to use the courts as a means of getting their demands met**, sometimes for compensation ('the culture of litigation').
- **An unwillingness on the part of politicians to deal with some sensitive issues**, including some matters that have clear moral implications (e.g. abortion, stem cell research); they are happy to leave these for the courts to resolve.

■ The administration of justice in the UK

For many years, some commentators have argued the case for having a Ministry of Justice. They pointed to inadequacies in the judicial system and difficulties in obtaining information in the House of Commons because of the division of legal functions between the Lord Chancellor and Home Secretary. They wanted to see a single 'Minister of Justice' at the head of a department with undivided responsibility for the administrative aspects of the judicial system.

Under the new arrangements that operate from 2007:

- The **Ministry of Justice** is the department which has assumed responsibility for sentencing policy, probation, prisons and prevention of re-offending in England and Wales. It is responsible for dealing with all suspected offenders from the time they are arrested, through until convicted offenders are released from prison.
- At its head is the Lord Chancellor who retains the roles and responsibilities given to him under the Constitutional Reform Act 2005. He or she is now known as the **Secretary of State for Justice and Lord Chancellor** (The Lord Chief Justice has responsibility for the system of courts and judges).
- The **Home Secretary** retains responsibility for the police and the security service, as well as oversight of crime reduction, counter terrorism and other crime-related areas.

Fig. 1 *Ticket of entry to the Hutton enquiry*

■ Further information

The Lord Chancellor and Lord Chief Justice

Since the passage of the CRA 2005 the Lord Chief Justice is the overall head of the judiciary. The office of Lord Chancellor has lost most of its judicial functions. He/she:

- is Secretary of State for Justice and Lord Chancellor
- is no longer a judge (but still exercises disciplinary authority over the judges, jointly with the Lord Chief Justice)
- has a role in appointing judges.

Fig. 2 *Lord Phillips, current Lord Chief Justice*

The Court Structure of Her Majesty's Courts Service (HMCS)

Her Majesty's Courts Service carries out administrative and support work for the Court of Appeal, the High Court, the Crown Court, the magistrates' courts, the county courts and the Probate Service.

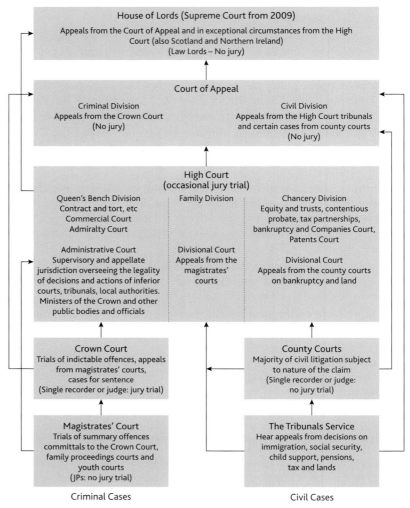

Fig. 3 *The court structure*

Key elements of the legal system

There are many different kinds of courts, judges and legal professionals.

Magistrates' courts are usually made up of three people from the local community who have no professional legal qualifications and are unpaid. They are known as lay magistrates or Justices of the Peace (JPs). They hear well over 95 per cent of all criminal cases in England and Wales. The magistrates receive training to give them sufficient knowledge of the law and of the nature and purpose of sentencing. A court clerk advises them on law and procedure. In some circumstances, district judges preside over magistrates' courts instead of JPs. Legally qualified and salaried, they tend to deal with longer and more complex cases and also have jurisdiction to hear cases involving extradition.

Judges preside over the Crown and County Courts and a range of higher courts. They may be assisted by a jury in the Crown Courts. There is no jury if the accused pleads guilty and the case is limited to the matter of sentencing.

In depth

Types of courts

- Crown courts deal with criminal offences. These are usually presided over by circuit judges, in the most serious and sensitive cases by High Court judges, and in less complex ones by recorders.

- County courts deal with civil offences, and these are presided over by circuit judges. In the case of substantial or complex cases, they are dealt with by the High Court.

- The Court of Appeal (Criminal Division) deals with appeals from Crown Courts. These are usually presided over by one Appeal Court and two senior High Court judges. The Civil Division hears appeals from the High Court and in some instances County Courts. It is usually presided over by two or three Appeal Court judges.

- The House of Lords (Supreme Court) is the highest court of appeal, presided over by law lords, known technically as Lords of Appeal in Ordinary. From October 2009, they will sit in the new Supreme Court.

Barristers and solicitors generally represent the interests of the disputing parties.

The Attorney General and the Solicitor-General are the government's main legal advisers. They may also represent the Crown in difficult or publicly important domestic and international cases.

In depth

The role of juries

- Juries have long been portrayed as bastions of British liberty. Trial by jury dates back to the period after the Norman Conquest and became customary during the reign of Henry II in the late twelfth century. It is seen as a cardinal feature of justice that the guilt of those charged with a criminal offence should be determined by their peers, bringing the law closer to the people. This is seen as a bulwark against oppression, particularly valuable when the decision involves a consideration of how actions or remarks would be interpreted by the everyday man or woman. Juries provide ordinary people with an opportunity for active participation in the affairs of government. If jurors make an error, it is more likely to be on the side of the accused. For these reasons, the public have faith in the jury system.

- Critics allege that juries are inappropriate to deal with highly technical cases and some civil cases involving the awarding of damages. ('Considerable' damages may mean different things according to the standards of living of those sitting in a particular court.) Sometimes, trials last over several days or weeks, so that jurors, equipped with no special training, have to follow arguments and evidence which can be highly complex.

■ Recent legislation, such as the Criminal Justice Act 2004, has restricted the right of jury trial in some cases.

■ Juries sit in a few civil cases, in particular, defamation and cases involving the state.

The independence of the judiciary and how it is secured

In many states, the constitution provides for an independent judiciary. Its existence is a fundamental characteristic of liberal democracies. Judicial independence implies that there should be a strict separation between the judiciary and other branches of government. It is expected that the judicial system will be able to function freely and without any interference from the government of the day.

In some states the judiciary is under constant pressure to deliver verdicts acceptable to the regime and those who exhibit a passion for justice can find themselves under considerable pressure. In other parts of the non-Western world such as India, there is a strong independent judiciary. The independence or otherwise of the judiciary is a key difference between authoritarian and liberal states.

Judicial independence in Britain

The independence of the British judiciary is supposed to be protected in three main ways:

■ the way in which judges are selected

■ their security of tenure

■ their political neutrality.

In addition:

■ There is a tradition that the remarks and sentences of judges in court cases should not be subject to parliamentary debate or criticism. In the words of Lord Hailsham, parliamentary criticism is 'subversive of the independence of the judiciary'. The tradition is sometimes breached because politicians sometimes become irritated by the observations of 'meddlesome' judges and especially by the allegedly lenient sentences they impose. They may make their views known in the House of Commons.

■ Those involved in court proceedings – judges, juries, lawyers, witnesses and the accused – are all granted immunity from the laws of defamation for any comments made in court that attack someone's good name or reputation.

■ The independence of the judiciary is also protected by the fact that judges receive fixed salaries not subject to parliamentary approval.

Summary questions

1 In what ways have the courts in many countries become increasingly involved in politics?

2 Is the British judiciary independent?

2 The selection and security of judges

Learning objectives:

- How have senior judges been appointed in the past?
- How has the method of appointment changed?
- What are the typical backgrounds of senior judges?
- Can judges be removed?

Key term

The Bar comprises lawyers who are qualified as barristers. They are collectively known as 'members of the bar'.

In Britain, judges have traditionally been appointed by the government of the day. The most senior ones were appointed by the Prime Minister following consultation with the Lord Chancellor. High Court judges, Circuit judges and magistrates were appointed by the Lord Chancellor, mostly from the ranks of senior barristers known as QCs (Queen's Council). The dangers were that appointment

- became a means of rewarding relatives and friends (nepotism) and
- meant that people were not chosen because of their judicial merit but rather because of their political leanings and known views on matters of public life (partisanship).

New arrangements were announced by the Lord Chancellor in mid-2003 and subsequently included within the framework of the Constitutional Reform Act 2005. A new Judicial Appointments Commission now examines the way in which judicial appointments are made. It puts forward nominations, and there are clear restrictions on the ability of the Lord Chancellor to reject them. For appointments to the new Supreme Court, the minister should receive only one name from the Commission.

What sort of people are appointed as judges?

Many judges reached their eminence having practised at **the Bar**, the membership of which has long been held to be elitist and unrepresentative. As a result of the manner of selection and the choice available, judges have usually been people born into the professional middle classes, often educated at public school and then Oxbridge. They have tended to be wealthy, conservative in their thinking, middle aged when first appointed (in their sixties before they attain a really powerful position in the House of Lords or Court of Appeal) and – like so many people in positions of power in British life – out of touch with the lives of people from different backgrounds. Critics have sometimes complained that they are unable to understand the habits and terminology of everyday life, reflecting instead the social thinking of 30 or 40 years ago. In particular, they have doubted the ability of such people to preside over cases involving highly politicised argument on issues of human rights and civil liberties. Of course, recruitment patterns are not necessarily a guide to judicial opinions. People from a privileged background can still hold socially liberal views.

Table 1 *Women and ethnic minorities on the Bench as at 1 April 2007*

Rank	No. of women	No. of ethnic minorities
Lords of Appeal in Ordinary (12)	1	0
Heads of Division (5)	0	0
Lord Justices of Appeal (37)	3	0
High Court judges (108)	10	1
Circuit judges (639)	73	9
Recorders (1201)	179	53
Recorders in training (5)	3	0
District judges (450)	101	14
Deputy district judges (780)	219	30
District judges in magistrates' court (139)	33	7
Deputy district judges in magistrates' court (169)	42	9
Overall total (3,545)	664	123

NB: Figures in brackets represent the total number of each category.

Source: Figures adapted from those provided by the Department for Constitutional Affairs

169

In depth

The reputation of British judges

Several decades ago, Lord Chief Justice Hewart told a gathering at the Lord Mayor's Banquet that: 'Her Majesty's judges are satisfied with the almost universal admiration in which they are held'. Today, the remark seems breathtakingly arrogant and complacent.

Some comments made by judges in the 1970s and 1980s stirred up considerable controversy:

- In the 1970s, Lord Denning suggested that 'blacks' should not serve on British juries because of their 'alien' cultural backgrounds.
- In a case involving attempted rape, one judge remarked: 'Women who say no do not always mean no. If she does not want it, she only has to keep her legs shut and she would not get it without force and there would be marks of force being used'.
- During a murder trial, Lord Donaldson (Denning's successor as Master of the Rolls) famously asked for an answer to his question: 'What is snogging?'

Such comments were made a generation ago. More optimistic observers would suggest that the values and opinions of judges have to some extent changed in the light of changing social attitudes.

Activity

Write a couple of paragraphs arguing the case for having:

- more women on the Bench and
- more members of ethnic minorities on the Bench.

The social background of judges has changed less than that of senior civil servants or even diplomats. Overwhelmingly, they are white, male, upper middle aged and upper middle class. At the turn of the 20th century all of the Law Lords were men, educated at Oxford or Cambridge, half of them were from three colleges that have a traditional reputation as 'nurseries for lawyers'. Their average age in mid-2003 was 68.5 years.

The security of tenure of judges

Once installed in office, judges normally retain their position, subject to their good conduct. They should not be liable to removal on the whim of particular governments or individuals.

In Britain, the Act of Settlement 1701 established that judges be appointed for life. They are very hard to remove and serve until the time of their retirement. Today, those who function in superior courts are only liable to dismissal on grounds of misbehaviour. This can be done only after a vote of both Houses of Parliament and has not actually happened in the 20th or 21st centuries. Neither are lower judges normally dismissed. Dismissal only applies in cases of dishonesty, incompetence or misbehaviour. In 1983, one judge was dismissed for whisky smuggling!

Summary questions

1. Does the background of judges matter?
2. Are judges out of touch with attitudes and behaviour in modern society?

3 Judicial neutrality

Learning objectives:

- Do judges simply administer the law?

- What is 'judicial activism'?

- Should judges keep out of politics?

- Why are politicians wary of judges?

Activity

Make a list of the ways in which judges become involved in our political life.

Key terms

Judicial activism is the idea that the courts should be active partners in shaping public policy. Supporters see the courts as having a role in looking after groups denied political influence or clout. Opponents portray them as being excessively liberal, pro criminal and soft on crime.

Kilmuir Guidelines are principles set out by the then Lord Chancellor that restricted the freedom of judges to speak out on matters of public policy.

By convention, judges are above and beyond politics, apolitical beings who interpret but do not make the law. As such, their discretion is limited. But such a view is naïve and a series of distinguished British judges from Denning to Devlin, from Radcliffe to Reid, has acknowledged that their role is much more creative than mere interpretation. This is because, apart from their work in relation to sentencing criminals, judges are involved in passing judgement in numerous cases relating to areas such as governmental secrecy, industrial relations, police powers, political protest, race relations and sexual behaviour. They are not simply administering the law in a passive way, there is much potential for them to make law as they interpret it, a process often known as **judicial activism**.

In fulfilling their role, judges are expected to be impartial and not vulnerable to political influence and pressure. They are expected to refrain from partisan activity and generally have refrained from commenting on matters of public policy. The 1955 **Kilmuir Guidelines** urged them to silence since 'every utterance which he [a judge] makes in public, except in the actual performance of his judicial duties, must necessarily bring him within the focus of criticism'. The Guidelines were later relaxed, allowing judges to give interviews. More recently, in a greater spirit of openness, senior judges have been willing to express their views on public policy, although this is not an attempt to show support for one party.

The separation of judges from the political process is not quite as clear-cut as the concept of an independent judiciary might suggest. Some holders of judicial office also have a political role, among them the Lord Chancellor, the Attorney General and the Solicitor-General. Although they are supposed to act in a non-partisan manner in their judicial capacity, at times this can be difficult. The legal advice given to the Blair government by the Solicitor-General over the legality of the decision to send troops into Iraq was especially controversial. Critics allege that he did everything he could to support the ministerial case for intervention.

Judges may find themselves caught up in political controversy in other ways too. They may be asked by the Prime Minister to chair important enquiries and make recommendations for future action. Lord Hutton was asked to enquire into the death of David Kelly, the former weapons inspector who committed suicide in 2003 after suggestions that the case for military action against Iraq had been 'sexed up'. Sometimes, the findings of such enquiries are contentious and inspire criticism of the judge involved. Hutton was accused of producing a report that 'whitewashed' the Blair administration whilst heaping blame upon the BBC which had carried the 'sexing-up' allegation.

The reason why judges should remain politically neutral is clear. If they make a partisan utterance, it is felt that this would undermine public confidence in their impartiality. They need to be beyond party politics, committed to the pursuit of justice.

Are judges neutral?

The issue of judicial neutrality has aroused much academic and political controversy. In practice there are real doubts as to whether judges can ever be totally neutral as all members of the Bench have their own leanings and preferences.

The Left in Britain has long been critical of judges and wary of the power they exercise. Throughout much of its history, many in the Labour movement have felt that their party has suffered from the decisions made by those on the Bench, particularly in the area of industrial relations. The most famous example of such treatment was the *Taff Vale* case (*Taff Vale Railway Co* v *Amalgamated Society of Railway Servants* (1901) AC 426) at the turn of the 20th century, in which the right of the unions to take strike action was seriously restricted. In the 1980s, a number of **sequestration** cases were heard, in which union funds were taken away as a result of judicial decisions. But the suspicion has not arisen solely as a result of the unfavourable verdicts that judges have often delivered in cases involving the Labour Movement. It derives from a feeling that their judgments in court are influenced by their backgrounds, attitudes and methods of selection. In other words, they are biased.

This view was expressed in a Labour document entitled *Manifesto* written in 1985: '[of judges] Their attitude to the political and social problems of our time is shaped and determined by their class, their upbringing and their professional life – their attitude is strongly conservative, respectful of property rights and highly authoritarian'. Other left-wing writers have suggested that in cases involving official secrecy, the performance of Labour councils and trade unions, the partiality of judges is evident. In their view, the nature of judicial backgrounds and the conservatism of their attitudes undermine the idea of judicial neutrality.

The most frequently quoted attack on the characteristics of judges was made by John Griffiths (1997). In his words, judges 'by their education and training and the pursuit of their profession as barristers, acquire a strikingly homogeneous collection of attitudes, beliefs and principles which to them represent the public interest'. He complains that in exercising their discretion, judges rather assume that the public interest favours law and order and the upholding of the interests of the state over any other considerations. He suggests that judges are more willing to defend property rights than wider human rights or personal liberties:

> They [judges] cannot be politically neutral because . . . their interpretation of what is in the public interest and therefore politically desirable is determined by the kind of people they are and the position they hold in our society: [and because] their position is part of established authority and so is necessarily conservative, not liberal.

According to this view, the backgrounds and attitudes of judges make them unsympathetic to – indeed, biased against – minorities (especially those that are particularly militant and outspoken), and opposed to ideas of social progress. Militant demonstrators have often received harsh words and stiff punishments from judges who dislike the causes and methods with which strikers and others are associated.

Key term

Sequestration is the removal of the financial assets from their owner, until he or she complies with a court order.

Activity

Write a paragraph to explain why the Left has traditionally been wary of judges.

Summary questions

1. Distinguish between judicial independence and judicial neutrality.
2. Are judges biased?
3. Should unelected judges interfere with the decisions of government in a modern democracy?

4 The growing importance of judicial review

Learning objectives:

- What is meant by judicial review?

- Why has the number of cases of judicial review grown rapidly in recent decades?

- What sort of cases arose involving judicial review during the Blair era?

Judicial review is the process that enables judges to override the decisions and laws of democratically elected governments. Specifically, it covers three main areas:

- rulings on whether specific laws are constitutional
- resolving conflicts between the state and the citizen over civil liberties
- resolving conflicts between different institutions or levels of government.

Judicial review gives judges a unique position, both in and above politics. In the US, judges have strong powers of judicial review, enabling them to strike down laws as unconstitutional. In Britain, interest in the process of judicial review has developed relatively recently. It operates in a weaker form. It enables the courts to monitor the way in which public officials carry out their duties and it empowers the courts to nullify (cancel out) those actions which are considered illegal and unconstitutional or in which a decision was irrational or unreasonable, or unfairly reached.

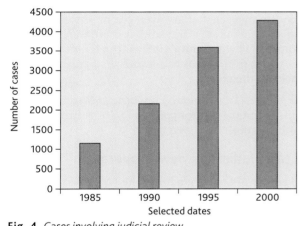

Fig. 4 *Cases involving judicial review*
Source: Derived from information in M. Sunkin, Public Policy and Management, 2001

The increased relevance of review was apparent when in 1987 government lawyers produced a document for Civil Servants entitled *The Judge over your Shoulder*. It showed them how to avoid the pitfalls. By then, there had been substantial growth in the number of cases involved. Between 1981 and 1996, the number of applications for judicial review rose from just over 500 to nearly 4,000; in 1996 alone, there were 1,748 immigration applications and 340 concerning homelessness.

The increasing resort to review and the decisions that judges reached in several cases caused resentment under the Major government. Home Secretary Michael Howard made several important decisions which were considered unlawful by senior judges on issues ranging from criminal injuries to the exclusion from the UK of the Rev. Moon (the leader of the Unification Church in the US – 'moonies' – and said to be involved in questionable financial activities).

Tension became acute. Ministers were overtly critical of judges and complained about judicial activism, whilst some judges felt there was a campaign to discredit them. The tabloid press joined in the so-called 'judge bashing', complaining of the 'galloping arrogance' of the judiciary.

Labour and judicial review

Under the Labour government there have been several cases in which the verdict of a judicial review has gone against the minister. Often, they have involved issues of immigration and the rights of asylum seekers. Some ministers have publicly expressed their concern about the activities of the courts in scrutinising government actions and striking them down with the regularity with which they do. Ex-minister Paul Boateng pointed out that 'the judges' job is to judge, the government's job is to govern'. At various times, the then Home Secretary David Blunkett accused judges of routinely rewriting the laws that parliament had passed and bluntly

Fig. 5 *Protest outside Belmarsh prison in south-east London*

made it clear that he did not agree with their findings. As he put it after the judges had declared that parts of the Nationality, Immigration and Asylum Act 2002 were in breach of the Human Rights Act 1998:

Frankly, I'm fed up with having to deal with a situation where parliament debates issues and the judges then overturn them . . . parliament did debate this, we were aware of the circumstances, we did mean what we said and, on behalf of the British people, we are going to implement it.

The legislation introduced by Labour in response to the perceived terrorist threat has fallen foul of the judges. In a review of the Anti-Terrorism Crime and Security Act 2001, they found that the detention of foreign terror suspects without trial was unlawful, both disproportionate (in that less-restrictive measures were available) and discriminatory (since UK nationals suspected of terrorism were not liable to indefinite detention). So too did ministerial attempts to amend the original legislation by the introduction of 'control orders' that applied to both UK and foreign nationals suspected of involvement in terrorism. Human rights groups argued that these were incompatible with both Article 5 (the right to liberty) and Article 6 (the right to a fair trial), a position upheld by the courts.

The law lords also ruled against the government on its immigration control policies re Roma migrants, Czech citizens of Romani origin.

Further information

Belmarsh 2004

Belmarsh – Britain's Guantanamo Bay?

You don't have to go to Cuba to find terror suspects controversially imprisoned. Nine foreigners have been held in London's Belmarsh Prison for almost three years without charge or trial. So is it the UK's Guantanamo Bay? . . . The nine . . . were not able to see the intelligence against them . . . under charges brought under anti-terrorist legislation.

Extract from *BBC News*, 6 October 2004

The Prague Airport case: judicial review in operation

In December 2004, the House of Lords ruled that the UK government had discriminated on racial grounds against Romas by preventing them from travelling to the UK in order to stop them from claiming asylum upon arrival (*Regina* v *Immigration Officer at Prague Airport* (2004) UKHL 55). In 2001, the Czech Republic agreed that the UK could station immigration officers at Prague Airport to screen all passengers travelling to the UK. The overwhelming number of passengers who were refused permission to enter the UK under this operation was Roma. Statistics showed that Roma were 400 times more likely to be refused entry to the UK than non-Roma. The practice was described by the Lords as 'inherently and systematically discriminatory' against Roma, and contrary to Article 3 of the 1951 Refugee Convention. The decision was highly significant in its condemnation of racial discrimination in the area of border regulation.

Summary questions

1. In what sorts of cases has judicial review caused problems for British governments?

2. Is judicial review a key element in British democracy?

3. Does judicial review bring judges too much into the political arena?

5 The trend towards judicial activism

Learning objectives:

- Why have judges in many countries become more involved in politics?

- How easy were the relations of the Thatcher/Major governments with the judges?

- Why and in what ways did the Blair administrations clash with judges?

- What are the arguments for and against increased judicial power?

Judicial activism is a phrase that describes situations in which the judges and the courts take a broad and active view of their role as interpreters of the constitution and reviewers of executive and legislative action. It refers to the willingness of judges to venture beyond narrow legal decisions so as to influence the evolution of public policy. In contrast, **judicial restraint** is a more conservative philosophy and approach. It maintains that judges should simply apply the law (including the constitution), irrespective of policy implications or the judges' own values.

The growing political involvement of judges

Throughout the Western world, judicial intervention in public policy has become more common over the last few decades. There has been an increase in the power of judges who have become far more willing to enter into political arenas that would in the past have been the preserve of politicians and national parliaments. When they strike down policies and laws passed by ministers, they seem to be trespassing into an area reserved for the elected representatives of the people.

In Britain in recent decades, the growing importance of judges and the courts has been one of the most significant political developments. Previously, the role of the courts in British politics had been restricted and sporadic, whereas it is now often said to be central and constant.

Key term

Judicial restraint is the idea that the courts should not seek to impose their views on other branches of government. Supporters favour a passive role for the courts which limits them to implementing legislative and executive intentions.

Judges and ministers at war!

The sickness sweeping through the senior judiciary – galloping arrogance

Does the judge think he's above democracy?

Fig. 6 *Some tabloid headlines from the Conservative years*

The British courts and the Thatcher/Major administrations

Particularly from the 1980s onwards, judges have become involved in many areas from which they were previously excluded, most notably local–national government relations and industrial relations. In the former, the growth of centralisation under the Thatcher government left many Labour-controlled local authorities seeking clarification and redress or defending their position in the courts, as their traditional rights were overridden. In industrial relations, the new laws restraining trade union action meant that judges were involved in deciding issues such as ballots prior to strike action, secondary picketing and sequestration of assets. The print workers' union, SOGAT 82, found itself on the receiving end of financial penalties for a technical breach of the law, without in its view sufficient allowance being made for the special circumstances of the case. Other unions too felt displeased with the treatment they received in the courts.

Yet if the growing political involvement of judges in these cases worked in favour of the Conservative government, this was not to be the case in the 1990s. We have seen that the increasing use of judicial review involved judges in conflict with ministers, for example the greater willingness of more European-minded judges to speak out in favour of the incorporation of the European Convention on Human Rights into British law and against ministerial policy on issues such as the sentencing of convicted criminals and prison conditions. The decisions of the Court of Human Rights in Strasbourg against the British government only added to ministerial misgivings during the Major administration, so that by the middle of the 1990s there was clear hostility between the politicians and the judges. Conservative spokespersons frequently denounced the trend towards increased judicial involvement in political controversies of the day.

The courts and the Blair administrations

We will legislate further including, if necessary, amending the Human Rights Act in respect of the European Convention on Human Rights.

Tony Blair to the press, 5 August 2005

> **Key term**
>
> **Politicisation of the judiciary** is the growing trend for judges to become involved in political issues.

Under the Labour government, it might have been anticipated that relations between the Blair administrations and the judges would have been better, given the promising start made by ministers by incorporating the European Convention into British law – in line with much judicial opinion. Yet the passage of the Human Rights Act 1998 itself has provided opportunities for further **politicisation of the judiciary**.

Judges have become more embroiled in the political arena, as they seek to decide on the interpretation and/or validity of a particular piece of legislation. As we have seen, in several cases of judicial review decisions have gone against ministers. Judges at the highest level have also been willing to speak out in criticism of the policies pursued on issues such as freedom of information and trial by jury.

Have judges become too powerful?

Yes, they have!

Many politicians and some academics regret the trend to politicisation of the judiciary. They feel uneasy about unelected judges stepping so boldly into political territory. They stress that under British constitutional arrangements, parliament is the main protector of our liberties. It is a sovereign body and its members alone should make decisions. Because they are elected, politicians need to remain sensitive to the wishes of the voters, whereas judges lack accountability and are seen as a group remote from present-day reality.

In other words, according to this view, the punishment for inappropriate behaviour by the government of the day should be in the polling booth rather than in the courtroom. Politicians should not rely on judges to make difficult decisions. In any case, they are inappropriate persons to do so given their narrow backgrounds and preference towards defending established interests in society.

No, they haven't!

The division of power between the three branches of government is a means of protecting people from arbitrary government, a safeguard against potential tyranny. An independent judiciary is well suited to deciding difficult issues of the day. If they are not elected, then at least – in the words of one US source – 'they read the returns too'. They are aware of the way people have voted in recent elections and are therefore not immune from what goes on in society. Moreover, they can offer a view that commands respect because of the broad esteem in which they are held. After all, they are held in higher regard than that currently enjoyed by politicians as a whole.

On issues relating to the liberties of the people in particular, judges have a role to play. Obviously it is a secondary role. The Executive has the initiative and introduces law, whereas judges react to the law, reviewing it once it is in place. But it is an important role in any modern democracy and an independent judiciary is an appropriate body to exercise it.

Summary questions

1. Is the conflict between politicians and the judges inevitable?
2. Should we worry about the power of judges in our democracy?

Activity

Judges are unelected and therefore unaccountable. In the light of what you have read, write a paragraph or two to explain whether there is a case for electing them. Would this make them more political?

6 The impact of the European Convention and the Human Rights Act 1998

Learning objectives:

- What is the European Convention on Human Rights?

- What sorts of freedoms does it protect?

- How did Britain fare in the European Court on Human Rights prior to the introduction of the Human Rights Act 1998?

- How did Labour attempt to ensure that parliamentary Sovereignty was preserved following the introduction of the Human Rights Act 1998?

- What has been the early impact of the Human Rights Act 1998?

The European Convention was a document drawn up mainly by British lawyers in the Home Office. The bodies responsible for its implementation (the European Commission on Human Rights and the European Court of Human Rights) began their work in 1953. The Commission and the Court pre-date, are not part of and should not be confused with the European Union, which is described in Chapter 17.

Britain was an early signatory of the document and from 1965 its citizens had the right of access to the European machinery. This meant that although the Convention was not part of British law, citizens who felt that their rights had been denied could take their case to Strasbourg to gain redress and possibly compensation.

In depth

How the HRA has failed: cases quoted by Michael Howard

Articles of the European Convention

1 Commitment of all signatories to secure the rights set out in the Articles below.
2 Right to life
3 Freedom from torture, inhuman or degrading treatment
4 Freedom from slavery or foreced labour
5 Right to liberty and security of person
6 Right to a fair trial by an impartial tribunal
7 Freedom from retrospective criminal laws
8 Right to respect for private and family life, home and correspondence
9 Freedom of thought, conscience and religion
10 Freedom of expression
11 Freedom of peaceful assembly and association, including the right to join a trade union
12 Right to marry and have a family
13 Right to an effective remedy before a national authority
14 Freedom from discrimination
15 Right of a country to derogate (exempt oneself) from its obligations in time of war or other public emergency

Further information

The need for the HRA
It takes on average five years to get an action into the European Court of Human Rights once all domestic remedies have been exhausted; and it costs an average of £30,000. Bringing these rights home will mean that the British people will be able to argue for their rights in the British courts – without this inordinate delay and cost.

1997 White Paper,
Rights Brought Home

Contents of the European Convention

Via the broad phrases of the 66 Articles and several Protocols, the Convention sets out a list of freedoms such as freedom of expression (Article 10) and prohibition of discrimination (Article 14). For each entitlement, the basic statement is followed by a series of qualifications that lists the exceptions to it. For example, freedom of expression is limited by considerations such as those 'necessary in a democratic society, in the interests of national security, for the prevention of disorder or crime, or for the protection of health or morals, for the protection of the rights of others'. The Court of Human Rights which sits in Strasbourg has the task of interpreting the Convention in a particular case. With the incorporation of the Convention into British law via the Human Rights Act 1998, British courts now have similar scope.

Britain and the Convention: the situation prior to the passage of the Human Rights Act 1998

The record of British governments in Strasbourg was for many years a poor one, especially prior to incorporation of the European Convention via the Human Rights Act 1998. They lost many cases in which the judgements came down on the side of the aggrieved individual. As a result:

Fig. 7 *The Court of Human Rights in Strasbourg*

- Prisoners won the right to consult a lawyer or write to an MP.
- Corporal punishment in schools was ruled out of order if parental views had not been taken into consideration.
- The armed forces were criticised for acting illegally by banning gays and lesbians from serving.
- It was said that the child killers of James Bulger did not receive a fair trial as they could not have understood the proceedings and that it was wrong for the Home Secretary to decide their final sentence.

The case for incorporation of the Convention was accepted by Labour back in the early 1990s, when John Smith was leader (1992–94). Along with many centre-left politicians, he and his successor, Tony Blair, recognised that the status of the Convention in Britain was unsatisfactory. Britain was ultimately bound by it, but citizens had difficulty in using it. Ministers were tempted to play for time and not give way when infringements of rights were alleged. This was because they knew that Strasbourg justice was slow, sometimes taking 5–6 years to get a court decision. Many people were tempted to give up the struggle rather than wait for a European verdict.

Labour: the Human Rights Act 1998

In October 1997, New Labour produced a White Paper showing how for the first time a declaration of fundamental human rights would be enshrined into British law. The detail of the proposals showed that the courts were not being empowered to strike down offending Acts of parliament as happens in Canada. Instead, judges would be able to declare a particular law incompatible with the Convention, enabling government and parliament to change it if they wished, and providing a fast-track procedure for them to so do. In this way, the proposed Act would not pose a threat to the principle of parliamentary sovereignty.

The resulting Human Rights Act (passed in 1998) became operative from October 2000. It provides the first written statement of the rights and obligations of British people, by incorporating most – but not all – of the European Convention on Human Rights into British law. It allows them to use the Convention as a means of securing justice in the British courts. Judges are now able to apply human rights law in their rulings.

Life under the Human Rights Act 1998

From 2000, the courts have had more power than ever before to hold the government and public bodies to account for their actions. Much

Activity

Using the internet to assist you, find out how the HRA has helped develop a law of privacy in the UK. You might look up cases such as those concerning:

- Footballer Garry Flitcroft, caught cheating on his wife with both a lap dancer and a nursery-school teacher.
- Gordon Kaye, the British television actor who wanted to block publication when a tabloid photographer and reporter entered his hospital room shortly after emergency brain surgery.
- Catherine Zeta-Jones and Michael Douglas and their suing of *Hello!* magazine for publishing unauthorised photographs of their wedding.
- Naomi Campbell's complaint against a tabloid which published details of her treatment for cocaine addiction at Narcotics Anonymous.

of the discussion of the new Act has surrounded the question of the extent to which the judges will embrace their new opportunity with enthusiasm and flex their muscles at the expense of parliament.

Used to poring over the precise wording of British statutes, judges are now required to interpret what the law is in a particular situation when a citizen brings a case under the 'broad brush' phraseology of the European Convention. Many precedents (i.e. earlier cases) that previously influenced their legal judgments have lost some of their former relevance.

At the time of the passage of the Human Rights Act 1998 (HRA), William Hague echoed many recent Conservative criticisms of allowing power to pass from an elected parliament to judges who cannot be dismissed. Tony Blair and his ministers, having overcome the party's long-term hostility to 'Tory judges', argued that the courts would provide an essential check upon the might of an overweening (i.e. unduly powerful) executive.

The HRA does appear to tilt the balance of the Constitution in favour of the judges. As Bogdanor (2003) puts it, the measure 'considerably alters the balance between parliament and the judiciary . . . for in effect the Human Rights Act makes the European Convention the fundamental law of the land'. Not all academics and commentators agree with his judgement. Some doubt that major social and political change will in future be driven by judges rather than legislators, noting that this has not happened in those countries which incorporated the Convention many years ago.

In depth

How the HRA has failed: cases quoted by Michael Howard

- The schoolboy arsonist allowed back into the classroom because enforcing discipline apparently denied his right to education.
- The convicted rapist given £4,000 compensation because his second appeal was delayed.
- The burglar given taxpayers' money to sue the man whose house he broke into.
- Travellers who thumb their nose at the law and are allowed to stay on green-belt sites they have occupied in defiance of planning laws.
- A convicted serial killer allowed hard-core porn in prison because of his right to information and freedom of expression.

In the Conservative 2005 election campaign, Howard vowed to 'overhaul or scrap' the HRA:

> The time has come to liberate the nation from the avalanche of political correctness, costly litigation, feeble justice, and culture of compensation running riot in Britain today . . . the regime ushered in by Labour's enthusiastic adoption of human rights legislation has turned the age-old principle of fairness on its head.

NB: David Cameron has also vowed to scrap the HRA if elected, instead replacing it with a 'Bill of Rights' for Britain.

Early impact

The effect of incorporation of the Convention is to introduce a new human rights culture into British politics. In general, decisions by parliament, a local authority or other public body must not infringe the rights guaranteed under the Act. Where rights conflict, such as privacy versus freedom of information, the courts will decide where the balance should lie. Judges have the task of deciding cases as they come before them.

There were some concerns that the Act would clog up the courts (particularly in the early stages) and that the chief beneficiaries would be lawyers. It was expected that the courts would be deluged with all kinds of cases, some of them extreme. In Scotland, where the European Convention was already in force, 98 per cent of the cases in the first year failed. In the event, there was no legal free-for-all. Between 2000 and 2002, of 431 cases involving human rights heard in the high courts, the claims were upheld in 94. Keir Starmer, a barrister much involved in such cases, has concluded that 'hand on heart, the Human Rights Act has changed the outcome of only a very few cases'.

 Summary questions

1. Compare Labour and Conservative attitudes to the Human Rights legislation.

2. Has the Human Rights Act 1998 been a force for good?

Further reading

Useful articles:

M Garnett, 'Judges versus Politicians', *Politics Review*, September 2004.

L Jeffries, 'The Judiciary', *Talking Politics*, January 2003.

P Norton, 'Judges in British Politics', *Talking Politics*, January 2004.

G Peele, 'The Human Rights Act', *Talking Politics*, September 2001.

M Ryan, 'A Supreme Court for the UK', *Talking Politics*, September 2004.

Useful books:

L Bridges, G Meszaros and M Sunkin, ***Judicial Review in Perspective***, Cavendish, 1995.

G Drewry, 'Judicial independence in Britain: challenges real and threats imagined' in P Norton (ed.), ***New Directions in British Politics?***, Elgar, 1991.

S Foster, ***The Judiciary, Human Rights and Civil Liberties***, EUP, 2006.

J Griffiths, ***The Politics of the Judiciary***, Fontana, six editions, latterly 1997.

A Sampson, ***Who Runs This Place? The Anatomy of Britain in the 21st Century***, Murray, 2004 (see the chapter on The Law).

Websites:

www.dca.gov.uk. Office of Secretary of State for Constitutional Affairs. Information relating to judiciary in general and judicial appointments.

www.justice.ie. The Department of Justice, Equality and Law Reform.

www.echr.coe.int. European Court on Human Rights (Council of Europe machinery).

www.lawsociety.org.uk. The Law Society.

www.justice.org.uk. A legal and human rights campaigning group.

AQA Examination-style questions

1 ☑ Read the extract and answer questions (a) to (c) which follow.

Need for a written Constitution

Government in Britain was becoming increasingly powerful and undemocratic. After 1979 in particular, some academics worried about the increasing centralisation of British government, a process being intensified by the era of one party (Conservative) dominance. Prime Minister Thatcher developed a very personal style of leadership; other agencies such as the Cabinet and the civil service lost power. Some pointed to the steady erosion of the functions and powers of local government, the increased power of quangos and the limitations on human rights. Given such dangers, if a fully-fledged written *constitution* was not a priority, we certainly needed measures to reform the second chamber, increase personal rights, bring in freedom of information legislation and other things which might shift power from Whitehall in favour of the citizen. As it was, the state was becoming too powerful, with too few checks and balances.

Source: adapted from Chapter 9 of this textbook

(a) Briefly explain the term *constitution* as it is used in the extract. *(5 marks)*

(b) Using your own knowledge as well as the extract, explain why the civil service is judged to have lost power in recent years. *(10 marks)*

(c) Assess the most important constitutional changes introduced in the UK since 1997.

(25 marks)

2 Read the extract and answer questions (a) to (c) which follow.

The judiciary and politics

Judicial review gives judges a unique position. In the US, judges have strong powers of judicial review, enabling them to strike down laws as unconstitutional. In Britain, interest in the process of judicial review has developed relatively recently. It operates in a weaker form. It enables the courts to monitor the way in which public officials carry out their duties and it empowers the courts to nullify (cancel out) those actions which are considered illegal and unconstitutional or in which a decision was irrational or unreasonable, or unfairly reached.

Source: adapted from Chapter 10 of this textbook

(a) Briefly explain the term *judicial review* as used in the extract. *(5 marks)*

(b) Using your own knowledge as well as the extract, consider whether the practice of judicial review compromises the doctrine of judicial neutrality. *(10 marks)*

(c) 'The passage of the Human Rights Act has provided opportunities for further politicisation of the judiciary.' Discuss. *(25 marks)*

11 The composition, role and function of parliament

1 Parliament's two chambers

Learning objectives:

- What are legislatures?

- What is the difference between unicameral and bicameral legislatures?

- What are the advantages and disadvantages of second chambers?

- What are the functions of legislatures?

Legislatures are representative bodies that reflect the sentiments and opinions of the public. Their members consider public issues and pass laws on them. Most countries have a legislature as part of their institutions of government.

The roots of the name of the first modern legislature, the British parliament, suggest the crucial function – *parler*, to talk. Most early legislatures were created to provide advice to the political executive, often a monarch, and to represent various political groups. Many legislatures have also been responsible for introducing public policies. The roots of the word 'legislature' are the Latin terms *legis* (law) and *latio* (bringing, carrying or proposing). Legislatures are the branch of government empowered to make law. Whether known as assemblies or parliaments, they are forums for debate and deliberation.

Legislatures may be unicameral or bicameral:

- Unicameral legislatures have one chamber, e.g. Bulgaria and Sweden.
- Bicameral legislatures have two chambers, e.g. Australia and the UK. Bicameral legislatures are more common in federal states than in unitary ones.

Bicameralism now operates in just over 60 countries. The existence of a second chamber is often said to have certain advantages. It can:

- act as a check upon first chambers, particularly important if one party has a landslide majority
- more effectively check the Executive
- broaden the basis of representation, especially in federal states giving representation to the regions
- allow for thorough scrutiny of legislation, providing more time for careful examination of bills
- act as a constitutional longstop, i.e. delaying the passage of bills and allowing time for debate.

On the other hand, critics allege that a second chamber:

- can be unnecessarily costly
- performs no useful role that cannot be covered by a streamlined lower house
- slows down the task of government, sometimes delaying much-needed legislation
- sometimes does not represent the electorate and often adopts a broadly conservative viewpoint
- is a recipe for constitutional stalemate or gridlock. It institutionalises conflict between the two houses.

ⓘ What legislatures do

Most elected legislatures perform three broad roles:

- **Legislation**. In fact, in most countries the dominant role in policy making has passed to the Executive, but legislatures still have an active and significant role. The essence of their power is that in most systems a majority of the members of the legislature needs to vote to authorise the passage of any law.
- **Representation**. Elected representatives represent public opinions and the public interests within the governing process and therefore play an important role in providing a link between government and the people.
- **Oversight of the Executive**. Legislatures normally oversee the actions of the Political Executive. This scrutiny means that there are regular procedures by which the legislature can question and even investigate whether the Executive has acted properly in its implementation of public policies. In this way, **accountability** is ensured.

A further function of legislatures is that they act as major channels of recruitment, providing a good pool of talent. In parliamentary systems, service in the assembly is the required career path for ministers and premiers. Assemblies recruit and train the next generation of political leaders.

On the floor of the chamber, apart from involvement in lawmaking, which takes up much of the time available, members also take part in other activities such as discussion of financial provisions, participation in general debates and asking questions. The latter is an activity more common in Britain and Commonwealth countries than it is elsewhere.

Several roles of parliament are listed above, but in essence the Lords and especially the elected House of Commons are concerned to provide legitimation. That is, in the words of Robins (in Coxall *et al.* (2003)), 'they authorise the actions of rulers, thereby justifying their acceptance by the ruled. It can fulfil this purpose because of its historic status, constantly renewed, as a unique forum for national representation, law-making, political criticism, debate and leadership recruitment'..

Key term

Accountability relates to the system of control and answerability which is seen as a key element of democratic and representative government. By various mechanisms, ministers have to account for their stewardship of the nation's affairs to the elected House of Commons.

Summary questions

1. Is it better to have one chamber rather than two?
2. What do you think is the most important function of parliament? Why?

2 The role, composition and reform of the House of Lords

Learning objectives:

- How was the House of Lords reformed in the 20th century?

- Who is now entitled to attend the House of Lords?

- What does the House of Lords do?

- Does the House of Lords need further reform?

- Along what lines might reform proceed?

Key terms

Life Peerages Act 1958: this permitted men and women to be created as peers for the duration of their lives. The purpose was to diversify membership of the chamber by bringing in people from various walks of life (without excluding their heirs from membership of the Commons).

The **Parliament Act 1911** removed the power of permanent veto over legislation, so that the Lords could not indefinitely delay legislation. In future, any bill which passed the Commons in three successive sessions would automatically become law. The House of Lords had lost its permanent veto.

The **Parliament Act 1949** further limited the delaying power of the Lords. Any bill that passed in two successive sessions became law. This effectively curtailed the delaying power to 8–9 months. The 1949 Act still applies. It has been used on four occasions, most recently for the passage of the bill that abolished fox-hunting.

For much of the 19th century, the membership of the House of Lords (sometimes referred to as the second chamber or upper house) was based on heredity and the chamber enjoyed equal status with the House of Commons. However, its position became increasingly inappropriate when the right to vote was extended and the lower house became more representative of the people. The Lords was able to survive the transition into a democratic age on the basis that its powers were trimmed and its membership modified.

Fig. 1 *The House of Lords in session. There is a gorgeousness in some of the rooms, a sense of tradition even though the building itself is mere C19. Those who work there are exceptionally pleasant and helpful. It would be easy to be seduced by this place. Barbara Castle [a now-deceased Labour ex-minister and member] advised me: 'Don't inhale', on the day of my induction.* – Lord Bragg of Wigton on the House of Lords

20th-century changes

In the 20th century, there were several changes to the composition and powers of the second chamber. The most important concerning membership was the introduction of Life Peers, under the terms of the **Life Peerages Act 1958**. The most important powers related to the **Parliament Act 1911** and the **Parliament Act 1949**. These seriously restricted the power of the upper chamber to block or delay legislation from the House of Commons.

It seemed difficult to achieve a fundamental reform of the second chamber that would tackle functions, powers and composition. Party agreement was hard to establish and the subject was not viewed as a priority. Indeed, the 1949 measure had to be passed under the terms of the Parliament Act 1911, because of the Opposition aroused in its passing.

Labour's 1998 change: Phase One of Lords reform

Before the 1997 election, Labour and the Liberal Democrats agreed on a first phase of Lords reform. The 1997 Labour manifesto committed the party to action to end by statute 'the right of hereditary peers to sit and vote in the House of Lords'. Phase one was to provide for the abolition

■ Further information

Lords' membership (July 2007)

748 Peers in total (of whom 143 were female)

604 Life Peers

92 elected hereditaries*

26 Law Lords

26 Bishops.

Party affiliation:

211 Labour

203 Conservatives

77 Liberal Democrats.

*hereditary peers allowed under the 1999 Act

of **hereditary peerages**, which was effectively carried out in October 1998. The House voted to remove all but 92 of the hereditaries who were elected by party groupings to serve in the revised chamber.

The House of Lords Act left the 'judicial' and 'spiritual' membership of the chamber untouched. The Lords Spiritual comprise the two Archbishops (Canterbury and York), as well as the 24 next most senior bishops. They retain their membership only for as long as they hold office within the Church. The Law Lords are members by virtue of their high judicial positions. They retain their seats until their death, so that there are always more Law Lords than are necessary to enable the House of Lords to fulfil its judicial functions.

■ The work performed by the House of Lords

In 1918, Lord Bryce distinguished four roles for the British second chamber:

■ **The consideration and revision of Bills from the House of Commons**. The House of Lords has the power to examine legislation in detail and may pass, amend or reject bills. Ministers may accept or reject amendments to government legislation, rejection leading to a process of negotiation between the two chambers. The Commons can use the Parliament Act 1949 to insist on getting its way. Revision is the key function today and the House spends much of its time on scrutiny of **public bills**, some of which have been badly drafted or inadequately discussed in the lower house. Many amendments are actually introduced by ministers after further consideration of the issues involved.

■ **The initiation of non-controversial legislation**. About a quarter of bills begin their parliamentary life in the upper house, although these are mainly non-controversial bills on which there is no strong party disagreement. The number has increased, in order to spread the parliamentary workload more evenly throughout the year. Back-bench peers can also introduce **Private Peers' Bills**. Few are passed, but they provide a chance to air topics ranging from social reform to the case for a Bill of Rights.

■ **The power of delay**. The Lords can hold up legislation under the Parliament Act 1949, the extra time being designed to provide a pause for reflection and reconsideration. (In the past, this power has been used to frustrate the wishes of more radical governments; Labour has traditionally been wary of it.)

■ **The holding of general debates**. Peers – under less pressure of time than MPs – can conduct useful discussions on matters such as leisure and the environment. There are many Life Peers who have expertise to contribute on issues ranging from education to race relations, health to policing. Such debates usually take up more than 25 per cent of the time of the Lords and are less noisy and partisan than those in the Commons.

Today, the Lords also does valuable work in scrutinising European legislation via its Select Committee on the European Union. The Committee has 19 members and an elaborate system of six sub-committees covering the principal areas of EU responsibility. There is a total working membership of around 70 peers. They examine the merits of proposals for legislation and undertake wide-ranging investigations of EU policy. Although some debates are held in the Lords, it is more common for its authoritative and well-written reports to be communicated to ministers by letter.

In its judicial capacity, the Lords also acts as the final court of appeal, a role performed by law lords who deal with cases that raise important

■ Key terms

Hereditary peerages are peerages that came about as a result of a title inherited within the family.

Public bills are bills which change the law as it applies to the whole community, being binding on everyone. They are the most common type of bill introduced in parliament.

Private Peers' Bills or Private Members' Bills are bills which are introduced by peers in the Lords. They go through the same stages as any other public bill. For further information on the various types of bill, see pp190–191.

points of law. In 2009, this role will be transferred to the new Supreme Court. The judges will be the current law lords, housed in a different building. They will no longer be peers (see p178).

The future of the Lords: unicameral or bicameral?

Some people would say that we do not need a second chamber of any type. Most Westminster-type parliaments are bicameral, but not all. The parliament of New Zealand for example has had only one chamber since the Legislative Council was abolished in 1951. However, most sizeable countries are bicameral. Although Denmark, Israel and Sweden – along with New Zealand – manage well with one chamber, these countries do not have the volume of work and particularly of legislation that is a feature of the British system. Unicameralism would be impossible without major streamlining of the House of Commons.

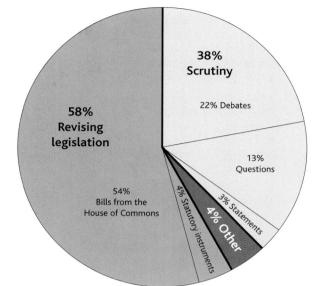

Fig. 2 *How the House of Lords spends its time*

Does the House of Lords need further reform?

Yes, it does!

■ **From a government point of view, the task of Lords reform is unfinished**. A phase two was always intended because although the major problem of the hereditaries has been removed, the present membership is still able to inflict damage on an elected centre-left government. On issues such as fox-hunting, the chamber has been only too willing to frustrate the wishes of the lower chamber. On three occasions since 1997 the Commons voted overwhelmingly to abolish blood sports, but the Lords proved obstructive. (Hence the need to use the Parliament Act 1949 in 2004 to get the measure onto the statute book.)

> The debates on statements from the Commons . . . are often of high quality, as are the Wednesday debates initiated by the different parties in rotation. But it is in the scrutinising of legislation that the House makes its true mark . . . [at night] a score of mostly lawyers [can be found] carefully clarifying Bills which had been whipped out hot and perhaps too hastily from the scrummage of the Commons.
>
> Lord Melvyn Bragg

■ **According to the critics, the present situation is not significantly better than it was**. Heredity may be an unacceptable basis for membership of a legislature today, but arguably so is appointment. At the present time, it is the Prime Minister who makes nominations and those appointed – several of them Labour, to boost the party's representation – are said to be 'Tony's cronies'. Given the method of appointment, the House of Lords does not have the legitimacy to show much independence, whereas with a democratic chamber real power could be exercised. Those who oppose an elected House of Lords are said to fear a second chamber that could delay legislation, hold ministers to account and scrutinise treaties and public

Fig. 3 *Lord Bragg, a traditional left-wing opponent of the Lords who underwent a change of heart after becoming a life peer*

Activities

Go to the parliament website (www.parliament.uk, Bills and Legislation) and find examples to illustrate the legislative work of the Lords. Examiners are keen to see evidence of up-to-date material!

1 What differences do you detect in the following manifesto pledges made by Labour in 1997 and 2005? Why might they be significant?

a 1997: 'We will make the House of Lords more democratic'.

b 2005: 'In our next term we will complete the reform of the Lords, so that it is a modern and effective second chamber'.

2 Write a paragraph outlining the case for making parliament unicameral.

appointments. Yet these are powers exercised by second chambers in most liberal democracies.

The current House of Lords should reflect Britain as it is today. Whereas bishops are present to represent the Church of England, there is currently no representation for several other denominations and faiths. Moreover, of the appointments made in 2001 only 17 per cent were women and 3.5 per cent were from an ethnic minority. Continuing to appoint members would ensure an upper house of ageing white men. An election – particularly one conducted under a 'fair voting' system – would yield an assembly that represents the people and in which women and ethnic and religious minorities would have a chance of election.

No, it does not!

The second chamber produces a valuable opportunity for careful scrutiny of government work. The House actually performs this role rather well. As Prime Minister, John Major used to say: 'If it ain't broke, don't fix it'. It has been fixed to some extent, in a way that has lessened the absurdity of heredity that was an affront to many people in a democratic era. The removal of the hereditaries means that members now are mostly Life Peers, chosen because they have something special to contribute.

The diversity of membership among the Life Peers means that there is normally someone who can speak with authority on even the most obscure subject. Relatively free from the constraints of time and able to speak in a less partisan atmosphere, debates do produce some interesting contributions from members with specialist knowledge and expertise, be it on education, the economy, welfare or a host of other topics. There is an impressive array of experience and talent. Many successful industrialists and businessmen become Life Peers, as do some trade unionists (especially after their retirement). Senior academics, people active in local government and in the charitable and voluntary fields, and people from the arts have also been given peerages.

The chamber has done useful work of revision and also shown a spirit of independence in the last couple of decades or so. The so-called resurgence of the Lords in that period has been attributed to the large number of Life Peers with their particular specialisms to feed into debates, the arrival of television (which created a little more interest in its proceedings) and the greater willingness of party members to defy the whips and vote with the cross-benchers. Governments of both parties have been frequently defeated. Tony Blair's first phase of reform has created a chamber more willing to flex its muscles.

The future of the Lords: an elected chamber?

We need an elected house!

Alternative methods of determining the membership have disadvantages. Heredity has gone out of fashion in a democratic age, most hereditary peers having now been removed under phase one of ministerial plans. Many people see appointment as being little better as it is open to partisan abuse and can allow the Prime Minister to pack the chamber with his supporters. Tony Benn, a one-time Labour MP and minister and long-term left-wing critic of the Blair administration, asks a central question of those who occupy positions of power: 'Can they be removed?' In Britain, the answer is no.

Elections are central to democracy, conferring legitimacy in modern government. They produce a chamber that represents the people's choice. Direct election is the most common method of choosing a second chamber, being used to choose nearly 30 of the world's second chambers. It is a good enough method for much of Europe, the US and Australia. Yet in the 'mother of democracies', the House of Lords currently lacks a democratic basis.

No we do not!

The main difficulty of having a fully elected second chamber is that it may prove to be a rival to the lower house, a danger which is increased in Britain if the upper body is elected by some scheme of proportional representation and can therefore claim to be more representative of the people. (Such dangers could be reduced to some extent by staggering the election process and allowing members to sit for a long term of perhaps 10 or 15 years.) Critics of an elected house concede that there is a good case for an elected chamber in a federal country because there it can serve the purpose of safeguarding the individual states from an all-powerful federal government. But this does not apply in Britain.

Another objection is that some people from various walks of public life, such as business and the public services, may make a useful contribution to the chamber as part-time Life Peers but would not want to become involved in electoral politics. Their specialist expertise is an asset that might be lost if they either had to choose between standing for election or playing no part in parliamentary life. This point really leads to the more fundamental objection to an elected chamber. Peers do not need to be elected for the tasks they perform. They primarily have a revising role and do not ultimately have the power to frustrate the House of Commons whose task it is to represent the people's will.

NB: A partially elected chamber would, of course, be a compromise. It would allow the House of Lords to retain members with experience of the world beyond Westminster politics, but would also provide it with greater legitimacy than at present. Various compromise schemes have been put forward, perhaps for a 50:50 or even a 20:80 split between appointed and elected peers.

■ The future of Lords reform: difficulties in reaching agreement

Lords reform has always been controversial and for this reason it tends to lose its priority the longer a government remains in office. It wins few votes in a general election and tends to generate opposition from members on either side of the House of Commons.

Summary questions

1. Do we need a House of Lords?
2. If so, should it be a more powerful check on the first chamber?
3. Should it also be smaller?

■ Further information

Second chambers elsewhere

Direct elected:

- Australian Senate – by STV (see pp49–50)
- Czech Republic – by party list (see pp48–49)
- US Senate – via FPTP (see pp44–45), two members per state.

Indirect elected (e.g. by lower house or local authorities):

- France – by local government
- India – by state assemblies.

Appointed:

- Canada – by Prime Minister
- Germany – by state governments
- UK – all but the 'elected' 92 members, by Prime Minister (see p186).

3 The roles of the House of Commons

Learning objectives:

- What are the functions of the House of Commons?
- What is the difference between public and private legislation?
- How do bills become laws?

The main functions of the House of Commons are legislation (i.e. making the law), controlling the raising and spending of public money, scrutinising the Executive (i.e. examining the activities of the government) and representing the people.

Legislation

The House of Commons is part of the legislature. At first glance, therefore, it might be assumed that passing laws is its main function. Indeed, most debate and argument in the chamber is about legislation, proposed or already passed. But virtually all legislative proposals originate from – and are shaped by – the Executive. The House does not normally overturn governmental proposals wholesale or even significantly change many of them. The government majority normally sees its programme through, broadly intact.

In depth

Types of bill that pass through the Commons

Public bills alter the general law of the land and affect public policy. They concern the whole community. Most public bills are government Bills and are brought in by the relevant departmental minister who pilots them through the House. Of public bills, Private Members' Bills are introduced by MPs and Private Peers' Bills by members of the upper house. The main legislative proposals that make the headlines are all public bills.

Private bills are promoted by organisations outside the House, such as a local authority or a company. They enable the organisation to obtain powers for themselves in excess of, or in conflict with, the general law. They therefore affect only a limited section of the community. They should not be confused with private Members' bills, which are a type of public bill. The procedure for private bills differs from that for public bills.

In depth

Private Members' Bills (PMBs)

- Introduced by MPs or peers (not ministers).
- As public bills, they aim to change the law for whole population.
- Can be introduced as a result of winning a place in 'top 20 ballot', held early in a new session.
- Can be 'ten-minute bills'. MP speaks for ten minutes outlining the purpose, another MP may briefly oppose. Raises the profile of an issue.
- Few PMBs become law, but they create publicity for an issue. Balloted bills have a better chance of becoming law.

- Difficulties surrounding PMBs include the lack of opportunities for their introduction, of time for their consideration and of civil service help in drafting them.
- PMBs often deal with socio-moral topics, on which there is no strict party view – issues that are often difficult for governments to handle (e.g. abortion).
- Some important PMBs have been enacted, perhaps most famously the Abortion Act 1967.

Activity

Make a list of five topics that might be suitable for PMBs. Remember that if they are less controversial, they may have more chance of success.

There is potential for amendment of legislation, but few changes are made against the wishes of ministers. Occasionally there may be a sizeable rebellion, and even less often a bill may be withdrawn. These occurrences are highly unusual. In other words, the impact on the form of legislation is modest.

In depth

How a public bill becomes law

Most government legislation originates in the party manifesto. Ministers have a mandate (see Chapter 3) to implement their proposals. They may produce a **Green Paper** or **White Paper** before the bill enters the House of Commons.

A bill passes through several stages – in both chambers – before becoming law:

- first reading (formal introduction of the bill)
- second reading (general debate on the principles of the bill)
- committee stage (detailed examination, debate and introduction/ consideration of amendments. In the Commons, this stage takes place in a **Standing Committee** or **Public Bill Committee**)
- report stage (the bill, as amended, is reported back to the whole chamber; last opportunity for new amendments)
- third reading (the whole bill, with all amendments, is considered for final approval; final opportunity for debate).

When a Bill has passed through both chambers, it is returned to the one in which it started (more usually the Commons) for the other chamber's amendments to be considered. If the House of Lords continues to reject a piece of government legislation, the government may resort to using the Parliament Act 1949 to get its legislation through parliament.

The bill receives the Royal Assent (granted by the monarch; no bill has been rejected since 1707).

Raising and spending public money

Parliament's permission is needed to raise and spend money, but this is virtually automatic. Key decisions are made by the government and although the House has the ultimate deterrent of rejecting proposals this does not happen in practice. The Commons plays a scrutinising role, mainly carried out in **Departmental Select Committees** and via the **Public Accounts Committee**. As Graham Thomas writes: 'Parliament has largely given up its role in financial matters to the Executive'.

Key terms

Green Paper: a document laid before the House of Commons by ministers, setting out the options that might be pursued in a given policy area; a consultative paper which invites opinions.

White Paper: a document issued by ministers that sets out their proposals on a topic of current concern, prior to the production of a bill.

Standing Committees are committees of the House of Commons which scrutinise and amend the details of bills, clause by clause. They comprise back-bench MPs of all parties, the number for each party depending on its relative strength in the chamber. From the beginning of the 2006–07 session, Standing Committees have been known as **Public Bill Committees**.

Departmental Select Committees: the 19 parliamentary scrutiny committees responsible for examining the expenditure, administration and policy of their relevant department, e.g. Defence. They comprise back-bench MPs of all parties, the number for each party depending on its relative strength in the chamber.

Public Accounts Committee: the Committee that examines the accounts, showing how money granted by parliament has been used in programmes involving public expenditure.

Scrutinising, influencing and acting as a watchdog over government

This role is exercised by MPs individually and by the House as a whole. The work of scrutiny and influence goes on all the time and finds expression in everything the House does (see Chapter 12).

Further information

Table 1 *Private Members' Bills which became law, 2001–06*

Year	Bills originating in Commons	Bills originating in Lords
2001–02	7	1
2002–03	13	0
2003–04	5	0
2004–05	0	0
2005–06	3	13

NB: In 2004–05 no bills had completed their passage by the time that parliament was dissolved. They had to be sacrificed.

Activity

Using the parliament site, find out more about the Bill, what it aimed to achieve and how far it proceeded.

Key term

Westland affair (1986): a highly contentious political issue that had to be handled by the Thatcher government, concerning the future ownership of the Westland helicopter company.

Other functions might be distinguished, notably:

- **Ensuring that the voices of citizens, individually and collectively, are heard** and that – where necessary – grievances are redressed.
- **Acting as a focus for national debate**, particularly at moments of great drama such as the **Westland affair** (1986). Over Iraq, the quality of the set-piece debates was generally high, with reputations at stake and the House appearing to rise above the more usual level of partisanship.
- **Recruiting a government**. Those seeking high office are elected to the House, make a reputation there, are spotted by the party whips and as a result of their success are chosen for advancement. Members become a pool of talent from which ministerial ranks are filled. This is especially true in Britain, more so than in many other democracies which are more likely to bring into government those who have made a reputation in academia or the business world.

Summary questions

1. What is the most important function of parliament? Why?
2. To what extent do bills get changed during their passage through parliament?

4   The roles of Members of parliament

Learning objectives:

- What is the difference between front-benchers and back-benchers?
- What are the roles of MPs?
- How might their responsibilities conflict?
- What did Burke think was their primary responsibility?

Further information

John Bercow, Conservative MP for Buckingham

- Main priorities as an MP: serving constituency and country.
- Causes supported: international development, special needs education and parliamentary reform.
- Allocation of time: roughly equal between constituency and Westminster.
- Workload: 70 hours a week, 35 in recess; 250–300 letters a week.
- Winner of *The Spectator's* 'Backbencher to Watch' award in 1998.'

MPs are each elected as representatives of a single-member constituency. The 2005 election returned 646 men and women to the House of Commons. Their constituencies varied enormously in size, socio-economic composition and economic activity. Some are concentrated in a small inner-city area with a high population density (e.g. Glasgow Kelvin), whereas others are spread across a vast rural territory (e.g. Ross, Skye and Inverness West, which runs from one side of Scotland to the other). Some have consistently large majorities for one party, so that the elected member may continue to represent constituents for many years (e.g. Sutton Coldfield for the Conservatives, Barnsley for Labour). Others are highly marginal and have a high turnover of MPs (e.g. Braintree, currently held by Labour, and Cheadle, currently held by the Liberal Democrats).

For their efforts, MPs are paid a salary of £60,675 from 1 April 2007 in addition to a range of allowances for office help, staffing and accommodation. Some members still voice criticism of the lack of constituency help they receive, whilst others feel they could benefit from additional research assistance at Westminster. Most MPs employ a couple of people to assist them, and also make use of the services of unpaid research assistants.

The duties and responsibilities of MPs

In depth

The work of which we are most proud

(Taken from a *Guardian* survey of 200 MPs, April 2001.)

The main responses were:

- 43 – introducing their own legislation
- 27 – securing new constituency investment, e.g. to save or build a hospital
- 25 – service on a select committee (see p207).

'Successfully piloting through parliament my Private Members' Bill – the Football (Offences and Disorder) Act 1999 – to tighten up the law on football hooligans.' Simon Burns, C, Chelmsford

'Inviting a man who was about to commit suicide to give me a week to solve his problems and contacting him after six days to say those problems had been solved.' T Taylor, C, Rochford and Southend East

'The successful campaign I led with shop stewards [trades union organisers] to win orders for Govan shipyard . . . The government listened and delivered vital work. We fought for Govan and won.' Mohammed Sarwar, L, Glasgow Govan

There is no formal job description available to MPs. Much depends on what individual members choose to make of their role. Elected under a party label, they operate in parliament as a collective body. However, each one represents a constituency, an individual role which has in recent years been of growing importance.

■ Further information

Front-benchers and back-benchers

In the House of Commons:

- ■ Seating is arranged in blocks or rows, with each political party grouped together.
- ■ The government benches are to the right of the Speaker, the Opposition ones to the left.
- ■ The leading spokespersons (front-benchers) for the government (ministers) and opposition (shadow ministers) sit on the benches at the front of their group.
- ■ Those MPs behind are known as back-benchers.

Today, MPs face increasing and wide-ranging demands upon their time. The sheer volume of requests made to them has risen substantially. In the early 20th century MPs occasionally took up issues with ministers and requested help in resolving some constituency matter. In the last few decades the burden of constituency correspondence has become onerous, particularly for members with inner-city constituents who need help with problems of housing, immigration and urban deprivation. In addition, MPs receive communications from pressure groups. Letters, phone calls and e-mails have all increased in number.

Members of parliament have several obligations that may occasionally conflict with each other. The four main spheres of responsibility are to:

1 **The party**. It was because of their party label that the overwhelming majority of MPs was elected. The party is entitled to demand loyalty in return. MPs are expected to 'toe the party line' in debates and votes, attend party committees and promote the party's outlook and policies – keeping the national leadership and local association satisfied with their performance. For many members, party is the predominant loyalty, but under the Blair administrations that loyalty was much tested. Many Labour MPs have found it difficult to support the leadership's policy on issues such as Iraq, foundation hospitals, tuition fees and anti-terrorist legislation.

2 **The constituency**. MPs are careful to nurse their constituencies, by holding regular surgeries, promoting any constituency interests (such as fishing or the motor industry), attending political meetings and various social functions, and receiving any constituents who visit Westminster. Much of their work today is taken up with welfare-type action on behalf of constituents. They are expected to handle grievances and problems, and ensure that they are dealt with at the appropriate level – perhaps by asking a question in the House or by seeing/writing to the relevant minister.

3 **The nation**. MPs have an obligation to the whole country. They serve in the national legislature and are expected to attend the House regularly and make a contribution in debates, take part in votes and serve on standing and/or select committees. They should inform themselves about the various problems on which they are called to vote and ensure that they bear in mind the national interest as well as those in points 1 and 2 above. NB: According to a survey in 1996, MPs spend on average just over 50 per cent of their working week on parliamentary as opposed to constituency work.

4 **Conscience and special interests**. MPs have their own ideas and preferences. They may wish to introduce Private Members' legislation on some area of concern. They have their own conscience to consider and cannot be expected to speak and act in defence of something they know is wrong. They may also act as spokespersons for outside interests. They are often lobbied by private companies to act on their behalf. Some have a particular concern for some sectional group and wish to articulate their problems and needs.

Of course, the responsibilities outlined above may conflict:

- ■ **MPs will be expected by their constituents to present the local viewpoint when there is a problem** such as an industry in decline (e.g. fishing in the South West) or the threat of closure of a car plant (e.g. the Rover plant at Longbridge). But they also need to see the problem in its national setting. It may be that economic reality dictates that particular goods can no longer be economically manufactured locally.

■ **Personal and party interests may conflict**. Some left-wing Labour MPs – for reasons of personal pacifism or practical policy – may be unable to accept their government's pursuit of a renewal/replacement of Britain's Trident nuclear deterrent. Personal and constituency interests may also differ. Pro-abortion MPs may find themselves out of step with their largely Roman Catholic constituents, just as 'liberals' on capital punishment may find their views create local difficulties. Similarly, a pro-European MP may find it difficult to represent a fishing port in which there is constant criticism of the damage done to the local trawlermen by the Common Fisheries Policy.

The proper role of an MP has been much debated. The classic case for allowing an MP to act as an individual, once elected, was set out in 1774 by a well-known political theorist of the day, Edmund Burke, who had just been elected for Bristol. In a famous, much-quoted letter to his new constituents, he informed them that MPs should not be considered merely as delegates or agents of the voters in the area for which they had been elected. Rather, they should be considered firstly as members of parliament, representing the one interest of the nation. They must define this according to their own judgement of the issues to be decided by parliament: 'Your representative owes you, not his industry [hard work] only, but his judgement: and he betrays, instead of serving you, if he sacrifices it to your opinion.'

Burke was of course writing before the development of the party system and the massive increase in constituency work of recent years. But many members would still argue that on issues of private morality, they have a duty to seek out information, listen to the speeches in the House and then make up their mind in light of what they hear and not because of the views expressed in their constituency postbag.

Summary questions

1 What is the most important responsibility of an MP?

2 If there were to be a division on the return of the death penalty and an abolitionist MP knew that his or her constituents overwhelmingly wanted it reintroduced, how should that MP vote?

3 How has the role of an MP changed in recent years?

5 In what sense is parliament representative of the nation?

Learning objectives:

- In what sense is parliament a representative assembly?
- What do we mean by saying an MP is 'a representative of the people'?
- How socially representative are our MPs?
- Why are women under-represented in the House of Commons?

Britain has a system of representative democracy. Representatives of the people – chosen at regular and free elections – meet together to advance the interests of the individuals and groups on whose behalf they are acting. As such, the system is distinctive from any dictatorship.

The House of Commons, the elected element in parliament, therefore has a key representative role. MPs are there to represent the ordinary people of Britain, a claim they can carry out more effectively since the introduction of the right to vote for all men and women over 18. They represent the people because they have been chosen by them. As such, the House of Commons – and its equivalent in other countries – is the institution that forms the basis of representative democracy. In Western democracies, it is the manner of choice – free elections – which is seen as the key component of representative government.

Electoral reformers such as the Liberal Democrats would probably wish to point out that the assembly chosen in any Westminster election is not truly representative as governments have been chosen by less than half of the voters in every post-war election and might therefore be said to have lacked legitimacy. Moreover, minority views are seriously under-represented (see Chapter 3). In the case of individual MPs, some two-thirds of those elected in 2005 lacked majority support in their constituency. They 'represented' under half of the eligible voters who turned out to vote.

MPs as representatives of the people

To say that MPs are 'representatives of the people' can have various meanings. It might mean that:

- they have been freely elected by their constituents whose interests they should represent
- they represent the interests of the voters as they understand them, rather than acting as a delegate for any particular organisation or group of voters
- they are socially representative of those whom they represent (i.e. 'typical of a class or group').

As we shall see, the membership of the House of Commons is not socially representative of the people because it is overwhelmingly more white, male, middle class and middle aged than the bulk of the population. In other words, it does not mirror or reflect the characteristics of the community as a whole.

How socially representative are MPs?

Elected assemblies of whatever type in most countries are often criticised as being not representative of society. MPs, peers, MEPs and members of devolved bodies tend to be middle class, young middle aged (40+) to elderly, male and unrepresentative of ethnic and religious minorities.

Activity

Perhaps using the internet to help you, find out what the *Jepson* case was about and why it mattered to the Labour party. How has the situation been subsequently changed?

This is true of all Europe's elected legislatures. In the case of women, there are huge variations across the continent, ranging from the good (one in three or more are women – Sweden) to the fairly good (almost one-third – the European parliament), the fair (around 20 per cent – the House of Commons), and the poor (around 10 per cent – France and Italy).

So legislatures are not a 'microcosm' or mirror image of the population on whose behalf they act. Moreover, as politics becomes more 'professionalised', many politicians are going straight into the world of national politics without ever having done an ordinary job of work. (These are **career politicians**.)

Key term

Career politicians are people committed to politics which they regard as their vocation. They know little else beyond the world of politics, policy making and elections.

Further information

Table 2 *Women in other legislatures*

Country	Women MPs (%)	Electoral system used
Rwanda	48.8	List PR
Sweden	47.3	List PR
Finland	42.0	List PR
Costa Rica	38.6	List PR
Norway	37.9	List PR
Denmark	36.9	List PR
Netherlands	36.7	List PR
Cuba	36.0	Double ballot
Spain	36.0	List PR
Mozambique	34.8	List PR
UK (world ranking: 52nd)	19.7	FPTP
USA (world ranking: 68th)	16.3	FPTP
World average (of 131 countries)	17.3	
European average	19.8	

Source: Derived from information provided by the Inter-parliamentary Union, June 2007 and based on lower houses in two-chamber countries

Following the 2003 devolved elections to the Welsh National Assembly, 30 out of 60 Assembly Members were women, the first time 50:50 representation had been achieved in a democratic assembly. Following a by-election, women were briefly in a majority. In 2007, the number of women fell to 28. In the European parliament in June 2007 238 out of 785 (30.4 per cent) MEPs are women.

To summarise, elected representatives are not a good cross-section of the community. But does this really matter? If 5 per cent of a population is Muslim, does the country need to have 5 per cent of its elected members of the same religion? Should there be the same proportion of gay people in parliament as in the community at large? Could there ever be?

■ **In depth**

The social backgrounds of the MPs elected in 2005

■ They are overwhelmingly white. A record number of ethnic minority MPs were returned. Whereas all ethnic minority members had in the past been elected to the Labour side, this time two Conservatives entered the House. Four MPs in the current House are Muslims, an increase on the previous parliament.

■ They are overwhelmingly middle class. Whereas Labour once saw it as its mission to bring 'workers' into parliament, this is no longer the case. Many of its MPs are now drawn from the professions. The pattern is similar to what has been happening with other social democratic and left-wing parties across much of Europe. The trend began in the 1960s with an influx of Labour academics. Today, teachers in universities and schools are still strongly represented, as are other public sector professionals, **political staffers** and lawyers. The legal profession is well represented, there being an obvious connection between lawyers who work in the law and parliaments which make it. The law provides a flexible work situation for candidates as they wage their campaign. Also, lawyers can leave their profession with relative ease and return to it as they wish.

■ Other than the law, many Conservative MPs derive from business and city backgrounds, and a fair proportion of professionals have worked in the media and public relations. Over half of them has been to public school, although far fewer have attended Eton than was the case a few decades ago. Many MPs of all parties have a degree, so that by occupation and education elected members are socially unrepresentative of those whom they serve.

■ They are overwhelmingly middle aged. Most become an MP having made their mark in some other employment. This can be said to provide them with experience of life, but it also means that the voice of young people is absent, causing some to feel alienated from the political system. In Britain, following the 2005 election, 11 members were aged over 70. The average age of Conservatives at Westminster is currently younger than their Labour counterparts (48 as opposed to 53). This was helped by the influx of some younger members in 2005. Three MPs (all Liberal Democrats) were under 30 at the time of the election.

■ They are overwhelmingly male. Progress on women's representation in the House of Commons was slow in the 20th century and did not increase to beyond 5 per cent of the membership until 1987. In 1997, the number of women elected to the Commons doubled to 120, a record improved upon eight years later when 128 were returned. This still leaves Britain with a lower proportion of female representation than many countries not known for their democratic credentials, from Mozambique to Rwanda and Argentina to Cuba. Other than in 1970 and 1983, the bulk of female MPs has been on the Labour side. Today, Labour is well ahead of the other parties in moving towards gender equality. There is a long way to go, but women make up more than one-quarter of the present parliamentary Labour party (98 MPs, 27.5 per cent).

■ **Key term**

Political staffers are those who have served a political apprenticeship working as assistants for MPs or at a party's headquarters.

The underrepresentation of women

Further information

Table 3 *The number of women MPs in selected elections since 1945*

Election	Conserv-ative	Labour	Lib/Lib Dem	Total number (%)
1945	1	21	1	24 (3.8)
1970	15	10	0	23 (4.1)
1992	20	37	2	60 (9.2)
1997	13	102	3	120 (18.2)
2005	17	98	10	128 (19.8)

Joni Lovenduski's survey of 83 current and recent women MPs (2004) found male MPs:

- asking to 'roger' colleagues
- juggling imaginary breasts
- crying 'melons' as women try to speak in the chamber.

'What worries me about my own party is the rampant "laddism". It's New Labour, new sexism, as far as I can see. You get it in the younger male MPs and the constituency parties.' Jenny Jones, ex-MP Wolverhampton

Women in the House of Commons: reactions

Several factors contribute to the under-representation of women in parliament:

- **Child-bearing and home-making responsibilities**, which have traditionally prevented many women from seeking a parliamentary career until the children have become teenagers, particularly given the long and still often unsociable hours that MPs work. Members of selection committees, particularly in the Conservative party, have often questioned women about their intentions and responsibilities with regard to their offspring.

- **The electoral system**. Whereas the use of proportional representation (see p50) encourages the adoption of a gender-balanced list of candidates, the use of single-member constituencies makes their selection less likely.

- **The nature of parliamentary life**, which tends to be masculine and aggressive. Would-be female politicians may find themselves out of sympathy with the atmosphere of the House of Commons. The macho approach of some members, obsessed as they are with point scoring and abuse, is unwelcoming to them. They may not feel comfortable about coping in such a traditionally male preserve.

The campaigning organisation, Fawcett, claims that there is active discrimination against women across the political parties, particularly in the candidate selection process. In addition, it suggests a neat summary of four other factors that can prevent women standing for parliament – the four 'Cs' of culture, childcare, cash and confidence. Partly as a result of its persistent campaigning, the Sex Discrimination Act 1975 was amended in 2002 to allow parties to use positive measures such as all-women shortlists to increase women's representation at all levels of politics.

Does it matter that MPs are not socially representative?

Most people would probably be relieved to know that MPs are experienced and have levels of educational attainment higher than among the population at large because members deal with complex issues of public policy. It is essential that they are literate and fluent, qualities not possessed by all UK inhabitants. Similarly, it is no bad thing that the small minority of persons in the community suffering from acute emotional disorders is not represented at Westminster. In other words, it is undesirable that the House of Commons should be an exact microcosm or mirror image of the whole population. Nor – in a chamber whose membership is elected – could that ever happen. Moreover, generally the people who come forward tend to be young to middle aged, highly educated, white and male.

But should there be more women and ethnic minority members?

Yes, there should:

- It is dangerous in a democracy if groups with less wealth and power are under-represented, not just women and members of ethnic minorities, but also young people and members of the poorest section of the community. If they feel excluded, they may regard the legislature with some contempt and turn to other forms of political action to get their message across.

- As long as certain groups are under-represented, there are likely to be fewer debates on issues affecting them, and the quality of debate may be poor as many members do not take the matters under discussion seriously. As a result, full scrutiny by the media of the impact of government policy on such groups may be largely absent from the political process.

- Legislatures need the services of the most able people available, but at present much talent goes unrecognised. The more women and members of ethnic minorities that get elected, the more role models there will be to encourage others of their own type to come forward and see politics as a realistic, attractive career option.

- All of the mainstream parties talk about their aspiration to achieve a society in which people are able to progress on merit. They claim to dislike discrimination and to wish to encourage equal opportunities. It is therefore hypocritical for the legislature not to reflect these worthy principles in their composition.

No, there should not:

- In a representative democracy, we select MPs broadly to reflect the wishes and interests of their constituents. To achieve this, it is not necessary for them to be a mirror image of British society. They do not have to belong to a particular group or interest in order to put a case on their behalf. As long as they possess an ability to empathise with the needs of all sections of the population, they are capable of advancing their viewpoint. You do not have to live in a slum to appreciate that slums need to be improved or removed, even if your recognition of the full horrors might be more acute if you have experienced them first hand. Neither do you need to be a woman to understand that discrimination against women is hurtful, wrong and damaging to society.

- Women and other social groups are not homogeneous. They do not all possess the same needs and views. For instance, some women are pro-choice on abortion, some favour divorce and others are ardent feminists. Many take a contrary view. Class, employment, age, locality and lifestyle may be more important in determining political views than gender or race. For this reason, it is impossible to represent all women or minority peoples as a group.

- Above all, what we need are competent and caring people to represent us. The personal ability and party allegiance of any candidate should be the main determinants of who gets elected. To draw attention to irrelevant factors such as gender in deciding on the selection of candidates may be unfair and result in reverse discrimination against the most suitable candidates for the job.

✓ Summary questions

1. Does parliament represent the nation?
2. Should it?
3. Can it ever do so?

Further reading

Useful articles:

S Childs, 'Parliament, Women and Representation', *Talking Politics*, April 2002.

I McAllister and D Studlar, 'Electoral Systems and Women's Representation: a Long-term Perspective', *Representation*, 39:1, 2002.

P Norton, 'Reforming the House of Lords: A View from the Parapets', *Representation*, 40:3, 2004.

Useful books:

A Adonis, ***Parliament Today***, MUP, 1993.

P Norton, 'The UK: Parliament under pressure' in P Norton (ed.) ***Parliaments and Pressure Groups in Western Europe***, 1999.

P Norton, 'Parliament' in A Seldon (ed.) ***The Blair Effect***, Little Brown, 2001.

P Norton, ***Parliament in British Politics***, Palgrave, 2005.

Websites:

www.fawcettsociety.org.uk. The Fawcett site, providing statistics and analysis of female representation in British politics at all levels.

www.parliament.uk. Parliament site, with links to both chambers.

Activities

Write a couple of paragraphs to explain your views on the following:

1. Why women are under-represented in the House of Commons.

2. The case for having more members of ethnic minorities in the House.

Further information

The social characteristics of peers

- Few belong to ethnic minorities or have a working-class background.

- Middle-aged to elderly people predominate, many having been appointed in middle age after achieving distinction in their chosen field.

- The average age of members is currently around 68.

- Women are under-represented, although at 19.1 per cent of the membership in July 2007, this is similar to the lower chamber.

12 The power and effectiveness of parliament

1 The doctrine of parliamentary sovereignty in theory and practice

Learning objectives:

- What is meant by sovereignty?
- What is meant by parliamentary sovereignty?
- What are the main political constraints on parliamentary sovereignty?
- How has parliamentary sovereignty been affected by membership of the EU and devolution?

Key term

International Monetary Fund: an international organisation of 185 member countries, established to promote international monetary cooperation, encourage economic growth and provide temporary financial assistance to countries to help ease balance of payments difficulties.

Sovereignty means ultimate political authority. Parliamentary sovereignty is said to be the key element of the British Constitution. In a legal sense, it means that parliament has absolute and unlimited authority, being the supreme law-making body in Great Britain. Only parliament can make, amend and unmake law. No other institution can override its decisions. Thus no one parliament can bind its successor.

Whatever the theory, the validity of the doctrine of parliamentary sovereignty has, in practice, been questioned for many years. It implies that parliament is supreme and all-powerful, yet it is widely agreed that in the 20th century power passed from parliament to the Executive. Sceptics argued that far from exercising real power, parliament simply endorsed governmental action. Any government armed with a large majority had a good chance of pushing its programme through the two chambers and seeing it passed into law.

In reality, there are political constraints on parliament's legal sovereignty. These include:

- membership of the EU
- the demands of the **International Monetary Fund** (where a government is seeking to borrow money, it may impose stringent conditions on policy to be followed in the future)
- the activities of pressure groups, the City and other economic bodies
- the powerful media
- the electorate which has ultimate political sovereignty in that it can vote a government out of office.

The need to gain and maintain public support is a crucial limitation on any group of ministers, especially prior to an election.

Parliamentary sovereignty is in practice modified by the nature of the political system. Ultimately, the people are sovereign. In a democracy, their wishes must ultimately prevail. Government and parliament need popular acquiescence (acceptance) and consent for their actions.

Membership of European bodies and parliamentary sovereignty

As a signatory to the European Convention on Human Rights and a member of the European Union, any British government must modify its law to take account of European wishes. European law ultimately prevails over British law.

In depth

The *Factortame* case

- Came to prominence when a Spanish fishing company appealed in the UK courts against restrictions imposed on them by the Merchant Shipping Act 1988 (MSA).
- The company claimed that their trawlers were entitled to fish in UK waters under EC law.
- The High Court granted an order to disapply the relevant part of the MSA.
- The Court of Appeal and House of Lords took the view that under the British Constitution the British courts did not have the power to suspend Acts of parliament.
- The European Court of Justice ruled that national courts could disapply legislation that conflicted with EC law.
- Consequently, the Lords ruled in favour of the company, Factortame.

When Britain joined the European Community (EC) as it then was, it accepted 47 volumes of existing legislation, so that many directives and regulations passed before we assumed membership were suddenly binding upon us. Since then, in several areas, British lawmaking has been influenced by the decisions of the European Court, most notably in the Factortame dispute concerning Spanish fishermen operating in British-registered vessels. The Merchant Shipping Act (MSA) was passed by the Conservative government in 1988 to define what was meant by a British-registered vessel. It was overturned by the European Court which found the legislation to be discriminatory and unfair and a breach of Community law. It was clear that in future, national law could be made to bow to Community law, and that British courts had the right to review and suspend any British law which seemed to infringe that of the EC.

Summary questions

1 What are the limits on the sovereignty of parliament?

2 How has membership of European organisations impacted upon parliamentary sovereignty?

2 The relationship between parliament and government

Learning objectives:

■ What is the difference between a parliamentary and a presidential system of government?

■ What is meant by accountability to the House of Commons and in what ways is it ensured in Britain?

■ In what ways do governments dominate the elected chamber?

■ What is meant by suggesting that Britain has an elected dictatorship?

■ Parliamentary and presidential government

A parliamentary system is one in which the Executive governs in and through the legislature. The government is chosen from the majority party or a combination of parties and is responsible to the elected assembly. There is therefore a fusion, rather than a separation, of powers (see Chapter 9).

By contrast, in a presidential system, the Executive is separately elected and in theory equal to the legislature (as in the US).

Most liberal democracies – ranging from Australia to Sweden, and India to New Zealand – have some kind of parliamentary government. So does Britain. Government ministers are chosen from the largest party in the House of Commons. They are dependent on the House for support and are answerable and accountable to it.

An example of the accountability of ministers is that they are expected to resign if the Commons passes a vote of 'no confidence' in their performance. This happened in 1979, when the Callaghan government was forced into calling a general election after losing such a vote by just one vote. Other examples of their accountability are that they have to respond to oral questions at Question Time, participate in debates and votes and be subjected to scrutiny by departmental select committees. The doctrine of ministerial responsibility ensures that ministers have to answer for their actions, both individually and collectively.

ⓘ The relationship of parliament and the Executive in Britain

Historically, Britain had an era of legislative supremacy over the Executive in the 19th century. The situation evolved into one in which there was a relatively even balance between the two branches of government. However, over several decades, commentators have suggested that we have moved towards executive supremacy. The Executive tends to dominate the Legislature because the party and electoral systems usually produce a strong majority government, opening up the possibility of what the Conservative peer, Lord Hailsham, called an 'elective dictatorship'.

Governmental domination of the House of Commons

Governments dominate the House in several ways:

■ **They almost always provide the majority of its membership**.

■ **They shape the agenda of the House**, after consultation with the Opposition over the management of Commons business – principally, government legislation, ministerial statements, motions by government or opposition, emergency debates, **private members' motions on the adjournment** and oral questions.

■ **They determine the legislative programme of the House**. The bulk of legislation is government initiated as opposed to the situation in the 19th century when great changes in the law were brought about by MPs or 'private members'. Most governments wish to pass vast

■ Key term

Private members' motions on the adjournment: half-hour debates at the end of each day's sitting in the chamber. MPs can initiate a debate and speak for 10–15 minutes, perhaps allowing an intervention by another MP for a few minutes before the minister responds. They provide an opportunity to raise constituency issues.

amounts of legislation to bring about changes in law, institutions, expenditure and taxation. The use of **delegated (or secondary) legislation** in the form of **statutory instruments** has grown significantly in recent decades. This allows ministers to introduce changes without the need to pass new legislation.

- **They shape the outcome as well as the timing of legislation**, in that most of the amendments to bills represent 'second thoughts' by ministers following representations made by pressure groups and MPs on their own side. Only rarely do they make concessions to criticism from the Opposition.
- **They almost always win**, when votes or 'divisions' take place.
- **They monopolise the time of the House**, much of it spent in consideration of the government's legislation, policies and actions.
- **They control the flow of information to parliament**. Ministers are at an advantage over their opposition counterparts as they are present when issues are discussed in Cabinet or Cabinet committees; they have the resources of their Whitehall departments to provide them with information (particularly important when highly technical issues are under consideration); they generally choose what material should be made known to MPs, sometimes withholding that which may be damaging; and they may even choose to release information to the media before telling parliament.

Key terms

Delegated (or secondary) legislation relates to laws made by ministers, under powers granted to them by parliament, e.g. to ministers. Such laws are technically known as statutory instruments.

Statutory instruments: many Acts are passed in outline form, allowing ministers (and other public bodies such as local authorities) to introduce the necessary orders or regulations, e.g. increasing levels of benefit payment, as authorised by Social Security legislation.

Do we have an elective dictatorship?

In 1976 in his Dimbleby Lecture, Lord Hailsham used the phrase 'elective dictatorship' to express his anxiety about the growth in executive power. He argued that with a flexible constitution, a majority government in control of a sovereign parliament could bring about fundamental changes almost at will, showing scant regard for the democratic process. He wanted to see the introduction of a reformed House of Lords and a Bill of Rights as possible 'longstops', i.e. safety mechanisms which might slow down a government in a hurry. They are reforms still under consideration more than 30 years later.

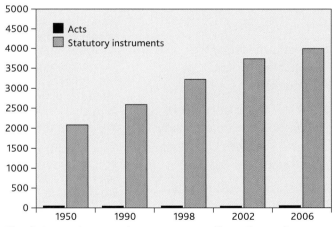

Fig. 1 *Acts and statutory instruments passed by parliament in recent years*

The suggestion behind the theory is that there is an imbalance in the constitution. Executive power has grown at the expense of parliamentary power. The only thing said to hold a government in check is its need to retain enough popularity to win the next election. Government is portrayed as all powerful, the checks and balances identified by Dicey and other constitutional lawyers having been eroded. Normally, a modern Cabinet need fear no defeat. Indeed, no majority government has been forced to resign following a defeat on a vote of confidence since 1880, showing just how strong the position of governments has become in an age of tight party discipline.

Hailsham was writing at a time when the 1974–79 Labour government was about to lose its already slender majority. It had been elected in October 1974 on the basis of the minority support of only 29 per cent of the whole electorate. Contentious bills were being pushed through

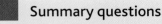

Key term

Whipping system: the system – enforced by the party whips (see p237) – by which party discipline is ensured, with MPs being expected to stay loyal in parliamentary votes.

Summary questions

1 How do governments dominate the House of Commons?

2 Do we currently have an elective dictatorship? If so, does it matter?

parliament and Hailsham was alarmed that government could use its strict **whipping system** to drive through legislation against the wishes of many MPs and the electorate. But the term 'elective dictatorship' has been subsequently picked up by other writers who note that such is the extent of governmental dominance of the House today that ministers can ride roughshod over the wishes of MPs and push through a controversial programme.

Critics of the Hailsham theory point out that there are nonetheless practical constraints on governmental dominance in parliament, such as the select committees and the possibility of back-bench revolt. Governments can be frustrated/defeated, as was the then Labour government (1974–79) on its first Devolution Bill soon after he gave his lecture. The history of the Major administration indicated how a persistent group of parliamentary rebels could cause havoc within the ruling party and make it difficult for ministers ever to dominate the House, particularly when the government has a small majority. In spite of its comfortable majority, the Blair government was actually defeated over its anti-terrorist legislation in 2005.

3 Parliamentary control of the Executive: the watchdog function

Learning objectives:

- What is meant by the 'watchdog function' of parliament?

- What is the importance of Question Time, particularly Prime Minister's Questions, to the scrutinising role?

- What is the role and value of departmental select committees?

- What is the role of HM Opposition party?

As we have seen on p214, much of the work of the House of Commons is concerned with scrutiny. Parliament is supposed to examine and debate governmental actions and policies, holding them up to criticism when they are found wanting, exposing errors that have been made, pointing out things that have been left undone and overall acting as a check upon the performance of ministers, both individually and collectively. It publicises the activities of the government and airs the views of the public on issues of the day.

The scrutiny of legislation is conducted mainly in Standing Committees or – as they are now more often known – Public Bill Committees which operate in a less formal and less adversarial way than the business conducted in the main chamber.

The more general scrutiny of the Executive is carried out via questions, letters, debates, **Early Day Motions** and parliamentary committees (in particular, via the departmental select committee system). In addition, the Opposition is granted 20 opposition days in the yearly timetable for debate and criticism of any aspect of government policy that the Opposition parties choose to highlight. Outside the House, there are also several opportunities for MPs to air criticism via the media.

Within the House of Commons, much of the scrutiny is highly adversarial, particularly if the issues under debate are ones of great political controversy. The most extreme version of gladiatorial combat is provided by Prime Minister's Question Time.

Question Time (QT)

The practice of MPs asking questions of ministers in the House developed substantially in the 20th century. Oral questions are put to departmental ministers on a rota basis. Some are asked to find out information, but others are often vehicles for making a party point – perhaps by raising a constituency problem. Those not answered in the House get a written reply. In addition, some 35,000 written questions are asked per session.

Prime Minister's Questions (PMQ) used to be held for 15 minutes twice a week. Originally introduced by Harold Macmillan, it was modified by Tony Blair in 1997 to its present once-weekly half-hour Wednesday session. There has been much criticism, particularly from the Opposition parties, of the revised format. They want to see the Prime Minister spend more time in the House, feeling that the new format 'lets him off the hook'.

PMQ remains the high point of the parliamentary week, a regular joust between the party leaders and one which is popular with members. It is also popular with the media. The arrival of the television cameras and the use of extracts on news bulletins have served to personalise politics even more. TV likes Prime Minister's Questions, an entertaining spectacle which often generates little light but considerable drama. Good performances by a party leader in this weekly jousting can enhance their reputation within the parliamentary party. A series of poor ones can be deeply damaging to party morale. They seriously undermined the leadership of Iain Duncan Smith as Conservative leader.

Fig. 2 *Prime Minister's Questions*

It is easy to focus only on the regular Wednesday sparring, but this gives a misleading picture of the reality of what Question Time is about. Norton (2005) reminds us that: 'Questions to departmental ministers will not necessarily be as sharply partisan and are characterised at times by informed questioning by members pursuing issues of concern to constituents and others in society'.

The role and merits of departmental select committees

Question Time is lively and confrontational because it takes place 'on the floor of the House'. Scrutiny which is conducted away from the partisan atmosphere of the chamber and in a smaller, more informal setting is

Key term

Early Day Motions: MPs may table motions for debate 'on an early day' which in most cases never comes, the purpose being to draw attention to an issue. Other MPs add their names to the motion, so making known to the government the extent of parliamentary feeling on the matter.

Activity

Look up departmental select committees on the parliament website. Make a list of those currently in existence. Find details about any one committee and write a paragraph on it. Remember that examiners appreciate the use of such up-to-date information.

likely to be less dramatic but more thorough and rigorous. The most effective form of scrutiny is carried out in committee.

A system of departmental select committees began to function in 1980. Fourteen committees were set up, each to monitor the work of one government department, e.g. one for Foreign Affairs, one for Home Affairs. Membership of the 19 current committees varies from 11 to 16 and reflects party strengths in the House. The Committee of Selection appoints members for the lifetime of a parliament. Often they are reappointed in the next parliament, if they get re-elected. This longevity enables them to acquire a real expertise on their subject. Select committees have powers to send for people, papers and records, receive evidence from ministers and civil servants, and can use the services of outside experts.

In depth

British and US committees

The idea for investigatory committees came from the US. The US Congress has uniquely powerful committees that are vital to its work. They are backed with huge resources, employing in all some 3,500 policy specialists. They decide the fate and shape of most legislation and have spawned many subcommittees. The chairpersons of congressional committees are often highly influential. Of course, in US government there is a separation of powers, with the three parts of government theoretically having equal status. The legislature is required to hold the Executive to account and strong committees serve an important purpose in carrying out this role. Given the weakness of the party system, it is no surprise that even members of the president's party may be active and vocal critics in committee.

By contrast, in party-dominated legislature such as the House of Commons, the Public Bill Committees do not challenge executive dominance in the legislative field and – in the case of the previous Standing Committees – were seriously under-resourced. The system of select committees of scrutiny do probe government policy and monitor its implementation, and they have been an important innovation of the last 30 years or so. However, they cannot match their US counterparts in terms of personnel, nor are their reports always taken as seriously. Many British politicians – particularly ministers – have expressed the fear that the introduction of US-style committees would be aimed at controlling rather than criticising the policy and actions of the department concerned.

Overall, the British parliament is floor oriented (in other words, what happens on the floor of the House of Commons is arguably more important), whereas the US Congress is committee-oriented (much of the important work takes place in committees).

Select committees are a good thing!

- They work in a less partisan way than happens in the chamber and try to produce an agreed report on their findings.
- Members are often well informed, developing a real specialism.
- Members can feed their knowledge back into House of Commons debates and so help to inform others.

- They have made government more open, evidence being taken in public and ministers being examined in a thorough way.
- They encourage government to have a pre-emptive impact, deterring ministers from behaviour that they might be unable to justify before a committee.
- They may manage to persuade government to change course.

Select committees are not particularly effective!

- In recent years, the whips have tried to keep more independent and effective MPs off committees and not reappoint those who are critical of government.
- Committees need more resources; their budget is too small to carry out substantial independent research.
- They generate much paperwork; their reports may be debated – then they are often shelved and forgotten.
- They need more powers. Ministers attend but sometimes refuse to answer and civil servants are often tempted to withhold information in the interests of national security or 'good government'.
- They have a majority of government party members, as their composition reflects the balance of party strength on the floor of the House.

In depth

The differences between standing (public) and select committees

- Duration: public bill committees (PCs) are appointed every session; select committees (SCs) are for the duration of the parliament.
- PCs are non-specialist, bills being allocated to the next one available; SCs are specialist, members tend to serve a long time and acquire expert knowledge.
- Work: PCs are concerned with a stage in the legislative process, examining detail of bills; SCs monitor and scrutinise the spending, policies and administration of a particular department.
- Size: PCs are fairly large bodies of 16–50 members; SCs are fairly small bodies, usually of 11 members but up to 16.
- Power: PCs are traditionally less investigatory (that is not their primary function), but they have had the power to take evidence from outside officials and experts since 2006 SCs are more powerful, equipped with powers to hold hearings and collect evidence.

The role of Her Majesty's Loyal Opposition

'Her Majesty's Loyal Opposition' or the 'Official Opposition' is the largest party on the Opposition benches as opposed to the term 'opposition parties' which includes all of those parties that oppose the government of the day.

The opposition plays an essential role in the day-to-day affairs of parliament, at best providing a structured and regular challenge to the measures and actions of government. It has three main functions:

Key term

Her Majesty's Loyal Opposition or the **Official Opposition** is the second-largest party in the House of Commons and a recognised part of the Constitution. Since May 1997, the Official Opposition has been the Conservative party.

Fig. 3 *Members of the Shadow Cabinet 2007 led by David Cameron*

Activity

Governments face two oppositions in parliament: the official opposition and that deriving from their own back-benchers. Think about this and write a few sentences explaining which is likely to exert the greater impact on ministers. Consider how effective you consider the present opposition party to be.

1 The opposition opposes the government. It stood at the last election on the basis of distinctive principles and policies, and naturally opposes ministers when they do things differently to the way it recommends. It needs to provide sustained scrutiny, questioning ministerial proposals and testing them through debate.

2 The opposition supports the government where appropriate, not opposing for the sake of it. This is the concept of responsible, constructive opposition. Careful scrutiny is given, but if ministers do things broadly seen as in the national interest (e.g. over Northern Ireland), then the Opposition will try to be bi-partisan and cooperative.

3 The opposition is also an alternative government. If its criticisms are not responsible and well thought out it will lack credibility and seem obstructive. It will need to review its policies as circumstances change and produce a coherent, convincing range of alternative courses for action.

The existence of an official opposition party is regarded as one of the litmus tests of a democracy. In Britain, the task is performed by the second-largest party in the House. Its importance is recognised by the payment of an official salary to the leader of the Opposition and opposition chief whip. The opposition also gets a share of the 'Short Money', the grant payable to help opposition parties carry out their work.

Problems for the Opposition

Life can be difficult for a party in opposition, especially in the early years following a long period in office. Among the problems:

- The opposition lacks the information available to the government. Ministers have civil servants/political advisers to brief them and know the state of the accounts. The opposition lacks help from officials in the civil service and does not have access to detailed information.

- Governments set the political agenda and the Opposition normally has to respond to it. Ministers can and sometimes do take over the best opposition policies. Moreover, it is the Prime Minister who determines the date of the next election.

- There may be pressure from dispirited activists to push the party back to a more fundamentalist position. Activists like to see clear water between themselves and ministerial policies, but of course abandoning a middle-of-the-road position may alienate moderate, centrist voters.

- Morale can be low, especially after a massive election defeat. After landslide election defeats such as those in 1997 and 2001, there seems little point in turning up to be defeated by a massive majority in every parliamentary vote. Party division may also set in.

- Prospects for re-election can seem dismal when the majority is vast. It seems to take a lot of work and a long time before the public forget the errors committed when the Opposition party was last in office.

- If the Opposition try to reverse party policy too quickly in order to expose governmental weakness, voters may ask why they did not get things right when they were in government.

Summary questions

1. As his premiership came to an end, Tony Blair was said to have used the term 'bollocks' to describe PMQ. Does it have as little value as he implied? What might the remark tell you about his attitude to parliament?

2. Assess the value of departmental select committees.

3. Have the Conservatives been a credible/convincing opposition party?

4 Do individual MPs make a difference?

Learning objectives:

- What opportunities are there both within and outside the House for MPs to influence the evolution of policy?

- What factors limit their influence?

- How restrictive is the whipping system on the independence of MPs?

- In what ways can individual MPs make an impact in the House?

Key terms

Westminster Hall was opened as an additional location for parliamentary debates in December 1999. It is aimed at introducing a different style of debate. Seating is in a horseshoe arrangement intended to encourage constructive rather than confrontational debate.

Motion for the adjournment: takes place prior to the recess, at the end of each day's sitting and in timed slots in the Tuesday and Wednesday morning sittings in Westminster Hall. MPs seek to adjourn the House in order to raise topics of constituency interest or public concern.

Catch the Speaker's eye: MPs signal that they wish to speak in a debate by standing up from their seat (a custom known as 'catching the Speaker's eye'. They can also notify the Speaker in writing in advance.

The demands of party loyalty: the expectation by the party leadership that party MPs will 'toe the line' (i.e. conform).

As we have seen, parliamentary time is monopolised by the government and to a much lesser extent by the Opposition. Ordinary back-bench MPs may feel powerless, some conscious of the fact that their main role is to serve as a cog in the party machine, voting as their party requires. Opportunities to make memorable contributions in debate or to initiate legislation are infrequent.

Yet there are limited ways in which MPs can make a difference mainly in the House but also in **Westminster Hall**. They can:

- **criticise policy** during Question Time, by ballot on the **motion for the adjournment** usually at 10pm and at the end of the parliamentary session before a recess and speak in debate (if they can **catch the Speaker's eye**)

- **initiate legislation** by winning a good position in the annual ballot of private members or by introducing a bill under the Ten-minute Rule

- **convey their views** via appearances and propaganda both inside the House and through the media by appearing at public functions and on national and local TV and radio programmes.

However, some MPs are conscious of the limitations upon their ability to do the job as well as they would wish. Their desire to advance their career may make them unwilling to speak out in opposition to their party's policy. If they wish to become a minister, then they may be reluctant to speak out against their party's policy for fear of falling foul of the party leadership. By being loyal and supportive, they can behave as trainee ministers, waiting for their time to come.

Factors influencing the effectiveness of MPs

The ability of MPs to act effectively and independently as free agents has been restricted by **the demands of party loyalty** and by increasing domination of the House of Commons by the government of the day.

MPs know that their parties expect them to show support in the voting lobbies as they were elected on a party manifesto. Opportunities for independent thought and action are few. Those who have been dissidents have often fallen foul of the party, so that the number of **mavericks** is relatively small. For those MPs who have no hopes of future promotion or whose parliamentary career is coming to an end, party discipline may not be a problem and some on the Labour benches are prone to rebellion (see below). For most, it is an obvious limitation on their freedom of manoeuvre or action.

An MP's ability to do his or her job well is also limited by the following:

- **Poor facilities**. These may have improved over the last generation, but MPs who have had experience of the worlds of commerce and industry will probably find the lack of office space, computerised equipment and assistance with handling constituency problems a real impediment.

- **The immense amount and complexity of government business**. Government was probably always complex to those involved and there never was a golden age in which MPs knew everything about every aspect of policy. In the 20th century, the role of government dramatically expanded and we now live in the age of the **managed economy** and welfare state. The voters have high expectations of their governments at home, and the demands of global interests and responsibilities (such as involvement in the European Union) create additional areas of ministerial activity. Faced by this situation, the MPs find it best to specialise in selected areas as it is unlikely that they can be informed about the whole range of policy issues. Their problem is not so much a lack of information but rather a lack of time in which to absorb that information.

- **The growing burden of constituency work**. Constituency work has now become so much more demanding. Constituents assume that their member will be active in taking up their personal and social problems. All MPs now have a very large postbag. Letters, faxes and e-mails are sent to them in ever-increasing numbers. Most MPs are dealing with correspondence for two or three hours every day. Also, constituency pressures upon an MP to take up a matter of concern to their locality or take a particular stance on a social issue such as abortion may conflict with party policy or personal belief – causing another problem for MPs.

- **Service on public bill and select committees**. This removes the member from the floor of the House which is the only place where ministers can really be challenged and governments placed under threat.

MPs, the whips and party loyalty

Critics of parliament often point to the strength of party discipline. Sometimes they portray MPs as 'lobby fodder', lacking in independent judgement and only too willing to conform. They dislike the tight whipping system which operates in the two main parties.

The whips

The whips are the officials who manage the supporters of their party in the House of Commons. The term is borrowed from the hunting-field, where one person traditionally had the task of 'whipping in' to the pack of hounds as they pursued their quarry. The whips are key figures in party organisation and they have responsibility for maintaining discipline and unity. In British politics, the chief whip in the House of Commons is assisted by between eight and 10 assistant whips all of whom are MPs. There are also whips in the Lords. But party discipline tends to be less strong in the second chamber and the whips are less exclusively concerned with party matters. (A number of cross-benches for peers are not associated with any political party.)

Whipped votes are votes in which the party whips instruct members on the line they are expected to adopt, the term 'whip' also being applied to the notice of business that requires attendance to vote with the party in divisions or votes coming up in the following week. Items are underlined once, twice or three times, according to their importance. For a 'three-line whip', MPs are expected to attend, absence only being approved if a member is out of the country on parliamentary business, seriously ill or has other exceptional reasons. On occasion, MPs may be allowed to miss votes if they can make an approved **pairing** arrangement.

Key terms

Pairing is an arrangement where an MP of one party agrees with an MP of an opposing party not to vote in a particular division. This gives both MPs the opportunity to absent themselves from Commons proceedings. Such arrangements have to be registered with the whips.

1922 Committee: this is made up of all Conservative back-bench MPs, although front-benchers, except the leader, can attend when the party is in opposition.

Parliamentary Labour party: the body of Labour MPs in parliament, the equivalent to the Conservatives' 1922 Committee.

Activity

Using the local press or the internet to assist you, find out what the MP in your area has been doing in recent weeks, both in the House and in the constituency. For more details, look at: www.theyworkforyou.com.

Maintaining unity is essential for any party because:

- Splits can mean the loss of the governing party's majority. For example, the survival of both the Callaghan and Major governments was often jeopardised.

- Governments wish to legislate on programmes on which they have fought the election in order to carry out their mandate. They need to be able to rely on the backing of their MPs in order to implement their policies.

- Divisions are harmful to parties as they provide opportunities for other parties and journalists to expose and exploit their differences.

- Parties which do face three ways in a division (some members for, some against and some abstaining) create confusion. They cause difficulty for the public and commentators who are unsure what party policy actually is.

Parties realise that there are inevitably internal differences among their MPs as parties are broad coalitions of sometimes quite widely differing viewpoints. But they expect that they will not often question party policy in public or be disloyal when crucial parliamentary votes are counted. Most MPs can accept these constraints. Why do MPs normally toe the party line?

- However much they doubt their own side's policy, the last thing they want to do is to endanger the government's survival and see the Opposition occupy the ministerial seats.

- They know that in the privacy of a back-bench meeting (in the **1922 Committee** or in the **parliamentary Labour party**) they can argue for a concession from the minister and – especially if its seems that their doubts are widely held – they will probably get one. The minister may well be flexible in order to ensure that his bill gets safely through. Several concessions were made during the passage of the bill providing for tuition fees for students in higher education (2003–04) in order to ensure that the government got the measure on the statute book.

- Finally, there is the 'carrot and the stick'. For some young MPs who hope to climb the ministerial ladder, the prospect of early promotion keeps them in line. Should there be persistent rebellion, then more formal sanctions may be applied such as loss of the whip – as happened to eight Euro-sceptics under the Major government. This means that they lose the privileges of membership of the parliamentary party, such as the right to attend its meetings.

Rebellions do occur

MPs were more assertive in Labour's second term than in the first. In 2003, when the invasion of Iraq was launched, its own members were in rebellious mood. At the beginning of the year, the largest rebellions that have ever occurred were recorded (121 and 137, both over Iraq). But on fox-hunting, foundation hospitals and hunting, high levels of dissent were recorded. In addition to those Labour MPs who voted against the government, many more abstained. The habit of rebellion became well established, as many Labour MPs seemed keen to inflict a 'bloody nose' on Tony Blair whose leadership style and policies they disliked.

In addition, of course, there are some free votes – primarily on socio-moral issues – in which MPs can choose to express their individual attitudes rather than toe the party line in the voting lobbies. Also in 2003, there was a free vote on fox-hunting in which 329 Labour members rejected the preferred ministerial option of licensed hunts. The abolition of hunting is one issue on which MPs undoubtedly got their way, a total ban being achieved against the wishes of the Prime Minister who found himself using the Parliament Act 1949 to enforce a measure about which he had grave doubts.

The significance of the average back-bench MP

There never was a golden age in which MPs were well informed about all aspects of government and were able to exercise judgement free of party pressures. But 150 years ago the demands upon them were much less than they are now and they also enjoyed much social standing within the community. Today, MPs are often held in low repute by the voters, many of whom are cynical about their ideas, performance and integrity. The opportunity for individual MPs to influence national events is limited by certain factors.

But MPs can make their mark. They may ask questions, speak in debates, be active in standing or select committees and crusade for good causes. Maybe a Private Members' Bill will be forever associated with their name. Although many MPs do not have a high profile, some are often seen on the media and can make an impact via broadcasting. Otherwise, much depends on what they regard as their primary tasks. There are different routes that they may follow, as described by Richards (1964). They can be:

- **Useful party members**. Such members tend to specialise in particular areas of policy and serve on the relevant committees and appear on the media to discuss issues on which they can contribute their expertise. They are useful to the party, often loyal in the lobbies, and may become a parliamentary private secretary or advance further.
- **Good constituency members**. Such MPs devote much of their time to constituency work, taking up personal cases and earning themselves a well-deserved reputation for diligence and effectiveness on behalf of those they seek to serve.
- **Individualists: independents within the system**. These MPs are often colourful characters who are not easily contained within the party system. Genuine independents are few, but there are some independently minded MPs in the main parties who make a name for themselves. Richard Shepherd (Con) is active in the areas of freedom of information/state secrecy and abuse of executive power. He is known as being a persistent and courageous member. Former Labour MP George Galloway, now of Respect (see p55), has been a fearless critic of government policy over many areas.
- **Part-timers**. Some MPs still seek to combine their parliamentary activity with an outside occupation, perhaps serving in journalism, the law or business. The number of part-timers diminished following Labour's landslide win in 1997. Many Conservatives with outside interests were voted out in that election.

For example, Richard Shepherd (Figure 04) has the following select committee membership:

- Human Rights (Joint Committee of two chambers).
- Modernisation of the House of Commons Committee.

He tends to ask questions about:

- Departments: Health, Home, Justice, Prime Minister, Leader of the House.

Further information

200 MPs and their proudest achievements

- 43 passing legislation, 18 a Private Members' Bill
- 27 securing better health provision in their constituencies
- 25 service on a select committee
- 18 helping constituents
- 15 helping to save/create jobs
- 13 securing better educational provision
- 9 securing regeneration money for their constituency
- 9 securing a new road or crossing.

Source: Survey for the *Guardian* (April 2001)

Fig. 4 *Richard Shepherd MP for Aldrige-Brownhills*

■ Subjects: North Sea Camp Prison, Sexual Health, Legislation, Walsall Primary Care Trust, Official Secrets Act.

Summary questions

1 Are MPs lobby fodder?

2 Why do you think that MPs on the government side have more influence on ministers than MPs on the Opposition side?

5 The reputation of parliament today

Learning objectives:

■ Why is parliament often said to be in decline?

■ In what ways has parliament been reformed in recent years?

■ What more could be done?

■ Should the activities of the whips be curtailed?

Hint

Remember that when talking about parliamentary – as opposed to House of Commons – reform, it is worth mentioning possible reform of the Lords as well as of the lower chamber. You might re-read the section on p209 about reform of the upper house.

Over recent decades, many writers have drawn attention to the alleged 'decline of legislatures'. In Britain, chapters have been written on the 'passing of parliament', 'parliament in decline' or 'the loss of parliamentary control'.

There are different ideas about parliament's role. They focus primarily on the House of Commons as the elected chamber:

1 Critics of the House tend to argue that it needs strengthening so that it can wield greater influence and more effectively hold the government to account for its work; it must act as a vigilant watchdog over the Executive. Back-benchers who are reform minded, academics and commentators often adopt this approach. They wish to see reforms that strengthen the chamber's powers.

2 Others expect a lesser role for the House of Commons. They see it as an important debating chamber, a forum where grievances are aired and where the party struggle is conducted. According to this view, it is more of a place to vent arguments than a body that is truly a check upon the Executive. Reforms to make the House work more efficiently and use its time more effectively might be welcome.

Interest in the subject of parliamentary reform has increased in recent years as part of a general concern about the health and vitality of British political institutions. Surveys have shown that many people now question the way in which parliament does its work. Some of the concern voiced by commentators and journalists is about the House of Commons as a collective entity, whilst at the popular level there is more scepticism about the conduct, performance and work of individual MPs. Such public disquiet has encouraged some people to seek to achieve their goals by extra-parliamentary means (direct action) rather than via traditional democratic channels.

Reforming parliament

In depth

The differing views of those who wish to reform parliament

- Ministers may wish to see government tackle its business more speedily so that they can get their programme through – the need for efficiency.

- Some MPs may wish to have an improved working environment and more reasonable hours – the demands of convenience.

- Other MPs may want to remove outdated practices and rituals, little understood by people outside the chamber – the removal of a cause of embarrassment about their workplace.

- Academics and commentators may feel that parliament needs to be strengthened, to provide a better check upon government – the argument for greater effectiveness.

Some of these motives may conflict with each other. The desire to get business through more quickly may conflict with the wish to see parliament provide greater scrutiny. The demands of scrutiny may also conflict with the desire to ease the lifestyle of members (convenience). The most important reason for reform must be to make parliament better able to hold government to account.

Writers such as Philip Norton argue that the decline and weakness of parliament can be over-stressed and point out that in recent years parliament has become more effective, with MPs becoming better-informed and professional, and the House more efficient. But even if they doubt some aspects of the diagnosis, they still see a need for further reforms to make parliament work better.

What has been done since 1997 (for good or ill)?

Changes have been made to:

- **modify the timetable of the House of Commons**. In 2002, the House voted to modify its antiquated sittings. The hours were made more 'family friendly', with proceedings starting and finishing earlier in the day. (In 2005, they were slightly revised to allow late sittings on Tuesdays.)

- **provide more office space**, via the opening of Portcullis House, next door to Westminster

- **Prime Minister's Questions**. There is now one half-hour session per week instead of two shorter ones

- **permit more effective questioning of the Prime Minister**. Beginning in 2003, Tony Blair began to answer questions from the chairpersons of the select committees, meeting as the **Commons' Liaison Committee**

- **provide for more pre-legislative scrutiny of legislation**, to ensure that the bill which is finally produced has already received careful analysis and taken account of possible problems

Key term

The **Commons' Liaison Committee** includes the 30 chairmen of select committees. It is appointed to consider general matters relating to the work of select committees and to report on them to the House.

Further information

Improved parliamentary scrutiny
Scrutiny . . . is now stronger than it was in 1997 . . . changes in procedure and improvements in the power of the House – including many more inquiries by select committee, the Public Bill system that we have established and much else besides . . . have strengthened its role. The number of parliamentary questions asked of the government has also nearly doubled.

Jack Straw, Leader of the House of Commons, addressing the chamber, 3 May 2007

Further information

Suggested reforms to make MPs more effective
Austin Mitchell, Labour MP since 1977, wants to see:

- well-resourced constituency and London offices
- a non-ministerial career path
- a greater role in the legislative process
- a change in the role/power of the whips
- more joint parliamentary committees to draw upon the expertise of MPs and peers
- better television coverage, perhaps some sort of current affairs channel.

Source: Address to Politics Association, 1994

- **allow for debates and occasionally questions sessions in Westminster Hall**, a specially converted room off the main hall, thus providing more opportunities for MPs to have their say.

What more could be done?

Academics and commentators advocate a range of ideas, some of which may be found in the following list:

1 **More powerful select committees**. Critics say that more resources are needed, with a better budget, more staffing by experts, stronger powers to make ministers and officials answer, more attention to and debate of committee reports and less influence by the whips over selection of membership. The House did introduce payment for select committee chairs to come into force for the 2003–04 session. Since 1 April 2007, £13,326 has been paid on top of the standard MPs' pay.

2 **Better pay and facilities for MPs**. Pay and facilities are much better than they were a few decades ago, but many MPs still find that they cannot get all of the secretarial and research help they need. Many point to the need for more constituency help and better computer links with their local base.

3 **Full-time MPs**. Given the size of Labour's majority, many MPs are full time and it is the Conservatives who tend to have second jobs. Critics say that no MP can do two jobs well; that membership of parliament and full engagement in its committee system is so demanding that it requires full-time attention; and that anyway some previous occupations (e.g. working on the shop floor in the manufacturing industry) cannot be combined with parliamentary duties. Pay and facilities should be such that all MPs can be full time; they can get experience of life outside Westminster in their holidays. Opponents argue that the House benefits from the experience and current knowledge gained from outside tasks; that a House of full-time members becomes a kind of monastery, detached from the public; and that hard-working people can find the time to perform their parliamentary and constituency duties as well as making a contribution in some other area.

4 **Less MPs**. Philip Norton, Michael Howard and others have called for a cut in number to around 450. This would reduce the current payroll and so enable more to be spent on better-resourcing fewer MPs to enable them to operate effectively. As there are now more full-time MPs, pressure on the existing institution is considerable. For instance, MPs ask far more questions today, hoping that this will win them constituency approval. Norton wants a smaller, more professional house and makes the point that the present one, organised for the days in which mainly gifted amateurs went into politics, is one of the largest elected chambers in the world.

5 **More free votes**. Strong party discipline seems to worry MPs much less than critics outside. They like free votes on social and moral topics, but accept that if governments are to push through their legislative programme then whipping is essential. Also, they know that there are other ways of influencing events.

In depth

Excessive whipping?

party has greatly undermined the independence and hence the prestige of individual members. It is difficult to have much interest in parliamentary debates when the outcome is known before the debate has even opened. It is no accident that the best debates which have taken place in the Commons . . . have been those on the moral and social subjects . . . where the party whip was not operating.

Lord St John Stevas, February 1980

The House of Commons is perceived by the electorate to be as putty in the hands of any government with a secure majority and a good whipping system.

John Major, in a Commons debate, 2000

Summary questions

1 Why do you think that parliament and its MPs are popularly held in low esteem?

2 Is further reform of the House desirable and necessary? If so, what reforms would you favour?

Activity

Write a couple of paragraphs in defence of the whipping system in the House of Commons.

Further reading

Useful articles:

P Cowley, 'The Marginalisation of Parliament', *Talking Politics*, Winter 2000.

P Cowley and M Stuart, 'Parliament: a few headaches and a dose of modernisation', *Parliamentary Affairs*, 54:3, 2001.

P Cowley and M Stuart, 'New Labour's Backbenchers', *Talking Politics*, September 2002.

M Grant, 'The Theory and Practice of Parliamentary Reform', *Talking Politics*, January 2004

P Norton, 'Parliamentary Reform in Labour's Second Term', *Talking Politics*, September 2001.

P Norton, 'Reforming the House of Lords: A View from the Parapets', *Representation*, 40:3, 2004.

C Ridsill-Smith, 'Parliamentary Reform', *Talking Politics*, September 2001.

'The Challenge for parliament: Making Government Accountable', *Hansard Society Commission Report*, 2001.

Useful books:

A Adonis, *Parliament Today*, MUP, 1993.

P Norton, 'The UK: Parliament under pressure', in P Norton (ed.) **Parliaments and Pressure Groups in Western Europe**, 1999.

P Norton, 'Parliament', in A Seldon (ed.) **The Blair Effect**, Little Brown, 2001.

P Norton, **Parliament in British Politics**, Palgrave, 2005.

Websites

www.parliament.uk. Parliament site, with links to both chambers.

AQA Examination-style questions

1   ☑ Read the extract and answer questions (a) to (c) which follow.

Problems for the Opposition

Life can be difficult for a party in opposition., especially in the early years following a long period in office. Among the problems are:

■   The Opposition lacks the information available to the government. Ministers have civil servants/ *political advisers* to brief them and know the state of the accounts. Oppositions lack help from the civil service and do not have access to detailed information.

■   Governments set the political agenda and the Opposition normally has to respond to it. Ministers can and sometimes do take over the best Opposition policies. Moreover it is the Prime Minister who determines the date of the next election.

Source: adapted from Chapter 12 of this textbook

(a)   Briefly explain the term *political advisers* as it is used in the extract.   *(5 marks)*

(b)   Using your own knowledge as well as the extract, explain what kind of help officials in the Civil Service may give ministers.   *(10 marks)*

(c)   Analyse what other difficulties the leaders of parties in Opposition are likely to encounter.   *(25 marks)*

2   Read the extract and answer questions (a) to (c) which follow.

The back-bench MP

MPs can make their mark. They may ask questions, speak in debates, be active in standing or select committees and crusade for good causes. Maybe a *Private Members' Bill* will be forever associated with their name. Although many MPs do not have a high profile, some are often seen on the media and can make an impact via broadcasting. Otherwise, much depends on what they regard as their primary tasks. There are different routes that they may follow.

Source: adapted from Chapter 12 of this textbook

(a)   Briefly explain the term *Private Member's Bill* used in the extract.   *(5 marks)*

(b)   Using your own knowledge as well as the extract, assess the role of select committees in the work of the House of Commons.   *(10 marks)*

(c)   Analyse the primary tasks of the back-bench MP.   *(25 marks)*

13 The Prime Minister and Cabinet

1 The Cabinet system

Learning objectives:

- What is meant by 'the core executive' in British politics?
- What is the Cabinet?
- What does the Cabinet do?
- Would smaller Cabinets be a good thing?
- What are the roles of the Cabinet Secretary and the Cabinet Office?

Key terms

The core executive in Britain is the network of key institutions, people and practices at the heart of government, including the Prime Minister, the Cabinet and its committees, the Prime Minister's and Cabinet office, the government's law officers and the security and intelligence services.

Civil servants: defined by the Tomlin Commission in 1931 in this way: 'Servants of the Crown, other than holders of political or judicial offices, who are employed in a civil capacity and whose remuneration is paid wholly and directly out of moneys voted by parliament.'

The core executive

The term 'executive' derives from the Latin *ex sequi*, meaning to 'follow out' or 'carry out'. The role of the Executive branch of government in the political system is to make policies and administer laws. As long as there have been political systems, there have been individuals or small groups who assume the role of leadership, formulating and implementing public policy.

Many writers use the phrase '**core executive**' to refer to the complex network of institutions and people at the centre that between them are charged with the day-to-day government of the country, the making of policies and the implementation of laws. The core comprises the first minister (in Britain, known as the Prime Minister), the Cabinet and its committees, the offices that serve the first minister and Cabinet, and the departments headed by senior ministers and including senior civil servants. These groups represent the pinnacle of the decision-making process.

All members of the core executive are involved in a power network with other influential people and organisations in Whitehall and Westminster. Membership of the core is liable to change and it is not always clear who should be included at any given time. During the build-up to and invasion and occupation of Iraq, it included members of the intelligence services and the leaders among the military, but they would probably not always be involved. In some listings, the chief whip and even those who chair back-bench parliamentary committees are also part of the core.

In the British system, executive leadership and political direction is in theory provided by the Cabinet, but in practice the Prime Minister is more powerful than any of his ministerial colleagues. However, the notion of the core executive is intended to stress that government is an activity that is constantly responding to new problems and changing circumstances. As Moran (2005) puts it:

> There is no fixed agenda of business for the core executive; demands for decision just flow in . . . neither are its boundaries fixed . . . An issue that was once routine (managing football fans who travel abroad) suddenly rises right to the top of the concerns of the core executive. Individuals who normally work in obscurity within the Home Office tribe suddenly find themselves at meetings with the senior ministers and officials trying to explain how best to manage the problem.

The idea of the core executive is useful in helping us to understand that government is not a kind of pyramid, with the Prime Minister at the helm, then the most prestigious Cabinet ministers, then those who lead departments carrying less status, all of whom are advised by the group at the bottom of the pyramid, the unelected permanent **civil servants**. It serves to remind us that government is a fluid process in which many different people, offices and relationships are involved. All are active in making decisions at the centre of government.

Activity

Go to the Downing Street website (www.number-10.gov.uk) and look at the membership of the present Cabinet. See if you can find any differences in the offices (e.g. Secretary of State for Health) included in the Cabinet and those included in the Blair administration (these can be found on the Wikipedia website under the heading 'Blair Ministry').

Key terms

Cabinet government is a system in which the Cabinet forms a collective political executive, with each member having in theory an equal influence, other than the Prime Minister who is 'first among equals'. The Cabinet makes or is consulted about all important political decisions.

Prime Ministerial government is a system in which the office of Prime Minister has become a power-house, executive power being concentrated in his or her hands. Policy making is dominated by the Prime Minister rather than by the collective will of the Cabinet.

The membership, role and operation of the Cabinet

The term 'Cabinet' relates to the group of the most senior ministers who are chosen by the Prime Minister and are at the centre of the British political system. They are collectively empowered to make all decisions on behalf of the government. Most members are heads of government departments with the title of Secretary of State. They are drawn from either chamber of parliament.

In traditional constitutional theory, the Cabinet was the key formal decision-making body of the Executive. It directed the work of government and coordinated the activities of individual departments. It was described in the 19th century by Walter Bagehot as the 'efficient secret' of the political system. In the early–mid 20th century it was labelled the 'core of the British constitutional system' and writers commonly referred to the system of **Cabinet government**. Today, the Cabinet has a reduced role as a decision-making body. Indeed, some commentators claim that power has passed into the hands of the Prime Minister. Academics now often debate the reality or otherwise of **Prime Ministerial government**.

Cabinet membership

Most Cabinet members are drawn from the House of Commons, the dominant elected chamber. Most run a department such as Education and Skills, Health, the Home Office and Communities and local government. Some are non-departmental ministers such as the Lord Privy Seal and Chancellor of the Duchy of Lancaster. Lacking specific responsibilities, they have the opportunity to rove over the whole area of government and are available to take on particular tasks as assigned by the Prime Minister. Although the Cabinet normally has more than 20 members, there have been experiments with a smaller number, especially in time of war. In the words of Denis Kavanagh (1994):

> Decisions about Cabinet size and composition have to balance the needs of decision making and deliberation against those of representativeness. It has to be small enough to allow ministers the opportunities to discuss, deliberate and coordinate major policies, yet it must also be large enough to include heads of major departments and accommodate different political views in the party.

In depth

For and against smaller Cabinets

In the First World War, it was realised that a large Cabinet could not direct war policy. A small War Cabinet of five members was created in 1916. Since then, numerous authorities have suggested that to allow for a proper distinction between day-to-day administration and long-term general planning, a smaller body is required in peacetime as well. The Heath government (1970–74) went some way to achieving this goal in its experiment with a number of super-ministries each of which encompassed large areas of government.

A smaller cabinet would consist chiefly of five or six coordinating ministers appointed on a functional basis to cover such matters as defence, economic affairs, the social services and the environment, with departmental ministers only attending when their input was needed.

Advantages claimed for a Cabinet along these lines are that:

- Cabinet members, freed from departmental responsibilities, would see national problems as a whole and be mentally fresh to formulate and implement a national policy.
- It could meet more frequently and thus be available to make important decisions.
- It would be easier for the Prime Minister to act as the driving force of such a body.
- Each Cabinet member would be able to direct the policies of departments under his or her supervision, in the light of broad Cabinet decisions, coordinating their work and settling any disputes that might arise between them.

Disadvantages are that:

- It is not always possible to separate policy from administration. In making broad policy decisions, the Cabinet would lack the experience of those involved in day-to-day administration.
- The arrangement might blur responsibility to parliament, the Cabinet 'supervisors' not actually being in charge of much of the departmental work.
- A small Cabinet would make it more difficult to include up-and-coming younger ministers and deprive them of valuable experience at the highest level.
- Because of its size, it would be difficult for the Prime Minister to include representatives of all shades of party opinion. There would be a danger that the Cabinet could easily lose touch with party and public opinion.

In evidence to the Select Committee on Public Administration in 2007, Lord Butler noted that Heathite super-ministries were created for reasons 'that seemed very good at the time but really did not work because the burden on the secretary of state . . . was found to be too great, so the thing fragmented again'.

In Cabinet meetings, the attitudes and preferences of more senior ministers normally carry greater weight than those of others present. The Prime Minister is at the helm, followed by the Chancellor of the Exchequer, the Foreign Secretary and then the Home Secretary. The relationship of the Prime Minister and Chancellor is crucial. If they are united in their stance on a particular issue, other ministers will find it hard to achieve any contrary objectives. In the Blair years, there was often friction between Tony Blair and Gordon Brown.

The chief whip will normally attend Cabinet meetings, although the office does not really carry full membership of the Cabinet. The chief whip is there to advise Cabinet ministers of the feeling on the back-benches of the party, in order to ensure that the leadership does not lose touch with other MPs. This will help prevent damaging revolts in the House of Commons.

The Blair Cabinets were noted for the number of women they included, five in the first one, six following a reshuffle in October 2002 and eight out of 23 in the final one as reshuffled in January 2007. Until the last reshuffle, none of the senior, more prestigious posts had been held by a woman, but on becoming Foreign Secretary Margaret Beckett set a precedent.

Fig. 1 *The Brown Cabinet*

The first Brown Cabinet has 22 members, but a further seven ministers attend its weekly meetings.

The role of the Cabinet

The work of the Cabinet involves:

- **Deciding on major policy to be followed at home and abroad**. Government policy has often been stated in the election manifesto and reflects prevailing party policy. But when in office, the priorities for action have to be decided and a legislative programme drawn up. Details of policy have to be filled in according to prevailing circumstances such as the financial state of the country and the advice received from key pressure groups.

- **Dealing with unforeseen major problems**. New problems arise from time to time. In former Premier Harold Macmillan's words, the main problem for governments is 'events, dear boy, events'. There may be a crisis in the European Union, a sudden invasion of a friendly state, a fuel crisis at home, the discovery of a major human or animal disease (e.g. Aids, BSE or foot-and-mouth) or a hospital bed shortage in a winter outbreak of a vicious strain of influenza.

- **Coordinating the policies of different departments**. If government is to function well and policy is to be successfully carried out, there needs to be coordination between government departments. In some cases, disputes may have to be resolved between departmental ministers or policies pulled together to ensure what Tony Blair termed 'joined up government'. There is a natural tension between Treasury representatives and spending ministers who want more money for defence, education, health, transport and other costly areas of policy. Ultimately, these disagreements may have to be settled at Cabinet level.

- **Planning for the long term**. Ideally, this is a key area of policy making, but governments are often preoccupied with the here and now. Moreover, ministers come and go, making it difficult to plan ahead with consistency of purpose. Yet some issues require long-term planning (e.g. the environment, defence and pension policy). Often this work is done in **Cabinet committees**.

The role of the Cabinet has diminished in recent years, the frequency of its meetings and their duration both being reduced. Clement Attlee, the post-war Labour premier, held two meetings per week, but from 1969 onwards there has only been one regular session, usually held on a Thursday morning. In the Attlee/Churchill years, there were often over 100 Cabinet meetings per year, most of them lasting for a couple of hours or more. In the 1970s, there were around 60 meetings per year. Tony Blair averaged about 40, many of which lasted under one hour. One held in 1997 lasted only 30 minutes, probably the briefest ever. Short meetings can reflect prime ministerial style. They may also be a sign that members are broadly agreed on what they wish to achieve and how they wish to achieve it. Significantly, the Callaghan and Major meetings were longer than average as there were often serious disagreements over the controversial issues in need of resolution.

The role of the Cabinet Secretariat and Cabinet Secretary

For these meetings, the Cabinet Secretariat of 30–40 senior civil servants timetable meetings, circulates papers, prepares the agenda (under the direction of the Prime Minister), writes and circulates the conclusions, and retains them for future reference and posterity. The Secretariat is so important that its head is the country's top civil servant, the Cabinet Secretary. He is in daily contact with the Prime Minister and Cabinet members. He attends Cabinet meetings (though not when party political items are being discussed) and some Cabinet committees. The relationship between the Prime Minister and the Cabinet Secretary is a crucial one. Many years ago, **Richard Crossman** revealed its importance, noting how the two men decided the Cabinet agenda and the order of the items on it, and agreed the minutes afterwards.

The Secretariat is assisted by a Cabinet Office of some 1,500 civil servants who prepare the work for committees and follow up their decisions. The term 'Cabinet Office' is now generally used to cover the whole machinery that services the Cabinet and the departments, and the word 'Secretariat' rarely features. The main tasks of the Cabinet Office are:

- to support the Prime Minister as leader of the government
- to support the Cabinet in its transaction of business
- to lead and support the reform and delivery programme
- to coordinate security and intelligence.

Apart from its traditional duties as outlined, since the Major years within the Cabinet Office there has been permanent machinery to cope with emergencies such as threats to fuel and water supplies, or terrorist activity. This is the Civil Contingencies Unit that can, as the occasion demands, transform itself into a mixed committee of ministers, officials, the military, the policy and the security services, with the Home Secretary in the chair.

From an early stage as PM, Tony Blair and his team were keen to see a 'dynamic centre'. This involved more power for the Prime Minister's Office which would work closely with the Cabinet Office. He answered a parliamentary question on the future of the Cabinet Office back in 1998. He said:

Further information

Recent Cabinet Secretaries

- 1979 Sir Robert Armstrong
- 1988 Sir Robin Butler
- 1998 Sir Richard Wilson
- 2003 Sir Andrew Turnbull
- 2005 Sir Gus O'Donnell.

The role of the Cabinet Office has traditionally been to help the Prime Minister and the government as a whole to reach collective decisions on government policy. Since the election, the three principal parts of the centre – my own office, the Cabinet Office and the Treasury – have worked closely and effectively together, and with other Departments, to take forward the government's comprehensive and ambitious policy agenda.

Since then, there has been a closer fusion than before between the Prime Minister's Office and the Cabinet Office. Tony Blair developed the Major emphasis on government by specialised unit. The Social Exclusion Unit and the Performance and Innovation Unit were created by him and housed in the Cabinet Office. They were given specific tasks and reported to him via the Cabinet Secretary.

The Cabinet Office is intended to support the Prime Minister. It helps him or her to ensure that the government delivers its priorities, particularly in relation to health, education, transport, crime and asylum policies. The department is currently headed by the Minister for the Cabinet Office, a key figure who is granted close access to the Premier. The incumbent is in charge of progress chasing across government departments. He or she reports directly to the Prime Minister and answers on the range of his or her departmental duties to the House of Commons.

Summary questions

1. What do you regard as the most important function of the Cabinet?

2. Would a smaller Cabinet function more effectively and allow for improved decision making?

3. What is the role of the Cabinet Office? In what ways did Tony Blair change its role and structure?

2 How the Cabinet operates

Learning objectives:

- Other than via Cabinet meetings, what are the main opportunities for members of the Cabinet to convey their views to the Prime Minister?

- What is the role and value of Cabinet committees?

- How can they be used to empower the Prime Minister?

- What is meant by Collective Cabinet Responsibility and how strongly is the convention enforced?

Key term

Task forces bring together civil servants and outside experts to tackle issues that do not easily fit within the orbit of any one department. An important innovation of the Blair government, they were designed to improve the quality of decision making in government and have been used to tackle issues such as football and disability rights.

Activity

Go to the Cabinet Office website (www.cabinetoffice.gov.uk) and investigate the number and range of current Cabinet committees.

The Cabinet in a wider sense

The term 'Cabinet' is generally used to refer to the formal meetings held each week. In recent years, these have become increasingly concerned with the exchange of information and the ratification of decisions already made elsewhere, so that when we speak of the Cabinet we may use the term as an umbrella one for other foci of decision-making. In this broad sense, the Cabinet is still of major significance in determining the direction and policy of government. These other focus points include:

- **The inner Cabinet**. In many Cabinets, there are informal gatherings of leading departmental ministers, among whom there is normally an established pecking order. The Deputy Prime Minister (if there is one), the Chancellor of the Exchequer and the Foreign Secretary are likely to be included, with others attending according to prime ministerial taste. The existence of such a body serves to strengthen prime ministerial dominance, as it allows him or her to involve a small body of important and/or like-minded colleagues in decision making.

- **The kitchen cabinet**. Most Prime Ministers also have a kitchen cabinet consisting of their own trusted advisers who may be Cabinet members but are often trusted personal advisers on their own staff.

- **Cabinet committees**. The Prime Minister determines the chair and composition of Cabinet committees. They usually comprise departmental ministers and a representative of the Treasury, although some also include officials. Those considered important to the direction of governmental policy are likely to be chaired by the Prime Minister or his deputy (if he has one), the Chancellor of the Exchequer, or sometimes (as in the early days of the Blair premiership) the Lord Chancellor. Decisions made in committee are often presented to the whole Cabinet as established government policy.

- **Bilaterals** These are meetings between the Prime Minister and the relevant Secretary of State.

Gillian Peele notes that in recent years there has been an increased use of subcommittees, which tend to have a narrower remit than Cabinet committees. Also:

> Since 1997 there has also been a much greater use of less-formal policy coordination devices. These include working groups, task forces and ad hoc meetings. Unlike Cabinet committees and subcommittees, which have the authority of the Cabinet as a whole, these groups have no formal status and cannot make binding decisions.

In depth

A note on Cabinet committees

Cabinet committees existed in an unsystematic form in the 19th century, but it was the impact of two world wars and the rapid expansion of governmental activity in the post-1945 era that created the present committee structure. Up until the 1970s, their existence

227

was officially denied, but within a decade academics and journalists had probed to find out more. Since 1992, the membership of Cabinet committees has been published.

There are two types of Cabinet committee:

1 Standing committees are named, permanent committees responsible for a particular policy area such as Northern Ireland, the European Union and local government. The most important is the Economic and Domestic Policy (EDP) Committee, chaired by the Prime Minister.

2 Ad hoc committees vary in number according to the preferences and style of the Prime Minister. They are concerned with particular policy areas, perhaps a sudden crisis or an issue of current importance. Once the crisis has passed or the event ceases to be relevant, ad hoc committees are disbanded. Some others continue to exist but meet only as necessary. In Tony Blair's first administration, there were ad hoc committees on celebration of the millennium, utility regulation, biotechnology, genetic modification and better government.

Important deliberative work is done in committees. They consider issues in more detail than a Cabinet meeting does. Decisions are made in committees and are not referred to the whole Cabinet which only becomes involved with prime ministerial approval and in cases where there are major differences of opinion between ministers and departments. But as the Prime Minister chairs several important committees, disagreement is not common. Tony Blair personally chaired the committees on Iraq, international terrorism and antisocial behaviour, all areas of importance to the standing of his administration. Under both Tony Blair and Margaret Thatcher, the creation and composition of committees has been a key element in strengthening prime ministerial power, although in the case of Tony Blair he also relied heavily on more informal sources of support.

The doctrine of collective cabinet responsibility

The convention of cabinet responsibility means that ministers are collectively responsible to the House of Commons for governmental policy. In public, they are required to stick to the agreed Cabinet line and stay united. As a 19th-century Prime Minister, Lord Melbourne, once cynically remarked: 'It doesn't matter what we say, as long as we all tell the same story'.

There will be times when Cabinet members feel uneasy about what is being proposed and there may be sharp controversy behind closed doors. They have the opportunity to voice their discontent. But when the policy is decided, they either resign because they cannot go along with it or they decide they can live with it and agree to stay silent about any reservations. The position was laid down clearly by Lord Salisbury more than a hundred years ago:

> For all that passes in Cabinet, every member of it who does not resign is absolutely and irretrievably responsible, and has no right afterwards to say that he agreed in one case to a compromise, while in another he was persuaded by his colleagues.

In recent decades, the policy has been extended downwards, well below Cabinet level. All members of the government are bound to back official policy, even though only Cabinet members will have been present at the time of decision. Today, even the lowest rank in the administration, the unpaid **parliamentary Private Secretaries (PPSs)**, are expected to toe the line. This means that ministers who did not participate in discussion of a particular issue, or may not even know that discussion had taken place, are bound by collective responsibility once the decision is made public.

The doctrine still has its uses as it:

- ensures that ministers all portray the same views and opinions thereby helping to make policy clear and coherent
- helps to maintain a united front in public, thereby increasing public confidence that the government is fully in control
- avoids the confusion that can arise when different members of an administration say different things, as happens sometimes under US administrations.

Yet today, collective responsibility lacks the force it once had and is applied in a way that suits the government of the day. For instance:

- Some ministers get round the obligation by leaking their views, perhaps in coded language.
- Others make speeches containing thinly veiled criticisms of government policy (Michael Portillo on European policy under John Major) or express personal views (Peter Mandelson on the desirability of Britain joining the eurozone, under Tony Blair.
- In the face of evident disunity, in 1975 Harold Wilson and in 1977 James Callaghan actually allowed ministers to agree to differ on divisive aspects of European policy.

The convention is liable to be waived when it suits the Prime Minister, which is why some commentators regard it as a constitutional myth. The doctrine purports to make the government responsible to the House of Commons, the implication being that if a serious blunder is committed then the government as a whole is liable to be defeated. Yet governments have survived countless crises from Westland to Iraq and no mass resignation of ministers has occurred. Party discipline ensures that MPs stay loyal in the voting lobbies, so that crises sometimes provide impressive demonstrations of unity.

Fig. 2 *Robin Cook*

Key term

Parliamentary Private Secretaries (PPSs) are unpaid assistants who serve as the parliamentary contact for their minister. Appointment to this rank is seen as the first step on the promotion ladder for an MP.

Further information

Iraq and collective responsibility

- Robin Cook resigned as Leader of the House of Commons (March 2003) over the decision to invade Iraq 'without international agreement or domestic support'.
- Clare Short, known to be uneasy about Iraq and other issues, stayed in office for a further two months, then resigned. She claimed that 'the errors . . . over Iraq . . . stem primarily from the style and organisation of our government'.

Summary questions

1. Are Cabinet committees an effective way of organising modern government? What are the dangers in their use?

2. For ministers in disagreement with government policy, what are the arguments for resignation or remaining in the Cabinet?

3. For Prime Ministers, what are the arguments for dismissing Cabinet ministers who are critical in public of government policy?

3 The importance of the Cabinet

Learning objectives:

- How important is the Cabinet as a decision-making body?
- What were the findings of the Butler Review on the way that Blairite Cabinets made decisions?

Further information

Cabinet decision making

'An increasingly small number of advisers . . . make decisions without proper discussion . . . There is no real collective responsibility . . . just diktats in favour of increasingly badly thought-through policy initiatives that come from on high.' Clare Short, May 2003

NB Shortly after, ministers made clear that the entire Cabinet would decide whether a referendum should be held on entry into the euro.

Activity

From all that you have read in this chapter, what evidence can you find to confirm or rebut Clare Short's observation above?

As we have seen, the importance of the weekly meeting has been downgraded in recent years. Nigel Lawson, a Chancellor under Margaret Thatcher, has written of its unsuitability as the body for thrashing out problems and making long-term plans:

> A normal Cabinet meeting has no chance of becoming a grave forum of statesmanlike debate. Twenty two people attending a two-and-a-half hour meeting can speak for just over six and a half minutes each on average. If there are three items of business – and there are usually more – the ration of time just exceeds two minutes, if everyone is determined to have his say. Small wonder then that most ministers keep silent on most issues.

It is widely recognised that rather than providing a forum for detailed discussion of a wide range of policies, the main role of the Cabinet is to facilitate cohesion and coordination of governmental policies generally, and to provide or establish the boundaries in which those policies are prepared and pursued. Many, if not most, government policies are developed in Cabinet committees and then reported back to the full Cabinet for approval. In other words, the Cabinet often rubber-stamp decisions made elsewhere. This was particularly true under Tony Blair, in whose administrations there was often discussion about the presentation of policy decisions rather than the actual making of them.

In the governments of the Thatcher–Blair eras, most key decisions have been made prior to full meetings of the cabinet. Former ministers such as Clare Short and Chris Smith, political commentators in the media and others 'in the know' have drawn attention to the trend, but in the Butler Review (see below) it was criticised. The Blairite style of government was viewed with some dismay. Peter Hennessy's verdict on life under the Blair administrations, delivered in 2001, was similarly unflattering:

> The Cabinet is no longer a central organ of government. Cabinet Ministers still matter as heads of Departments, but Cabinet meetings no longer really count. The system is no longer collective. It is a centralised system directed by 10 Downing Street.

Hennessy (2005) confirms that very few decisions are now made in the Cabinet, even if most major policy issues come before the Cabinet at some time. It is the final court of appeal for ministerial and departmental disagreements, the place where formal approval of decisions made elsewhere is given and from where crisis management at a time of national emergencies and political controversy is likely to be conducted.

Butler on the Cabinet

In Butler's opinion, there were too many sofa chats and too many occasions when minutes were not taken. This led to a subsequent lack of clarity about what had been decided. In restrained language, the ex-Cabinet Secretary barely concealed his dislike of 'the informality and circumscribed procedures' which marginalised the Cabinet's role in decision making over Iraq in the run-up to war. He noted that the Cabinet discussed the subject on 24 occasions in the tense year before war broke out, but he disapproved of the fact that the frequent reports of the foreign and defence secretaries and the Prime Minister were often unscripted; the defence and overseas committee did not meet at all. He concluded:

> Without papers circulated in advance, it remains possible but is obviously much more difficult for the cabinet outside the small circle directly involved to bring their political judgement and experience
> to bear.

Summary questions

1. What evidence is there to support the idea that Cabinet government is in decline?

2. When referring to the Cabinet, is it wise to focus attention on the weekly Cabinet meetings?

3. Has the Cabinet now become a 'dignified part of the Constitution'?

4 The role and increased power of the Prime Minister

Learning objectives:

- What are the main duties of the Prime Minister?

- What is the role and importance of the Prime Minister's Office?

- Why has there been a growth of prime ministerial power?

- To what extent is prime ministerial power subject to constraints?

The Prime Minister (PM) is nominally chosen by the Queen, but by convention she chooses the leader of the majority party in the House of Commons. His or her powers derive from the royal prerogative and rest on convention rather than law.

The Prime Minister is head of the Executive branch of government and chairman of the Cabinet. He or she has several responsibilities ranging from oversight of the security services to liaising with the Monarch in a weekly meeting, keeping her informed of what the government is doing and advising on matters such as the constitutional implications of a royal marriage or divorce. Among the chief tasks of the Prime Minister are the following:

- **Leader of his party in the country and in parliament**. The Prime Minister owes his or her position to the party and in carrying out duties cannot afford to forget that connection. He or she will use the powers of leadership to keep the party united, working out compromise solutions as necessary. As leader of the majority party, the PM retains the support of parliament. As long as the majority is a workable one, the PM and his or her Cabinet colleagues are in a position to persuade the House to adopt party policies. When the majority is small, the government is vulnerable, particularly if there is a sizeable block of MPs who reject key themes of the leadership's policy. This role of managing the party is crucial to the Premier's prospects of survival. The PM cannot afford to lose touch with the people he or she leads.

Activities

1 Make a list of any factors that might be taken into account when a Prime Minister forms or reshuffles his or her Cabinet. What do you think is meant by the idea of a balanced Cabinet?

2 Why do you think that Tony Blair chose St Olave's (see Fig. 3 on opposite page) as the setting for his election announcement?

Key terms

Patronage: political patronage is the granting of favours or rewards, in this case the right to appoint people to important and often highly prestigious public offices.

The **Privy Council** comprises all members of the Cabinet, former Cabinet ministers and other distinguished persons appointed by the Monarch. It issues Orders in Council (legislation in Commonwealth countries made in the name of the Queen), grants Royal Charters and acts as a court of appeal from British courts in overseas territories.

Responsibility for the appointment and dismissal of members of the Cabinet, acting as its chairman; appointment of other members of the government. The ability to hire, fire and reshuffle colleagues and thereby make or break their careers is a formidable one. In relation to the Cabinet, this also includes appointing members of Cabinet committees, many of which the PM also chairs. Chairmanship of the Cabinet involves drawing up its agenda – in partnership with the Cabinet Secretary – and agreeing the minutes after the weekly meeting.

Leader of the government at home and abroad. The PM answers questions in the House at Prime Minister's Question Time on Wednesdays; acts as the country's voice on occasions such as the death of Princess Diana or some national disaster; and represents Britain in summit conferences with European leaders, the US president and other world statespeople. In this role of national leadership he will sometimes appear on TV and address the nation directly.

Responsibility for a wide range of appointments, exercising a considerable power of patronage. Appointments once made by the Monarch are now mostly made on the advice of the Prime Minister. He appoints people from bishops to peers, from the Chairman of the BBC to members of the **Privy Council**.

He determines the date of the next general election. The Prime Minister alone decides when to ask the Monarch to dissolve parliament and consequently the timing of polling day. Normally, this will be after around four years in office, although John Major fought his two elections after a five-year term had been completed. The Prime Minister will choose a time when victory looks most likely and his choice is likely to be influenced by his party's performance in the polls, in by-elections and other tests of opinion such as local government and European elections.

He exercises powers under the royal prerogative, including the decision to go to war (although Gordon Brown has indicated that in future parliament will be allowed to decide).

In these tasks, the political and administrative support available to Prime Ministers has historically been rather limited, though often effective. Although the Cabinet Office is primarily there to service the Cabinet as a whole, it has often been responsive to a Prime Ministerial lead. Assistance has always been available at Number 10 as well, but only since the Thatcher/Major era has the provision of help become more systematic. Under Tony Blair, the Prime Minister's Office (see below) has been greatly expanded and politicised in order to enhance its capacity to support his personal approach to the premiership.

In depth

The Prime Minister's Office

Unlike other ministers, the Prime Minister has no department. However, the Prime Minister's Office, made up of permanent civil servants and political advisers, has increased in size and its membership is divided into five components:

The Private Office, which handles the Prime Minister's official engagements and his relationship with parliament and government departments.

- The Policy Unit, comprising outside specialists brought in to advise on specific aspects of government policy.
- The Political Unit, which exists to create a bridge between the party (its MPs and members in the country) and the Prime Minister.
- The Press Office, there to handle relations with the media, a role of major importance in the Blair era given the importance attached to policy presentation and image.
- The Strategic Communications Unit, there to spot pitfalls and coordinate ministerial announcements, ensuring that Downing Street is ahead of the game and in control of the overall direction of government.

Fig. 3 *Tony Blair at St Olave's Catholic school South London, announcing that an election was to be held in 2001*

The growth in prime ministerial power

The Prime Minister is the most powerful politician in the country. He or she heads a group of powerful figures some of whom have a party or national standing in their own right. The way in which they work together will depend upon the mix of personalities involved.

At the beginning of the 20th century, the Prime Minister was thought to be *primus inter pares* – first among equals. This suggested that in spite of the Prime Minister exercising powers denied to other ministers (such as those of patronage and appointment), the Cabinet reached its decisions collectively and on a majority basis, even though the Prime Minister summed up the sense of the meeting. The phrase suggested that the Prime Minister's status as the person at the helm was of a formal nature, with little additional power attached to the office. The description 'Cabinet government' seemed appropriate, even though some Prime Ministers were much stronger than this picture suggests and were capable of dominating their administration – especially in time of war (e.g. Lloyd George during the First World War).

Since the early 20th century, the power of the Executive branch of government in Britain has grown – as in most democracies – although the distribution of power within the Executive is liable to change at any time. If there has been a gradual trend to prime ministerial dominance, it has been characterised by an ebb and flow of power rather than a continuous increase. A much-quoted observation made in 1928 by Lord Oxford (formerly known as Liberal PM Asquith) reflects the varying nature of political power. He judged that: 'The office of Prime Minister is what its holder chooses and is able to make of it'. His emphasis on the ability, character and preference of the incumbent is generally accepted, as is the role of particular circumstances.

Prime ministers do not have unlimited power. If they did, they would be behaving as dictators. It is one thing to have dictatorial tendencies, it is another to be a dictator. Dictators cannot be removed other than by a military coup or similar event. Prime ministers can always be evicted from Number 10 at the next election. The electorate is the ultimate limitation on even the most powerful premier. If leaders are seen as too powerful, remote, out of touch or untrustworthy, voters can react against them and bring their party down. There are, of course, other constraints too, some of which are itemised below.

Activity

Britain has no Prime Minister's Department as the Prime Minister has no department to run. How has the Prime Minister's Office been developed in recent years? How does this serve to empower the Prime Minister?

Activities

Consider Lord Oxford's observation. Why might aspects of a Prime Minister's personality have an impact on his or her power?

1 Use the internet to look up details of Margaret Thatcher's handling of the Falklands War:

  a Find out what impact it had on her power as Prime Minister.

  b What qualities does war leadership require?

2 If her handling of the war was good for her reputation, why did events in Iraq prove so damaging to that of Tony Blair?

In depth

Constraints on the British Prime Minister

All Prime Ministers have been subject to some constraints, among them:

- **The Cabinet**. On major issues, even a strong Prime Minister will wish to keep his or her Cabinet united behind him/her. It normally comprises some figures of public and party standing, potential rivals if they are ignored or antagonised. In the build-up to the invasion of Iraq, it was essential for Tony Blair that he could count upon the support of Gordon Brown, John Prescott and Jack Straw. The way in which Prime Ministers and their colleagues work together will depend upon the mix of personalities involved, the relationships being complex and fluid. Much depends on the issues and problems with which they are faced.

- **Party**. Strong premiers can be hard on party back-benchers, expecting loyalty in the voting lobbies even for policies they dislike. When ministers are going through a difficult period – and especially when party MPs fear for their seats in the next election – they may find that support melts away. Prime ministers who lose back-bench backing may find that they cannot rely on continued consent to their leadership, as Margaret Thatcher found out in 1990. In the case of Tony Blair, even before the 2005 election, he faced some serious revolts. After he had announced that he would not serve a full term if re-elected, his critics were regularly willing to challenge him in parliamentary divisions and his authority was seriously undermined.

- **Parliament**. Prime ministers need to retain support in parliament to get their policies through the chamber. Even a Prime Minister who makes only limited other appearances in the House still has to appear every Wednesday to be grilled at Question Time, defend his policies to occasional select committee hearings and sell his policies on contentious issues such as Iraq and tuition fees. In March 2003, Tony Blair could not have gone ahead with his backing for President Bush if MPs had rejected his case for war. Primarily, getting parliamentary support means keeping government MPs happy, but over Iraq he wanted to ensure that there was sufficient agreement from the Opposition to his policy to help him defeat the Labour rebellion.

- **Events**. It was Harold Macmillan, the Conservative Prime Minister of the 1950s and 1960s, who saw 'events, dear boy, events' as his greatest danger. No Prime Minister knows what hazards are around the corner, issues ranging from war in Iraq to an outbreak of foot-and-mouth disease that can derail or at least threaten the administration.

- **Hostility in the media**. Even an incumbent who is good on television can have a tough ride when the novelty wears off. A poor performer on television will soon find that the medium is useful to charismatic politicians but a problem for the less articulate or persuasive. Whereas Tony Blair had a remarkable degree of press support in 1997 and 2001, in 2005 war and other issues inspired marked hostility from sections of the Tory press, especially the *Daily Mail*.

The central elements in prime ministerial power today are well known but difficult to measure. They include:

- the power of appointment and dismissal of Cabinet and other ministerial offices
- power over the structure and membership of Cabinet committees, any of which the PM may chair
- the central, overseeing non-departmental nature of the office
- leadership of the party
- single-party government
- the distribution of patronage
- wartime leadership (for some)
- increasing use of special advisers
- bureaucratic support from the PM's office and Cabinet office
- a high degree of public visibility, which has been much increased by the tendency of the media (especially television) to focus on personalities.

These features have operated for much of the 20th century, but in recent decades some have assumed a growing significance. For instance, Prime Ministers are now much more visible than ever before because of the growing trend towards the use of international summit conferences and a high degree of television exposure. No modern occupant of Number 10 since the last World War has been anything less than very powerful. Any Prime Minister today has a formidable display of powers at his or her disposal.

Activities

For each of these three features of prime ministerial power, write down one or more limitations on that power:

1. The freedom to hire and fire colleagues.
2. The opportunity to appear on television.
3. The ability to dominate the House of Commons, because of leadership of the majority party.

Summary questions

1. Would you support the idea that there has been a centralisation of power in the hands of the Prime Minister over recent decades? Explain your answer.

2. To what extent is it true to say that the power of the Prime Minister has increased, is increasing and ought to be diminished?

3. What are your impressions of the Brown approach to the office of Prime Minister?

5 Prime ministerial or Cabinet government?

Learning objectives:

- Why has a widespread belief developed that Britain now has 'government by Prime Minister'?

- Is the thesis of prime ministerial government a convincing one?

- What is meant by the notion of a British presidency?

- What evidence is there to support the idea that Tony Blair was a presidential Prime Minister?

Activity

We have used three labels for the British political system: Cabinet government, prime ministerial government and presidential government. For each of them, write down two pieces of evidence to suggest that the label is an appropriate one. Then write a paragraph about the label that you think is most convincing.

Crossman (1976) explained the thesis of prime ministerial government in this way: 'The postwar epoch has seen the final transformation of Cabinet government into Prime Ministerial government; with the effect that "the Cabinet now joins the dignified elements in the Constitution".' His views were confirmed by Professor John Mackintosh (1977) who similarly noted the supreme importance of the Prime Minister, with the Cabinet becoming 'a clearing house and court of appeal'. Such claims have often been repeated since the early 1960s. But it was the premiership of Margaret Thatcher which provided renewed impetus in the debate about whether we have 'government by Prime Minister'. Tony Blair has also often been accused of operating via a system of personal rule, of operating 'too presidentially'.

The thesis can be over-stated and suffers from the tendency to over-generalisation. As we have seen, the power of Prime Ministers is limited by a range of factors and dependent on the circumstances of the time. It is not merely that some Prime Ministers are more powerful than others (a 'strong' Thatcher being followed by a 'weak' Major, who in turn was followed by a 'strong' Tony Blair), but that any single incumbent will be more powerful at certain times than at others in the course of the premiership. Even the strongest among them are not always able to sustain the same degree of performance throughout their term. Certainly, the last 18 months of the Blair premiership saw a leader beset with difficulties which began in November 2005 with a humiliating and larger-than-expected defeat over his plan to allow the police to detain suspected terrorists for up to 90 days without charge. Then there were difficulties over loans for peerages, the ongoing problems surrounding the occupation of Iraq and increasing disquiet in the parliamentary party as the polls revealed the loss of faith in Labour and its leader and the revival of the Conservative party. His authority drained away.

It is difficult to apply one label to the system of government. Prime ministerial government seems inappropriate as a description of the Major years but more relevant to the experience of life under Tony Blair. An old exam question invites discussion of the quotation: 'The power of the Prime Minister has increased, is increasing and ought to be diminished'. But as we have seen, there has not been an uninterrupted trend to prime ministerial dominance.

There are checks upon prime ministerial dominance, in particular the need to retain party support and the backing of Cabinet colleagues. When the government is doing well and is in control of events, the Prime Minister may seem to be effortlessly in charge. When policy is in disarray and the prospects for re-election appear to be in jeopardy, then a challenge to the leadership can be mounted and power may melt away.

Presidential government?

In the words of Kavanagh and Seldon, 'every Prime Minister from Gladstone onwards has been accused of being "dictatorial" or "presidential".' There have been some exceptions, most notably – in the post-1945 period – Sir Alec Douglas-Home, the Conservative Prime Minister 1963–64, who lacked the inclination or mastery of affairs to be in a position to dominate his administration. However, as a generalisation the comment is broadly correct. But in the cases of Margaret Thatcher and Tony Blair the allegation intensified the longer they remained in office, as they became more domineering and arguably more detached from their colleagues around the Cabinet table.

In depth

Comparing the offices of Prime Minister and US President

Both offices provide substantial powers of patronage, opportunities to manipulate the media, substantial control over policy-making support and the ability/tendency to act as a truly national leader over and above the party battle. But:

- Britain has separated 'pomp from power' and has a separate head of state; the US President combines the roles of head of the Executive and head of state.
- A British Prime Minister can be brought down (e.g. Margaret Thatcher). The president has more security of tenure, having a fixed term. Of course, the PM has the opportunity to choose the timing of the election.
- Britain has a plural executive, with the PM and cabinet both responsible to the Commons. The US has a single executive and the US Cabinet is not a significant body in policy deliberations and policy making.
- PMs are leaders of strong, centralised parties. Party discipline enables them to pass much of their legislative programme. This is not true of the US President.
- Whereas the PM is the leader of a significant country in the world, the President has a major global role as leader of the 'free world'. Tony Blair initially had more difficulty over Iraq than did George W Bush.

Activity

Re-read this chapter and then note down the key points that might help you decide how far the Blair government has contributed to the downgrading of the Cabinet.

Those who detected presidential qualities in Tony Blair pointed to:

- **The large apparatus in Downing Street with which he equipped himself**. In particular, Tony Blair developed the Prime Minister's office, which has become a de facto if not formalised Prime Minister's department. Presidents – lacking the degree of backing that a Prime Minister derives from the Cabinet – rely heavily upon an array of advisers and consultants, many of whom are located in the Executive Office of the President.
- **His pre-eminence in shaping policy especially on overseas issues**. After consultation with his political advisers, he decided what needed to be done and imposed his inclinations upon Cabinet colleagues.
- **The priority attached to the presentation of policy and the manipulation of the media** in order to get the ministerial message across directly to the people. He and his advisers understood that television is a medium which likes to dwell on personalities and broad themes which are easier to portray than complex matters of policy. They were keen to emphasise his personal characteristics. In the case of Alistair Campbell, his role went beyond concern with the Prime Minister's image, communicating the government's

Further reading

Useful articles:

C Brady and P Catterall, 'Inside the Engine Room: Assessing Cabinet Committee', *Talking Politics*, April 2000.

M Foley, 'Presidential Government in Britain', *Talking Politics*, 6:3, 1994.

N Jackson, 'The Blair Style: Presidential, Bilateral or Trilateral Government', *Talking Politics*, January 2003.

D Kavanagh, 'Tony Blair as Prime Minister', *Politics Review*, 11:1, 2001.

N McNaughton, 'Prime ministerial power', *Talking Politics*, September 2002.

M Rathbone, 'The British Cabinet Today', *Talking Politics*, September 2003.

M Smith, 'The Core Executive', *Politics Review*, 10:1, 2000.

Useful books:

S Buckley, **The Prime Minister and Cabinet**, EUP, 2006.

M Foley, **The Rise of the British Presidency**, MUP, 1993.

P Hennessy, **The Prime Ministers: The Office and its Holders Since 1945**, Allen Lane, 2000.

Websites:

www.cabinet-office.gov.uk. The Cabinet Office site.

www.number-10.gov.uk. The Downing Street site.

views and trying to control the news agenda; he was a key member of the Blairite kitchen cabinet and therefore a key source of political advice.

- **The tendency of making key policy announcements at staged and televised public events** rather than in the House of Commons. His record of attendance and voting in the chamber suggested a lack of interest in parliamentary proceedings.

- **The quality of what Michael Foley has called spatial leadership**, a technique whereby some Prime Ministers like to appear 'above the fray' of battle, sometimes talking about the government and what it must do as though they were not the key force in shaping its direction and policies. This was a technique adopted by President Reagan who seemed able to escape from the difficulties of his administration. 'Teflon Tony' was a label applied to Tony Blair to draw attention to his ability in the early years to retain an aura of dignity and authority, unsullied by the events that happened to his ministers. The label lost much of its relevance when his credibility and reputation were tarnished by the events surrounding the Iraq war.

Foley (2000) concluded that Prime Ministers such as Margaret Thatcher and Tony Blair did become presidential, but in a uniquely British way. Tony Blair was not a head of state, nor – unlike the US president – did he derive his power directly from the people. Writing of the Prime Minister, Foley explained that:

> He cannot ignore the Cabinet, even if it is sometimes by-passed on individual policy matters. The constitutional position in the two countries does not make for real convergence. There is a fundamental difference between presidential and parliamentary government.

✓ Summary questions

1. Is Cabinet government dead or is it alive and well?

2. 'The present centralisation of power into the hands of one person has gone too far and amounts to a system of personal rule in the very heart of our system of . . . parliamentary democracy' (T Benn, ex-Labour MP and Cabinet minister). Do you agree?

3. Do we want a British presidency?

14 Ministers and civil servants

1 Government departments and the civil servants who work in them

Learning objectives:

- What is the civil service?
- What is the difference between ministerial and non-ministerial departments?
- What sort of people are to be found in the higher civil service?
- What do higher civil servants do?
- What are the traditional principles by which higher civil servants work?

Key terms

Bureaucracy: government by non-elected salaried administrative officers. Such officials conduct the detailed business of public administration and advise on and apply ministerial decisions. In Britain, it is more usual to speak of the civil service.

Civil servants were defined by the Tomlin Commission in 1931 in this way: Servants of the Crown, other than holders of political or judicial offices, who are employed in a civil capacity and whose remuneration is paid wholly and directly out of moneys voted by parliament.

The civil service is the governmental **bureaucracy**. Most government departments are run by ministers who are elected politicians, but they are administered by professional and permanent paid officials. Many of these are clerical or managerial staff, distributed in government offices up and down the country. The ones who concern us most are those who belong to the top administrative grades, often referred to as the 'mandarins' or, collectively, as 'the higher civil service'.

These senior officials are based mainly in the large Whitehall ministries, known usually as departments. The top **civil servant** is the Cabinet Secretary, but in a typical department there will be a Permanent Secretary at the helm, and below this rank a number of Deputy Secretaries, Under Secretaries, Assistant Secretaries, Senior Principals and Principals. The majority of the civil service staff in fact now works in **executive agencies**, which are separate operational organisations reporting to particular government departments.

'Whitehall' is often used as a synonym for the central core of the civil service. This is because most government departments have headquarters in and around the former Royal Palace of Whitehall.

Government departments

Ministerial departments are led politically by a government minister and cover matters that require direct political oversight. In most departments, the minister in question is known as a Secretary of State and is a member of the Cabinet. He or she is generally supported by a team of junior ministers. The administrative management of the department is led by the Permanent Secretary.

As we have seen, executive agencies are subordinate to these ministerial departments. An executive agency has a degree of autonomy to perform an operational function. Her Majesty's Prison Service looks after prisons for the Home Office, the Driver and Vehicle Licensing Agency deals with vehicle licensing for the Department of Transport and Jobcentre Plus (the largest agency in terms of staff numbers) is linked to the Department for Work and Pensions. Agencies report to one or more specific government departments which will establish their funding and strategic policy. The Chief Executive of the agency, however, is usually responsible for efficient management of the organisation and for meeting ministerially imposed targets.

Non-ministerial departments generally cover matters for which direct political oversight is judged unnecessary or inappropriate. They are headed by senior civil servants. Some fulfil a regulatory or inspection function, and their status is therefore intended to protect them from political interference. Some are headed by Permanent Secretaries or Second Permanent Secretaries. Examples are the Assets Recovery Agency, the British Council, the Charity Commissioners for England and Wales and the Export Credits Guarantee Department.

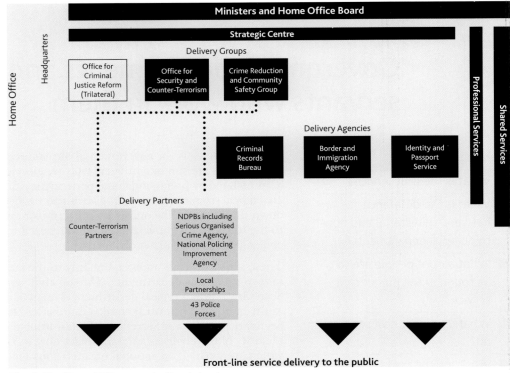

Fig. 1 *The Home Office organisational structure*

Key term

Executive agencies carry out some of the administrative functions of government previously the responsibility of civil service departments. They operate as semi-autonomous agencies at arm's length from the sponsoring department. Aka 'Next step' agencies because they were first suggested in the 1988 report: 'Improving management in government: the next steps'.

Activities

Use the internet to help you answer the following questions:

1. Find out about how any one ministerial department is organised. Who are the ministers involved?

2. How many executive agencies are there? Find some examples to quote in response to examination questions.

In depth

Ministerial departments under the Brown administration include:

- Business, Enterprise and Regulatory Reform
- Cabinet Office
- Children, Schools and Families
- Communities and Local Government
- Culture, Media and Sport
- Defence
- Environment, Food and Rural Affairs
- Foreign and Commonwealth Office
- Health
- Home Office
- Innovation, Universities and Skills
- International Development
- Justice
- Northern Ireland Office
- Office of the Leader of the House of Commons
- Privy Council
- Transport
- Treasury
- Wales Office

- Scotland Office
- Work and Pensions.

The civil service

Size

The civil service comprises all government departments and executive agencies in Great Britain and includes the Diplomatic Service. Numbers have fallen from a peak in 1976 when approximately three-quarters of a million civil servants were employed. By April 1999, this number had fallen to a record low of 459,600 due to **privatisation**, **outsourcing** and cutbacks, although it has risen since then. On 1 April 2004 there were some 523,580 permanent civil servants (full-time equivalent), of which 503,550 were non-industrial staff and 20,030 were industrial staff. (The distinction is similar to that which exists in the private sector between white- and blue-collar workers. The Ministry of Defence is the largest employer of staff in industrial grades within the civil service, employing around 80 per cent of the total.) There were also 10,820 casual staff.

Higher civil servants: their role and backgrounds

The senior civil servants, often known as higher civil servants, comprise around 750–800 leading officials. Only this group will really be involved in working with ministers on policy. On a typical day, considerably fewer are likely to have much direct contact with ministers.

At the head of the civil servants in each department is the Permanent Secretary, below whom will be the Deputy and Assistant Secretaries.

Of course, a number of senior civil servants now work in agencies which are formally detached from the process of policy making. However, some key officials in those agencies are involved in offering guidance to the Chief Executive on the advice that should be given to ministers.

What sort of people become higher civil servants?

Civil servants have been recruited on merit (by passing competitive examinations) since the middle of the 19th century. Often, those who were selected for entry were among the brightest and best graduates, with first class degrees from older and more prestigious universities. However, by the 1960s, academics and commentators increasingly lamented their lack of relevant training and skills and the narrow and unrepresentative social background from which they emerged. Their ability was not doubted, but the sort of degrees for which they studied (for instance, history and the classics) seemed to be of doubtful relevance to the work they would be doing in Whitehall. Moreover, they lacked experience of the outside world, having gone into the civil service on completion of their academic courses. The 1968 Fulton Report called for changes so that there might be a movement away from this 'cult of the amateur' in favour of greater professionalism.

Since the 1990s, more has been done to ensure that there are more temporary secondments between commerce, industry and Whitehall, and more extensive recruitment from the private sector. Under the Blair government, an attempt was made to ensure that there were a greater number of shorter and flexible secondments from the civil service into industry, especially civil servants at the junior level who operate outside of London.

Key terms

Privatisation is the process of converting public amenities and services into private ones, a feature of Conservative economic policy in the 1980s and 1990s.

Outsourcing is the practice of contracting out (paying a private provider to deliver) a service either to itself or to the public that was once provided 'in house'.

Activity

Make a list of the possible reasons why the recruitment process of higher civil servants seems to favour people who have a public school/Oxbridge background. Write a paragraph to say whether this typical background matters.

The persistent bias in favour of public school students who become Oxbridge graduates has been difficult to address, although since the early 1990s the issue has been taken especially seriously. There has been a broadening of the basis of recruitment with:

- increased recruitment from non-Oxbridge universities
- a movement away from the arts subjects
- greater scope for women and members of ethnic minorities.

It is increasingly considered important to ensure that those who advise ministers and influence policy making should be more representative of the community, although there is still a long way to go before this can be achieved.

It remains the fact that many higher civil servants are still public school/Oxbridge educated and drawn from a narrow section of society. Various enquiries into this 'bias' have suggested that it may not be a conscious preference for a certain type of character, more that young people with those backgrounds tend to apply to join the civil service. Also, such candidates tend to perform well in interviews, usually being confident, well spoken and endowed with plenty of *savoir faire* (i.e. they know what to say and do in any situation).

The role of higher civil servants

The role of those core higher civil servants who work in Whitehall is concerned with:

- **Preparing legislation**, drawing up answers to parliamentary questions and briefing the particular minister.
- **Administration** – overseeing and carrying out the day-to-day work of the department or some part of it. This may involve meeting up with representatives of pressure groups or dealing with difficult, non-routine casework.
- **Helping to develop the department's attitudes and work**, looking at alternative lines of policy, surveying the advantages and difficulties of these, foreseeing practical problems.
- **Policy implementation/management**, the latter of which has been increasingly important in the Thatcher and post-Thatcher years.

The role of the Permanent Secretary is crucial. He or she is a member of the highest grade of the civil service and is the leading official in the department. They are responsible to the minister for what goes on. Because of the minister's heavy involvement in political work, the Permanent Secretary has to direct and supervise most of the department's normal work, perhaps 85–90 per cent of it.

The principles according to which higher civil servants work

Traditionally, the civil service is run according to three interlinked features that are still important but no longer carry the force they once did:

- **Permanence**. In Britain, civil servants are career officials prepared to serve a government of any party. They do not change at election time as they do in the US. This permanence is associated with experience and continuity, so that an inexperienced incoming government will be able to count on official expertise. Permanence, coupled with confidentiality, means that civil servants can speak frankly to ministers without fear of dismissal. It makes a civil service career seem attractive. However, that permanence means 'no change at the top', which may well stifle fresh thinking and new initiatives.

- **Neutrality**. Officials are required to be politically impartial, and not let their personal political leanings affect their actions. They must carry out decisions with which they personally may disagree, and they must not involve themselves in any partisan activity. If they were to be partisan, this would make it difficult for them to remain in office and serve as permanent officials. Some critics would suggest that neutrality puts it too strongly, as they are expected to further the policies of the elected government – be 'neutral on the government's side'.

Indeed, in the last decades of the 20th century, some political observers claimed that the British civil service has become increasingly politicised. The main complaint relates to an increase in the number of **Special Advisers** in the 1980s and 1990s, particularly under the Labour government. Critics also note the involvement of ministers in the appointment of senior civil servants. The Prime Minister has final say over very senior appointments such as Permanent Secretaries and the Cabinet Secretary, but the PM is supposed to choose from a handful of shortlisted candidates purely on the basis of merit without political consideration. Some observers claim that recent Prime Ministers, particularly Margaret Thatcher, exercised these powers of patronage unfairly to appoint Permanent Secretaries whom she regarded as efficient managers and who were sympathetic to her government's aims.

- **Anonymity**. Ministers are answerable for what happens in their departments. The role of civil servants is to offer confidential advice, in secret. If officials became public figures, this would endanger their reputation for neutrality as they could become identified with a particular policy. They might then be unacceptable to a new administration. Identification might also prevent them from offering frank advice to ministers; if they knew they could be named, they might feel the need to be very discreet. On the other hand, anonymity may conceal poor advice, give less incentive for officials to improve their effectiveness and shield them from the consequences of any inadequacy. In recent years, civil servants have become less anonymous. They are sometimes named or easily recognisable from investigatory reports, and they appear before select committees of the House of Commons.

A new civil service code was launched on 6 June 2006 to outline the core values and standards expected of civil servants. The core values are defined as integrity, honesty, objectivity and impartiality. A key change from previous values is the removal of anonymity within the core values.

Summary questions

1 Why have higher civil servants often been criticised?

2 Why are their backgrounds and roles important?

Key term

Special advisers are advisers appointed to provide political advice, assessment and support to ministers, offering an alternative perspective to those provided by civil servants.

Table 1 *The increase in the number of special advisers*

Financial Year (a)	
1994/95	34
1995/96	38
1996/97	38
1997/98	70
1998/99	74
1999/00	78
2000/01	79
2001/02	81
2002/03	70
2003/04	72
2004/05	84
2005/06	82
2006/07	68

2 Ministers: their backgrounds and roles

Learning objectives:

- Which categories of people are included within the term 'ministers'?

- What are the main tasks of ministers?

- What factors may limit the powers and effectiveness of ministers?

By ministers, we are referring to around 100 government members, including Cabinet ministers, ministers of state and parliamentary under-secretaries. In accordance with constitutional convention, all ministers within the government have traditionally been either members of parliament or peers in the House of Lords, although Gordon Brown has brought in non-political outsiders. Among five new non-Labour ministers included in his administration was Sir Digby Jones, the former director general of the CBI (Confederation of British Industry), who became minister of state for trade and investment in the Department for Business, Enterprise and Regulatory Reform.

In depth

The route to becoming a government minister

- As we have a parliamentary system, Cabinet and other ministers are members of the legislature and accountable to it.

- Normally, politicians need to prove themselves in the House of Commons before getting ministerial office, and as a junior minister before entering the Cabinet.

- Ministers have no training, though they may have had responsibility for an area of policy in opposition. They study their new brief quickly and then need to work themselves into their job.

- Some ministers are peers, with no background in the Commons.

- Very occasionally, ministers are appointed to the Cabinet for a specific purpose, having had no previous parliamentary or ministerial experience. Such parliamentary inexperience can be a handicap and the experiment has not been particularly successful.

- Ambition, talent, skill in debate, managerial skills, a record of loyalty to – and allies in – the leadership, and good fortune, all of these things help advancement.

Members of the government work in departments of state or ministries, most of which are headed by non-Cabinet ministers. The major ministries, usually 17–18 of them, are headed by Cabinet ministers. These include departments such as the Treasury, the Home Office, the Department for Innovation, Universities and Skills, and the Foreign Office.

Such is the volume of work in departments run by a Cabinet minister that other layers of ministers have been created. The 30 or so ministers of state and the same number of parliamentary under-secretaries are collectively known as 'junior ministers'. Below them, are the 40–50 parliamentary private secretaries (PPSs) who are the general assistants of ministers and really act as 'dogsbodies'. They are unpaid for their work. Broadly, the more important the government department, the more ministers and junior ministers it will have. At the Department of Health, under the Brown administration there is one Cabinet minister backed by five other ministers. At the Department of Transport, one minister is supported by three other ministers.

As we have seen, below these ministers there is a hierarchy of civil servants. The Cabinet minister usually deals with them via his or her private secretary (normally a bright, up-and-coming civil servant charged with the responsibility for organising the minister's busy schedule) or through his or her Permanent Secretary.

Ministers are very reliant on the performance of the civil servants who work in their department. They are the people who organise the minister's day, arrange appointments, write letters on their behalf, draft replies to parliamentary questions, arrange meetings and offer advice on how to deal with political issues as they arise. Yet the minister does not choose the civil servants. Ministers work with the people who are there when they come to office. For personal support in their dealings with officials, ministers rely on their junior ministers and their political advisers.

The roles of the minister

The minister has two main roles. He or she is a politician with duties in Cabinet and parliament, and also the administrator of a large Whitehall Department consisting of civil servants (officials).

As politicians, ministers have their normal constituency duties as MPs, but they also speak in the House of Commons in debates, appear before the relevant select committee, take their turn at the Despatch Box in Question Time and pilot any legislation through the House concerning the department. Ministers are also in the Cabinet if they are senior party figures. Here, they will argue the case for their department on any issues that arise and take part in more general discussions of government policy.

As heads of a Whitehall department, their role is to supervise and take a keen interest in the work being done. They are the ministers responsible for ensuring that their departments are managed efficiently. They make the key decisions and take responsibility for the actions of their civil servants. In theory, they listen to the advice put before them and use their judgement. In practice, in a large department such as the Home Office, they perhaps decide only 10–15 per cent of the vast array of issues that come up. But they need to ensure that they run a smooth, well-oiled machine, have competent people on whom they can rely, and are vigilant to see that they are getting the best advice.

Since the development of the **Next Step programme**, the areas of policy making and implementation have been separated for efficiency. This has reduced the minister's direct responsibility for what happens in whole areas of government work. Although ministers answer in the Commons on matters covered by an agency, the day-to-day management of such enterprises is left to Chief Executives who take a share of responsibility for what happens.

Possible limitations on the power of ministers

- They are outnumbered by their senior officials, by around six or seven to one.
- They lack permanency, having an average period in any ministerial office of two years (in some departments, movement of ministers is particularly frequent: in the Conservative years 1979–97 there were 12 Trade and Industry Secretaries of State).

Further information

The Ministerial Code

The Ministerial Code, as amended in 1995, places a clear demand on ministers to watch their behaviour carefully. Ministers must not knowingly mislead parliament and the public, and they should correct any inadvertent errors at the earliest opportunity. They must be as open as possible with parliament and the public, withholding information only when disclosure would not be in the public interest.

Key term

Next Step programmes advanced in the late 1980s to transform civil service institutional arrangements following publication of the Ibbs Report ('Improving management in government: the next steps'), most notably the creation of executive agencies. See p266.

- They are non-specialist, often lacking any knowledge of the departments' work. This means that they rarely possess clearly defined objectives and priorities on taking over.
- They have multiple demands upon their time, from Cabinet, parliament, the media and (in the case of several departments) Britain's role as a member of the European Union. Around 65 per cent of their work is on non-departmental matters.
- They may find it difficult to get key information as they are dependent on what their officials tell them or the data with which they are presented. Officials control the supply of information and may even choose to embarrass the minister by leaking stories to journalists.
- They may find it difficult to get their policies implemented and their decisions carried out as officials have over many decades developed the art of delay and frustration of ministerial initiatives.

Summary questions

1. What qualities does a minister need?
2. Why might it be hard to master their brief?

3 The relationship of ministers and civil servants: who dominates?

Learning objectives:

- What are the main perspectives for examining the minister–civil servant relationship?
- What sort of factors shape the relationship?

For many years, academics, journalists, politicians and top officials have engaged in discussion about where power lies in British government. Is it with the politicians or with the bureaucrats who serve them? In responding, much depends on the perspective of those who analyse the relationship. Kevin Theakston (1999) has detected four models or theories of the relationship:

1. **The traditional, public administration model,** namely that ministers decide issues in the light of the advice they are given by their civil servants ('civil servants advise, ministers decide'). The officials have a passive, neutral role, loyally setting out to serve their ministers' wishes and implement the decisions made. This model is reinforced by the convention of individual ministerial responsibility, in which ministers have the lead role. They take the praise or blame for what has been done, for good or ill.

2. **The adversarial model (sometimes referred to as the radical perspective)** adopted especially in the past by critics on the Left, which concentrates on the social background and attitudes of powerful civil servants who use their establishment connections and their wiles (i.e. cunning) to frustrate left-wing ministers who want to change the direction of policy in a way that sharply challenges the status quo. This model sees the relationship as a power struggle based on the separate agendas of ministers and their officials, suggesting that the elected politicians may be frustrated by a 'departmental view'.

3   **The Whitehall community model** first developed in the US, which sees the minister/official relationship as being more of an alliance of mutual interest. According to this view, civil servants favour strong rather than weak ministers because they recognise that within a department they have common interests with the elected politicians. Civil servants have expertise and links to organised group interests, while ministers contribute their political judgement and ideological commitment in arguing the departmental case with their Cabinet colleagues. In effect, in the small, enclosed Whitehall community or village in which there is a competition for limited resources between different departments, there is much to be said for ministers and civil servants having a cooperative rather than a conflictual relationship. For instance, in the Treasury, both are likely to see merit in curbing public expenditure, an approach which is at variance with that in a spending department such as health in which ministers and officials wish to argue for a larger share of funds.

4   **The public choice model**, which is part of the more general New Right critique of public sector provision. This suggests that bureaucracies tend towards inefficiency and needless growth, based on empire building, immune as they are from the market pressures that influence people in business and commerce. Establishment civil servants have a vested interest in the expansion of public services and ministers connive with them in support of this agenda.

Although they have a different vision and different objectives, non-consensus politicians of the Left and Right are liable to be frustrated by the way in which the civil service operates and may wish to see changes in Whitehall.

Some factors in the relationship

■ **'Ministers decide, civil servants advise'**. This is the classic statement of the relationship, the civil servants being 'on tap, but not on top'. Officials are supposed to be non-partisan and impartial. They are there to serve any government, offering advice and suggestions but allowing the minister to make decisions – after all, the minister takes responsibility for what goes wrong. It is the minister who is responsible to parliament; he or she has to be able to justify what has been done.

■ **Further information**

Table 2 *Turnover of cabinet ministers and civil service heads, 1945–2004*

Department	Ministerial head (number of changes), e.g. Secretary of State	Civil service head (number of changes), e.g. Permanent Secretary
Education	27	11
Foreign Office	21	15
Home office	21	10
Industry	33	12
Treasury	21	11

Source: Adapted from data provided in M Moran, *Politics and Governance in the UK*, Palgrave, 2005

■ **Further information**

Three views of the relationship

'I realise the tremendous effort it requires not to be taken over by the civil service.' Richard Crossman in *The Crossman Diaries*

'... the minister who complains that his civil servants are too powerful is either a weak minister or an incompetent one.' Dennis Healey, Labour Chancellor during the Wilson/Callaghan governments

(Of civil servants) 'There is nothing they dislike more than a minister whom they feel is weak, who does not know his mind.' Edward Heath, ex-Conservative Prime Minister

■ **Further information**

The advantages of civil servants over ministers

■ Their vast numbers.

■ Their relative permanence.

■ Their experience and expertise.

■ The network of interdepartmental committees of officials.

■ Their effective control of the administrative processes.

■ Their close involvement in national security/intelligence matters.

■ Their powers of patronage over thousands of appointments nominally made by the Prime Minister.

■ UK membership of the EU, which has necessitated much preparatory work and coordination.

Based on an article by Peter Kellner

Ministers are of course transient. They come and go, perhaps serving for a full administration or maybe moving on after a couple of years. By contrast, their officials may have been in the department for a long time and have developed considerable expertise. They become familiar with the realistic range of policy choices available and know the advantages or otherwise of various lines of policy. Their views will reflect a 'departmental view', but this may conflict with the government's or minister's priorities. In this situation there is scope for conflict between them.

A good period in office is important for any minister, as this enables him or her to acquire experience, master details and become involved in shaping rather than presiding over departmental policy. But as the figures in the Table indicate, the turnover of ministers is roughly double that of their senior civil servant counterparts. In some cases, turnover is rapid, especially in departments lacking high status in Whitehall. They tend to serve as staging posts for politicians on the way up. Education and Industry both have this reputation.

Much has been written about 'mandarin power', mandarins being the very senior officials who have close and regular contact with ministers. It is suggested that often, because of their ability, experience and expertise, they exert a powerful influence over what happens in a department, especially over the policies that emerge. Radical commentators and MPs (and Prime Ministers such as Margaret Thatcher who wanted to get things done) are wary of mandarins, seeing them as a cautious group hostile to necessary innovation. At worst, they may frustrate the minister and be obstructive, concealing information. Wariness about their character and outlook is increased because of their rather privileged public school, Oxbridge background; some are to be seen in the best gentlemen's clubs in London. They form an elite group.

Strong ministers will insist on their policy. It is often said that the first 48 hours will reveal whether a minister will assert his individuality and strength, or whether he will be a pushover, excessively dependent on his officials. At best, there is a constructive relationship between both sides.

In depth

Gerald Kaufman, Labour MP and ex-minister, on life as a minister

Before the meeting [of the Cabinet committee] you will receive the departmental briefing . . . Your departmental briefings are works of art. They will analyse the issue and the papers concerned not from the standpoint of the government as a whole, but purely from the departmental point of view. They will advise you of the "line to take", the sentences beginning with masterly injunctions such as "The Minister will wish to say . . ." . . . They will even include speaking notes which the minister can read out without having taken the trouble to study the Cabinet papers at all.

Though your officials would be perfectly happy for you to remain permanently in your department and totally in their thrall, fortunately for you (and in fact for them) you will have many duties to perform in the House of Commons. Indeed, your department will have a parliamentary branch especially established to facilitate your dealings with both Houses.

Extract from G Kaufman, *How to be a Minister*, Faber, 1997

Fig. 2 *Gerald Kaufman*

Summary questions

1. Why do radical ministers sometimes find their relationships with civil servants frustrating?

2. Do civil servants have too much power?

4 Individual ministerial responsibility

Learning objectives:

- What does the convention mean?

- What factors have undermined its importance?

- Why is it important?

- When and why do ministers resign?

Key terms

The **Crichel Down Affair**: a dispute in the early 1950s concerning an aggrieved landowner whose acreage had been requisitioned in wartime and was later sold off without him being given the chance to re-purchase it. Such were his social influence, wealth and connections that the issue brought about the resignation of the Minister for Agriculture (Sir Thomas Dugdale) who lost support among Conservative MPs.

The **Falklands War** (1982) resulted from the conflict between the UK and Argentina over ownership of the Falkland Islands, but was precipitated by the Argentinian invasion of South Georgia. Lord Carrington took full responsibility for the complacency and failures in the Foreign Office which might have been expected to foresee this development. He and his ministerial team resigned.

The theory

Individual responsibility refers to the responsibility of each government minister for the work of his or her department. Ministers are answerable to parliament for all that happens within it. The positive benefit of this is that MPs know that there is someone to whom they can direct their questions and anxieties about policy, e.g. at question time, in committees, in debates, and privately to the minister responsible. The negative benefit is that thereby civil servants are kept out of the political arena and shielded from controversy, making it possible for any future administration to have confidence in civil service neutrality.

Brazier (1988) has summarised the main areas of individual responsibility as those concerning private conduct, the general conduct of the department, and acts done or left undone by officials in the department. He might have added policy, a main area of responsibility, but its absence is recognition of the fact that ministers rarely resign over it. As to whether or not they do take responsibility, he has recognised that 'the principles which have developed are at best elastic, and in testing how far they will stretch the personal determination of particular ministers can be crucial, especially when they are trying to defend themselves against demands for their resignation'.

Individual responsibility is a convention and its operation is not therefore regulated by statute. There are few binding rules governing ministerial responsibility unless ministers have been guilty of a gross deception of the House of Commons. Precedent and guidance have some impact on how ministers behave, but as we shall see, political considerations are highly relevant. Much depends on the circumstances of the individual case.

The responsibility of individual ministers for their own conduct and that of their departments is regarded as a vital aspect of accountable and democratic parliamentary government.

What does 'responsible' actually mean? It means on the one hand that ministers are required to inform parliament about the work and conduct of their departments, explaining and if necessary making amends for their own and their officials' actions. They take the praise for what is well done and the blame for what goes wrong. In this sense, answerability and accountability still apply. But 'responsibility' goes further and implies liability to lose office if the fault is sufficiently serious.

The practice: erosion of the doctrine

Resignations for political or administrative misjudgements and mistakes have in recent decades become extremely unusual. In the 19th century, such resignations were not uncommon; only two (Dugdale over the **Crichel Down affair** and Carrington over the outbreak of the **Falklands War**) have occurred since the Second World War. In the Carrington case, in which he and other members of his foreign office ministerial team resigned, this was arguably done to protect the Prime Minister and other ministers. It was perhaps convenient for one key member of the Cabinet to accept individual responsibility in order to protect the government as a whole. Without a resignation, the government would have been in greater political difficulty.

Many political blunders, misjudgements and departmental administrative failings are committed, but they go unpunished by the ultimate sanction. Whether or not a minister resigns under the convention will depend on his or her support from the party, Prime Minister and Cabinet colleagues. If there is prolonged adverse publicity that may be damaging to the government, a resignation is more likely to occur.

In practice, the convention does not normally apply in the sense of ministers being liable to resign when blunders or wrongdoing are exposed. Its application has been watered down as:

- Often MPs on the government side rally behind a minister in difficulty.
- Many commentators are sympathetic to ministers who find themselves in political trouble over an episode in which they had no direct involvement.
- In the Home Office, which deals with controversial issues that create much public anxiety, the volume of mail received every day is massive. It would be unreasonable to assume that ministers can read it all or know the details of every response sent out in their name.
- The creation of executive (Next Step) agencies has blurred responsibility. They have a degree of autonomy, so that when a problem occurs – perhaps a mass prison break-out – there is an issue of who is to be held responsible, the head of the Prison Agency (responsible for administration and operations) or the Home Secretary (responsible for the broad lines of policy).
- In the case of the Parkhurst gaol break (1995), neither Michael Howard nor Sir Derek Lewis were willing to accept responsibility, each blaming the other. In this latter episode, as in many others, governments have sometimes distinguished between the duty of ministers to account to parliament for the work of their departments and their individual responsibility. In the complex world of modern government and decision making, they cannot be held responsible for every action of every departmental official. This point has particular application to agencies which are responsible for many operational issues. However, purists counter-argue that it is impossible to distinguish between areas for which ministers are personally responsible and those for which they are constitutionally accountable.

Merits of the doctrine

1   **It ensures that someone is accountable**, in that there is a minister to answer questions. In this way, it facilitates the work of MPs to investigate the grievances and press the claims of their constituents.

2 **It keeps civil servants on their toes**. Civil servants are not normally named when any error has occurred, but the knowledge that if they make a misjudgement then their minister will be answerable in the House, helps to ensure that they act with care in handling departmental issues.

3 **It facilitates the work of opposition**, in that it forces someone to justify government policy to those seeking to expose departmental or policy failings.

Fig. 3 *Why do ministers resign? Stephen Byers, Secretary of State for Transport in 2002 after a troubled tenure at the office, including the Jo Moore episode*

Why do ministers resign?

Ministerial resignations were fairly frequent under the Major and Blair administrations. Some have been high-profile ones, such as those of Peter Mandelson and David Blunkett. Most resignations have little to do with ministers taking responsibility for the work of their department under the principle of ministerial responsibility. They tend to fall into one of three categories:

1 **Sexual or financial impropriety**, e.g. Tim Yeo resigned after fathering a 'love-child' (1994) and Ron Davies resigned having experienced a 'moment of madness' on Clapham Common which led to an assault upon him (1998).

2 **Political misjudgements and mistakes**. Peter Mandelson resigned after failing to declare receipt of a large loan from a fellow minister to facilitate a house purchase. A potential conflict of interest was involved (1998). He resigned again three years later, after suggestions that he intervened to secure a fast-track passport application for the Hinduja brothers, financiers who contributed generously to the Labour party. David Blunkett's first resignation (as Home Secretary in December 2004) came after an affair in which he had been involved became high profile. More seriously, he had intervened to fast-track a visa application from his lover's nanny, thereby using his departmental influence to secure a personal favour.

Activities

Below are some ministerial resignations of the Blair era. Choose any two of them and use the internet to find out the circumstances surrounding the cases.

Table 3 *Ministerial resignations during the Blair era*

Minister	Date of resignation
Ron Davies	October 1998
Peter Mandelson, Geoffrey Robinson	December 1998
Peter Mandelson	January 2001
Stephen Byers	May 2002
Estelle Morris	October 2002
Robin Cook	March 2003
Clare Short	May 2003
Alan Milburn	July 2003
David Blunkett	December 2004
David Blunkett	November 2005

3 **Policy differences with the government**. On occasion, ministers can no longer support the policy of the Cabinet. We have seen that Robin Cook resigned shortly before the invasion of Iraq (2003) because he felt the policy was dangerous and ill-conceived. He could not accept collective responsibility for what was being done.

Summary questions

1 Does responsibility mean 'liability to lose office'?

2 Is the convention still operative?

3 Can it still be preserved in an age of executive agencies?

4 What factors determine whether a minister does or does not resign after committing some blunder or indiscretion?

5 Changes in the civil service in recent decades

Learning objectives:

- Why was there growing disquiet with the performance of the civil service in the pre-Thatcher era?

- What changes did Prime Minister Margaret Thatcher bring about in the civil service?

- What was Tony Blair's view of the civil service?

- What has been the impact of New Labour on the civil service?

- What are the benefits and disadvantages of using special advisers in government departments?

For many years the British civil service was highly regarded, often being likened to a Rolls Royce in terms of its skill in handling policy issues and the transition from one government to another. Its professionalism and integrity were seen as sturdy virtues. But by the 1960s and 1970s, there was a growing feeling that change was needed to bring the civil service into the late 20th century:

- **Civil service elitism was much criticised**, particularly on the Left which was wary of the social composition and rigid structure of the organisation. It was hoped that fundamental reform would improve the quality of personnel within the civil service and that this in turn would improve the quality of advice given to ministers.

- **The service was increasingly seen as a barrier to radical change**, not just on the Left but also by reform-minded Conservatives of the Thatcherite variety.

- **Members of the civil service were also thought to lack the necessary qualities for running a modern state**. As the role of government expanded in the days of the Welfare State and Managed Economy, special expertise was needed if the best possible advice was to be available to ministers. There was a feeling that civil servants were insufficiently innovative and business-minded.

The Fulton Report (1968) – whose recommendations were broadly accepted by the Labour government – tackled some of these issues, particularly the rigidity of the structure and the need for improved recruitment and training of personnel. But in the Thatcher and Major years, the pace of reform was accelerated. In particular, the Thatcher era saw the most profound modern reforms of the civil service. The principles of Thatcherism were applied to government administration, a guiding one being that as much decision making as possible should be made according to market principles. Margaret Thatcher's well-known dislike of the public sector stimulated several major changes to the size, organisation and functions of the civil service.

The Thatcher impact

Margaret Thatcher was instinctively suspicious of the civil service and the culture traditionally associated with it. She had no obvious admiration for the alleged qualities of the British civil service machine. In her view, a large bureaucracy went hand in hand with the 'big government' which she so despised. She wanted to roll back the frontiers of the state. This involved curbing a civil service which had become unnecessarily large and was urging/pursuing misguided policies.

Margaret Thatcher was also suspicious of the power and type of senior civil servants, some of whom might use their permanence and expertise to develop their own view of what was needed rather than assist in carrying out the wishes of the government of the day. Not only were they excessively powerful, they were also sometimes poor managers, ill-equipped for the task of running a large department. They often lacked training in management skills, many being generalist all-rounders rather than expert administrators.

Among other things, as Prime Minister she:

- achieved substantial cuts in the number of personnel
- tried to bring in people at the top who were 'one of us'; a number of early retirements enabled her to sweep away several long-serving officials
- brought in outside advisers such as Sir John Hoskyns and Sir Derek Rayner who challenged the attitudes and outlook of many senior officials and were responsible for cost-conscious policies and efficiency savings
- appointed Sir Derek Ibbs to run the Efficiency Unit. His influential report, 'Improving management in government: the next steps' argued for the creation of a slimmed-down, better-managed civil service. New agencies would be responsible for 'blocks' of executive work (operational matters), and a smaller 'core' civil service would work in the departments to 'sponsor' the agencies and to service ministers with policy advice and help.

The New Labour impact

By the time of Labour's arrival in office, it looked as though Whitehall was in a state of continuous upheaval. The old days of hierarchical departments staffed by permanent officials had long gone. The incoming administration accepted the idea of executive agencies.

Like his predecessor, Tony Blair wished to deliver effective public services. He was anxious to achieve performance targets and was more interested in reaching them than in worrying about the means by which this might happen. Thus cutting waiting lists for hospital appointments was a goal, as was cutting class sizes in infant schools. Ministers were less interested in the department or agency that delivered the outcome than in ensuring that it was attained.

To improve policy coordination and implementation and get away from the short-termism of traditional governmental thinking, the Blair government established the Performance and Innovation Unit in the Cabinet Office. Specifically, it was to examine cross-governmental policies, sorting out departmental disputes. The Prime Minister was

Activity
Write a paragraph to explain why Margaret Thatcher was instinctively hostile to aspects of the civil service.

Activity
Compare the approach to civil service reform of Margaret Thatcher and Tony Blair.

committed to 'joined-up' government. Before Lord Falconer became a Departmental Secretary, the Prime Minister used him and others to ensure that officials planned for the future and worked with those in other departments.

To open up government, the Prime Minister was keen to change the culture of senior civil servants. He suspected that many were resistant to new thinking and in some cases doubted their quality. He and his advisers made the comparison with the New Labour machine then at Millbank, which had served the party well in opposition. They wanted to see the same efficiency in Whitehall. Above all, he feared 'departmentalitis', the idea that civil servants tended to adopt a policy view and keep to it whichever party was in power. To break the stranglehold of traditional attitudes, he brought in new people from outside the service. His fondness for political advisers illustrated his enthusiasm for changed thinking.

Following the example of his two predecessors, Tony Blair made extensive use of political advisers. He increased their overall number from 38 in the Major years to 80 or so by the time of his departure. The idea was to enable ministers to get a grip on their officials. Advisers add a political dimension to the opinions gained from civil servants and are there to help ministers who may be too susceptible to official advice. Most ministers are keen on this independent source of advice. Former minister Mo Mowlam felt that they give 'strong central support and political focus'.

Advisers are usually appointed for the lifetime of an administration. During that period they create some opposition within Whitehall as some civil servants see them as trespassing into their domain. The best officials probably see them as an aid, but others feel threatened. Critics also point to the rapid increase in the number of advisers. The Neill Committee recommended in 2000 that their number should be limited to a maximum of 100. Neill rejected the view that special advisers had broken Whitehall rules or that there has been an unhealthy 'politicisation' of the civil service, but wanted to ensure that they operate to a code of conduct which sets out the relationship between special advisers, officials, ministers and the media.

■ **Further information**

The growing use of special advisers
- 1979: 6
- 1994: 34
- 1998: 74
- 2002: 81.

■ **Activities**

1. A report by the Public Administration select committee in 2002 on special advisers was subtitled 'Boon or bane?' Which do you think they are?

2. Using the internet to assist you, find details about the so-called 'turf wars' in the Department of Transport, Local Government and Region, following the 'Jo Moore incident'.

Fig. 4 *Jo Moore, whose e-mail exposed bitter conflicts within the Transport Department: 'It's now a very good day to get out anything we want to bury. Councillors' expenses?'*

Tory critics include MP Andrew Tyrie (a former special adviser) who claims that: 'They are effectively unelected ministers. They are the people who are really running the country and I don't think that is acceptable'. Critics have also pointed to instances of conflict between Special Advisers and members of the civil service. There has been one well-publicised incident – the tensions between Martin Sixsmith and Jo Moore, who both worked for Stephen Byers when he was Transport Secretary. Both resigned following a scandal relating to an e-mail sent by Jo Moore on the day of the terrorist attacks on 11 September 2001, which was widely felt to be inappropriate.

Defenders of the Blair government acknowledge the upward trend in the number of special advisers, but argue that this began before Labour came into office. They point out that the total number still amounts to no more than three or four individuals in each Ministry. A Select Committee enquiry by the Public Administration Committee in 2002 heard from civil servants themselves that advisers 'protect civil servants by carrying out work that might raise doubts about civil service neutrality'.

Summary questions

1. 'Continuous revolution' – is that a fair description of what has been happening within the civil service over the last generation?

2. Why do you think that both Margaret Thatcher and Tony Blair saw a need to place more emphasis on managerial efficiency in the civil service than their predecessors?

3. Has the experiment with special advisers been a success?

Further reading

S Buckley, *The Prime Minister and Cabinet*, EUP, 2006.

www.homeoffice.gov.uk. The Home Office

AQA Examination-style questions

1   ✓ Read the extract and answer questions (a) to (c) which follow.

Ministers and Civil Servants

Ministers of the Crown head government departments. Those departments are extensive and complex bodies. Ministers enjoy substantial formal as well as political powers. The extent to which they are able to utilise those powers will depend upon the purpose and skill of the individual minister as well as power situation, climate of expectation and international developments. Ministers face considerable constraints.

Source: Bill Jones et al., *Politics UK*, 4th edn, Pearson Education, 2001

(a)   Briefly explain the term *Ministers of the Crown* used in the extract.   *(5 marks)*

(b)   Using your own knowledge as well as the extract, assess the main factors that influence the power of a minister.   *(10 marks)*

(c)   What should be the relationship between a minister and his or her civil servants?   *(25 marks)*

2   Read the extract and answer questions (a) to (c) which follow.

The Cabinet and Cabinet committees

Rather than providing a forum for detailed discussion of a wide range of policies, the main role of the Cabinet is to facilitate cohesion and coordination of government policies generally, and to provide or establish the boundaries within which those policies are prepared or pursued. Many, if not most, government policies are developed in *Cabinet committees* and then reported back to the full Cabinet for approval. In other words, the Cabinet tends to rubber-stamp decisions made elsewhere.

Source: adapted from Chapter 13 of this textbook

(a)   Briefly explain the term *Cabinet committees* used in the extract.   *(5 marks)*

(b)   Using your own knowledge as well as the extract, consider how significant the doctrine of collective Cabinet responsibility is in modern British politics.   *(10 marks)*

(c)   'The Cabinet's role in decision making has been marginalised in recent governments.' Discuss.   *(25 marks)*

15 Local government

1 Local government: does anyone care?

Learning objectives:

- What is the difference between local government and local governance?

- Why do we need local government?

- Why is it important?

- Should we be anxious about the state of local democracy?

- Why does local government have a poor image?

Key term

Democratic deficit is a situation in which there is a deficiency in the democratic process, usually where a governing body is insufficiently accountable to an elected institution.

Further information

Local elections: turnout

- Turnouts are lower than in many western democracies.

- They have been falling steadily since 1945.

- In 1999, average turnout was 29 per cent, around 12 per cent in some inner-city wards.

- Since then, the average figure has hovered just under 30 per cent, only higher when polling is held on the same day as general or European elections.

Further information

The Blairite case for local government

Good local government makes a huge difference to our lives. From the moment we step outside our front door it is about how our neighbourhoods look and feel, to the quality of our schools and the facilities in our local park. Good local authorities benefit from strong and accountable leaders who are in touch with confident communities who will fight for what is best.

Tony Blair, October 2006

Local government is part of the framework of multi-level governance in the UK, with its European, national and devolved dimensions. Many people agree that it is a good idea to have a tier of administration close to them, but they show little interest in or enthusiasm for the actual work of their councils.

A recurring theme in much of the discussion about local government is the extent to which local government is in decline. It has been bypassed by the creation of appointed agencies, sometimes known as the 'new magistracy' or 'local quangocracy'. The reference to magistracy for this element of unelected local government dates back to the 19th century, when Justices of the Peace performed many administrative tasks at the community level. Many critics feel that the developing trend towards a 'new magistracy' leaves a serious **democratic deficit** in local administration.

What is meant by local government?

By local government, we mean the government traditionally provided by elected local authorities, usually known as councils. These councils originally provided many of the local public services, but they do not do so today. As Tony Blair indicated back in 1998: 'There are all sorts of players on the local pitch, jostling for position where previously the local council was the main game in town'.

In these changing circumstances, we now often use the term 'local governance' which seems a more appropriate label to describe the various agencies (public, private and voluntary) other than local authorities that are involved in providing services at the local level. This wider term emphasises the importance of the processes of government rather than its institutions. It also embraces the relations between the various participant organisations and the local community.

The case for local government

The case for local government is based on two interrelated themes – policy effectiveness and democracy. Local government is based on the principle that public policy decisions should be made as close to the

Activities

1. Check if it is possible to arrange a visit to your local council chamber and offices. Maybe a local councillor or official would lead a group on a tour round the council offices or into the council chamber and explain how the procedures work.

2. Using the internet to assist you, look up the local government election results for 2008. What were their key features?

3. Go to the Local Democracy Campaign website (www.campaigns.lga.gov.uk/localdemocracy). Find out what is being done in Local Democracy Week to arouse interest among young people in civic affairs.

people as possible. The reason for this is that centrally imposed solutions may prove inappropriate in many areas. Local councils can provide the most appropriate local response to a particular situation, based on their local knowledge, matching services to particular needs. Councils are also more accessible to local people who can more easily seek redress for any problems they face. Finally, individual councils can be used to experiment with new ideas and policy innovations. Overall, local government allows for diversity and flexibility.

In addition, because local government is closer to the people than central government, it is therefore more accountable. Elected local councils help to strengthen the democratic process, encouraging as they do the participation of citizens, by voting or standing for office. Moreover, the network of councils means that there are multiple centres of power, acting therefore as an important safeguard against an over-powerful central state.

Should local government matter?

It plays an important part in our lives. Although it has lost functions and powers in recent decades, its expenditure – adjusted for inflation – remains at about six times the level it was in 1900, the number of council houses is still around 3.5 million and the vast majority of schools is state-provided via local authorities. According to the Local Government Association, some 2.1 million staff work in local government and it provides around 700 different functions. Local authorities educate our children, provide social services for people who are vulnerable or in need of support, safeguard and protect the environment, and provide libraries, cultural and leisure facilities. They are at the very heart of our daily lives. Current spending is around £70bn per annum, about 25 per cent of all public expenditure.

The principle of local democracy is an important one. Whether or not people turn out and vote in council elections, local government still matters precisely because it is local government. People who know the area are more likely to be sensitive to local needs and be able to respond when action is needed than someone who operates from Whitehall. It also provides scope for community government and local participation. Some residents may choose to stand for office, others may be content to be voters. Either way, the chance for participation is provided and via local involvement some people will go on to engage in national politics. Such involvement means that government has local support, and this helps to strengthen democratic values.

Anxieties about the quality of local democracy

In depth

Local government: dying or still very much alive?

Dying:

- poor public image, lack of popular and media interest
- turnouts are low
- elections are fought mainly on national rather than local issues
- loss of functions to other bodies
- little financial independence, excessively dependent on central government.

But still very much alive:

- newer parties are gaining seats as main ones have lost backing, e.g. greens
- more parties are involved in running local councils
- councils have gained a greater role in economic renewal
- some councils are keen to innovate, e.g. on recycling and congestion charging
- some councils have boldly sought out European funding for civic projects
- councils are still responsible for key services, sometimes as enablers rather than providers
- local government is still a large employer and spender.

There are several grounds for anxiety about the health of local democracy. These include:

- the loss of powers to unelected alternatives
- poor turnouts
- the tendency for voters to cast their vote on national grounds
- the use of the FPTP electoral system
- low levels of interest and participation in local government
- widespread ignorance of what it actually does.

Add in the criticism of the quality of many local councils and councillors, and the number of scandals that has seriously undermined public confidence, and the picture of local democracy in action may seem a dispiriting one.

Why does local government not arouse more enthusiasm?

Several explanations have been offered:

- **Local government lacks glamour**. Many people feel that all of the interesting and important things are decided nationally. In contrast, local councils can do so little that their work hardly inspires any effort to vote. Their powers have been curtailed by central government, successive pieces of legislation having severely restricted the functions and powers of local authorities.

- **Some voters might think that voting is not worthwhile because in their area control never changes**. For several decades after 1945, Labour dominated in places such as Doncaster, Manchester, Sheffield and Stoke. If people feel that there is a chance that they might be represented by a candidate standing for their own party, there might seem more point in turning out.

- **Local government has a poor image**. Often because of one-party dominance, there have been many stories in recent years of cronyism, sleaze, contentious land deals and wasteful 'junkets' (trips made at public expense) by councillors. The media has often focused on such 'negative' stories, partly because they are good items for local news bulletins and partly because local authorities do little which seems interesting or exciting.

Summary questions

1. What do we mean by saying that local government has evolved into local governance?

2. Has local government had its day?

3. Can (should) local democracy be revitalised?

4. Should we care about local politics?

🔏 How could people be made to care more about local government?

▪ Create smaller authorities to encourage local democracy – but turnout is not always related to size and in any case this might not allow for the efficient provision of services.

▪ Use a proportional voting system (see Chapter 3), which is arguably more fair – but this is unlikely to improve turnout very much.

▪ Encourage local authorities to create small area committees (the Local Government Act 2000 actually allows them) – but such community councils do little to arouse enthusiasm.

▪ Grant local government more powers, so that voters know that key decisions are made locally.

▪ Create a local supremo to get things done, as some authorities have by choosing to have an elected mayor for their region.

2 The shape and scope of local government and what it does

Learning objectives:

▪ What is the structure of local government in England and Wales?

▪ What are the benefits of unitary councils?

▪ What are the functions of the different types of authorities?

▪ The present structure of local government

The Conservatives were responsible for the introduction of a largely two-tier system of local government during the Heath administration (1972–74). Under Margaret Thatcher, the structure was modified by the removal of five metropolitan counties and – most famously – of the Greater London Council (GLC) in the mid-1980s. With the abolition of these authorities, functions were either passed down to the London borough councils and metropolitan districts beneath them, or to new quangos.

Across the rest of England, the structure was unchanged until 1992, when the Local Government Review under John Banham was created. Its task was to examine local government reorganisation in England on a case-by-case basis. The commission engaged in widespread consultation and found a surprisingly high degree of satisfaction with the existing structure. As a result of this third Conservative reorganisation, most of the two-tier system was retained. Counties (34) and district councils (238) exist in many areas, so that in a shire county such as Staffordshire, there is a county council and below it a series of district councils such as Lichfield DC. A few large county councils which had never won public admiration (e.g. Avon and Humberside, creations of the 1970s) disappeared. Also, some large towns and cities such as Bristol, Milton Keynes and Reading, became **unitary authorities**. But these were only created where there was obvious public support for the idea.

The result of all this activity over the last generation is that there is now a patchwork of unitary authorities and the two tiers of counties and districts in other parts. The unitary ones include those which were created in the large metropolitan areas in 1974 (36), such as Birmingham, Coventry and Walsall, and the new 'Banham' ones in the rest of England (46). Scotland and Wales both have a system of unitary authorities.

Unitary authorities are said by their admirers to have certain advantages. Notably, they:

- promote local democracy by placing responsibility on one authority for the whole range of local services
- reduce administrative costs
- improve the quality of local services.

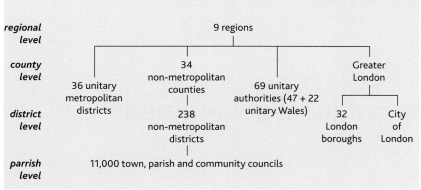

Fig. 1 *Structure of local government in the United Kingdom*

The two-tier system has been strengthened by the Labour proposal, backed in a capital-wide referendum in 1998, to recreate an all-London assembly led by a directly elected mayor responsible for overall strategy in Greater London. The new system of London government began to operate in 2000. London retains its 32 borough councils (which have a status similar to the metropolitan district councils in shire England) and the Corporation of the City of London.

At the time of writing, there were 410 local councils in England and Wales that were designated as 'principal authorities' under the terms of the Local Government Act 1972 (see below). A historic and diverse tier of around 10,000 sub-principal authorities also exists in the form of community, parish and town councils, made up of nearly 100,000 councillors. These first-tier councils can respond to the needs of the local community. Many are involved in planning, promoting tourism, licensing, community halls, representation, management of town and village centres and providing community halls, etc.

The difficulty of local government reform since 1945 has been to achieve a balance between promoting efficiency and maintaining a sense of community. Units need to be large enough to be viable and able to operate and sustain a broad range of services. But they also need to match the local communities with which people easily identify.

What local authorities do: functions

- Districts are responsible for leisure, environmental health, housing (including the provision of social housing and housing benefit), refuse collection and local roads.
- Counties are responsible for more strategic services such as education, fire and ambulances, libraries, main roads, refuse disposal, social services, trading standards and transport.
- Unitary authorities exercise all of these functions.

Summary questions

1. Would very large local authorities be better than small ones?

2. Is it true that local government no longer has any worthwhile functions?

Local authorities sometimes provide services on a joint basis with other authorities through bodies known as joint boards. Joint boards are not directly elected but are made up of councillors appointed from the authorities which are covered by the service. Typically joint boards are created to avoid splitting up certain services when unitary authorities are created or a county or regional council is abolished. In other cases, if several authorities are considered too small (either in terms of geographic size or population) to run a service effectively by themselves, joint boards are established. Typical services run by joint boards include fire services, public transport and sometimes waste-disposal authorities.

3 The powers of local government

Learning objectives:

- What is the constitutional position of local government in Britain?

- Why was the period from 1945 to the 1970s a heyday for local government?

- In what ways has the relationship between local and central government changed since the 1970s?

- How has Britain's membership of the European Union impacted on local government?

The constitutional position

Local government in Britain has no constitutionally secured powers as the UK lacks a written constitution. The political system is a unitary one, with constitutional authority deriving from Westminster. All local authorities have been created by Acts of parliament, and parliament is free to change boundaries and remove functions from local councils as it wishes. Indeed, it could abolish the whole system if it so wished. Local government can only act in those areas specifically laid down by parliament.

So parliament is the source of all local authority powers. See the list of some of the things over which it has control below.

In depth

How parliament legislates and controls local authorities

Parliament:

- determines the structure of local government
- creates or abolishes new authorities
- lays down certain compulsory features in their internal workings, compelling them to establish various committees
- controls the terms under which councillors hold office (e.g. matters of payment)
- requires councils to provide certain services such as education and care of the elderly
- lays down minimum standards of provision in those services
- forbids councils from undertaking activities such as commercial trading
- approves or overrules by-laws made by them
- grants discretionary powers to ministers and other public bodies to make orders concerning their operation and allows them to issue circulars that have to be complied with

■ approves the bulk of money for local authorities (see p264) and can change the system of local taxation.

The post-war years to the 1970s: the high point of local authority influence

Although the British system of local councils is controlled by Westminster and Whitehall, for many years it was an active and vibrant system. It reached its heyday in the period after 1945, in what now seems to have been in some respects a golden period for local government. The growth in local spending coincided with the creation and expansion of the welfare state. Councils assumed additional responsibilities particularly in areas such as social services, spending a growing share of the national income, employing more people and enjoying a considerable degree of freedom to determine local policy responses. The broad parameters of policy were laid down in London, but local government was responsible for the direct delivery of the majority of public services that directly impacted upon people's lives, notably in education and housing.

Broadly speaking, in this expansionist phase, both local and central government directed their efforts at achieving the same goals, and relations were straightforward and lacking in tension. Central government was concerned to see that there was in place a pattern of local councils that was large and powerful enough to deliver a wide range of expanding services. It assumed the main role in policy making, but left detailed implementation to local government. As for the delivery of services, it laid down specified requirements and standards. However, there was ample scope for authorities to adapt the specifics of public policy to local conditions according to the mandate they received from their local electorate. Generally speaking, local councillors and officials were sympathetic to increasing local spending to provide a better range of services.

■ Central pressure on local government since the mid-1970s

The situation began to alter in the mid–late-1970s, when the expansion of provision came to an end. But most noticeably, it was impact of Thatcherism that began to change the political agenda as far as local councils were concerned.

The relationship between central government and local authorities relates primarily to issues such as the arrangements for local government finance and the balance of national and local influence in policy making. The arrangements in these areas became more sharply politicised after 1979. Profound changes affected the structure of local government and the way it was financed, and led to the more rapid creation of non-elected quangos.

Conservative ministers wanted a greater role for the private sector in the delivery of local services, stressing the enabling rather than the direct service provision role of local government. In the field of public housing, in addition to the policy of selling council houses, active encouragement was given to the involvement of non-governmental agencies such as housing associations. In education too, previously an area of relative local **autonomy**, central control was increased in several ways, most obviously by the introduction of the national curriculum. The government placed the emphasis on consistency and efficiency rather than diversity and choice.

Activity

List the ways in which local government autonomy has declined since the 1970s.

Key term

Autonomy: self-government, allowing freedom to subordinate authorities to shape the character of their community.

During the Conservative era, more than 100 separate Acts of parliament included provisions that made changes to local government in the UK. Broadly, they fell into three categories, those relating to:

1 finance, particularly how local authorities raised or received their income and the rules and legislation concerned with how they spent their money

2 activities in which local government was engaged. Under compulsory competitive tendering (CCT) regulations, councils were required to put certain services (e.g. grounds and vehicle maintenance and refuse collection) out to public tender

3 the framework of local government, affecting its structure (the abolition of the six existing Metropolitan councils and the Greater London Council in 1986, as well as the creation of a number of entirely new authorities). In addition to structural changes, there were other developments:

   a the development of the concept of local councils as enabling authorities which did not provide services directly. Instead, they allocated contracts for service delivery to competing providers

   b raft of policy changes that tightened control just in the areas in which councils had previously had much discretion – namely education and housing.

Local councils were seriously undermined by such measures. The most significant powers lost were in the areas of education and housing. The former polytechnics (now mostly universities) were removed from local authority control, the management of schools was devolved to school governors and some schools were allowed to opt out of local government funding altogether. In housing, there was a massive transfer of housing units (some 2.2m council houses were sold) and in other cases council estates were allowed to choose a different future, run by housing associations.

The situation since 1997

As a result of the changes made, many commentators felt that after 1979 there was increased central control over local councils, involving a reduction in the degree of local autonomy. In 1997, the new Blair government was committed to giving councils a higher profile and restoring life and vigour into the way they functioned. The Prime Minister was keen to revive this failing area of British democracy. It would be 'modernised . . . re-invigorated . . . reborn and energised' under Labour rule. New Labour's plans for reviving local democracy included:

■ the proposal for an elected Mayor of London and a new assembly

■ allowing councils throughout England the chance to consult the people in their vicinity about how they would operate in future

■ replacing Compulsory Competitive Tendering (CCT) with Best Value in 1998, retaining the principle of competition, but allowing contracts to be awarded on the basis of other factors as well as price.

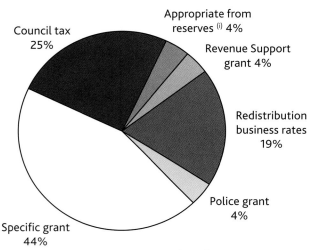

Fig. 1 *Where the money comes from (2006)*

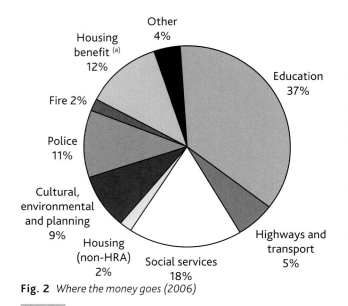

Fig. 2 *Where the money goes (2006)*

There was much interest among commentators as to how the wider policy of massive constitutional change would impact on the world of local government as policies such as devolution, electoral reform and the use of elected mayors all had clear implications for the existing form of local government.

In depth

The powers of local government

- Local authorities exercise power within statutory restrictions laid down by Westminster.

- In certain cases, ministers have powers to secure uniformity in standards to safeguard public health or to protect the rights of individual citizens. Where local authorities exceed their statutory powers, they are regarded as ultra vires (acting outside the law) and can be challenged in court.

- All types of councils also have a general power under the Local Government Act 2000 to 'promote economic, social and environmental well-being' of their area. Councils may promote legislation in parliament (see private bills, p190) in order to acquire special powers. The general power does not allow local authorities to expand their money-raising powers. Any specific use of it can be overridden by the Secretary of State.

- The ability to raise money is the key to the exercise of power. In the post-1945 era, local government lost much of its financial independence and became increasingly dependent on central government for its revenue. It now gets only around one-third of its funding from local sources.

So what can local government do?

- Although it has lost many of its functions, local government is still a major deliverer of services, even if it now delivers considerably less than in the past.

- Given the arrival of new players on the service provision scene (housing action trusts, registered social landlords (housing associations) and private companies etc.), councils have increasingly become enablers rather than providers, in the words of Osborne and Gaebler (1992), 'steering rather than rowing'.

The impact of Europe on local government

A further development since the 1980s has been the growing impact of Europe upon British local government. For a number of reasons, British local authorities began to develop a direct relationship with the institutions of the European Union and with partner local authorities on the continent. In the main, these evaded British central government, indicating that a new dimension was emerging in central–local relations. The developing relationship between local authorities and the European Union took two principal forms:

1 The provision of EU funding through programmes such as the European regional and social funds. Some authorities such as Birmingham were notably effective in attracting European money to finance major construction projects.

2 Local authorities began to participate in European networks, working with councils in other countries in the search for common solutions and in a bid to influence the direction of EU policy.

Summary questions

1 In what ways was the period from 1945 to the 1970s one of expansion in local government?

2 Has local government sufficient powers to do a worthwhile job today?

4　Financing local government

Learning objectives:

- Where do local authorities get their money from?

- What are the arguments for and against (a) the community charge, and (b) the council tax?

- What are the main possible alternatives?

The subject of local government finance is an important one because local councils are responsible for approximately a quarter of all public spending. National government, which wishes to monitor the overall level of public expenditure, seeks control over the volume of local spending. It is also interested in the ways by which local authorities are financed. These methods may prove harmful to a significant element among the supporters of the party in power at Westminster. Voters might blame national government when they are asked to pay more in local taxation.

Over the past few decades there have been many suggestions about the most desirable way by which people should pay for the local services they use. On paper, any proposed system may seem preferable to the existing one, but in time they all founder on the fact that some group in the community seems particularly burdened by them. All have their winners and losers. In time, the losers begin to complain loudly about the unfairness they endure.

Today, under the Local Government Finance Act 1992, local authorities have four main ways of financing their current (revenue) expenditure which is used for spending on pay and the day-to-day costs of running services such as education:

- the Council Tax
- income from fees and charges for services such as use of swimming pools and parking meters
- grants from central government (or the devolved administrations in Scotland, Wales and Northern Ireland). These are in the form of the Revenue Support Grant (RSG), the main block grant to local authorities, and Special or Specific grants, money allocated for a particular purpose such as policing
- income redistributed from central government, deriving from the Uniform Business Rate (the property tax levied on businesses and other non-domestic properties) for the area; the rate is determined by central government (see further information on p293).

The trends in financing revenue expenditure over recent years are that central government grants have significantly increased in importance (thus reducing the financial independence of local authorities) and that the impact of locally raised resources has diminished.

Past methods of financing local government

Until the 1980s, local government was financed out of the rates, a tax paid by property owners and based on the value of residential and commercial accommodation. Shortfalls in income were made up by money from central government in the form of the Rate Support Grant (RSG). As local government expanded in scope, so the need for an ever-increasing RSG was apparent. In the late 1930s, it represented about 30 per cent of local government spending. By the late 1970s, the figure was over 65 per cent. Furthermore, as home ownership became more widespread, so too the proportion of the population that paid rates increased and it became clear how **regressive** the rating system really was.

Key term

Regressive: disproportionately hitting lower rather than higher income groups in taxation.

Fig. 3 *Community Charge protest in the Thatcher years*

The Thatcher/Major years: from Community Charge to the Council Tax

The Conservatives disliked the rating system, which was a form of local taxation, and the 1974 manifesto pledged to reform it. But they did not win the election. When Margaret Thatcher became Prime Minister five years later, they had their chance. She had never liked the rating system and was committed to changing it. She wanted to see a new method of financing local authorities. Her administration opted for the Community Charge – better known as the Poll Tax. The Charge came into operation in 1990, having been trialled for a year in Scotland, much to the Scots' anger. Ministers had chosen the alternative that was the most likely to arouse opposition.

The Community Charge in action

The idea of the Community Charge was simple enough, that every adult living in a particular area should pay a flat charge to the local council. Occupants of stately homes who had previously received high rates bills now paid the same as occupants of tiny council flats. Some 17 million people who had never had to pay rates now found themselves contributing to their local council. This, it was argued, was fair because it meant that people who used local services would now contribute towards their maintenance. It would also make local authorities more accountable as the results of their high spending would be apparent to everyone. They would be reluctant to spend money too freely and raise the level of the Charge because potential voters might punish them at the ballot box.

The trouble was that the Poll Tax was regressive. There was some relief for the poor and disadvantaged, but most people paid the same as their neighbours however much better-off they were. Of course, in houses where only one person had formerly paid the rates, there might now be four or five paying the new tax – a considerable increase in the outgoings of the household.

Critics – including some in the Cabinet – were quick to point out the impact that the Community Charge would have, but the Prime Minister was not to be deflected from her mission. The innovation

Activity

Write a paragraph in defence of the Community Charge and another to explain to what extent the Council Tax represents an improvement.

was highly unpopular, provoking riots in some areas and much voter hostility. As such, its introduction stands out as one of her most serious miscalculations, one that contributed significantly to her downfall.

The Council Tax

When John Major became Prime Minister in 1990, a new local tax was the first priority of his government. He quickly established a review team to find an immediate replacement for the Community Charge. It was abolished by the passage of the Local Government Finance Act 1992.

Two recommendations were advanced, both of which were put into effect:

1 The introduction of a Uniform Business Rate, much like the old rating system. It is assessed and collected nationally, the money then being allocated to the relevant local authority. It has proved controversial because it falls heavily on small businesses and has increased sharply in recent years.

2 The introduction of the Council Tax, which is a kind of hybrid, blending elements of the rating system, a tax on income and the Poll Tax. Every property is rated according to value in eight bands, A–H, but the tax falls on the current occupant of the property, not the owner, and is progressive in as much as it is related to the wealth of the individual – as judged by the value of the house. (Better-off people tend to live in more expensive houses.) There are rebates for the disadvantaged, including the least well-off and those who live alone.

At first, the Council Tax seemed to work fairly well and there were no serious problems in collecting it. Its basis was generally accepted as fairer than its predecessor. However, more recently, the tax has become highly unpopular and there have been calls for its replacement. Those who dislike it talk of its 'unfairness', wondering why we cannot have a system more geared to people's ability to pay. In particular, many older voters have felt unduly penalised.

NB: The Council Tax differs from the Community Charge because the latter taxed people; it was a head tax. The Council Tax taxes property. The Council Tax differs from the rates because that was based on a notional rental value of the property and was paid by the owner. The present system is based on the capital value of the property, is paid by the occupier and calculated on the basis of two adults.

Further information

Council Tax banding

Present bands (which are based on property values at a specific time):

Band A = up to £40,000

Band B = £40,000–£52,000

Band C = £52,000–£68,000

Band D = £68,000–£88,000

Band E = £88,000–£120,000

Band F = £120,000–£160,000

Band G = £160,000–£320,000

Band H = £320,000 upwards

Fig. 4 *Axe the Tax: the Liberal Democrat campaign to replace council tax with a fairer alternative*

In depth

For and against the Council Tax

It is a good thing:

- It is relatively simple, difficult to avoid and easy to collect: council tax collection rates – at 96.8 per cent – are at their highest level ever.

- It is levied on households, nonetheless the amount payable is determined by the capital value of the property as placed in one of the above bands. It has an element of broad fairness, in that the tax is weighted more towards occupants of more expensive properties. In other words, occupiers of Band A, B and C properties pay only a proportion of the tax, Band D pays the full tax (this is the level used by local authorities in calculating the charge), while Bands E to H pay progressively more than the full tax.

- It assumes a two-person household but caters for single people, the poor and disadvantaged who all pay less.

No, it is not a good thing:

- The banding can be arbitrary, based as it is on the original assessment of a passing estate agent who travelled down the road and categorised properties.

- The progressive element is linked to property values rather than income or ability to pay. A widower who is not very well off and still lives in the family home after his wife has died may find himself paying quite heavily even though his income is low. Lower-income families pay a larger amount of their disposable income in council tax than better-off ones do.
- Levels of council tax have recently been rising faster than inflation.
- Property values can change between valuations, so that after a few years the banding system can become out of date.

What are the alternatives?

The present government is currently examining the options with which the Council Tax can be supplemented or replaced. Two possibilities are:

1 Local income tax. As proposed by the Liberal Democrats and supported by several commentators, this is seen as easy to collect and adjust according to spending needs. It is strongly linked to the ability to pay and makes all taxpayers conscious of the local services they use. But from a ministerial point of view, it is not easy for central government to control and it could be inflationary and encourage spending. Also, the very areas that need most money to improve their infrastructure are likely to be those in which incomes are low.

In depth

Lyons on a local income tax

- In principle, many people like the idea, nearly half of respondents thinking that it should fully or partly replace Council Tax. It was widely seen as fair, as it reflected ability to pay. It would be more progressive than Council Tax, even with full take-up of Council Tax Benefit.

- Support may be high because of a lack of understanding of its implications for people's own bills. They think that pensioners will do well, but do not realise that they may pay more themselves. As earnings increase, so more is paid and more money raised. (Of course, revenue could fall in bad times, so that local authorities would need to be equipped to manage this risk should this happen.)

- Applied to the basic rate of income tax, on average an additional 7.7p in the pound would have to be paid to raise the same amount as Council Tax raises now. An extra 1p in the pound would have yielded £2.9bn in 2006–07, but if this had been used as a supplement to Council Tax many people surveyed saw this as paying twice for the same services.

2 Local sales tax. This has the advantage of being hidden in the overall price (like VAT) and is therefore perhaps less unpopular. It is easy to collect and the families that spend the most on their shopping bill are going to pay more than disadvantaged families, many of whom will spend less. But it is not directly related to the ability to pay and could be burdensome for poor people who have to buy basic goods. Also it does not encourage local residents to think about the cost and desirability of the services they use. Again, it offers ministers less scope than the present arrangements to control local expenditure.

Further information

The Lyons inquiry into local government, March 2007

Recommendations:

- Retaining the Council Tax in the short term.

- Tackling its 'unfairness' (harshness on the poorest) via more generous benefits (short term) and revaluation to make it more progressive (medium term), with new bands at the top and bottom.

- More consistency over charges for services which currently raise more money than Council Tax in several councils.

- No local income tax at the present time.

Summary questions

1 Should the Council Tax be reformed if it is not replaced altogether?

2 What is the case for a local income tax?

5 The role and backgrounds of councillors

Learning objectives:

- What is the typical background of a councillor?
- Why are women and members of ethnic minorities under-represented?

Activity

Check how often your local councillors hold surgeries and where they take place. The information is often available in the local newspaper or from the library. Check the papers for stories that illustrate the sort of issues councillors take up.

Further information

Conveying views to councillors

- Sending letters, e-mails and faxes, and via phone calls.
- Attending surgeries held by councillors to discuss community issues.
- Attending those council meetings open to the public, where there may be a chance to speak.
- Attending any public question-time sessions, as held in several areas every few months.
- Responding to public consultation exercises, e.g. on development plans.

Becoming a councillor is a rewarding form of public service that puts people in a privileged position where they can make a difference to the quality of other people's daily lives. However, being an effective councillor requires hard work. Every day, councillors have to balance the needs and interests of their residents, voters, political parties and the council. All of these groups will make legitimate demands on the councillor's time on top of their personal responsibilities to family, workplace and friends.

The roles of councillors

The councillor's role includes representing his or her ward and its residents, decision making, policy and strategy review and development, overview and scrutiny, regulatory duties, and community leadership and engagement. However, the primary role of a councillor is to represent their ward and the people who live in it and to communicate council policy and decisions to them. Councillors representing political parties (as the overwhelming majority do) may find that their party offers advice and guidance on doing this.

Councillors cannot do the work of the council themselves and so are responsible for the appointment and oversight of officers, who are delegated to perform most tasks. Local authorities nowadays have to appoint a Chief Executive Officer, with overall responsibility for council employees, and who operates in conjunction with department heads.

The rewards and backgrounds of councillors

Councillors are not paid for their duties. However, regulations issued in 2004 allow authorities to provide basic, special responsibility and childcare and dependants' carers' allowances. The amounts payable are a matter for local determination. In this way, councils can take full account of their particular circumstances. The lack of payment discourages less well-off individuals in the community from coming forward, ensuring that many councillors tend to be self-employed or retired people who can make time available for council work.

The backgrounds of councillors

A new study by Professor Alice Brown, Amy Jones and Dr Fiona Mackay of Edinburgh University for the Rowntree Trust has examined the 'representativeness' of councillors. Their key findings are:

- The majority of councillors are still white, male and middle-aged.
- Barriers to participation are varied, complex and interconnected. Political systems, recruitment and selection procedures, local government cultures and practices are such that it is difficult for women, young people, those with full-time jobs, people from minority ethnic backgrounds, and disabled people to get involved and stay involved.
- Party policies to open up opportunities for participation are not fully developed and in some parties no specific policies exist.
- The willingness of individual political parties to use positive action measures to ensure fairer social representativeness is limited.

■ Creating socially representative councils is seen by many to enhance local democracy and increase the legitimacy of the local government system. Support for reform is also given on the grounds of equity and fairness.

According to the researchers, the key reasons why certain groups are under-represented include:

■ The political system and the structure of opportunities that it provides. A key factor discouraging members of minority groups from coming forward as candidates is the image and standing of national and local politics, and the perception that 'people like them' are unlikely to be selected or build a career. Local government has a particular 'image' problem.

■ Recruitment factors, such as selection procedures for candidates. Measures of positive discrimination are the most likely to ensure greater representation of marginalised groups. These are not widely used.

■ Individual supply and demand factors which influence whether people are able or willing to put themselves forward for selection (supply) and the decisions of those selecting potential candidates (demand). There are barriers to the recruitment of candidates from under-represented groups, such as the lack of time, money, childcare facilities and allowances for carers. Those who select candidates often do not do enough to ensure that marginalised groups are not discouraged from coming forward.

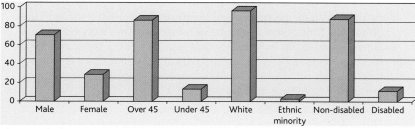

Fig. 5 *Who becomes a councillor*
Source: Figures taken from the National Census of Local Authority Councillors in England, 2004

 Summary questions

1 How can local councillors help those whom they represent?

2 Should local councillors be more socially representative than at present?

Further reading

Websites:

www.lga.gov.uk. Local Government Association. Useful section on 'about local government'.

www.local.gov.uk. Useful government information site.

16 Devolution

1 Getting the terms right

Learning objectives:

- What are the differences between unitary and federal states?
- What is a confederation?
- What are the respective advantages and disadvantages of unitary and federal government?

In most political systems, it has been found necessary to create governmental structures below central administration, with some scope for regional or local initiative. It would be impractical for national governments to govern entirely from the centre and involve themselves in the details of administration in every part of the country. However, the amount of power exercised by regional and local tiers of government varies considerably.

Different ways of distributing power

Broadly, there are three types of governmental system: unitary states, federations and confederations.

1 In classic unitary states such as Greece, there is no regional structure other than for centrally controlled administrative purposes, although there is likely to be a system of local government. In recent years, devolving unitary states (i.e. those intent on devolving powers to their regions) have become more common. These have some elected regional machinery with a degree of autonomy (not necessarily uniform) in addition to a tier of local government. Examples include France and the UK. Devolution usually comes about as a result of dissatisfaction with centralised government when ministers appear to be unwilling to recognise local needs.

In unitary states of either type, all legitimate power is concentrated at the centre. Central government has indivisible sovereignty. Some devolution of power, involving the transfer of power to subordinate elected bodies is possible, but this does not change the fact that control derives from the national legislature. Devolved governments exist only with the consent of central government, which can revoke the functions and powers at its convenience. (However, bear in mind that political reality can differ from constitutional theory. No London government is likely to try and abolish the Scottish parliament as to do so would provoke a storm of controversy north of the border and be a certain vote-loser!)

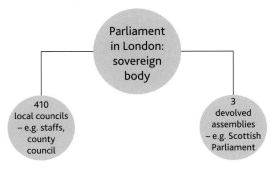

Fig. 1 *Unitary states, federations and confederations*

272

2 In federal states, there is a sharing of functions and powers between different tiers of government, a federal (central) government and regional governments, set out in a written constitution which provides for any disputes to be settled by a supreme court. The regions may have different names, being known as Lander in Germany and states in the US.

The different levels have guaranteed spheres of responsibility, the states enjoying autonomy within their sphere of responsibility and the central government conducting those functions of major importance which require policy to be made for the whole country. The essence of federalism is coordination rather than hierarchy between the levels of government.

Under federalism, it is still likely that there will also be a system of local government, although it can vary significantly in form. In the US, the federal government has little role in regulating the functioning of the local tier, which falls under the direction of the states.

Federalism
(power divided according to a written constitution)

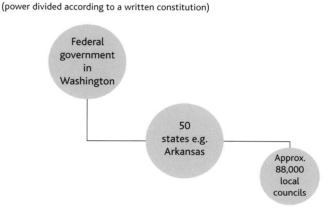

3 Confederal states have a looser form of federalism, in which central control is modest and the component elements (i.e. the states) retain primary power. Switzerland is often described as a confederation. Its 26 cantons exercise substantial power and the Berne government exerts relatively little influence over key aspects of Swiss life.

Confederalism
(power divided according to a written constitution)

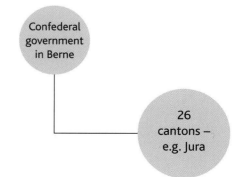

Advantages and disadvantages of unitary and federal states

	Advantages	Disadvantages
Unitary states	Clear ranking of authority, with centre supreme and few tensions between the centre and the regions	Excessive concentration of power at the Centre
	Provide clear focus of loyalty for all citizens who identify with country as a whole	Inadequate representation of regional and minority diversity
Federal states	Act as check on central power, the states preventing undue concentration of power at the centre	Some overlap of powers: possible competition and conflict between centre and states, resulting in gridlock or stalemate
	Provide national unity in large countries, but cater for diversity and regional/local responsibility. In so doing, they offer an acceptable compromise between the need for effective government and for strong regional/local recognition	Broad tendency for power to be increasingly exercised at centre, especially on key economic issues. Trend towards central control over much of US history, up until the decentralisation beginning in the 1980s
	States are useful as 'laboratories for democracy', where policy experimentation can proceed and politicians be groomed for the national stage	Sluggishness – difficulty in getting things done quickly, as over the US government in Washington's attempt to enforce civil rights legislation in the 1960s

Summary questions

1 'Unitaryism is good for the UK, federalism for the US.' Why might this be so?

2 What benefits and disadvantages does devolving unitaryism offer the UK?

2 How and why devolution came onto the political agenda

Learning objectives:

- How were Scotland and Wales governed before devolution?

- Why was there a growth in Scottish and Welsh nationalism from the 1960s and 1970s?

- Why did Labour offer Scotland and Wales devolution?

- What happened in the referendums of 1979?

Activity

Explain the attitudes to self-government in Scotland for each of the following parties: Labour, the Conservatives, the Liberal Democrats and the SNP.

How Scotland, Wales and Northern Ireland were governed prior to devolution

Pre 1707, Scotland was a sovereign state. Following the Act of Union of that year, it was governed as part of the UK although it retained distinctive features, such as its own legal system. After the Scottish Office was created in 1939, there was in place a system of **administrative devolution**. There was also a Secretary of State for Scotland, with a seat in the Cabinet. But decisions were still made in Westminster and implemented in St Andrew's House, Edinburgh, where the Office was located. What pro-devolutionists wanted to see was a transfer of decision making to Scotland, so that decisions would be made by a Scottish parliament subject to democratic control. They wanted **legislative devolution**, the power to make laws.

Wales, unlike Scotland, had never been a sovereign state, having effectively been ruled by England for several centuries. After 1964, it also had a Welsh Office and its Secretary of State had a Cabinet seat. But again, there was administrative devolution only.

Northern Ireland was a very different case having a distinctive history and culture. Under the terms of the government of Northern Ireland (1920), the island of Ireland had been partitioned. The six counties of the North remained part of the UK. They had their own parliament at Stormont (legislative devolution), but as a result of **'the troubles'**, the British government abandoned the Stormont parliament and introduced **direct rule** from Westminster.

Fig. 2 *Scottish National party (SNP)*

The growth of Scottish and Welsh nationalism

From the late 1960s onwards, there was evidence that many people in Scotland and Wales were dissatisfied with the way in which they were governed. Economic discontent was a common factor. Nationalist feeling tends to flourish when people feel that their area suffers from unfair burdens, perhaps bearing the worst impact of economic recession, industrial decline, higher unemployment, poor housing or an infrastructure in need of regeneration. Another factor was remoteness

■ **Key terms**

Administrative devolution is the transfer of administrative offices and responsibilities from central government in Whitehall to outlets around the country. It represents a decentralisation of the government machine.

Legislative devolution is the transfer of the power to legislate in certain areas from the national parliament at Westminster to subordinate elected bodies in the regions.

'The troubles': the period of conflict from the late 1960s to the mid-1990s in Northern Ireland in which there was communal violence, rioting and the threat of disorder involving Republican and Loyalist paramilitary organisations, the Royal Ulster Constabulary (RUC), the British Army and others.

Direct rule: the imposition in 1969 of rule from Whitehall/Westminster over the six provinces of Northern Ireland. It lasted until the final implementation of the Good Friday Agreement in 2007.

Nationalism is the desire of a nation to be recognised as a state.

Home Rule is a degree of self-government or devolution, which allows peoples in the constituent parts of the UK to be governed according to their own preferences and laws.

from London. There was a developing feeling that those who made the decisions knew or cared little about those who would be affected by them. For the Scots, there was in the early 1970s a new argument, the discovery of oil in the North Sea. To the nationalists, 'Scotland's Oil' made the idea of a self-governing Scotland more viable.

In addition, in Scotland there was a growing sense of national pride, a feeling that Scotland was a nation capable of governing itself. It had done so before the Act of Union, which is why it still has distinctive features in the UK, e.g. its own currency and legal system. For many Scots, it was time to regain control of their national destiny.

In hard times, nationalist parties often pick up the protest votes of those who wish to register their dissatisfaction with the government. Most Scots who voted for the SNP probably wanted to vote for a party which more obviously put Scottish interests first, just as voting for Plaid Cymru was another way of expressing 'Welshness'. Many of them did not necessarily want national independence, complete separation from the rest of the UK, which was the stated policy goal of the SNP and the Welsh Nationalists.

■ How the main parties in Britain reacted to the growth of Scottish and Welsh nationalism

For many years, neither Labour nor the Conservatives had shown much interest in the demands of the Scots and Welsh for a greater say in running their own lives. Labour was the dominant party in both countries. It had the most to lose if nationalist parties began to win seats at Westminster because it often relied on its large number of Scottish and Welsh MPs in order to achieve a majority in the House of Commons. It had always had some sympathisers for the idea of **Home Rule** for Scotland within its ranks, but it was the nationalist upsurge of the mid–late-1960s and again in the February 1974 election that made the party reconsider its position. In the late 1970s, Labour was willing to act and tried to introduce devolution for Scotland and Wales – but the proposals were not carried in the 1979 referendums.

Thereafter, Labour and the Liberal Democrats worked with interested bodies on the Scottish Constitutional Convention in 1989 to hammer out an agreed proposal for Scottish devolution. Following their agreement on a package of constitutional proposals in early 1997, they cooperated after the election. The pro-change argument was overwhelmingly endorsed by the Scottish voters in referendums held in September 1997. The Liberals and their successors have always been sympathetic to the decentralisation of power, favouring parliaments for Scotland and Wales.

The Conservatives, true to their full title which is the Conservative and Unionist party, resisted devolution proposals, seeing them as a 'slippery slope' leading to outright independence. However, following the referendums of 1997, the party accepted that devolution was a fact of life, the expressed desire of the majority of the Scottish and Welsh people.

■ **Summary questions**

1 'The growth of nationalism in Scotland and Wales was just a response to economic troubles.' Is this true?

2 How did the main three parties differ in their approach to the growth of Scottish and Welsh nationalism?

3 Devolution in Scotland: how it works

Learning objectives:

- What powers were granted to the Scottish parliament under the Scotland Act 1998?

- How were the new arrangements for devolved government justified by ministers?

- In what sense(s) has the Scottish parliament made a difference to the people of Scotland?

Key term

Reserved powers are powers 'reserved' to Westminster, in other words subjects still dealt with by the UK parliament and not devolved to the Scottish parliament. These include matters concerning the Constitution, foreign policy, defence and national security, employment and (controversially) the exploitation of North Sea oil and abortion.

Further information

Powers of the Scottish parliament

The 47 devolved matters include:

- Health
- Education and Training
- Local government
- Social Work and Housing
- Economic Development and Transport
- Law and Home Affairs
- Sport and the Arts
- Agriculture, Fisheries and Forestry
- Environment

Plus other legislative powers over 'all matters which are not reserved'.

In Scotland and Wales, the voters had backed the government's proposals for devolution in referendums. The Scotland Act and the Wales Act, both passed in 1998, gave expression to these demands.

Under the Scotland Act 1998, Scotland has a parliament of 129 members elected by the additional member system (AMS). The leader of the largest party in the chamber becomes First Minister, the equivalent position of Prime Minister. He or she chooses an Executive (since the 2007 elections, more often referred to as the Scottish government) that acts as a cabinet and is responsible to parliament. The powers granted to the new devolved machinery cover broadly the same areas as those provided by the old Scottish Office, ranging from criminal law to education and policing to local government, etc. '**Reserved powers**' remain with Westminster.

The Scottish parliament's power to make and amend laws means that it can shape a nation that is very different from England. Moreover, the tax-varying power of up to 3p in the pound gives the Scots greater flexibility in planning their social provision and the chance to offer more generous help to various groups than exists south of the border. The Executive manages an annual budget which in 2007–08 is more than £30 billion.

The Scottish Office (now more often called the Scotland office), continues to exist, but as much of its work has been taken over by the parliament it operates on a much reduced scale and fulfils a different role. Headed up by the Secretary of State for Scotland, it is now part of the Ministry of Justice, based in Whitehall, London. The Office's key roles are to:

- represent Scotland's interests at Westminster
- act as guardian to the devolution settlement, i.e. ensure that devolution works as it was intended to.

In depth

The role of the Secretary of State for Scotland

The primary role of the Secretary of State for Scotland is his or her political responsibility for the fulfilment of the two key roles of the Scottish Office. More specifically, the incumbent:

- promotes partnership between the UK government and the Scottish Executive and between the two parliaments
- continues to represent Scottish interests in reserved matters within the UK government, advising colleagues about any distinctive Scottish aspects and supporting them in presenting government policies in Scotland
- retains certain limited executive functions, notably in relation to the financial transactions between the government and the Scottish Executive and in relation to parliamentary elections
- makes orders (secondary legislation) under the Scotland Act 1998. These orders are needed, occasionally to amend, and more frequently to implement, Scotland's devolution settlement.

In his foreword to the White Paper on Scotland's parliament, the then Secretary of State for Scotland and later First Minister, Donald Dewar, justified the devolution proposals on two grounds. They would:

- strengthen democratic control
- make government more accountable.

Further information

Joint Ministerial Committee (JMC)

The JMC is the forum whereby the UK government and the devolved administrations (including those of Wales and Northern Ireland) meet to discuss matters concerning devolution. Terms of reference include:

- non-devolved matters which impinge on devolved responsibilities, and devolved matters which impinge on non-devolved responsibilities
- the treatment of devolved matters in different parts of the UK
- disputes between devolved administrations
- arrangements for liaison between the UK government and the devolved administration, to see if change is necessary.

Distinctive Scottish policies under devolution

In pre-devolution literature, there was discussion of 'a new style of government'. The suggestion was made that too often in the past those who made decisions on Scotland's behalf were out of touch with the prevailing views of the Scottish people. The new Scottish parliament would differ from Westminster in that it would be responsive to the wishes and values of the Scottish people. In particular, the new electoral system, designed to produce greater proportionality, would contribute to a more consensual style of decision making. It would thwart any tendency towards an 'elective dictatorship' by majoritarian governments resting on a minority of votes.

The elections have confirmed these hopes and expectations. Those held in 1999 and 2003 resulted in Labour being the largest party, but lacking an overall majority. It ruled in coalition with the Liberal Democrats for eight years. Minority parties also gained representation. Since 2007, Alex Salmond has been First Minister of an SNP minority government, backed by the Greens on a 'policy-by-policy' basis. An early move was to abolish the graduate endowment fees paid by Scottish students studying at Scottish universities.

The number of Scottish decisions on Scottish issues has significantly increased since 1999, as the Scottish parliament and Executive have assumed responsibility for decisions previously carried out by UK institutions. Several of the policies introduced by the coalitions have been distinctive from those pursued in England and Wales. Between 1999 and 2007:

- student tuition fees have been rejected in Scotland
- Clause 28 (on the teaching of homosexuality in schools) was abolished before other parts of the UK followed suit
- foundation hospitals have not been introduced
- elderly people have received entirely free care in nursing and residential homes

- fox-hunting has been abolished
- teachers' pay and conditions have been improved
- there has been a gradual cull of the number of unelected quangos.

The merits and demerits of Scottish devolution

After eight years, it is possible to offer some initial assessment of the case for devolution and how it is working in practice.

In favour

1 Devolution **is widely seen as democratic**, in that it allows people to express their distinctive identity and have a say in the development of the life of their own particular regions. The new system has 'strengthened democratic control' and 'made government more accountable', as Dewar intended. Control of decision makers and their accountability to an elected body are key criteria in any democratic system.

Devolution has promoted these themes. The number of Scottish decisions on Scottish issues has been greatly increased, as the new parliament and Executive take over functions previously carried out by 'British' institutions. Ministers have to defend their decisions and policies before the elected representatives of the people, the members of the Scottish parliament (MSPs).

2 Devolution **provides 'legitimate' government**. Because the electoral system includes a strong element of proportionality, it is said by its supporters to provide more representative government. The Executive can therefore claim 'legitimacy' for its actions in a way that the UK government, elected under First Past the Post, cannot. Whereas in general elections, no post-war government has based its support on more than 50 per cent of the popular vote, in Scotland the 1999 Executive (a Labour–Lib Dem coalition) had 53 per cent backing from the electorate. In 2003, the figure was 50 per cent. This compares favourably with the 42 per cent and 35 per cent achieved by Labour at Westminster in the elections of 2001 and 2005. (The SNP administration lacks majority support from the voters, with only 32.9 per cent backing.)

3 Devolution **provides a socially representative chamber**. The list system of proportional representation that elects 56 MSPs enables the voters to opt in greater numbers for minority parties and groups such as women and ethnic minorities who otherwise might fare badly under FPTP. The social composition of the Scottish parliament has an impressive gender balance relative to that at Westminster. Of the 120 MSPs elected in 2003, 51 (39.5 per cent) were women. In Labour's case, the number constituted more than half (28/50) of its intake. In 2007, 43 women were returned, as was the parliament's first ethnic minority member (a retired India-born businessman, who was brought up in Pakistan, became an SNP representative).

4 It **preserves the UK as a political entity**. If it works, it could be the saviour of the UK, granting just enough power to satisfy legitimate national aspirations. Many people believe that the four nations count for more in the world by being part of a single entity than they would individually. Also, they claim that interdependence is both inevitable and desirable in an island the size of mainland Britain.

5 It **has resulted in distinctively Scottish policies**. The Labour-dominated Executive, influenced by its coalition partners, introduced

Activity

Write a couple of paragraphs to argue the case for an independent Scotland, as favoured by the SNP.

a range of measures that differed from those introduced by ministers at Westminster. Since the introduction of devolution, political leaders in London have been forced to accept that it is an inevitable consequence of devolution that policies in Edinburgh and London can diverge, even when the same party is in control in both capitals.

Against

1 Devolution **got off to a poor start**. Disputes over the leadership of the Executive and the soaring costs of the parliament building served to discredit the cause in the short term. These may not be matters of substantial long-term political significance, but they caused initial controversy and damaged the reputation of those who operate the new devolved machinery.

2 It **is fraught with danger**, in that once parts of the UK are allowed to enjoy a measure of self-government there is a danger of the whole edifice splintering apart, in a kind of 'Balkanisation' of the UK. Such fears have been expressed by the Conservatives, who resisted the Blairite proposals in the 1997 election and referendum. They suggested that there was no real necessity for change, because unlike the situation in some other countries, the UK has not developed as a result of previously autonomous states coming together recently. They feared the ultimate disintegration of the UK if parts were able to go their separate ways, because the Scottish Nationalists would not be satisfied with devolution, a halfway house between unity and independence.

Indeed, the SNP does its best to expose the flaws in devolution as introduced, in the hope that this will fuel pressure for separation. Its long-term goal is national independence for Scotland. It views with envy the experiences of the Baltic states that have in recent years gained their independence and argues that – given its resources – Scotland also has the potential to exist as a viable state. Leader Alex Salmond is strongly critical of an Executive 'which takes its policy and its motivation from London'. He notes the frequent use of **Sewel motions** as a means of preventing the making of Scottish decisions on Scottish issues, instead 'making unsuitable English policy apply in Scotland'.

3 Devolution **has created a constitutional anomaly**, the **West Lothian Question (WLQ)**, which examines whether it is just that members of the UK parliament elected from Scotland can vote on issues only affecting England, whereas English MPs cannot vote on these same aspects in relation to Scotland. Moreover, it raises the issue of how it can be right that MPs elected to Westminster from Scottish constituencies can vote on educational policy for England, but not on educational policy affecting their own constituencies (a devolved matter handled by the Scottish parliament).

The WLQ is a consequential feature of devolution, of treating a part or parts of the UK differently from the whole. There is no easy answer to the situation, but a consequence of Conservative campaigning on the issue has been to make some English people feel that they are being treated less well. After all, Scotland has a parliament (unlike England), plus a Secretary of State in the Cabinet, over-generous representation at Westminster (until 2005) and a subsidy from the Exchequer.

4 Devolution **is a recipe for future tension**. As long as Labour was in office north and south of the border, then there was unlikely to be difficulty between Edinburgh and London. However, the recent change of party control in Scotland and probable change at Westminster at

---

■ **Further information**

Edinburgh–London conflict

A Conservative government at Westminster and Labour-dominated Executive in the Scottish capital could be a recipe for tension and ill-will. Prior to the 2005 election the Labour chairman recognised this. He warned that the prospect of a Conservative victory posed 'a threat to devolution because it would undermine the positive partnership that exists between both parliaments. Only Labour can be trusted to ensure a strong and stable UK.'

■ **Key terms**

Sewel motions are a mechanism provided for in the Scotland Act 1998 which allows the Executive to hand a decision or debate on a devolved matter over to Westminster, perhaps because it finds it too controversial or difficult to deal with, or when change might have UK-wide implications.

The **West Lothian Question (WLQ)**: 'For how long will English constituencies and English Honourable members tolerate ... at least 119 Honourable Members from Scotland, Wales and Northern Ireland exercising an important, and probably often decisive, effect on British politics while they themselves have no say in the same matters in Scotland, Wales and Northern Ireland?' (Tam Dalyell, Labour MP for West Lothian)

some time in the future mean that it is possible/inevitable that the wishes of the devolved and central administrations will come into conflict. If relations are not harmonious, then this could increase disillusionment with devolution in England and pressure for independence in Scotland. As we have seen, the SNP has no incentive to make the situation work smoothly.

In depth

The West Lothian Question: What can be done about it?

The question was never a source of contention when, prior to Direct Rule, Northern Ireland had its own parliament at Stormont while the province sent members to the House of Commons. (The situation arises again now that the Assembly and an Executive are up and running.) However, logic does not always apply in these matters. Some English people feel disadvantaged and resent the fact that an issue primarily relevant to England can be decided on the basis of Scottish votes in the House of Commons. Already, critics of the Labour government have expressed doubts about the Scottish Labour contingent at Westminster who have helped ministers push through contentious policies on tuition fees and foundation hospitals. Conservatives argue that only English MPs should be allowed to vote on English legislation.

Some supporters of devolution suggest that in reality there is no problem for England, because the overwhelming majority of UK MPs is elected in English constituencies, so that English views still predominate in debates and discussions at Westminster. Bogdanor (1999) makes the additional point that the difficulties inherent in the West Lothian Question have been resolved – or at least accommodated – elsewhere without much difficulty. Devolution has proved perfectly feasible in countries such as France, Italy, Portugal and Spain. For instance, in Italy 15/20 regions have no exclusive legislative powers, but the other five have wide responsibilities in economic and social affairs: in Spain, 7/17 have greater autonomy than the others. But 'there is no West Sardinian Question nor any West Catalonian Question'.

Of course, the dilemma of the WLQ would not arise under a federal system, as under federalism the division of functions is clear-cut. If ministers had opted for a system of elected regional councils for England, then each region (and Scotland and Wales) would have similar devolved powers, leaving the UK parliament to deal with the residue of issues, those key ones affecting the four countries collectively. Meanwhile, the reduction of Scottish representation at Westminster – carried out before the 2005 election – has at least gone some way to modify the impact of the West Lothian Question. There are now less Scottish MPs at Westminster to influence 'English' policies.

Summary questions

1. Has devolution been good for Scotland?

2. Might devolution lead to the eventual break-up of the UK? How might this come about?

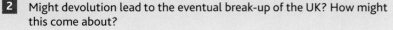

4 Devolution in Wales

Learning objectives:

- What powers were granted to the Welsh National Assembly by the Wales Act 1998?

- Why was Wales treated less generously than Scotland by the post-1997 Labour government?

- How well has Welsh devolution worked?

- How have the powers of the National Assembly evolved?

Under the terms of the Wales Act 1998, Wales was granted a 60-strong National Assembly rather than a parliament. Elections are held under the AMS system and as in Scotland there is a First Minister and Executive, since 2001 more usually known as the Welsh Assembly government.

The National Assembly is a less powerful body than the Scottish parliament, as its name implies. It was not granted primary law-making powers, although in 18 areas it was given responsibility for secondary legislation and empowered to flesh out bills already passed at Westminster. It was also envisaged that it might act as a pressure group on the London government for greater consideration of Welsh interests.

Most of the powers of the Welsh Office were handed over to the National Assembly for Wales, but a Wales Office remains as part of the recently formed Department of Justice. Based in Whitehall, the Secretary of State for Wales who heads the Office is the key government figure liaising with the devolved administration in Wales and represents Wales' interests in the Cabinet and in parliament.

In depth

Devolution in Scotland and Wales: why was Wales treated less favourably?

Welsh supporters of devolution pointed out that their country too has a distinctive identity and that even if their country lacked the distinctive institutions characteristic of the Scottish tradition, nonetheless they had something that Scotland lacked – a distinctive language. Ministers took a different view, arguing that – unlike Scotland – Wales did not have a tradition of independent nationhood. They were aware of its history as a conquered territory and of its smaller size. They were also aware that nationalism in Wales was always more about preserving the Welsh culture and language than it was about some form of home rule. Moreover, the demand for some form of self-government was more strongly established and had a longer history in Scotland. The referendum results in 1979 and 1997 showed the seeming lack of enthusiasm in the principality for devolution.

The difference between the situation in Scotland and Wales is clear. In Scotland, there was a clear demand for some form of home rule long before it was eventually granted. In Wales, machinery had to be offered to, and almost pressed upon, the Welsh people, before there were many indications that political devolution was wanted. Now that modest autonomy has been granted, there is a meaningful debate about the future direction that devolution should take. Welsh enthusiasts cast envious eyes upon the degree of self-government that the Scots have achieved.

Further information

Responsibilities of the Welsh Assembly government include:

- Health and food
- Social care
- Education and culture
- Local government, social justice and regeneration
- Economic development
- Planning and environment
- Agriculture and rural affairs.

The merits and demerits of Welsh devolution

Fig. 3 *Welsh National Assembly in Cardiff*

Since devolution, Wales has experienced both minority and coalition governments. Labour has been in office, the Executive currently being led by First Minister Rhodri Morgan. Critics have dismissed the devolved machinery as a 'talking shop', pointing to its lack of effective power. It is true that the powers are limited, but this has not stopped Wales from embarking on some policy initiatives that distinguish Welsh arrangements from those in England. SATs tests for seven-year-olds and prescription charges have been abolished, and the first Children's Commissioner has been established in the UK. In addition, the **quangocracy** in Wales (much disliked by many Welsh people) has been tackled. Even before the new machinery was established, the Wales Act 1998 had provided for the removal of nine quangos and more were due to be abolished at a later date.

As in Scotland, the early history of Welsh devolution was not a triumphant success story. There was much dissension within the Welsh Labour party over the way in which party managers in London arranged the electoral process so that a Blairite leader (Alun Michael) emerged as party leader and eventual First Minister. In 2000, he lost a 'no confidence' vote and the more popular Morgan took over. There were disputes within the Executive over controversial policies regarding EU funding, agriculture and teachers' pay, etc.

Recent changes

Plaid Cymru, as an officially nationalist party, believes in separation as a long-term goal, although in the short term it has pressed for greater recognition of Welsh identity and interests. In the light of early experience, some Labour Ministers of the Welsh Assembly (MWAs) were also keen to see more legislative power located in Cardiff. A review of current arrangements was undertaken against a background of increasing support for the idea of devolution, with more effective legislative powers and budgetary discretion being under consideration. The former Secretary of State for Wales, Ron Davies, always claimed that devolution 'was a process, not an event'. The review was an indication that movement was likely in the not-too-distant future.

> **Key term**
>
> **Quangocracy** is the collective name for the many unelected quangos that make up the quango state.

In the White Paper, Better government for Wales, published in mid-2005 the UK government proposed a half-way house between the status quo and giving the National Assembly full Scottish parliament-style legislative powers. The resulting government of Wales Act 2006 reformed the National Assembly for Wales and allowed further powers to be granted to it more easily. It created a system more akin to that of Westminster. Some of its provisions were:

- To make the Executive body – the Welsh Assembly government – separate from the legislative body, the National Assembly for Wales. Previously, it was in effect a committee of the Assembly.
- To forbid candidates from standing as a constituency candidate and being on the regional list.
- To grant the Assembly a greater legislative role, more similar to that in other devolved legislatures. In particular, it provided a mechanism for Orders in Council to delegate power from the Westminster parliament to the Assembly, giving it more power to make 'Measures', although Order-in-Council requests were made subject to the veto of Westminster.

Since the 2007 elections, Rhodri Morgan, the First Minister in the third Assembly term, has led a Labour–Plaid coalition administration, the first Welsh Assembly government to be in a position to utilise the increased powers.

Summary questions

1. What evidence is there that Welsh devolution has been 'a process', rather than 'an event'?

2. Should Wales be treated in the same way as Scotland?

5 Devolution in Northern Ireland

Learning objectives:

- What is distinctive about the politics of Northern Ireland?

- How was the province governed from 1920 to 1969? What brought these arrangements to an end?

- How has it been governed since 2007?

Northern Ireland is the least integrated part of the UK. It is often viewed as 'a place apart' because the province has a distinctive history and political culture. Different political parties stand for election and the issues over which they contest are not based around those that influence the voters elsewhere. Religion is a significant force in voting behaviour, with protestant and catholic parties taking different views over the very existence of the six counties. Hatreds based on events that took place long ago still linger in people's memories, and the emblems, flags, rituals and annual marches are always there to remind those who would forget the historical and religious differences.

Northern Ireland poses a unique constitutional problem. The Protestant majority conclude that the province should be governed as part of the UK, whilst a large, predominantly Catholic minority would prefer to see the island united as one Irish republic, or so they claim. Protestant

Loyalists are proud to be British; Catholic Republicans prefer to be considered Irish. Reaching any accommodation between two groups that adopt a very different outlook has been extremely difficult despite the efforts in recent years of the British and Irish governments to bring about a resolution of the problems. Whatever their religious allegiance, many inhabitants of the province would like to see a resolution of its problems, but the discussion is dominated by hard-line politicians on either side who are reluctant to compromise in order to reach an agreement.

From the creation of the original Stormont parliament to direct rule, 1920–69

Under the terms of the government of Northern Ireland Act of 1920, the island was partitioned. This gave the Protestants of the six counties their own parliament at Stormont, a chamber that was for years dominated by and organised in the interests of the majority Protestants. By the 1960s, many Catholics – who had been discriminated against in employment and housing and were denied their full political rights – became dissatisfied and by the end of the decade were pressing for an end to their mistreatment. Severe rioting and the threat of a serious breakdown of order led the British government to send in troops, initially much to the relief of many Catholics who feared for their lives. However, as the situation deteriorated, the British government abandoned the Stormont parliament in 1969, replacing it with Direct Rule from Westminster.

From the beginnings of the peace process to the present day

The peace process that resulted in the present governing arrangements was initiated by the Major government in 1993. For the first time, Sinn Fein – the political wing of the republican movement – had the chance to become involved in the negotiations about the future of the province. After 1997, the Blair government gave the by then stalled peace process a new momentum which culminated in the publication of the Good Friday Agreement in April 1998.

Under the terms of the Agreement, as ratified by the people in referendums on either side of the border, there was to be, among other terms:

- a devolved assembly with law-making powers in the province, elected on the basis of proportional representation
- an executive of 10 ministers who would operate on the basis of power-sharing between the leaders of the two communities.

Following the conclusion of the Agreement, there was conflict over the decommissioning of IRA weapons, the reform of the police service, the continued presence of British troops and several other issues. The Assembly and Executive were established, although they were suspended on four occasions. However, in May 2007 the machinery was re-activated, the Executive being jointly run by an unlikely coalition of the two hard-line groups within the political community, the Democratic Unionists and Sinn Fein.

Further information

The government of Northern Ireland

- The degree of devolution granted to Northern Ireland is somewhere in between that granted to the Scots and the Welsh.
- The Northern Ireland Assembly has legislative powers (like the Scottish parliament), but it has no tax-varying powers.
- Members of the Assembly decide on many matters affecting the province that continues to send 18 MPs to Westminster. Irish MPs can vote on English issues.

Summary question

1 Suggest why there has been greater devolution in Northern Ireland than in Wales.

6 The future of the UK

Learning objectives:

- What steps have been taken towards a more federal UK?

- What is the difference between devolution and federalism?

- Would federalism work in the UK?

- How might rising English nationalism be tackled?

Key term

Decentralisation is the process of transferring responsibilities and powers from national bodies to more local ones.

Britain remains a unitary state, but the important changes of recent years seem to indicate a move in the direction of a kind of federalism. Devolution has been the British route to the **decentralisation**. Ultimate power remains in Westminster's hands, although it is hard to imagine that it would be politically acceptable in Scotland, Wales or Northern Ireland if any administration in London tried to retrieve control over areas of policy that have been delegated to Edinburgh, Cardiff or Belfast.

Table 2 *The differing powers of UK devolved bodies*

Type of devolution	SP	WNA	NIA
Administrative devolution:			
■ Execute services			
■ Allocate funds			
■ Organise administration			
Legislative devolution:			
■ Make, repeal and amend laws			
Financial devolution:			
■ Ability to raise taxes			
■ Vary taxation independently			

SP = Scottish parliament
WNA = Welsh National Assembly
NIA = Northern Ireland Assembly

We now have a parliament for Scotland, a National Assembly for Wales, an Assembly for Northern Ireland, along with appointed Regional Development Agencies (RDAs) and indirectly-elected Regional Chambers around England. Each of these authorities has a different degree of power, even those of similar names. Another development has been the introduction of an elected mayor and assembly for London, followed by the creation of the office of elected mayor in several other towns and cities. Coxall and Robins (2003) wrote of '[the development from] a unitary state to a mosaic of federal, devolved and joint authority relationships between core and periphery, with the English core becoming more decentralised as regional and urban entities find political expression'. Elected regional government seems to have stalled since they wrote this, but the broad point remains. There appears to have been a move towards a more federal type of structure, even if it falls well short of the reality of federalism as generally understood. What we have is something not unlike what the Liberal party was proposing in the late 19th century, a kind of 'Home Rule All Round'.

Because we are moving in a decentralist direction, with power devolved to the component parts of the UK, some writers talk of 'creeping federalism'. Bogdanor (1999) uses the phrase 'federal devolution'

Above	Global	United Nations and its institutions (e.g. International Monetary Fund)
	Trans Atlantic	North Atlantic Treaty organisation
	European	European Union Council of Europe/Court of Human Rights
		The Centre Whitehall Westminster
Below	Devolved	Scottish, Welsh and Northern Irish devolved bodies
	Regional	Regional Development Agencies, Regional Chambers
	Local	410 councils, below which are parish/community councils

Fig. 4 *UK government, upwards and downwards from Westminster*

to describe the present British situation. As in Spain, it is not an even spread of power around the country. We have **asymmetric devolution**, with different parts enjoying different degrees of autonomy. The country is a devolving unitary state which lacks a uniform pattern of devolution.

What is the difference between devolution and federalism?

Devolution takes part in a unitary state. In the case of the UK, power is devolved from the centre to subordinate authorities as a means of meeting dissatisfaction with an over-centralised government. What Westminster has given, it can in theory take back. Legally, the devolved assemblies exist as long as Westminster allows them to. In a federal situation, a written constitution clearly defines division of responsibility between the role of central government and the role of the states or regions. Effectively, in federalism sovereignty is divided, whereas under devolution it remains at the centre.

Federalism is often seen as a system that allows for the benefits of union, without requiring total uniformity. It is especially appropriate for large states, often diverse in character. Thus, as we have seen, Switzerland is a very loose federation (because of its very weak centre, it is often labelled as 'confederal'), which is suitable because the country has two religions, three nationalities and three 'official' languages. Australia, Canada and the US, all federal countries, are geographically extensive and have obvious sectional diversities.

Might federalism work in the UK?

In depth

Labour's regional machinery after 1997

- When Labour came to office there was no strong tradition of regional government in England and a complete absence of elected representative regional institutions.
- The party was sympathetic to regional development, but settled for eight RDAs (plus a later one in London, from 2000).
- RDAs are appointed by and directly accountable to ministers in Whitehall.
- RDAs are supposed to further economic development and the regeneration of the regions, as well as promote a regional strategy.
- Indirectly-elected Regional Chambers (usually called assemblies) were established in each RDA region to provide a modicum of democratic oversight and accountability.
- From 2003, each region could establish an elected assembly if approved by the voters in a referendum.
- In 2004, the North East voted overwhelmingly against such an assembly. Other referendums were postponed/abandoned.
- As we saw on p316, Greater London was treated as a special entity and granted an Assembly and Mayor.

Activity

You are now in a position to fill in the blanks in Table 2 on page 286, comparing the degrees of devolution granted in Scotland, Wales and Northern Ireland. Have a go, writing 'yes' or 'no' as appropriate.

Key term

Asymmetric devolution relates to a situation in which the transfer of powers to a devolved body has occurred on a piecemeal or evolutionary basis, and in which different regions are granted different levels of autonomy.

The attraction of a federal solution to the problem of governing the four countries of the UK is that it offers such a clear-cut division of responsibility that would be neatly applied all round. There need be no jealousies between component parts, because all would have the same powers and be represented in the same way in the Westminster parliament.

A federal UK could be applied in two ways:

1 We could have parliaments or Assemblies for England, Northern Ireland, Scotland and Wales, with these bodies looking after the main 'internal' policies such as education, welfare and transport. There would also be a UK parliament still at Westminster. The trouble here is that England would predominate in the UK parliament because if representation was worked out on a population basis, England would need about 84 per cent of the seats. English representatives would be able to force any policy through, in spite of the Opposition of the other three countries. It would be unreal to expect England to accept that these three should be over-represented or have a blocking mechanism.

2 A better solution might be to recast England on the basis of 8–10 regions, perhaps similar to the ones used for the present Regional Chambers. Each region would have its own budget to provide its own educational, transport and other services, in the same way as would Scotland, Wales and Northern Ireland. This would mean that parts of England, especially those more remote from London (such as the North East), would have their needs and demands taken care of.

This might look like a logical way of dividing up the UK. It is certainly a very decentralist approach. But in the present situation, is there enough regional consciousness to make regional government of this type worthwhile? Would it enthuse the voters? The government made it clear that it would permit indirectly-elected chambers to opt to become elected should they wish to do so in the future. As we have seen, the voters in the North East overwhelmingly rejected this solution in a referendum held in September 2004.

Similar referenda had been planned in north-west England, Yorkshire and the Humber. Following the rejection of the proposal in the North East, Deputy Prime Minister John Prescott ruled out holding further referenda in other regions for the foreseeable future. Ministers appear to have lost any enthusiasm for the idea which would have provided a clearer, neater division of responsibility than currently exists.

The position of England within the UK today: the development of English nationalism

English nationalism is the name given to a nationalist political movement in England that demands self-government for England via a devolved English parliament. It has its roots in a perception amongst many people in England that they are English, rather than (or merely before) being British. Furthermore, it can be seen as a reaction to the establishment of devolved administrations in Scotland, Wales, Northern Ireland and in other historic European nations such as Catalonia and Flanders. Currently, the English regions do not have a Secretary of State or an English Office in Whitehall, nor do they have distinctive English committees at Westminster. (Although nationalists in Scotland and Wales might for their own reasons portray Westminster as an English parliament, it is in reality the parliament of the entire UK.) Of particular importance to the rise of English nationalism has been the publicity surrounding the West Lothian Question, which is widely seen as being hard to justify on a logical basis.

Opinion polls indicate that support for the creation of an English parliament with the same powers as the existing Scottish parliament has risen in recent years. There appears to be a widespread feeling that the Scots in particular have done well out of devolution – having a parliament, retaining a voice in the Cabinet and benefiting from a higher level of UK spending per head than applies in England.

In depth

The Campaign for an English parliament

[What we want is] a devolved parliament with all the powers of the Scottish parliament, maintaining the unity and the identity of England as a distinct nation with her people receiving the same advantageous and generous financial deal as Scotland and Wales receive. If Wales also had its own parliament, there would be parity between the three nations of the island of Britain, resolving the West Lothian Question. It would be for the English parliament to decide its own location (it does not have to be in London), what form of local government it should have, be it counties, unitaries or regions . . . An English parliament would be full devolution for England as England, constituting the most radical, genuine and progressive decentralisation of power in the history of the UK.

www.thecep.org.uk

Further information

England's disadvantage?

'The people of England now find themselves governed by political institutions that are manifestly unfair to them. First, the English are under-represented in parliament . . . second, the English do not have an exclusive say over English laws.' (William Hague, Conservative MP)

Some Conservatives believe that at Westminster, only English MPs should be able to vote on English legislation, a proposal that would make defeat of a Labour government likely on its more contentious legislation. The government responds by questioning the existence of purely English legislation.

Fig. 5 *The Campaign for an English parliament*
Source: www.thecep.org.uk

Further reading

Useful articles:

D Denver, 'The devolution project', *Politics Review*, September 2001.

P Dorey, 'The West Lothian Question', *Talking Politics*, September 2002.

M Rathbone, 'The National Assembly for Wales', *Talking Politics*, April 2003.

Useful books:

V Bogdanor, ***Devolution in the UK***, OUP, 1999.

R Deacon and A Sandry, ***Devolution in the UK***, EUP, 2007.

R Hazell, ***Constitutional Futures: A History of the Next Ten Years***, OUP, 1999.

P Lynch, ***Scottish Government and Politics***, EUP, 2001.

J McEvoy, ***The Politics of Northern Ireland***, EUP, 2008.

A Trench (ed), ***Has Devolution Made a Difference? The State of the Nation***, The Constitutional Unit, 2004.

A Ward, 'Devolution: Labour's Strange Constitutional Design', in J Jowell and D Oliver (eds), ***The Changing Constitution***, OUP, 2000.

Websites:

www.scottish.parliament.uk.

www.wales.gov.uk.

The Scottish National party (www.snp.org.uk) and Plaid Cymru (www.plaid.co.uk) sites offer a different insight into the governance of the two countries.

 Summary questions

1 What is meant by describing the governmental system of the UK as federal?

2 Were the people of the North East unwise to reject an elected assembly?

3 Does England need its own parliament?

17 The European Union

1 The development of the European Union

Learning objectives:

- What were the aims of the pioneers of post-war cooperation in Europe?

- Why was the European Economic Community created?

- What was the importance of the Single European Act 1986 and Maastricht Treaty?

- What are the main characteristics of the EU today?

Fig. 1 *Jean Monnet, one of the founding fathers of the European Union*

Key terms

US of Europe: the Churchillian vision of a re-creation of the 'European family' which would unify the continent.

Supranationalists are supporters of the idea that there should be decision making by processes or institutions that are 'above nations or states' and largely independent of them.

The Second World War was a catastrophe which discredited the old international order in Europe. The continent was in ruins. France, Germany and Italy were reduced to chaos, their people were without work and sometimes starving or homeless. It was necessary to rebuild Europe on new lines:

- to bring about economic recovery and provide a decent standard of living for the people of Europe

- to bring about reconciliation and a new stability on the continent, so that old hatred would not resurface. In particular, it was necessary to ensure that France and Germany should live and work together in peaceful harmony.

A brief history: from the European Coal and Steel Community to today's European Union

This was the background to the moves to develop closer cooperation in post-1945 Europe. There was at the time an unusual willingness to think in European rather than in national terms. Some leading continental thinkers and politicians were idealists who had a vision of a Europe in which countries would work towards the achievement of economic, political and military union. One was Jean Monnet, one of the founding fathers of the European Union, who took the view that the sovereign states of the past could no longer solve the problems of the day.

In the years after 1945, Monnet and others wished to see definite movement towards their grand design, complete political unification as implied by the term 'a **US of Europe**'. Some of these **supranationalists** wanted to see the speedy establishment of a federal Europe. Others saw federalism as the ultimate goal but were prepared to work to achieve it over a longer period via functional cooperation in particular areas.

Monnet was the architect of the Schuman Declaration (1950). This was a step forward in one sector as it set out a plan for a new supranational body to manage all coal and steel production in Germany and France, an organisation open to all other countries. The short-term aim was economic, to create a tariff-free market in which there would be no customs barriers to restrict trade in coal and steel across western Europe, but the pioneers of what became the European Coal and Steel Community (ECSC) had in mind a greater goal – political union.

France, Germany, Italy and the **Benelux countries** were members of the ECSC. The success of the enterprise inspired the same six nations to take a further step along the road to greater unity. They agreed to develop the peaceful use of atomic energy via a new body, Euratom. At the same time, in March 1957 they signed the Treaty of Rome which established the European Economic Community (EEC). The Treaty still forms the basis of the European Union today. Beyond its immediate goals (a customs union in which all internal barriers to trade would be removed), it aimed

Key terms

Benelux countries: the collective name for three countries, Belgium, Luxembourg and the Netherlands, which together formed a customs union in 1948 and have remained closely identified ever since.

European parliament: the only directly elected EU institution, made up of 785 members of the European parliament (MEPs) who are the voice of the people in European decision making but who traditionally have lacked collective power.

Qualified Majority Voting (QMV) is the usual method of voting within the Council of Ministers. Large states have more votes than small ones. Specified numbers of votes constitute 'qualified majorities', e.g. the UK has 29 votes, Romania 14 and Malta three. A QMV decision must have 73.9 per cent of the votes and be supported by a majority of the Member States.

Social Chapter: a protocol of the Maastricht Treaty committing Member States to a range of measures concerned with the social protection of employees. Subsequently incorporated into the Treaty of Rome at the Amsterdam summit. Britain originally had an opt-out, but the Blair government soon signed the Chapter.

Intergovernmental union is a union in which decisions are reached by cooperation between or among governments, by bargaining and often on the basis of consensus. It is often contrasted with supranationalism.

Commission: a hybrid organisation which makes decisions in some areas and carries out decisions made by the Council in others. Among other things, it has powers to initiate policies and represent the general interest of the Union.

for 'a harmonious development of economic activities, a continuous and balanced expansion, an increased stability, an accelerated raising of the standard of living, and closer relations between its member states' (Article 2). The Common Market (as the EEC was widely known) was a means to an end, not the end in itself.

In 1967, the three communities (the ECSC, Euratom and the EEC) merged into a single European Community (EC). The next major change came in 1986 when all Member States (by then including the UK) signed the Single European Act 1986 (SEA). According to the terms of the SEA:

- Trade barriers and customs duties between members of the enlarged Community were removed, thereby creating a single market.
- There would be free movement of goods, persons, services and capital.
- The powers of the **European parliament** would be increased.
- The principle of **Qualified Majority Voting (QMV)** would be introduced in EC decision-making.

The 12 states that signed the Single European Act 1986 agreed in its preamble that it marked another step towards 'ever-closer-union' of the European peoples. In 1992, Member States went further and signed the Maastricht Treaty which created the European Union (EU), as we know it today. They planned for the creation of a single currency (what was to become today's eurozone); promised social legislation via a new **Social Chapter**; extended cooperation into the areas of justice and internal security, and defence and foreign affairs; and introduced the concept of citizenship of the EU. All of us are citizens of the European Union.

Since then, the EU has continued to develop and expand. Further treaties signed at Amsterdam (1997) and Nice (2000) developed the Union by, among other things:

- extending the powers of the parliament and the use of QMV
- introducing new and more transparent decision-making procedures
- planning for enlargement
- assuming greater powers over a number of policy areas such as justice and home affairs and the environment.

What then is the European Union?

The EU is a supranational and **intergovernmental union** of 27 states and it is an economic and political organisation. Established in 1993 by the implementation of the Treaty on European Union (the Maastricht Treaty), it is one of the largest economic and political entities in the world, having a total population of 494 million. Since its formation, new accessions have increased its membership, and its competences (areas of policy responsibility) have expanded.

It is supranational in that decisions made at European level have the force of law in member countries, European law being superior to domestic law. The **Commission** has the power to make decisions and particularly to issue **regulations** and **directives** which are binding on member countries. Moreover, the growth of majority voting and the increasing powers of the European parliament suggest that the element of supranationalism is on the increase. The more integrationist nations (the original six) have strongly backed such developments, seeing the supranational approach as the way forward.

An enlarging Union

Table 1 *Enlargements to the EU, 1973–2007*

Enlargement	Countries joining (number of members in brackets)
First (1973)	Britain, Denmark and Ireland (9)
Second (1981)	Greece (10)
Third (1986)	Portugal, Spain (12)
Fourth (1995)	Austria, Finland, Sweden (15)
Fifth: part one (2004)	Cyprus, Czech Republic, Estonia, Hungary, Latvia, Lithuania, Malta, Poland, Slovakia, Slovenia (25)
Fifth: part two (2007)	Bulgaria, Romania (27)

Key terms

Regulations: secondary legislation that is binding on all states without the need for national legislation.

Directives: secondary legislation that is binding as to the result to be achieved, but can be implemented in a way suitable to each individual country.

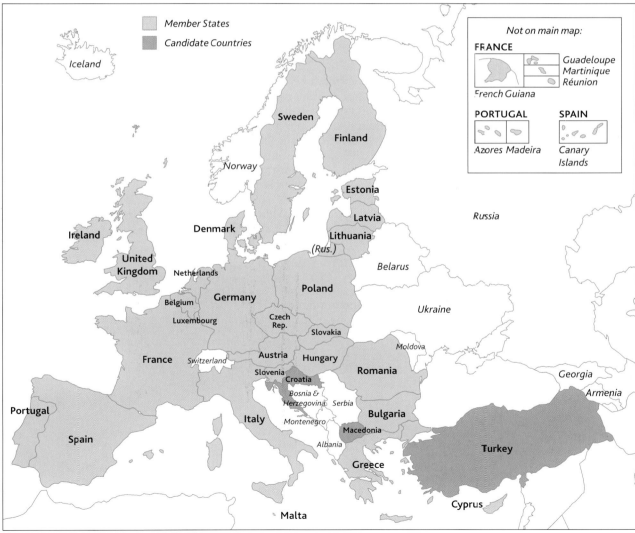

Fig. 2 *The 27 Member States of the EU*

Key terms

Council of Ministers: officially now the Council of the European Union, but this is not the name usually applied. The primary decision-making body of the EU, comprising a representative of each Member State with responsibility for whatever policy area is under consideration, e.g. environment ministers when the environment is being discussed.

Right of veto: the right of any country to block a proposed initiative or law in the Council of Ministers (undermined by the extension of QMV in several policy areas).

Intergovernmental Conferences (IGCs): gatherings that bring together representatives of EU Member States in order to hammer out the details of amendments to the treaties or other history-making initiatives on issues such as enlargement.

Activities

Using the internet to assist you if necessary, mark the names of the capital cities of Member States in the appropriate places on the map.

The EU is intergovernmental in that in many key areas of policy today, decisions are still made at the national level. Decisions on the broad direction and priorities of the EU are made by the **Council of Ministers** (officially entitled the Council of the European Union), which is made up of national ministers. Even where QMV is employed there is an attempt to achieve consensus. This is an approach that suits British politicians well. Within the EU, they have always been keen to retain certain sensitive EU policy areas (such as immigration and national security) firmly under the control of the Council where they can employ their **right of veto**. Moreover, in preparation for major treaty revisions Member States send national representatives to participate in **Intergovernmental Conferences (IGCs)** in which all Member States need to be in agreement with the final treaty or communiqué. Individual national leaders bargain amongst themselves on many of their negotiating positions, making compromises in one place in order to secure concessions in another.

A unique institution

The European Union is a distinctive creation. There have been several examples of countries that have joined with one another in ventures of mutual benefit, but in aim, method and achievement this one has gone much further than the others. From the signing of the Treaty of Rome, the Community always aspired to be more than just a customs union. It aimed for an ever-closer union of its peoples and developed supranational institutions with powers binding upon Member States.

Today, the European Union is difficult to characterise. It is neither a state nor just another international organisation, but it has elements of both. EU members have transferred considerable sovereignty to it, more than to any other non-sovereign regional organisation. But in legal terms, the states remain the masters, in as much as the Union does not have the power to transfer additional powers from states to itself without their agreement through further international treaties. Indeed in some key areas, Member States have given up little national sovereignty, particularly in the matters of foreign relations and defence. Because of this unique structure, writers tend to simply classify the European Union as *sui generis* (i.e. a unique body, of its own kind).

Summary questions

1. Why has there been a movement to bring about political union in Europe since 1945?

2. What are the differences between supranationalism and intergovernmentalism? How have they both influenced the development of the EU?

2 Britain in the European Union: the intergovernmentalist approach

Learning objectives:

- Why was Britain reluctant to join European organisations in the early years after the Second World War?

- How did the British outlook to Europe change when New Labour came to power?

- What are the elements of continuity in the British approach to Europe in the post-war era?

Further information

The approach of Winston Churchill to the relations between Britain and Europe

- 'We must build a kind of United States of Europe.' (1946)

- 'If Britain must choose between Europe and the open sea, she must always choose the open sea.' (1944)

- 'We have our own dream and our own task. We are linked, but not comprised . . . we are with Europe, but not of it.' (1946)

Key terms

Atlanticist: someone who is sympathetic to the US and favours a strong and positive relationship with it.

Special relationship: the term used to describe the warm political and diplomatic relations between the US and some Western nations, particularly Great Britain. The relationship has been the centrepiece of British foreign policy in the post-1945 era.

In Britain, from the earliest days of post-war cooperation, there were doubts about the wisdom or desirability of the closer union that Monnet favoured. British ministers of either main party preferred the idea of cooperation in appropriate areas, where nations found working together to be to their mutual benefit.

Britain within the Community

Britain stood aside from the early European developments. It had worldwide interests, there being 'three circles' in our foreign policy: the relationships with the US, the Commonwealth and – less importantly – Europe. In addition, there was the fact that Britain was – and remains – separated from the continent by geography, language and culture.

Yet by the early 1960s a growing number of British politicians began to reconsider Britain's aloof position, seeing dangers in isolating ourselves from events on the European mainland. They came to believe that there were good economic reasons for Britain to seek membership of the EC. Many of them also concluded that Britain would have more chance of influencing world events from inside the Community. After General de Gaulle had twice blocked British moves to join, the government of Edward Heath was successful at the third attempt and joined in 1973. In a referendum held to confirm British membership in 1975, there was a majority of two to one in favour of continued membership on renegotiated terms. Many people believed that Britain would have a better future inside the Community than outside. However, there was little evidence of widespread popular enthusiasm for working in partnership with other Member States.

Developing unease

The broad sympathy for British involvement was already beginning to change in the Thatcher years of the 1980s, but it gained momentum after the Maastricht agreement had been signed. There was a widespread popular feeling – fed by elements of the tabloid press – that after several years in the EC membership was bringing difficulties rather than benefits. Moreover, Brussels seemed to be too fond of interfering in our national life.

In office (and subsequently), Margaret Thatcher was a strong supporter of intergovernmentalism. She disliked the integrationist tendencies within the EC, her preference being for an enlarged Community, one that was broader and looser. She always remained a firm **Atlanticist**, seeing merit in the **'special relationship'** that her government developed with US President Ronald Reagan during the 1980s. Subsequent Conservative leaders have shared her broad outlook. Her views were set out clearly in her speech at Bruges, in which she called for 'willing and active co-operation between independent sovereign states' as 'the best way to build a successful European Community'.

Further information

Tony Blair, Britain and Europe

- I am a 'passionate European . . . Without being active in the Union, Britain will forfeit any chance of global influence'. (1994)

- '[We believe in] an alliance of independent nations choosing to co-operate to achieve the goals they cannot achieve alone.' (Labour manifesto, 1997)

- 'I happen to share the European idealism. I am by instinct internationalist . . . Britain's future lies in being full partners in Europe.' (1998)

- 'First, we should remain the closest ally of the US . . . But we must be at the centre of Europe . . . Europe should partner the US and not be its rival.' (2003)

Fig. 3 *Tony Blair and George Bush remained strong allies during the Blair era*

New Labour: the Blair approach

In opposition and office, New Labour has been broadly supportive of the EU. As Prime Minister, Tony Blair employed pro-European rhetoric and argued for 'constructive engagement' in the Union, a position which was at first well received by continental leaders. Yet the language used in the 1997 election was not markedly different from that of the Conservatives, the stated preference being for 'an alliance of independent nations choosing to co-operate to achieve the goals they cannot achieve alone'. Within a few years, several issues arose on which he found himself firmly defending national interests and in opposition to our European partners.

Looking back over the Blair era, two strands remain significant, namely the emphasis on intergovernmentalism and the value attached to the 'special relationship'. The preference for cooperation between nation states cooperating for their mutual benefit was reinforced by the fifth enlargement, which offered the prospect of support from new entrants for the British outlook in a wider and looser Union. As for the relationship with the White House, it was evident from the early days of the Blair premiership that Bill Clinton and the Prime Minister were personal as well as political friends. The relationship survived the change of personnel in the Oval Office, with George Bush and Tony Blair working together over many areas of policy. A series of events brought the two countries into active cooperation. Tony Blair publicly backed the US position over the terrorist attacks on the World Trade Center on 11 September, the formation of the 'coalition of the willing' to fight Al-Qaeda type terrorism and the decision to invade Iraq.

Tony Blair liked to use the 'bridge' metaphor to describe the British position in foreign policy, portraying Britain as being the pivot at the axis of a range of international relationships. According to this view, Britain has a unique position, one for which the country is well qualified by past history and circumstance. The thinking is that in this role Britain never has to make a choice between the US and Europe; it is linked to, yet similarly distant from, both continents. But over Iraq, a serious rift began to develop and widen between Europe and the US. Britain was unable to reconcile the two sides and had to make a choice. The divide could not be bridged by the Prime Minister's determined efforts to bring about agreement. Britain ultimately proved itself to be more Atlanticist than European.

The Blair era illustrated the difficulty of trying to be a key player in Union affairs whilst at the same time firmly standing up for British interests on matters such tax harmonisation, the euro and common policies on security and foreign affairs. Tony Blair recognised that he was operating in a country where enthusiasm for the Union was limited and sometimes reluctant, and in which membership was often seen as a necessity rather than a cause for celebration.

Summary questions

1. Why have British politicians been reluctant to commit the country wholeheartedly to a European destiny in the post-1945 era?

2. Is it fair to describe Tony Blair as 'a practical pro-European'?

3 The institutions of the European Union: a democratic deficit?

Learning objectives:

- What are the five key institutions of the European Union and what do they do?

- Why do many critics and some supporters of British membership of the EU complain about its 'democratic deficit'?

- How might the democratic deficit be overcome?

Fig. 4 *The European parliament*

There are five main institutions in the European Union. Three are supranational, involving a transfer of some national sovereignty to an organisation that acts on behalf of all the countries involved. Members are supposed to forget their national allegiances and see issues from a European perspective. The other two are intergovernmental, providing opportunities for national governments to cooperate over a range of issues without surrendering national sovereignty.

The three supranational bodies are as follows:

1 The European Commission is the Executive of the EU. It not only acts as a civil service carrying out particular policies such as the running of the **Common Agricultural Policy**, but it also makes some policy decisions. Its political arm is represented by the 27 commissioners who collectively form the College of Commissioners. The administrative arm is the EU civil service of around 20,000 officials who are based in 26 Directorates-General, each dealing with a different area of responsibility.

Each Commissioner is nominated by the government of one of the Member States (e.g. the UK Commissioner, Peter Mandelson, was nominated by the Blair administration). Once appointed, Commissioners are placed in charge of some function of the Commission's work, such as health and consumer affairs or development and humanitarian aid. They are expected to adopt a European attitude and not be preoccupied with national loyalties.

Key term

Common Agricultural Policy (CAP): a system of subsidies paid to EU farmers. Its main purposes are to guarantee minimum levels of production (so that Europeans have enough food to eat) and to ensure a fair standard of living for those dependent on agriculture.

297

The President of the Commission, currently José Barroso, is the nearest thing the EU has to a head of government, attending European Council meetings and representing the EU at international gatherings. The president chairs weekly meetings of the College of Commissioners and coordinates the work of its members.

2   The European parliament meets in Strasbourg. It receives reports from Commissioners and holds debates and a question time. Much of its important work is done in committees that meet in Brussels. Parliament's legislative role was initially only advisory, but in every major EU treaty (e.g. the SEA, Maastricht, Amsterdam and Nice) its powers have been increased. On key areas such as the CAP and taxation it only gives an opinion, but under the **co-decision procedure** it can veto Union legislation in some important areas such as the single market and consumer protection. It has the power to dismiss the entire Commission (in 1999, it brought about the resignation of the Santer-led Commission, en masse, after serious allegations of fraud and impropriety against individual commissioners) and to accept or reject a new President of the Commission. The 785 members are elected five-yearly, 1999, 2004, etc. (the UK has 78 MEPs).

3   The Court of Justice is based in Luxembourg. The 27 judges rule on matters of Union law as it is laid down in the treaties and can arbitrate in disputes between major states and on those between the Commission and Member States. It can levy fines on those states found to be in breach of Union law and on those which do not carry out treaty obligations. (The UK has one member.)

The two intergovernmental bodies are as follows:

1   The Council of Ministers (officially now the Council of the European Union) makes all policy decisions and issues directives like a government of the EU. One minister represents each of the 27 countries. Usually this is the Foreign Minister though it can be the Minister of Agriculture if agricultural affairs are being discussed, or the Secretary of State for the Environment if appropriate. Preparations for its meetings are handled by COREPER, the Council of Permanent Representatives of Member States, which comprises national ambassadors who speak and act on behalf of their member countries on lesser issues. (The UK has one Council member.)

Each Member State in turn acts as President of the European Union for six months (January–June and July–December). During those six months, all Council meetings are chaired by the relevant minister from the country holding the presidency.

Key term

The co-decision procedure is the main legislative procedure by which law can be adopted in the EU. It gives the European parliament the power to adopt legislation jointly with the Council of Ministers, requiring the two bodies to agree on an identical text before any proposal can become law.

Further information

EU law

There are two categories of law in the EU:

- Primary legislation is the body of law established by the founding treaties of the EC, together with all later amendments and protocols attached to those treaties.

- Secondary legislation relates to all laws passed by EC/EU institutions. The main forms are regulations and directives.

Further information

Table 2 *The rotating EU presidency, 2007–12*

Year	January–June	July–December
2007	Germany	Portugal
2008	Slovenia	France
2009	Czech Republic	Sweden
2010	Spain	Belgium
2011	Hungary	Poland
2012	Denmark	Cyprus

2 The European Council meets every six months at 'summit meetings' held in the country holding the presidency at that time. It includes the 27 Prime Ministers or their equivalents from each country. They discuss broad areas of policy and help move the EU forward by resolving disagreements between states and progressing difficult policy matters. (The UK has one representative.)

Finally, there are three other bodies of note (British membership of the total is shown in brackets):

1 The Court of Auditors which audits all EU revenue and expenditure (1/27).

2 The Economic and Social Committee has an advisory role and gives opinions on various proposals to the Council of Ministers. It includes representatives from groups such as employers and trades unions (24/344).

3 The Committee of the Regions includes people from each area of the member countries. It must be consulted by the Council to represent regional concerns (24/344).

Is there a democratic deficit in the workings of the Union?

A democratic deficit is a situation in which there is a deficiency in the democratic process, usually where a governing body is insufficiently accountable to an elected institution. The term often refers to the lack of accountability in the decision-making processes of the European Union. The result is that there is a developing gap between those who are governed and those who seek to govern them. This is partly a consequence of the way in which the EC/EU evolved.

Monnet and his co-founders were not primarily concerned with the issue of democratic legitimacy. Their more urgent task was to create the Communities at the earliest opportunity and to ensure that effective supranational practices were in place. They had a tendency to think that they understood best what was good for the continent and its inhabitants. Whilst public support was welcomed, it was not regarded as being essential. However, in recent years, there has been a growing feeling that the EU has been developing in ways that are out of step with popular opinion and that the Union needs to be representative of the people and their concerns.

Three specific issues have been singled out for criticism:

1 the feeling that Brussels interferes where it should not

2 the absence of knowledge about what is going on in the central decision-making bodies

3 the belief that Brussels lacks sufficient democratic legitimacy.

The Union has taken some action to overcome the first two deficiencies via:

- the doctrine of subsidiarity, which says that the functions of government should be carried out at the lowest appropriate level for efficient administration, i.e. at the closest level possible to the people affected by the decision. From a British perspective, it is usually interpreted as meaning the decentralisation of power from Brussels back to national governments wherever this is appropriate

- simpler legislation and better public information and by allowing organisations representing citizens a greater say in policy making.

Activity

Make a table to show the number of British representatives in the eight bodies mentioned in the text. In the case of the first four, the Commission, Council of Ministers, European Council and Court of Justice, see if you can find out the name of the British representative. Seek out the names of five MEPs.

The third deficiency is more difficult to address. Those who point to the democratic deficit make several points:

1 The way the pioneers of closer cooperation worked in the early years was to impose their vision on the peoples of Europe. Monnet and his co-founders were not primarily concerned with the democratic legitimacy of the institutions created.

2 The five-yearly elections to the parliament have many weaknesses. People vote primarily on national issues rather than European ones; they are 'second order' elections, with voters sometimes opting for smaller, even sometimes extremist parties to register a protest; turnouts are low; and there are no effective transnational parties, so that fighting the campaigns is left to national parties some of which are not really committed to the cause.

3 More seriously, there are concerns over the way in which institutions operate and the lack of democratic control over those who have the power to make decisions. As the EU has assumed more responsibilities, the power of its decision-making institutions has been increased and there has been a shift away from issues being examined in national parliaments. But the Council of Ministers is not elected, nor is the Commission. The Strasbourg parliament is elected, but it has traditionally lacked teeth. The result is that there is still no very credible system of democratic control within the Union. There is no effective accountability of the Council or Commission to either the national parliaments or to the European parliament.

So what could be done?

1 **The Commission could be democratised**. The elected European parliament could be responsible for the initial choice of the Commission instead of national governments nominating their commissioner. Or the European public could be allowed to vote for the Union's commissioners, perhaps on the same day as the European elections. A variation would be to allow parliament to choose the Commission but for the public to vote for its president.

2 **The powers of parliament could be increased**. The problem here is that those who strongly criticise the democratic deficit are often the very same people who are most reluctant to make parliament a more effective watchdog. British governments have been particularly keen to ensure that control is firmly maintained in Westminster hands.

3 **The role of national parliaments could be strengthened**. Most national parliaments do not have adequate opportunities to influence the decisions at community level. The Danish chamber, the Folketing, is better placed than others in this respect. It has the reputation of keeping a watchful eye over any European initiatives. In Britain, apart from the committees which have been established in the two chambers of parliament (e.g. the House of Lords European Union Committee), there are rare occasions when MEPs are invited to meet with their national colleagues in party committee meetings and informally. Yet keeping up with the burden of work coming from Brussels is a difficult task for the British parliament. This is an issue of parliamentary reform, ensuring that there is more effective and thorough scrutiny of what goes on in Brussels.

Activity

Write a couple of paragraphs to say how you would like to see the democratic deficit tackled.

In depth

How the Westminster parliament monitors EU developments

We have seen on pp202–203 that the sovereignty of parliament has been much affected by membership of the EU. So too has its workload as every year hundreds of proposals are being initiated by the Commission. Many are relatively important and non-contentious, but the time available in both chambers to sift and scrutinise them is inevitably limited. When the Commission proposals are sent to the Council of Ministers, the relevant British government department prepares a summary and sends this to the two houses.

The House of Lords has the Select Committee on the European Communities (see p186), which considers all Union proposals and reports to the House on those raising important questions of principle or policy. In the House of Commons, the Select Committee on European Legislation acts as a filter for the Commission's proposals and draws the attention of the House to those requiring further debate. The government of the day makes time available to consider reports of the Select Committee, though there have been criticisms that debates often get a low priority in the timetable and are relegated to late evening when the House may be poorly attended.

Such complaints about the inadequate opportunities to examine European legislation are commonly heard in other EU countries, all of them having difficulty in coping with the immense volume of EU work. The House of Commons tackled this dissatisfaction in 1991 by agreeing to establish two permanent standing committees which examine any documentation from the EU that has been recommended for further consideration by the House.

The House also tackles European issues in debates and at Question Time. When a treaty such as Maastricht needs ratification, the process is very time consuming.

4   **Europe-wide referendums could be introduced**. These have been employed in some countries as a means of claiming popular backing for treaty developments. As some countries make little use of the device or have no provision for them, it is unlikely that we shall see anything like a Europe-wide referendum as a means of finding out what the public thinks about European developments.

Some observers are not unduly concerned about the alleged democratic deficit. They argue that the Union is as democratic as it can or should be. They suggest that because of the nature of its functions, there is no reason to force democratic mechanisms upon the Union. Moreover, when judged against the practices of existing nation states, they claim that there is little evidence that the EU suffers from a lack of democracy in its workings.

Summary questions

1   Is there a case for strengthening the powers of the European parliament?

2   Does the democratic deficit matter?

4 Policies and policy making

Learning objectives:

■ How is responsibility for policy areas allocated between national governments and Brussels?

■ What impact has EU environmental policy had on Britain?

■ What is the British position on membership of the eurozone?

■ How is policy made within the European Union?

■ How does the EU pass legislation?

The European Union is not a giant super-state determining the outcome of all areas of policy. The responsibility for policy is shared between the Union and the national states. However, the EU has evolved over time from being a primarily economic community to an increasingly political one. An increasing number of policy areas fall within its competence. Political power has tended to shift upwards from the Member States to the EU.

Just as the range of policies undertaken by the Union is a wide one, so is the degree to which the EU becomes involved in their management. In some areas, such as agriculture, industry and trade, many important decisions are now made at European level, which is why national pressure groups spend so much of their time on European policy. In others, including some of those dealt with in the **Second and Third** (intergovernmental) **Pillars of the Maastricht Treaty**, EU involvement is increasing. This is also the case with many aspects of social policy, particularly those relating to labour relations, working conditions and employment practices more generally. In a few areas, there is little or no Union involvement in national policy. This is true of issues relating to policy on education, health, pension and social welfare, as well as to some matters affecting the personal and moral outlook of Europe's citizens, such as policy on abortion and alcohol consumption.

So the nature and extent of EU involvement in policy making differs from issue to issue. In some areas, national governments have been more willing to relinquish some of their capacity to determine policy than in others. The representatives of any country inevitably have to ask themselves what benefits are to be derived from a common approach and to balance possible gains for Europe as a whole against pressing national considerations. They also have to bear in mind what public opinion at home will stand.

Table 3 *The level of EU involvement in a range of key policy areas*

Policy area	Strong	Joint	Little/none
Agriculture	X		
Fishing	X		
Trade	X		
Drugs		X	
Environment		X	
Regions		X	
Working conditions		X	
Foreign affairs and security		X	
Education			X
Health			X
Housing			X
Welfare			X

NB: Defence policy was not on the agenda a generation ago, but today there is limited involvement. In the whole area of foreign and security policy, the trend is towards greater EU interest.

■ Two EU policy areas: their differing impact on Britain

The environment: Britain directly involved

Green politics did not get underway until the 1960s, so there was no mention of environmental policy in the Treaty of Rome. However, as concern developed about damage to the atmosphere, fauna, flora, habitats, health and landscape, the Community began to adopt a range of initiatives in the 1970s and 1980s.

Above all, it was the passage of the Single European Act 1986 that marked the new departure in Community policy. The EC obtained formal authority to legislate on the environment in its own right. It laid down minimum standards in a number of areas. Three principles were put forward: prevention, remedying damage at source and the 'polluter pays for damage done'. The Maastricht Treaty added a fourth principle, namely that there should be 'sustainable and non-inflationary growth respecting the environment', as part of an attempt to reconcile economic progress with environmental concern. Sustainability has been defined as 'development that meets the needs of the present without compromising the ability of future generations to meet their own needs'.

In the 1980s and 1990s, Britain fell foul of EU requirements in several areas, most notably those involving water quality. There was a longstanding dispute over the standard of bathing water on British beaches, which in many cases failed to meet strict guidelines on water quality. In 1993, Lancashire County Council actually took the British government to the European Court of Justice for failing to clean up beaches at Blackpool, Morecambe and Southport. By the turn of the century, there were significant improvements in beach quality. Beaches judged to be safe for bathing are entitled to fly the EU Blue Flag.

Most measures of environmental protection now originate in Brussels, so that British environmental policy is to a large extent dictated by EU directives.

The euro: Britain not directly involved

At Maastricht, various **convergence criteria** were agreed. Any would-be member of the single-currency zone would have to meet these before qualifying for entry. Eleven states were deemed to have met the convergence criteria in 1999 and proceeded to adopt the euro as their common currency. From day one the European Central Bank set a single interest rate for the entire eurozone. Four countries did not join: Britain, Denmark, Greece and Sweden. Greece became the twelfth country to join and Slovenia was the first of the most recent batch of Member States to join in 2007, followed by Cyprus and Malta a year later. Euro banknotes and coins have been in circulation since January 2002 and are now a part of daily life for 316 million Europeans living in the euro area.

Conservative ministers adopted a 'wait and see' approach to membership of the proposed single currency in the early–mid-1990s, some sceptical as to whether it would really happen. After the 1997 election, the Labour government advanced the position to 'prepare and decide'. As Chancellor of the Exchequer, Gordon Brown argued for Britain to wait until it was absolutely clear that Britain had satisfied the five criteria that he and his Treasury team had laid down as conditions for British entry. In October 1997, he told the House that he favoured entry in principle, but when he delivered his verdict in June 2003 he announced that only one of the five tests had been passed. Prime Minister Blair always seemed more enthusiastic about entry, but was aware of the lack of popular support for entry into the eurozone as well as the political opposition the issue aroused. Membership of 'euroland' seems unlikely in the near future.

Policy making in the Union

Proposals for and decisions on Union action come about in various ways. Sometimes the impetus derives from within the Community's institutions (the Community method) and sometimes it results from the expressed wishes of the Member States who give a strong lead (the intergovernmental method). So there is no fixed process by which policies emerge. At times in EU history, national governments have been actively involved in pushing forward new initiatives, but in other phases of the

Key term

Second and Third Pillars of the Maastricht Treaty: the parts of the Maastricht Treaty dealing with foreign and security, and justice and home affairs policy, respectively. The first pillar was concerned with developing the pre-existing European Community, for example by the adoption of a single currency.

Fig. 5 *The euro – Europe's currency*

Key term

Convergence criteria: the principles agreed at Maastricht to determine whether the economic performance of individual Member States is sufficiently strong to enable them to qualify for membership of the single currency.

Further information

The legislative process within the Union

When the Union decides to legislate, the procedure is broadly as follows, although there are significant variations at stages 2 and 3 according to the procedure involved:

1. The Commission proposes new legislation.

2. The Council consults on the proposal with the parliament, which scrutinises (and may suggest amendments) and with the Economic and Social Committee which advises.

3. The Council decides whether to go ahead.

4. The Commission implements the proposal.

5. The Court of Justice arbitrates on any infringement of the law and resolves any disputes.

Union's development there has been a greater interest in supranational policy making.

The Commission remains the starting point of the decision-making process. However, with the passage of the SEA, the Treaty of European Union (TEU) and subsequent treaties, the powers of the parliament have been increased, so that what was a dialogue between two institutions (the Council and Commission) has become more of a partnership between three of them.

When the proposal has been approved under whichever of the procedures is relevant, it is then introduced in the form of a regulation, directive or decision.

The main procedures for policy making are:

1 The Consultation procedure via which parliament gives an opinion on Commission proposals. This has gradually been reduced but still covers important fields such as the CAP, taxation and certain aspects of economic and monetary union.

2 The cooperation procedure. The SEA extended the role of the parliament which was given a second opportunity to examine any proposal, which it could accept, amend or reject. If it opted for rejection, the Council could override the objection, but only on the basis of a unanimous vote. This now applies only to limited areas of policy on economic and monetary union.

3 The Assent Procedure. The SEA also introduced the assent procedure which required the approval of parliament on any proposed enlargement of the EC. Under the TEU, it now covers other items such as policies with important budgetary implications for the Union as a whole. Parliament may give or withhold its agreement on the proposal laid before it, but it has no power of amendment.

4 The co-decision procedure. Article 189b of the Maastricht Treaty introduced co-decision. Under the co-decision procedure, parliament and the Council adopt legislative initiatives on the basis of joint agreement. Parliament has an absolute right of veto if it rejects the approved position of the Council, though in a conciliation stage a committee made up of representatives from the parliament and the Commission can look for a compromise satisfactory to both institutions.

Although there were fears about the likely time and complexity of co-decision making, it has worked well and enabled decisions to be made reasonably quickly on a number of issues. Originally, the procedure was used in decision making on consumer protection, culture, education, free movement of workers, health, freedom to provide services, the single market and the adoption of guidelines or programmes covering trans-European networks, research and the environment. However, since the Treaty of Amsterdam, it has applied to most of the fields of Community legislation.

Summary questions

1 To what extent are the policies of the British government determined by Brussels?

2 How does the EU make policy?

3 Is the co-decision procedure a good thing?

5 The future of the EU

Learning objectives:

- What was meant by the 'widening or deepening' disagreement within the EU?

- What is meant by a federal Europe?

- Has the EU become a super-state?

- What is meant by a flexible approach to integration?

- Why did several continental leaders conclude that the EU needed its own constitution?

Widening or deepening?

In the late twentieth century there were two lines of argument within the Union about how it should move forward. Some states wanted to cement the bonds between existing states as a top priority. Others were more interested in extending the EU into central and Eastern Europe.

Not surprisingly, Member States took different views about the admission of new entrants. France has traditionally been less enthusiastic, fearing a setback to the progress strengthening the links between present members. It has also been uneasy about the prospect of having first- and second-class applicants. Germany believes in enlargement but has been more committed to the accession of economically advanced countries such as the Czech Republic and Slovenia.

The British have long been supporters of enlargement. Under the Thatcher and Major governments, they liked the idea of extending deregulated trading areas and welcomed the fact that the new democracies saw free market solutions as being British driven. The Blair governments continued with the same policy. Above all, perhaps, the British have been attracted to the idea of enlargement to the East because ministers have felt that it might help to slow down the pace of integration in the West. Being more committed to closer economic rather than political union, enlargement makes sense. It caters for the first, whilst making the second less certain.

The widening or deepening controversy became largely irrelevant in the early 21st century, with the admission of 10 and eventually 12 new Member States. The expansion has had benefits. It has strengthened the EU by increasing its attraction as an export market for non-Union countries; enabled the organisation to have more say in world affairs; and helped to increase stability on the continent by promoting prosperity among the new states.

A more federal Europe

One of the most contentious issues concerning the future of the Union is the extent to which it moves in a federal direction. Lady Thatcher expressed the fear that a creeping federal system was being achieved without it being fully appreciated. She urged the need to halt this 'conveyor-belt to federalism'. In the eyes of many right-wing British politicians the word 'federal' remains deeply worrying because they see ideas of federalism and national sovereignty as fundamentally incompatible. Labour also shunned federal rhetoric and remained committed to the intergovernmentalism that has enabled it to defend British national interests and draw 'red lines' over which it was not prepared to cross. Tony Blair was no federalist preferring an enlarged and looser EU to the organisation envisaged by those who dreamed of European integration after the Second World War. That preference for cooperation between nation states cooperating for their mutual benefit has been reinforced by the latest EU enlargement.

Further information

Continued expansion?

Other than in 1981, the enlargements of the Union to date have tended to take place in 'waves' of multiple entrants all joining at once. A more individual approach will be adopted in future.

- Croatia is expected to join in 2010.
- Albania, Bosnia and Herzegovina, the Republic of Macedonia, Montenegro, Serbia, and Turkey are all likely future members.
- Turkey's membership is contentious. It is regarded as a European state, but there are concerns over its record on human rights, its continued occupation of Northern Cyprus and its strong leanings towards Islamicism. The country is regarded as too big, too poor (rapidly growing population and low average income) and too culturally different from the other Member States.
- Britain supports Turkish entry, arguing that its rejection could have negative consequences on relations between Islam and the West. Rather, we should embrace religious social and economic differences, not shun them. It would send a strong signal to Muslims to admit a predominantly Islamic country. To do so would create a force for stability in the region and bolster democratic institutions in Turkey. In addition, entry would strengthen the EU economy and reward Turkey for its pro-Western stance.

Key terms

Super-state: the idea of a centralised European state that is considerably more powerful than individual nation states. It represents the fear of those who detect the creation of a United States of Europe which some see as the inevitable outcome of the integrationist trends of recent years, e.g. the creation of a single currency.

The *Concise Oxford Dictionary* describes the word 'federal' as meaning 'an association of units that are largely independent' and 'a system of government in which several states unite under a central authority but remain independent in internal affairs'. As such, federalism is designed to allow the maximum devolution of decision making possible consistent with the needs of a workable union. However, the media in Britain, especially the popular press, have often used the term in the way that some Conservatives do, as if it implied the removal of power from the nation state to some **super-state**. It is seen as implying a move to centralisation and deeper integration. Some British MPs pounce on any proposal from the Commission suspecting that it brings the dreaded 'f' word ever nearer. On the continent, 'federal' arouses no such anxieties because it implies quite the opposite. To a German, subsidiarity is the very essence of federalism. It is a key element in the division of power between the different layers of government, European, national and regional.

'Federal' has become a slogan for all those who fear the drift of events in Europe, with Brussels having an ever-greater impact on national governments. In denying its use, British opponents are not only rejecting the formal structure of a fully fledged federal European state, but all the moves such as the single currency, the stronger European institutions and the increasing search for a common approach to many matters of policy.

Is the EU a giant super-state?

Several British Conservatives have expressed the fear that Britain is in danger of being dragged into some European monstrosity, a form of super-state. In the Labour party, such a view surfaces less frequently, although it was evident in the discussions over the desirability of a European constitution.

William Hague vividly described these feelings when he outlined his 'elephant test'. Simplistically expressed, his view was that if it looks, smells and sounds like an elephant, then it probably is an elephant. Applied to the emerging shape of the European Union, he detected the characteristics of a future super-state, among them a proposed president, a parliament, a court and a single currency. Recognising the possibility of such a state being created without remedial action, a *Mail on Sunday* writer expressed the more extravagant view that this outcome would 'be worse than Stalin's Soviet Union'.

Elements of doubt

Academics, constitutional experts, diplomats and European officials are divided in their views about what form the EU will eventually take, but the general view is that the Union will fall far short of being a super-state. We live in a world where more and more states are banding together – whether in Europe, the Americas or Asia – to make policies that benefit the member states. That does not mean new super-states are being created, rather that we are living in a world where layers of governance overlap in many different ways.

Historian Norman Davies points out that what is evolving is something of an in-between situation rather than one of either of the extremes sometimes presented. On the one hand, Europe is not going to be just the Common Market created by the Treaty of Rome, a free trading area designed to maximise economic advantage. Neither is it going to be a classic super-state 'which would have a head of state, an executive in permanent session, a legislative assembly to whom it is answerable and its own individual judiciary'. In his view, we are seeing a new kind of organisation emerge, but still one in which the intergovernmental Council of Ministers rather than the supranational European Commission has the final say: 'those ministers represent their national interests, not the interests of a super-state'.

Finally, the point has been made by Larry Siedentop (2000) that it is hard to imagine any super-state in which the size of the budget was limited by treaty to 1.27 per cent of the Member States' GDP: 'No large state uses less than 30 per cent'.

A more flexible approach to integration?

In order to overcome the many problems associated with progress for the European Union, the idea of **variable geometry** has re-emerged in recent years as a desirable possibility. Sometimes today it is known by an alternative name of 'enhanced cooperation' (*coopération renforcée* or flexible integration). This is seen as a way of catering for the economic weakness of some new members and the reluctance of larger states such as Britain to surrender part of their sovereignty, as represented by the national veto.

The Major government took the view that Member States should be allowed to adopt differentiated approaches to the wide range of EU policies, just as Denmark and the UK had adopted a different approach to monetary union. The key word was flexibility, enabling the creation of a Europe á la carte' in which countries could participate in the policies that suited their national needs. The difficulty was that when so many items on the agenda were unacceptable to London, then leaders in other capitals were likely to hesitate before agreeing to such an approach. They feared that if one or more countries such as Britain opted out of nearly all initiatives, the result would be a 'two-speed' or 'two-tier Europe' in which some countries moved ahead to integration at a rapid pace, whilst others which did not wish to go so far or so quickly trailed behind.

In its early years, the Blair government, not wishing to see Britain left behind, showed little enthusiasm for any variant of variable geometry. Its rhetoric implied that the intention was to join the euro 'when the time was right' and that it would seek to cooperate in other fields unless essential interests were at stake. But as yet, in spite of it having two massive majorities and one comfortable one in the House of Commons, the time has not been right. Moreover, Britain has found itself resisting the thrust of integration in other areas favoured by the powerful Franco-German alliance that is usually in the vanguard of further progress.

After the talks over the constitution (see p308), Tony Blair conceded that in order to preserve his red lines, it was necessary to agree that other states could be allowed to forge ahead with integration, including a common tax policy. Some states, particularly from the former Soviet bloc, shared his approach, indicating that what is beginning to emerge is a complex patchwork of alliances that form and reform over different issues and come and go with changing governments. The outcome seems likely to be a looser Union in which the integrationists form a core group who will drive things forward, with other nations choosing how and when they will participate as national interests and pressures permit.

Key term

Variable geometry: a model of integration in which not every Member State takes part in every EU policy area. Members can decide whether or not they wish to participate in any particular policy, subject to them taking part in a basic core of activities.

Further information

The Blair government's four red lines

Ministers wanted to see that:

- the EU's Charter of Fundamental Rights was not made legally binding
- there could be a right to opt in to majority voting decisions on criminal justice matters
- the veto on matters of taxation and social security systems was preserved
- the new 'high representative', who will coordinate foreign policy and represent the EU to the rest of the world, should not chair regular meetings of EU foreign ministers nor take over the resources of the European Commissioner for Foreign Affairs.

Further information

The fate of the amending treaty
- Prime Minister Brown signed the amending treaty, better known as the Reform or Lisbon Treaty, in December 2007.
- All member countries had to ratify it before it could come into force by the intended target date, in time for te European elections in 2009.
- Fifteen had done so by the end of May 2008, but then in June the Irish voters rejected it in the only referendum on the subject held in a member state.
- A few days later, it passed through the British parliament, making Britain the 19th country to approve it. Actual ratification was delayed by two legal challenges.
- However, as a result of the Irish vote, the future of the EU was plunged into uncertainty.

Further reading

E Bomberg and A Stubb, *The European Union: How Does it Work?*, OUP, 2003.

A Geddes, *The European Union and British Politics*, Palgrave, 2004.

S George, *An Awkward Partner: Britain in the European Community*, OUP, 1998.

A Jones, *Britain in the European Union*, EUP, 2007.

J McCormick, *Understanding the European Union: A Concise Introduction*, Palgrave, 2002.

D Watts and C Pilkington, *Britain in the European Union Today*, MUP, 2005.

D Watts, *The European Union*, EUP, 2008.

Websites:

www.europa.eu. Massive site on the European Union, basic information on all aspects.

www.europarl.eu.int. The UK Office of the European parliament.

A constitution for Europe?

At Brussels in 2004, an agreement was reached on the creation of a new constitution for the European Union. It was primarily concerned with defining and clarifying who did what, and streamlining decision-making procedures to cater for enlargement. Most of the EU powers were already in existence, although there was a modest extension of majority voting in some areas. In all sensitive new areas such as justice and home affairs or social security, Britain could not be outvoted. There was only one new area where the EU obtained the power to act (jointly with other governments): energy. Again, even on this issue, the Union already had some role through its environmental policy.

Had the constitutional treaty been ratified, it would have entered into force on 1 November 2006. However, the failure of supporters of the constitution treaty to win popular support for their work in some Member States (especially France and the Netherlands, where referendums were held and lost) caused other countries to postpone or halt their ratification procedures. As of February 2007, 20 countries had approved it in its original form, either by popular vote or parliamentary procedure.

Rejection of the constitution in two traditionally enthusiastic Member States caused uncertainty about the future direction of Europe, which continues at the time of writing. A Europe of 27 members cannot easily continue as it is at present because it is difficult to work with machinery that operates in the same way that was possible when there was only a handful of members. The difficulty is that in order to reach agreement on any initiative, the Commission has to seek the lowest common denominator among the different national positions. Together with the Union's slow economic growth, the failure of the constitutional treaty cast doubt on whether the EU would in the future be ready to accept new, far poorer members.

Any intention of reviving the constitutional treaty in its full 400-page form was out of the question. However, in 2007, there was agreement on a mini 'amending treaty' which would allow the EU to function better. Opponents, many on the British Conservative benches, felt that in agreeing to it, Tony Blair had conceded too much, in other words that it was the constitution by another name. He insisted that his four 'red lines' had been preserved. Moreover, because this was an amending treaty rather than the full-blown original version, he argued that it was no longer necessary to hold the referendum that he had promised voters before the 2004 European elections.

Summary questions

1. Are the British right to fear the creation of a federal Europe?
2. Is the EU a giant super-state?
3. Does Europe need a constitution?
4. One of the founding fathers of the Community, Robert Schuman, observed that: 'Europe will not be created at a stroke . . . [but] built through concrete achievements'. In Britain, should we admire the achievements or beware of the pitfalls?

AQA Examination-style questions

1 ☑ Read the extract below and answer questions (a) to (c) which follow.

Multi-level governance

In the UK today multi-level governance is a reality. The time has long passed when it was possible to understand the workings of the UK system of government and politics with reference only to White-hall, Westminster and *elected local councils*. Beyond this the workings of the European Union and the emerging system of devolved government are now integral parts of the system. In important respects, therefore, it now makes sense to discuss the UK in terms of multi-level governance. The European Parliament, however, is a relatively weak body, with limited powers to check the Commission and the Council of Ministers. The latter, although unelected, is the real decision-making body of the EU, and UK Cabinet ministers participate continuously in its work.

Source: adapted from J Greenwood, R Pyper and D Wilson, *New Public Administration in Britain*, Routledge, 2002

(a) Briefly explain the term *elected local councils* used in the extract. *(5 marks)*

(b) Using your own knowledge as well as the extract, explain the statement that 'in the UK today multi-level governance is a reality'. *(10 marks)*

(c) 'The European Council of Ministers is the real decision-making body of the EU.' Discuss. *(25 marks)*

AQA specimen question

2 Read the extract and answer questions (a) to (c) which follow.

Devolution

Britain remains a *unitary state*, but the important changes of recent years seem to indicate a move in the direction of a kind of federalism. Devolution has been the British route to decentralisation. Ultimate power remains in Westminster's hands, although it would be hard to imagine that it would be politically acceptable in Scotland, Wales or Northern Ireland if any administration in London tried to retrieve control over areas of policy that have been delegated to Edinburgh, Cardiff or Belfast.

Source: adapted from Chapter 16 of this textbook

(a) Briefly explain the term *unitary state* used in the extract. *(5 marks)*

(b) Using your own knowledge as well as the extract, analyse the differences between federal and devolved systems of government. *(10 marks)*

(c) Assess the arrangements for devolved government in any two countries of the UK. *(25 marks)*

References

A Adonis, *Parliament Today*, MUP, 1993

S Arnstein, 'A Ladder of Citizen Participation', *Journal of the American Planning Association*, 35:4, July 1969

W Bagehot, *The English Constitution*, (re-issued) Fontana, 1963

R Baggott, *Pressure Groups and the Policy Process*, Politics Association/SHU Press, 2000

T Bale, *European Politics: A Comparative Introduction*, Palgrave, 2005

D Bell, *The End of Ideology? On the Exhaustion of Political Ideas in the 1950s*, Free Press, 1960

T Blair, the *Guardian*, 10 September 1995

T Blair, as quoted in P Hennessy, *The Prime Minister: The Office and its Holders Since 1945*, Allen Lane, 2000

V Bogdanor, 'Western Europe' in D Butler and A Ranney (eds), *Referendums Around the World: The Growing Use of Direct Democracy*, Macmillan, 1994

V Bogdanor, *Devolution in the United Kingdom*, OUP, 1999

V Bogdanor, *The British Constitution in the Twentieth Century*, Clarendon Press, 2003

R Brazier, *Constitutional Practice*, Clarendon, 1988

D Broder, *The Party's Over*, Harper and Row, 1972

A Brown, A Jones and F Mackay, *The 'representativeness' of councillors*, Rowntree Trust, 1999

Lord Bryce, *Modern Democracies*, Macmillan, 1921

I Budge, I Crewe, D McKay and K Newton, *The New British Politics*, Longman, 2005

D Butler and D Kavanagh, *The British General Election of 2005*, Palgrave, 2005

D Butler and D Stokes, *Political Change in Britain*, Macmillan, 1969

H Clarke, M Stewart and P Whiteley, 'The Dynamics of Partisanship in Britain: Evidence and Implications for Critical Election Theory', *British Elections and Parties Review 11*, 2001

B Coxall, L Robins and R Leach, *Contemporary British Politics*, Palgrave, 2003

I Crewe, 'Has the electorate become Thatcherite?' in R Skidelsky (ed.), *Thatcherism*, Blackwell, 1988

I Crewe, *Comparative Research on Attitudes of Young People*, Wiley, 1996

R Crossman, in the Introduction to W Bagehot, *The English Constitution*, Fontana, 1963

R Crossman, *The Diaries of a Cabinet Minister Vol ii*, Hamish Hamilton/Jonathan Cape, 1976

N Davies, and L Siedentop, 'Towards a European superstate?' the *Mail on Sunday*, all as quoted in The *Observer*, 10 December 2000

D Denver, *Elections and Voters in Britain*, Palgrave, 2003

A Dicey, *Introduction to the Study of the Law and the Constitution*, Macmillan, 1885

P Dunleavy and C Husbands, *British Democracy at the Crossroads*, Allen & Unwin, 1985

M Duverger, *Political Parties*, Methuen, 1962

M Evans, *Political Participation, Developments in British Politics 5*, Macmillan, 1997

D Farrell, *Comparing Electoral System*, Harvester Wheatsheaf, 1997

F Fukuyama, *The End of History and the Last Man*, Penguin, 1989

M Foley, *The Rise of the British Presidency*, MUP, 1993

M Foley, *The British Presidency: Tony Blair and the Politics of Public Leadership*, MUP, 2000

I Gilmour, *Inside Right*, Quartet, 1978

Glasgow University Media Group, *Bad News and More Bad News*, Routledge and Kegan Paul, 1976 and 1980, respectively

W Grant, *Pressure Groups and British Politics*, Palgrave, 2000

J Griffiths, *The Politics of the Judiciary*, Fontana,1997

W Hague, speech on Europe, 6 December 2000

R Hague and M Harrop, *Comparative Government and Politics: An Introduction*, Palgrave, 2004

Lord Hailsham (Q Hogg), *The Purpose of Parliament*, Blandford Press, 1946

Lord Hailsham, 'Elective Dictatorship', BBC Dimbleby Lecture, 1976

A Hanson and M Walles, *Governing Britain*, Fontana, 1997

C Hay, *Political Analysis: A Critical Introduction*, Palgrave, 2002

P Hennessy, 'The Blair style of government', the *Guardian*, 28 February 2005

H Himmelweit, P Humphries, M Jaegar and M Katz, *How Voters Decide*, Academic Press, 1981

Lord Howe, 'Where next for the Lords?', *Citizenship PA*, January 2004

W Hutton, *The State We're In*, Vintage, 1996

Jenkins enquiry, 'The Report of the Independent Commission on Voting Systems', chaired by Lord Jenkins, HMSO, 1998

D Kavanagh and A Seldon, *The Major Effect*, Macmillan, 1994

G Kaufman, *How to be a Minister*, Faber, 1997

P Kellner, *New Society*, 2 June 1983

P Kellner and N Crowther-Hunt, *The Civil Servants*, Macdonald Futura, 1980

A King, in P Norris and C Wlezien (eds) *Britain Votes 2005*, OUP, 2005

N Lawson, *The View From No. 11*, Bantam, 1992

P Lazarsfeld, *The People's Choice*, Columbia University Press, 1968

J Lovenduski, 'Women and candidate selection in Britain', as quoted in the *Guardian*, 7 December 2004

J Mackintosh, *The British Cabinet*, Stevens, 1977

E May, *Parliamentary Practice: Treatise on the Law, Privileges, Proceedings and Usage of Parliament*, (re-issued) Butterworths Law, 2004

R McKenzie, *British Political Parties*, Heinemann, 1955

R Michels, *Political Parties*, Dover Publications, 1911

L Milbrath and M Goel, *Political Participation: How and Why Do People Get Involved in Politics?*, Rand McNally, 1977

M Moran, *Politics and Governance in the UK*, Palgrave, 2005

P Norton, 'Constitutional Change: A Response to Elcock', *Talking Politics*, September 1996

P Norton, *Parliament in British Politics*, Palgrave, 2005

D Osbourne and T Gaebler, *Reinventing Government*, Addison-Wesley, 1992

T Paine's pamphlet *Common Sense* (1776) and book *The Rights of Man* (§1791) are contained in *Collected Works*, Library of America, 1995

G Parry, *British Government*, Butterworths, 1969

G Parry, G Moyser and N Day, *Political Participation and Democracy in Britain*, Cambridge University Press, 1992

G Peele, *Governing the UK*, Blackwell, 2004

B Pimlott, *Contemporary Record*, May 1989

P Pulzer, *Political Representation and Elections in Britain*, Allen & Unwin, 1967

R Punnett, *British Government and Politics*, Gower, 1971

W Putnam, *Bowling Alone: The Collapse and Revival of American Community*, Simon & Schuster, 2000

P Richards, *Honourable Members*, Faber & Faber, 1964

M Rush, *Parliament and Pressure Groups*, Clarendon, 1990

S Saggar, *Race and Electoral Politics in Britain*, UCL Press, 2000

D Sanders, 'It's the Economy, Stupid: the economy and support for the Conservative Party, 1979–1994', *Talking Politics*, 7:3, April 1996

B Sarlvik and I Crewe, *Decade of Dealignment*, Cambridge University Press, 1983

P Seyd, P Whitely and J Richardson, *True Blues: The Politics of Conservative Party Membership*, Clarendon Press, 1994

K Starmer, 'Two Years of the Human Rights Act', *European Human Rights Law Review*, vol. 1, 2003

The Directory of British Associations, CBD Research Ltd, 2004

K Theakston, 'Ministers and mandarins', *Talking Politics*, 4:2, 1992

K Theakston, *Leadership in Whitehall*, Macmillan, 1999

G Thomas, *Parliament in an Age of Reform*, Politics Association/SHU Press, 2000

D Truman, *The Governmental Process: Political Interests and Public Opinion*, Knopf, 1958

A Tyrie, *Presentation: What is the legitimate role of special advisers?*, www.parliament.uk

E Wade and G Philips, *Constitutional Law*, (re-issued) Longman, 1998

T Wright, 'The Candidate' in A Geddes and J Tonge, *Britain Decides: the UK General Election, 2005*, Palgrave, 2005

Index

Page numbers in **bold** refer to **Key terms**